The Atlantic Monthly Press
~
New York

Sports Afield

TROUT FISHER'S
ALMANAC

Sports Afield

TROUT FISHER'S ALMANAC

Expert Advice from America's Greatest Anglers

EDITED BY SID EVANS

The Atlantic Monthly Press
~
New York

Published simultaneously in Canada.
Printed in the United States of America.

Library of Congress Cataloging-in-Publication Data

Trout fisher's almanac: expert advice from America's greatest anglers
/edited by Sid Evans.
p. cm.
Includes bibliographical references and index.
ISBN 0-87113-676-7
1. Trout fishing--United States. I. Evans, Sid. II. Sports afield
SH688.U6S66 1997
799.1'757--dc21   97-13971

Atlantic Monthly Press
841 Broadway
New York, NY 10003

1 3 5 7 9 10 8 6 4 2

Design by Michael Lawton

In Memory of Dr. J. D. Evans

Contents

~

Acknowledgments

~

It takes a lot of people to put together a book like this one, many more than I can list on one page. However, there are certain people who were intimately involved in the project from start to finish, and they deserve enormous thanks—especially Carol Cammero, Frank Golad, Michael Lawton, and Christina Wynn, all members of the *Sports Afield* staff. Each of them brought a great deal of energy to the book, a lot of ideas, and many, many hours of work. Thanks are also due to Georgia Andrews, for her wise counsel, Mike Toth, for his expert fishing advice, and especially Terry McDonell, whose confidence in the project made it not only possible, but enjoyable. I'd like to thank all the photographers and illustrators who contributed to the book, including Andy Anderson, Archive Film, Valentine Atkinson, Barry and Cathy Beck, the Catskill Flyfishing Museum, Soc Clay, John Dyess, John Flagg, Ed Lipinski, Richard Procopio, Tom Rafalovich, Dale Spartas, Greg Sweney, Steve Sanford, Doug Schermer, and Glenn Wolff. Lissa Smith was particularly helpful with the introduction, as was Miwa Messer, and Eric Price, my editor at The Atlantic Monthly Press, guided the book from start to finish. Thanks are due to John Mazurkiewicz at Scientific Anglers, Ryan Shadrin at Orvis, and Ed Lusch at Windsor Publications, for their assistance with illustrations and other materials; also Pete Rafle at Trout Unlimited, and Dr. Robert Behnke at Colorado State University, who were a great help with regard to numerous trout names and species. Freelancer Peter Zwiebach was did an excellent job of selecting and organizing art for the book. Finally, I suppose the most credit goes to the many contributors who dedicated so much of their lives to the study of trout, and then decided to write about it—from Anthony Acerrano to Lee Wulff. Without them, we probably wouldn't catch a thing.

"Obviously this is the pursuit of madmen."

—ROBERT TRAVER, 1964

Introduction

~

LAST YEAR IN the middle of February I went trout
fishing on the famous White River in Arkansas with my
father, my uncle Goodloe, and their friend Clyde. I'd been
invited on the trip because the usual fourth in their group couldn't
come, and I was excited not only about the legendary fishing on
the White, but about the fact that I might become a character in
one of their amazing fishing stories, which I'd heard for most of
my life. They had made a point of trying to fish every great trout
river they could get to in North America—the Gunnison, the
Green, the Madison, the Big Horn, the San Juan—and in recent
years their trips had become more frequent and their fishing more
intense. I really didn't deserve to fish with them, but I thought that
being in their presence for a weekend might teach me a few
things. I remember us packing all of the gear into the back of
Goodloe's Suburban—putting my fly rod in with theirs—and

feeling as confident and trout-worthy as Lee Wulff. We talked about trout fishing the entire four-hour drive from Memphis, and even though it was snowing when we arrived at the motel in Salesville, I felt like the great fishing had already begun.

The next morning we met with our guides, Fox Statler and Jim Lipscomb, who rigged us all with the exact same fly, a #16 Sow Bug, and then told us that if we fished it properly on a dead drift, we would catch so many trout we'd get tired of hauling them in. They were right. I heard music in the trees, and every little riffle was bulging with possibility. The sky was an exquisite shade of blue. The Trout God was with us. I could have caught trout with my eyes closed. It was extremely cold, and the guides on our 4- and 6-weight rods would freeze so often we had to dunk them in the river every cast, but the four of us caught and released more than 100 trout that day. Clyde caught the most, but I had hooked and landed at least a couple dozen. It felt good to be so good.

We woke up early on the second day, a little hungover from a trout celebration—that was Goodloe's fault—but cocky, nonetheless. We went to the same spot, tied on #16 Sow Bugs, and started fishing.

Nothing bit.

I was fishing with my father that day, and we tied on other flies, adjusted our leaders, fished the pools, the riffles, the banks. We tried every method we could think of to tempt a trout, but nothing would take. We asked the guide what was wrong, but he just shrugged his shoulders and smiled. "These trout are sometimes hard to figure," he said.

Then the guide pointed downstream. "Look," he said, "Clyde's got a fish."

We made our way down to Clyde's spot, and proceeded to watch him catch a trout on almost every cast. He was still fishing with a Sow Bug, and he'd found a little pool that was full of rainbows and browns.

"You guys should try over here," he said.

But we tried there and a lot of other places, and though we caught a few, we couldn't keep up with Clyde. After he had caught four or five in a particular spot, he would move so that someone else could fish there, but of course there never seemed to be as many once he had left the hole. What amazed me the most was the way Clyde seemed to move in slow motion, and the way he always looked certain that a trout was about to bite. I couldn't discern anything about his cast or his line or his fly that was any different from mine. It was simply the fact that he looked more at home on the water. He had found some kind of rhythm that I didn't quite get, and I knew I was in the presence of a better fisherman. I haven't ever felt this way before or since, but that day I wanted to be inside the man's head. I wanted to know what Clyde knew about trout.

This book is about getting inside the heads of the best trout fishermen of all time—Lee Wulff, Lefty Kreh, Thomas McGuane, Ernest Schwiebert, A. J. McClane, and many others. A lot of them devoted their lives to learning about trout and how to catch them, and collectively they have written down the most sophisticated and exacting information about trout ever published. It can be a humbling experience to expose yourself to such a panel of experts, but it can also be uplifting. Part of what makes the sport so compelling is the fact that you can never really learn it all. The fishermen in this book are some of the smartest in history, but they are also the ones who have been the most perplexed by trout, the most baffled, the most amazed, and it's obvious from these pages that they love the mysteries more than the solutions.

The *Trout Fisher's Almanac* is a compilation of 110 years of *Sports Afield* articles about trout fishing history, tactics, techniques, philosophies, and lore. *Sports Afield* readers have been passionate about trout fishing since the magazine was founded in 1887, so the editors have always been certain to include detailed articles by the most informed fishermen of the day. In some ways, the *Trout Fisher's Almanac* is a chronicle of the evolution of the sport, covering everything from the first artificial flies to the age of graphite. But read Lee Wulff's article, "The Finer Points of Playing Fish," from 1978, or Ted Trueblood's "A New Theory of Leaders," from 1951, and you will see that the basic elements of trout fishing have stayed the same, namely the fishermen and the fish. The only thing that has really changed is the technology, and even with the inventions of superior flylines, Gore-Tex waders, and high-tech multiplier flyreels, you can still find yourself standing in the middle of a beautiful trout stream with absolutely no idea how to hook one.

I went trout fishing again with my father, my uncle Goodloe, and Clyde about six months later on a wonderful river in Alaska that empties into Kuskokwim Bay. The last day Clyde caught a rainbow trout that must have been 26 inches long and weighed about eight pounds, while my father and the guide were eating lunch on the shore. It was far and away the biggest trout of our week long trip. No one was surprised. I didn't see him catch it but I've seen the photograph. The trout has an exceptionally brilliant red stripe running down its flank—they call it a "leopard" rainbow in Alaska—and Clyde is holding it up for the camera, just like you might see in a thousand other fishing pictures. My father is standing next to him, as if he had caught the fish, too, and both of them, of course, are smiling.

I don't think Clyde would call himself a great fisherman, and I'm not so sure my father or my uncle Goodloe would call him one, either. They have had their days on the stream, too. But both times I have fished with that trio, we have used the exact same rods; gone to the same rivers; used the same guides; and somehow, Clyde has managed to catch more and bigger trout. If you asked him how he did it, he would probably just throw up his hands and start telling stories about all the trout that he couldn't catch, the ones he never figured out. He would never tell you that had a particular strategy, or that he had mastered some technique—but that, I think, is his secret. As soon as you can admit that you don't really know anything, you start to learn.

—Sid Evans, February 1997

Trout Fishing History and Lore

~

"War, murrain, famine, pestilence, dictators, the rise and fall of empires or republics may defeat the game fisherman temporarily, but he rises again to invade the streams and the sea. More people have gone fishing over more centuries than for any other human recreation."

—*President Herbert Hoover*, Sports Afield, *June 1944*

◀◀◀ *President Herbert Hoover shows off one of many "spotted" trout—
probably a brookie—he took at Catootin Creek in Catootin Furnace,
Maryland, on May 16, 1936.*—**Photo from the Bettmann Archive**

A Trout Fishing Timeline

1496

The fishing nun, Dame Juliana Berners.

English nun and noble-woman Dame Juliana Berners publishes *A Treatyse of Fysshynge Wyth an Angle* in *The Book of St. Albans*, which is thought to be the first book devoted solely to sportfishing.

1651

In London, Charles Kirby creates new methods to temper and harden metal fishhooks and invents the Kirby hook-shape, which is still in use today, not only for fresh- and saltwater baitfishing, but also for fly hooks.

Trout in Ancient Times

IN THE THIRD century, **Claudius Aelianus**, a Roman nature writer, described the brown trout—"the fish with speckled skin"—and provided an account of flyfishing for trout on a Macedonian river. The passage is remarkable, for it is history's first mention of angling with an artificial fly, and a dry fly at that. Considering the short rod and the use of a tight rather than running line, it seems likely that the Macedonian angler filled his basket by dapping.

In addition to his description of trout fishing, Aelianus, who lived circa A.D. 170-230, wrote a revealing reference to grayling fishing as practiced by the ancient Romans.

Found on an Egyptian tomb, this petroglyph is the earliest known pictorial record of fishing with a rod and line. It has been dated by archaeologists at around 2000 B.C.

"In the river Tecinus in the north of Italy there is found a fish called thymalus (thyme-fish), about eighteen inches long, and in appearance something between a bass and a grey mullet. When taken, it has a scent which is very remarkable . . . you would think you were handling a bunch of freshly gathered thyme—indeed the scent is delicious—and anyone would believe that the creature was stuffed full of the herb . . . [the grayling] cannot be caught with a baited hook, either with pig's fat or winged ant, shell fish, or fish gut, or snail's tendon, the only successful bait being the mosquito—that detestable animal which is man's enemy by day and night alike by reason of its sting and its buzzing, but which is the only delight for the grayling, and does capture him."

The passage may seem confusing at first, but there is little doubt that the river Aelianus referred to is the present-day Ticino, or that the fish is indeed the arctic grayling. Over the centuries, the grayling's picturesque thyme legend has been passed on from writer to writer, and Izaak Walton claimed to have observed the same phenomenon some 1400 years later. From it has come the grayling's name, *Thymallus arcticus*.

But could a mosquito really have been used for bait? It seems doubtful that one could have implanted one on a hook. Perhaps Aelianus is imprecise in his insect identification, or, probably, the writer has simply showed us that Roman anglers knew the best lure for Ticino grayling to be none other than an artificial fly.

Other passages in Aelianus' writings provide considerable information concerning the tackle required by a well-equipped angler of the times. Aelianus' works suggest that the angler was familiar with the use of artificial lures in general, for example. He went on to discuss the materials and equipment an angler should use for fresh- and saltwater fishing. The freshwater angler, Aelianus stated, must have "horsehair of black, white, chestnut, and light grey color: of dyed colors light blue and purple are preferred; and all others are said to be worthless. Wild boar's bristles are also used and rosin: plenty of bronze and lead: string and feathers, black, white, and variegated. Anglers also require crimson and purple wools . . . a well-trimmed light rod and a rod of cornel wood."

This passage provides an illuminating glimpse of the contents of the second-century angler's tacklebox. A number of the items—string (probably

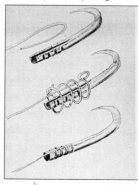

By carving notches in bone (left), primitive fishermen developed an effective method for attaching line to a hollow bone hook. Shown at right are three steps for making an ancient fish spear.

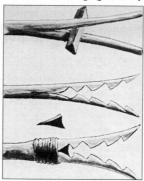

more like thread), feathers of different colors, bright wool—are strikingly similar to those that would be found in a 20th-century flytier's cabinet. It seems plain that Aelianus regarded the materials for making artificial flies as a basic part of the ordinary angler's equipment.

Line selection was quite sophisticated. The line was generally of finely twisted horsehair, and the colors—black, white, reddish, and gray—represented adaptations to different rivers or water conditions. Some lines were of twisted flax, but horsehair seems to have been more common. The angler's knowledge of the properties of his line was further refined by **Plutarch** (circa A.D. 80), who advised the use of hairs from the tail of a stallion, since they were longest and strongest. Those from the tail of a gelding were next and those from a mare least of all, due to the weakness imparted to them from urine. Plutarch

1653

Hundreds of editions of The Compleat Angler *have been published since 1653.*

The Compleat Angler by Izaak Walton is published in Britain and becomes the classic on the art and pleasures of angling. More than 400 English-language editions have since been printed.

1832

A box of 100 Hollow Point Mustad hooks, from the early 1920s.

The Mustad Company begins manufacturing fishhooks in Norway, which is still one of the two largest hook-producing nations in the world, England being the other.

1846

The modern-style cane flyrod is born as Sam Phillipe, a gunsmith and violin maker from Easton, Pennsylvania, breaks with British tradition and invents a new and much-improved flyrod, its blank made entirely of tapered, laminated split-bamboo.

1854

Theodore Gordon, considered by many to be the father of modern American dry-fly fishing, is born in Pittsburg, Pennsylvania.

1856

Orvis in his later years: He died in 1915 at age 84.

Charles Orvis of Vermont establishes the C. F. Orvis & Company,

also suggested the hair next to the hook be taken from a white horse to render it less visible to the fish. The soundness of this advice is reflected in its longevity. Fourteen hundred years later, **Dame Juliana Berners**, in her famous *A Treatyse of Fysshynge Wyth an Angle*, counseled the same practice and offered detailed instructions on coloring horsehair to meet different conditions. Plutarch cautioned against too many knots in the line as well.

Ancient anglers fished with a "tight" rather than with a "running" line. It is somewhat puzzling that people as inventive as the Greeks and the Romans failed to come up with a method for realizing the advantages offered by extra line, but all evidence indicates that fastening the line to the tip of the rod was a practice unchanged from the time of Egyptian anglers some 2000 years earlier. The reel does not make its appearance in angling literature until the middle of the 17th century, and it waited even longer for common acceptance.

The history of the fishhook is a study in itself, and from the earliest times men have used fishhooks made of bone, wood, stone, horn, ivory, and shell. Bronze was probably the most widely used hook material by classical times, and references to it are numerous. Hook making among the Greeks and Romans must have been quite advanced, for many bronze hooks excavated at Pompeii and Herculaneum are nicely made and correctly shaped, exhibiting fine craftsmanship.

Of all ancient tackle, it is perhaps the angler's rod that is shrouded in the greatest mystery. It seems fairly clear that it was of one-piece construction, although fowlers are believed to have used jointed rods in their efforts to snare birds from their perches. Some sophistication in rod selection is evident from those passages that speak of light rods of cane and heavier rods of wood, the selection depending on the application and the size of the fish sought.

Light rods were often made of a cane native to the Mediterranean region. Known today as *Arundo donax*, it is botanically a reed but has long been called "the bamboo of Europe." Stronger and more powerful rods were often made of something called cornel wood, a tough and slender growth that also furnished material for wheel spokes, javelin shafts, and arrows. Probably similar to the greenheart rods of the late 19th and early 20th centuries, the cornel wood rod provided the angler of ancient times with a stiffer and more powerful instrument for landing heavier fish. Most evidence suggests that such rods were quite short, probably averaging six to eight feet in length, as Aelianus states. The line was roughly the length of the rod.

Due to a lack of records, little is known of the angling practices in the centuries between the end of the classical period and the appearance of the earliest English angling writers. It can only be assumed that men continued to enjoy sport with rod and line just as they had for hundreds of years. It must

also be assumed that the practices detailed by Berners and Walton did not begin with them, but represented techniques that had been passed down.
–Paul Rundell, November 1984

The First Compleat Angler

Angle of repose: Izaak Walton.

OF THE 53.9 million anglers in the United States today [it's now closer to 50 million], I doubt if one percent has read **Izaak Walton's** *The Compleat Angler*. The Elizabethan prose of 17th-century England is long dead, and with the book's interlocutory form of Piscator talking to Venator, the words echo from its pages like a Gallagher and Sheen vaudeville act—although part of the instructional dialogue is contemporary *("Go to yonder sycamore tree and hide your bottle of drink under it")*. Despite this, it remains one of the most published and collected books in the world. An original Marriot edition that sold for 18 cents would, according to Colonel Hank Siegel of the Angler's and Shooter's Bookshelf, demand $8000 on the present market. Obviously, Walton's book has endured, as his blithe spirit is synonymous with the term *"angler."*

Izaak Walton died in 1683 at the age of 90, and in a commemorative sense we are in the triennial year of the Father of Fishermen. A decade from now we can celebrate his 400th birthday, but it's *The Compleat Angler* that became his passport to immortality: At last count this venerable book had appeared in about 400 different English editions, or reissues in paperback and hardback, and uncounted foreign translations. Actually, any serious collector of Walton is lost without one or two reference works—Peter Oliver's *A New Chronicle of The Compleat Angler* or Bernard Horne's *The Compleat Angler 1653–1967*—just to keep various editions in perspective. According to some book lists, it's the third most reprinted book in publishing history, exceeded only by the *Holy Bible* and *Pilgrim's Progress*.

I don't know what I expected to see in Walton's final home at No. 7 Dome Alley in the city of Winchester—maybe a quill pen or a stuffed carp—but the lady who owns the place let me wander around like an ignorant tourist. She had no interest in fishing, but was fascinated by his ghost—who apparently stumbles about the upstairs bedroom, moaning, I suppose, over all those uncollected royalties. The broad green lawn behind her house was a mass burial ground during the Great Plague, and there are nights when other ghosts materialize, but she seemed to know which one was "the fishing chap."

and quickly becomes known as a builder of excellent, though less expensive, flyrods.

1868

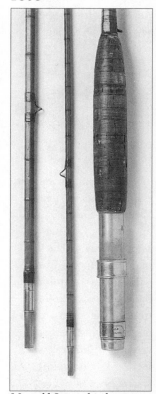

Most old Leonard rods are now worth a small fortune.

Outdoorsman Hiram Leonard reinvents the split-bamboo flyrod by making a lighter, better-tapered blank designed to cast in balance with the new silk lines that replace braided horsehair. The result is a remarkable

improvement over the heavy, unresponsive rods of previous makers like Sam Phillipe. The idea of building a rod to balance with a line for smooth and efficient casting begins a new era in flyfishing.

1874

Rainbows spawn all spring in 50 to 60°F tributaries.

Seth Green, former Fish Commisioner of New York, fish culturist, and outstanding flycaster (in 1864 he became the first man ever recorded to cast a fly 100 feet), introduces the California (rainbow) trout to the eastern United States, hoping the hardier species can thrive in the increasingly despoiled waters once home to native, pollution-sensitive brook trout. The transplant is more successful than even Green expects, leading to a rainbow trout fishery that expands to the East and upper Midwest.

1883

On February 24, the German liner *Werra* docks

The Compleat Angler was penned in an era when 15- to 18-foot spliced ash and hazelwood rods and horsehair lines were standard tackle. When free of urine stains and "without scabs or galls," hair from a brewery horse was considered top-quality; lengths of it were twisted, then joined with a water knot, each link having fewer and fewer hairs, starting perhaps with 12 and terminating in a twist of four hairs—in effect, a tapered line. The mark of an expert was capturing a trout on two hairs, for as Charles Cotton stated: "He that cannot kill a trout of 20 inches on two deserves not the name angler." **Thomas Barke**r, in his *Art of Angling* (1651), suggested a single hair next to the fly, as "you shall have more rises." He neglected to add that you wouldn't land too many fish.

Those lads weren't even using a reel either. The line was tied to the rod tip, and if a tug-of-war went in the fish's favor, Walton admitted to throwing his rod in the river when hooked to an overgrown trout, then recovering it later. The flyline was usually the same length as the rod, and was sent "flying before you up or down the river as the wind serves." Without a breeze it was simply swished back and forth and the fly dapped on the water. Dry-fly fishing didn't exist as a definitive method (flies were tied in a wet-fly configuration), but with the line dancing on the wind, letting no part of it touch the water "but your fly only," it would be impossible not to catch an occasional trout on the surface.

As a practical handbook for modern anglers, *The Compleat Angler* can't even rub bindings with works by Flick, Kreh, Wulff, Sosin, Whitlock, Schwiebert, Boyle, LaFontaine, and many other modern authors. Izaak himself was primarily a baitfisherman addicted to grasshoppers and worms, and he relied heavily on other people's experience to the point of plagiary, which was then fashionable when instructional books were being compiled. Walton did cite other authors, sometimes the wrong one, and for that matter his own name doesn't even appear on the first edition. When it did, his Christian name, Isaac, was spelled with the now familiar "z" and "k." His baptismal certificate in the register of St. Mary's Church in Straffordshire read Isaac filius Jervis Walton. I went to Winchester Cathedral where Walton is buried and the inscription on his crypt, carved in black marble, is almost illegible after being walked upon for three centuries. I borrowed a mop and bucket from the sexton, who seemed delighted to have his floor cleaned, and swabbed away layers of dirt and grimy footprints. He went out the way he came in—Isaac. Possibly "Izaak" began as one of those typographical gremlins that haunt every editor (the classic was in the suddenly popular 1631 King James edition of the Bible, which commanded "Thou shalt commit adultery"). But more likely the spelling was personal whim.

Little of angling value can be learned from *The Compleat Angler* today. There is nothing here on boron rods, bassboats, fathometers, magna-force reels, or microsphered plastics. But in the words of Charles Lamb, "it will sweeten a man's temper any time to read it."

—A. J. McClane, January 1983

Flyrod Lengths, 1862-1943

WITH EFFICIENCY AND comfort the prime moving factors, flyrod lengths have been continually shortened over the years.

In the days of Rube Wood and Seth Green, 1862-1875, rod lengths averaged well over 12 feet. From 1882 to 1890, during the life of the National Rod and Reel Association, the favored length was 11 1/2 to 11 feet. From 1895 to 1905 another foot was lost. The maximum tournament length was 11 feet. Fred Peet's favorite rod, with which he won in 1905-6 the delicacy and accuracy championships, was 10 feet in length and weighed 5 3/4 ounces.

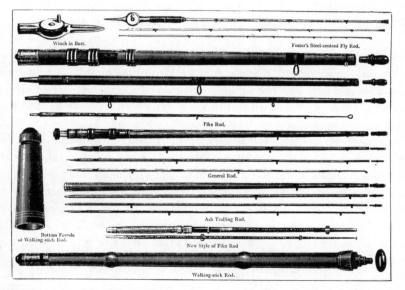

J. Harrington Keene's classic book Fishing Tackle *(1886), illustrates a few essential rods.*

By 1915 the favorite fishing rod was down to 9 1/2 feet. Ten years later it was 9 feet and today there are more and more fishermen going to 8 1/2- and 8-foot rods.

Many anglers are now making up matched sets of rods for a variety of weather and terrain conditions or various types of fishing. Most sets will or

in New York with 80,000 brown trout eggs—sent by Baron Lucius von Behr—which one month later will hatch into the "founding fathers" of the American brown trout fishery.

1884

The fixed-spool Malloch reel.

In Perth, Scotland, Peter Malloch invents the first fixed-spool fishing reel, precursor to the modern spinning reel.

1886

The appearance of *Floating Flies and How to Dress Them*, by British author Frederic M. Halford, fuels the dry-fly revolution in American flyfishing.

1909

Horton Manufacturing of Bristol, Connecticut, begins making tubular steel rods in the early 1900s. By 1909, they offer

tackle dealers a complete
line of Bristol rods.

Winter 1930-31

Lee Wulff wears his Tak-L-Pak fishing vest—the first of its kind—in the late 1940s.

**A passionate, creative
young fisherman named
Lee Wulff sews the first
modern flyfishing vest—
multipocketed and worn
over an angler's clothing
for comfort and easy
access. A refinement of
this vest first hits the
market immediately after
World War II as the Lee
Wulff Tak-L-Pak, made
by Masland of Carlisle,
Pennsylvania. Wulff would
go on to become a book
and magazine author,
filmmaker, and founder of
the Wulff flyfishing school**

should include a 7 1/2- or 7-foot rod. It is doubtful that rods will ever get
much shorter and still remain practical.

—H. H. Smedley, Sports Afield Fishing Annual, 1943

A Brief History of Flyfishing

A VISIT TO THE American Museum of Flyfishing in Manchester,
Vermont, is a nostalgic return to the days when fishermen sought
tranquility rather than excitement. In the quiet rooms of the museum, there
are delicate split-cane flyrods made by every major rodbuilder back to **Charles
Murphy** of Newark, New Jersey, who made and marketed the first commercial
six-strip split-cane rods in the 1860s. In another exhibit are the much older
and longer "buggy whip" rods, which sport pool-cue handles and tiny brass
reels that anglers of the early 1800s loaded with lines made of woven horsehair,
grass, and silk.

The old rods of greenheart, lancewood, hickory, and ash were wonderfully
crafted. Though most of them had slow actions, they were quite delicate, and
a skilled caster could use rollcasts and figure-eights to reach distant fish.

The evolution of flyfishing in America comes into focus as you pass from
one display to the next. The immense influence of the H. L. Leonard Rod
Company is immediately apparent. Old **Hiram Leonard**, a wilderness
merchant and gunsmith from Bangor, Maine, was a contemporary of Henry
David Thoreau; after the two met in the north woods, Thoreau recalled that
Leonard was a great hunter who would paddle down the Allagash and St. John,
then travel up some New Brunswick river and cross overland to the
Restigouche, and finally head down into the Bay of Chaleur, working as an
itinerant gunsmith and trader in the wilderness settlements along the way.

Leonard assembled a crew of bright young men and taught them how to
build flyrods. He used a beveling machine that he and a nephew, Loman
Hawes, had invented but never patented in order to keep the design secret. The
men who worked for Leonard in Bangor and later moved with him to Central
Valley, New York, to be closer to the market are the most impressive names in
rodbuilding history; Fred Thomas, Ed Payne, Eustis Edwards, and Hiram and
Loman Hawes. Thomas Chubb and George Varney were other famous early
employees. All of these men left Leonard's employ during the 1890s to set up
shops of their own, and all went on to establish themselves and their sons as
the finest rodmakers America has produced.

By the turn of the century, rodmakers were using direct flame or kiln ovens
to temper split cane to the springiness of steel. This enabled them to build rods
that could meet the demands of the new dry-fly fishermen. Clearing of land

and damming of streams had raised water temperatures and eliminated shy and delicate brook trout from the Eastern streams closest to the cities, and brown trout were being introduced to replace them. The brown trout were capable of tolerating dirtier and warmer water, but 400 years of existence under sportfishing pressure in Europe had selectively bred the species into a much more difficult fish to catch.

Any bright fly would take a brook trout, but you had to imitate the insect on which fish were feeding to catch a brown.

The museum collection contains a number of flies tied by **Theodore Gordon**, known to many as the father of American dry-fly fishing. Also included is Gordon's personal library of fishing books.

Gordon tied stiff-hackled flies that imitated the local insect life found in the fast Catskill waters. The obscure Catskill flytier once traded 39 dozen of his imitative flies to obtain his favorite flyrod, a 9 1/2-foot Payne.

As the new faster-action flyrods were developed, other changes were happening as well. Vacuum-coated braided-silk flylines were developed to slide through rod guides with less friction. In 1874 **Charles F. Orvis** of Manchester, Vermont, had patented a narrow-spooled, ventilated fly reel that became a prototype. The narrow spool made the reel a multiplier that took up line more quickly than the tiny wide-spooled reels in use at the time. The new reel also mounted beneath the rod grip rather than on the side, thus improving rod balance. Earlier ventilated reels were usually wire-framed "bird-cage" designs that did nothing more than store line. Of these, the early Billinghursts and Folletts are rare finds for the collector and have increased in value by hundreds of dollars despite the frugality of their design. The Billinghurst patented in 1859 was the first American reel designed for flyfishing.

The first disciplined study of American trout stream entomology appeared in 1935, when Derrydale Press came out with **Preston Jennings's** *Book of Trout Flies.* The book, now a valuable collector's item because it revolutionized flytying, expounded the theory that mayflies in American streams were entirely different from those in Great Britain. Thus ended the American tendency to copy the fly patterns in use overseas.

Jennings's book offered scientific identification of the major American trout-stream insects and described how to tie their imitations. The Derrydale Press volume and a collection of flies tied by Jennings are treasures of the museum collection. One of Jennings's favorite Catskill haunts was the West Kill Tavern operated by **Art Flick**, who made his mark on flyfishing in 1947 when his book, *A Streamside Guide to Naturals and Their Imitations,* studied the selectivity of trout and limited to a handful the really important flies that every trout fisherman should carry.

in Lew Beach, New York. He died in 1991 at the age of 86.

1935

An early Luxor spinning reel.

The Luxor spinning reel, an odd piece of European-manufactured tackle, is first introduced to the United States.

Derrydale Press publishes Preston Jennings's *Book of Trout Flies,* the first disciplined study of American trout stream entomology.

1938

The amazing Mepps spinner.

In France, André Meulnart designs a

weighted, in-line spinner that he names "Mepps"— the acronym for his company, Manufacturier d'Engins Précision Pour Peche Sportive. The new spinner is discovered and brought home by American GIs, but not until the early 1950s does the effective spinner become wildly popular in the United States.

George Mason convinces Dow Corning to manufacture a new kind of fishing line using the polymer Saran (commonly used in plastic wrap). The new product is called Monofilament Spinning Line, and though stiff and prone to coiling, is widely considered an improvement over the braided linen, silk, and cotton lines of the day.

Ray Bergman's *Trout*, considered by many to be the first comprehensive book on trout fishing in America, is published by Alfred A. Knopf.

1940

Tired of picking out backlashes, Texas watchmaker R. D. Hull invents

Though the collection has already reached a great magnitude through donations of old tackle and occasional purchases of rare finds, the museum continues to seek more. Who knows which attic may contain a dusty, long-forgotten flyrod by Phillipe, the first to pioneer the six-strip split-cane rod, or a gold-plated Orvis reel catalogued in 1876 but never found, or a rod whose grip was shaped to the hand of George Washington?

—*Jerome Robinson, September 1980*

Origin of a Species

AMERICA GOT HER first brown trout through the collaboration of **Fred Mather**, Superintendent of the New York State Hatchery at Cold Spring Harbor, Long Island, and **Baron Lucius von Behr**, president of the German fishing club (Deutscher Fischerei Verein).

The two men met at the 1880 International Fisheries Exhibition in Berlin, where they talked trout and went fishing in the Black Forest. Mather was very impressed with the fishing, and von Behr promised to send him some brown trout eggs.

Big and beautiful: a 16-inch brown trout taken from Montana's Gibbon River.

Von Behr did not, like many fishermen, simply make loose plans around the dinner table without much thought of going through with them. On February 24, 1883, the German liner *Werra* docked in New York, and 80,000 trout eggs in moss-lined wooden trays were taken immediately to the new hatchery out at Cold Spring Harbor, Long Island.

The browns were off to an auspicious start. However, the "founding fathers" of brown trout in America would need much help in the new land, and they were fortunate in having Fred Mather here to help the fish get through the winter. He was 50, goateed, the first lieutenant of the Seventh New York Heavy Artillery, fish commissioner, flyfisherman, and a humorist whose outdoor writings are still worth a reading today. A fish breeder with new and good ideas, he kept the world posted with a barrage of articles, press releases, displays, and lectures. In his efforts to popularize a little understood science, Mather was to trout culture what Cousteau is to oceanography.

Although Mather was busy with many projects in the early 1880s—designing better hatcheries, raising scallops, dreaming about returning Atlantic salmon to the Hudson—he gave the brown trout his special attention. They rewarded him by hatching in March 1883.

Mather's trout grew like dandelions. Brown trout fry were poured into hundreds of waters, and within a decade they were taking territory in lakes and streams from coast to coast. Besides the German strain, the silvery Loch Leven trout of Scotland was also tried. Eventually the heavily spotted German type would come to dominate, breeding the Scottish strain into obscurity. As early as 1885 the German trout showed their complete satisfaction with our waters by spawning.

By the mid-1880s, fishermen started hooking heavy yellow-bellied trout. The newspapers were filled with stories of strange and extraordinary catches. According to the *Rochester Democrat* for August 6, 1885, Frank J. Amsden caught a 14-ounce trout "covered with bright vermillion spots" in a creek near Mumford. A year later Amsden was taking browns up to three pounds, sometimes spending half an hour landing a fish. In July 1888 the same man caught a 5 1/4-pound brown in Caledonia Creek on a "light six-ounce rod"—a fish that could not have been more than four years old, and of a size unlike anything seen since before the war.

A year later the editor of the *American Angler*, **William C. Harris**, wrote that "the German or brown trout is particularly bidding fair to become an acclimatized and exceptionally popular gamefish."

Tarleton H. Bean wrote in *Forest and Stream* that the brown was "thriving and constantly gaining favor."

This pride in the new fish came from German-Americans, too, one of whom wrote in *Sports Afield* in 1899: "This fish is the German Bachfureilin, and I think it was a shame that the U.S. Fish Commission did not give it that name, but we Germans may hold to the mother tongue name."

the prototype for the modern spincasting reel.

1943

The Shakespeare Company introduces Wonderods, the first tubular fishing rods made of fiberglass, a material that quickly eclipses all other rod-making materials on the popular market.

1948

An early Zebco spincast reel.

R. D. Hull convinces the Zero Hour Bomb Company of Tulsa, Oklahoma, to manufacture his no-backlash reel. The company name is condensed to Zebco, and the first spincast reels hit the market.

1953

Cortland Line Company introduces the 333 Non-Sinkable Fly Line, the first modern-style, plastic-coated floating flyline, which quickly replaces silk lines and makes flyfishing more efficient, pleasurable, and hassle-free.

1955

Schwiebert with a world-record Atlantic salmon.

Ernest Schwiebert's *Matching the Hatch* **is published, spurring the trend toward "scientific" dry-fly fishing for trout in America.**

1957

Berkley introduces the first modern-style monofilament fishing line, made of nylon. It soon dominates the fishing world.

1962

The American Fishing Tackle Manufacturers'

What did people a century ago expect of the brown trout? We can never know for sure, but it must have been a lot. When the brown trout programs failed to bring back streams teeming with fish that were easy to catch, the fishermen grumbled. Letters of complaint began to pile up on the desktops of magazine editors, and a debate was building between the many anglers who misunderstood the fish and the few who recognized its worth. Around the turn of the century the brown trout was described as "big, gluttonous and sluggish" (*Outing* magazine) and "not so highly regarded as our native trouts" (*National Geographic*).

The vast fishing public despised the brown trout, even to the point of brawling in bars over it. But it was too late for anyone to do anything. By 1900 the trout had been introduced into 25 states. The wagons had crawled into every corner of the country: in the devastated Great Lakes region where the brook trout had been wiped out as ruthlessly as the white pine; in Montana and Wyoming, where some of the most fertile trout niches in the world were waiting to be filled—where a nearly fishless Firehole River would take the new trout and become an almost sacred place for anglers; in the rain forests of Oregon where old stump-filled reservoirs would grow monsters "you'd need a hay hook to pull into the boat."

It's a shame that the greater moments in brown trout history were not witnessed by Fred Mather. His death came in 1900, when the fish's reputation was at its lowest. He who had introduced them to America was putting up with a mountain of negative criticism. In a biography written to promote one of Mather's last books, his editors listed all his accomplishments—great and not so great—but they made no mention of the brown trout.

Mather, of course, defended his fish to the end. In the last year of his life he wrote, "Some anglers have objected to the introduction of the brown trout in our streams because they grow too fast and might eventually kill our native fish. To this I say, 'Let 'em do it if they can and the fittest will survive.'"

—Greg Roberts, February 1983

Age of the Wooden Rod

TODAY, TECHNOLOGICAL ADVANCES find frequent application in the production of tackle, especially rods. Highly sophisticated fishing gear is made of boron, graphite, and fiberglass. But it was the now-classic split-bamboo rod that sounded the death knell for the wooden rod over a century ago. Wooden rods are of little interest except to antique-tackle collectors and historians of angling. For centuries, however, wood was virtually the only rod material available, and it served the angler well.

As the use of reels became more common during the 18th century, lighter, shorter, and more delicate rods were built. By the early decades of the 19th century, the making of wooden rods had become a highly refined craft almost as demanding as the procedures employed in making split-bamboo rods.

The superior quality of split bamboo to other rod-making woods became clear to the angling fraternity before 1900. Introduced on a commercial basis in the 1860s, the split-bamboo rod was gradually perfected by such famous American makers as Leonard, Payne, Orvis, Thomas, and Edwards. However, it did not entirely replace other woods for many years because some fishermen, both in America and England, remained faithful to solid wood rods.

In the 1830s and 1840s anonymous American craftsmen were turning out beautifully executed wooden rods. A good example is the greenheart and lancewood flyrod on display in the American Museum of Fly Fishing in Manchester, Vermont. The fittings on this rod are of German silver and it dates from 1832. The quality of American rods of the day was discussed by **John J. Brown** in his classic *The American Angler's Guide* (1845):

"The best rods were formerly imported from England, and made from hazel or hickory, but they were little adapted to our modes of fishing. . . . American rod makers have introduced great improvements in the article within the last ten years, and can now turn out rods which, for workmanship and beauty of finish, cannot be surpassed. They are made to suit the tastes of all anglers, from the single ferruled rod for the novice, at the cost of from $2 to $5, to the more expensive one of the scientific angler, varying from $5 to $50."

England was a great seafaring and colonial power during the 18th and 19th centuries, so British rod makers had access to exotic raw materials from the far-flung corners of the empire. American rod builders of Brown's day relied extensively on native woods, and ash was popular for the butt and mid sections of rods. Other materials were often used for tip sections in ash rods, sometimes whalebone but more frequently lancewood. A fine-grained yellow wood imported from South America and the West Indies, lancewood was widely regarded as the most suitable material for the light and flexible tips of flyrods. By 1885 the ash and lancewood rod seemed to have lost popularity, for in that year **Henry P. Wells** wrote in his comprehensive work *Fly-Rods and Fly-Tackle*:

"The ash and lancewood rod has gone out of fashion in late years, and has fallen in general estimation to a position by no means commensurate with its merits. Some still think that, taking it all in all, this combination makes the best of wooden rods, and it seems to me they are not very far wrong."

Wells went on to describe the time he watched an angler using an ash and lancewood rod land a seven-pound trout after a half-hour battle. A rod of these

Association creates a standard for measuring the weight of flylines based on the weight of their first 30 feet.

1965

McClane with a giant rainbow trout . . . and his encyclopedia.

A. J. McClane publishes his massive *McClane's Standard Fishing Encyclopedia*, the largest, most comprehensive text on sportfishing ever.

1967

Richard Brautigan's *Trout Fishing in America*, which has little to do with actual trout fishing, is first published by City Lights Books.

1973

The Fenwick Company introduces graphite fishing rods, which lead to the graphite revolution in fishing tackle.

Endangered Species Act established; the greenback cutthroat trout is the first fish listed.

1976

On the set of A River Runs Through It.

At the age of 73, retired English professor Norman Maclean publishes his first book, *A River Runs Through It*, a fictionalized memoir of family and trout fishing in his home state of Montana. In 1992, the book is made into an Oscar-winning movie (directed by Robert Redford) that glamourizes flyfishing and nearly doubles the sale of fly tackle nationwide.

materials was still the safest investment for the angler with a modest purse, Wells said, but he cautioned the purchaser to select one in which the ash was white and wide-grained and the lancewood free from bluish streaks or stains.

Around the mid-19th century, American rod makers began to produce rods that were shorter, lighter, and more delicate. Rods built before mid-century were apt to be long (12 to 18 feet or more) with heavy, tapering solid wood butt sections.

Then as now there was disagreement over the proper dimensions of rods, but recommended lengths for 19th-century fly and bait rods are surprising. John Brown's *The American Angler's Guide* suggested a rod of 18 to 20 feet in length for salmon fishing. A bait rod, he wrote, should have the butt section of maple, midsections of ash, and the tip section of lancewood, bamboo, and whalebone. He recommended similar construction and materials for the trout rod but scaled down its length to 12 to 16 feet. **Thaddeus Norris**, author of *The American Angler's Book* (1865), urged the use of a 12 1/2-foot, 12-ounce rod for flyfishing where the trout ran large; where the fish were smaller, a smaller 12-foot, 7- to 9-ounce rod could be used to good advantage. Norris felt that the proper flyrod for trout should have white ash in the butt section, ironwood in the middle section, and split and glued Malacca cane in the tip.

The shift toward shorter and lighter rods had become evident by 1885 when Wells wrote, again in *Fly-Rods and Fly-Tackle*: ". . . confirmed by practical experience with rods from twelve feet six inches to nine feet eight inches in length, the writer is fixed in the belief that ten feet is an ample length for any single-handed fly-rod. . . ."

As rods lost some of their length and resemblance to billiard-cue shafts, rod builders began to experiment with various woods from all over the world as well as with more novel designs. Because anglers could now travel considerable distances to fish, rods that broke down into several sections came into use. These were called suitcase, trunk, or valise rods, and they were the ancestors of today's pack rods.

The list of both native and exotic woods employed in building rods lengthened with the march of time. Some of these were held in high esteem, while others were abandoned as impractical. Hickory was a favorite among native woods; ironwood achieved a degree of popularity. Cedar was praised by some for its lightness and quick action, but its lack of strength dictated extreme care when casting or attempting to set a hook.

Who made the best wooden rods? No single maker in the Age of Wood seems to have gained a better reputation over any other. We do know the names of prominent 19th-century rod craftsmen such as **William Mitchell**, **Robert Welch**, and **Henry Pritchard**. **Hiram Leonard** and **Charles Orvis**, remembered for their fine split-bamboo flyrods, began their careers turning out wooden rods. But the makers of many fine pieces owned by collectors are unknown.

What was it like to cast and to fish with a wooden flyrod?

Martin Keane of Stockbridge, Massachussetts, is well qualified to answer that question. He is the author of *Classic Rods and Rodmakers*, the definitive work on the history and development of the bamboo flyrod in America. He has tested numerous wooden rods and has found many of them to be rather surprising fishing tools. A greenheart rod, he notes, has a rather slow but powerful and rhythmic action that is pleasant to use. Testing a 10 1/2-foot, 9 1/2-ounce ironwood rod with lancewood tips, he made the following observations:

"Using an HCH silk line, the rod was worked back and forth in graceful arcs to lengthen the line through the rings. Even though the reel, line and rod weighed around 18 ounces, the outfit retained a delicate, light feeling. . . . I tried a modern weight-forward line, which instantly improved the casting distance to 75 feet; by accelerating the action with a mild doublehaul . . . I began shooting line out beyond 80 and 85 feet. Obviously, our early fishermen weren't as handicapped as many of us believed, for even when using a silk line, they could easily reach 60 feet or more."

Although the time of the wooden rod has passed forever, undoubtedly many lovely old rods are hidden in dusty attics or cluttered garages. Sometimes they appear at lawn sales, in antique shops, or at auctions. The possibility of finding a fine example of the rod maker's art is intriguing. To the thoughtful angler the delicately formed rod shafts, the soft luster of the finish, the natural warmth and beauty of the wood, can bring to mind a simpler, less hurried era. As instruments of our angling heritage, wooden rods should be remembered. As tributes to the men who built them, they should be preserved.

—Paul Rundell, February 1984

A Line about Flylines

FLYLINES WERE ONCE designated by letters. The letters stood for line diameter. An A line was .060 inch in diameter, and each letter further along in the alphabet was .005 inch smaller. An HEH line, recommended for many light eight-foot rods, had a tip of .025, tapered up to a belly of .040, then narrowed back down to a tip of .025. The method worked because the lines were made of silk and had an average specific gravity of 1.3.

The use of nylon in flylines created a problem. The manufacturers' claim that nylon lines would float better than silk ones was true, but only because the nylon line had a specific gravity of approximately 1.0, the same as water's.

1995

A whirling-disease infected trout with deformed cartilage.

Articles appear in *The New York Times* and *The Washington Post* about whirling disease (first discovered in Colorado in 1987), a deadly parasitic affliction that causes trout to whirl in place and ultimately die.

1996

James Prosek's book, *Trout: An Illustrated History,* is published by Alfred A. Knopf. *The New York Times* calls him "a fair bid to become the Audubon of the fishing world."

1997

Whirling disease continues to spread, especially in the western United States, but scientists isolate genes specific to the parasite, *Myxobolus cerebralis*, that causes it.

Fishermen soon found that an eight-foot rod wouldn't work with an HEH nylon line. It needed an HDH.

In the late 1940s line makers started improving the floatability of their products. New plastic finishes let them control the specific gravity of the lines. That eight-foot rod probably needed an HCH to work properly.

Line makers then turned around and made line that sank better because they were made of Dacron. That same eight-foot rod probably needed an IFI in a Dacron line.

A fisherman then probably had to remember a dozen different line sizes for one rod, depending on material and taper type. The odds of winning at Russian roulette were probably better than those of getting the right line for your rod.

In 1962, the American Fishing Tackle Manufacturers' Association (AFTMA) stepped in to bring order out of chaos. Flylines were assigned a number based on the weight of their first 30 feet. With flylines at last being sized according to weight, the problems of different materials and finishes were eliminated. The fisherman who owns that eight-foot rod now has to remember only one number instead of 12 sets of letters.

—Maurice Mellon, May 1989

Great Steven's Ghost

F EW TROUT AND salmon anglers fishing the famous Rangeley Lakes region of Maine realize they are within a few canoe-paddle strokes of the home of the Gray Ghost, one of the most popular flies ever tied. Still fewer have heard of **Carrie Stevens**, the creator of the fly.

Stevens lived with her husband, a Maine fishing guide, in a modest cottage beside a portage trail between Mooselookmeguntic and Upper Richardson lakes, both noted for brook and landlocked salmon. On July 1, 1924, she was busy with housework when she got an idea for a streamer. "I suddenly had an inspiration of dressing a streamer fly with gray wings to imitate a smelt," she said. To this day the smelt is the primary forage fish in both lakes. It didn't take Stevens long to fashion a creation that had two hackle wings and an underbody of white bucktail. As an afterthought she added several other feathers "which I thought enhanced its appearance and its resemblance to a baitfish," she said.

Carrie Stevens took it immediately to the nearby upper Dam pool where she landed a six-pound 13-ounce brook trout. A Connecticut banker also fishing the pool that day witnessed her catch and suggested she name the fly Gray Ghost. Word of the amazing Gray Ghost spread quickly through the angling world and Stevens was swamped with orders for the fly. "Soon I found I was in the flytying business," she said.

Carrie Stevens continued to tie her popular flies until her death in 1970. Her friends and admirers have erected a plaque in her memory across the portage trail from the Stevens cottage.

–Robert M. Gooch, July 1995

Flyfishing Reels

"Ah, the shriek of the reel, the trout fisher's reel!
No sound is so sweet to the ear;
The hum of the line, the buzz of the wheel!
Where the crystalline brook runs so clear."

THUS SANG OUR venerable poet, Isaac McClellan, the bard of the out-of-doors some 40-odd years ago. He is remembered by the dignified verse from his pen which appeared in the earlier annals of sport in this country. I am calling the attention of my readers to this first stanza of this celebrated poem, "The Angler's Chant," which has appeared conspicuously in an anthology of fishing verse selected from the times of Chaucer into the present day.

The phrase, "the shriek of the reel," stands out and begs the question. Now far be it from me to criticize that delightful contemporary of Herbert, Longfellow, and Whittier; nevertheless to straighten out a tangle which has always vexed me, I am laying bare a perplexing subject: that of flyfishing reels which sing and otherwise give vocal exhibitions of their prowess, much to the gratification of the angler. I have been aware for years that there are reels given to music, but to the present date none of these have come to my attention. What I am looking for is a reel such as Stoddart immortalizes:

"Hark to the music of the reel!
'Tis welcome, it is glorious;
It wanders round the exultant wheel,
Returning and victorious."

Then again, I want to meet up with what one writer mentions as a "ringing reel." I could spend many delightful hours with a ringing reel and I am quite sure a number of my readers who have not had the pleasure of hearing a ringing reel will agree with me that such a winch should be in every Waltonian's tackle box; a reel, in fact, as designated by another writer which "sings forth its song." But I do not think I could bear to have a flyfishing reel which goes into "hysterics," as one writer has stated; and if I live to be 104 years old, I never hope to hear a "whistling line."

A Historical Fact

John Adams (second president of the United States) left Harvard, in 1755, the best trout fisherman in his class. The peaceful spirit of those early college days made much of trout-fishing, and young Adams had a reputation. So firmly did this sport cling to him that after his Presidency he retired to Braintree, Massachusetts, to spend the remainder of his days "along stream."
Editors, July 1888

Voracious Trout

Grey trout or togue are noted for their appetite, but word comes to us from Sherbrooke Lake in Lunenburg County, Nova Scotia, of a particularly greedy fellow. Noticing that a six-pound togue seemed very fat and well rounded after being caught, George Grimm performed an operation to discover what it was all about. Inside the fish's stomach was found 17 fish, one of which was a yellow perch five and one-half inches in length. That's what we call "all hog or none."

—Cal Johnson, September 1936

A typical lake trout.

I think that I should like a reel that purrs; or one of those reels that just quivers with human emotion.

—Robert Page Lincoln, March 1931

The Origin of Western Brookies

THE EASTERN BROOK trout was unknown to the waters of the Rocky Mountains until the year 1874, at which time Gordon Land, Esquire, received some 5000 spawn from James Annin, of Caledonia, New York, and hatched them in Trout Creek, in Monument Park. In 1875, Messrs. Cashman and Denison hatched some 25,000 at Georgetown in a cellar and placed them in Green Lake, and subsequently the same gentlemen erected an expensive hatching house just below their lake, and continued their work of reproduction in connection with others of the salmon tribe for several years. I found the lake well stocked with natives and with *Salvelinus* in 1878, and there were also a few *Salmo quinnat* from the McCloud River, California, to be seen. I carried 18 Eastern trout from Green Lake to Bear Creek in 1879, and placed them in ponds eight miles above Morrison, and I hatched 15,000 for the benefit of that stream, but I question whether my action was a real benefit—it certainly was an improvement of the fishing. Since that time a great many people have imported eggs of the New York and Massachusetts char, the State of Colorado alone probably having been instrumental in placing three million small fry in the public waters. There is hardly a stream, at least on the eastern slope of the mountains, which has not received from 5000 to 100,000, and I think a fair estimate would give 500,000 to the South Platte alone, coming from all sources.

—W. R. Scott, February 1888

The Origin of Western Brookies, Disputed

I AM PLEASED with *Sports Afield* and will cheerfully do what I can to aid you. However, you must be patient with me, for I have more than 100,000 young trout to teach to feed and rear them to weigh three to the pound by next December. I also have a Fly Factory in which I propagate the festive blue-bottle and feed his numerous progeny; they in turn to serve as food for my fish.

I notice an error in W. R. Scott's article wherein it gives me the credit of introducing 5000 Eastern brook trout into the waters of Monument Park, in 1875. The facts in regard to the first introduction of *Salvelinus fontinalis* into Colorado waters are these: In the winter of 1871-2 James M. Broadwell brought from Boscobel, Wisconsin, the first eggs of the Eastern brook trout and hatched them in a small hatchery containing one or two gravel troughs fed by springs from the bank about 300 yards below where the present Colorado State Hatchery is now located, eight miles down the Platte from Denver. The following winter, 1872-3, the writer had shipped to him at Alden's Ranch, 16 miles from Fairplay in the South Park, 5000 eggs of *Salvelinus Fontinalis* from Seth Green's trout ponds in Caledonia, New York. At this place was constructed the first regular hatchery and trout ponds ever built in the State. Unlike those introduced at the Broadwell ranch, the fry were well cared for and grew to be fine, vigorous trout; they were placed into properly prepared ponds, while Mr. Broadwell permitted all of his to be lost; no ponds were constructed for the fry and the few that were turned into a long, shallow ditch were never again seen after the first season. The second introduction by the writer was a lot of 100,000, also from the Seth Green Ponds, placed in the hatchery at "Fish Ranch" in Manitou Park during the winter of 1874-5. From these 83,000 fry were obtained and used to stock the ponds prepared for them on the property. This hatchery is still in use after 14 years of service; 100,000 fry are now being fed beneath its roof, and since it was built it has done a great service to the State, inasmuch as the trout grown below its sheltering shingles have from time to time been turned out to stock the adjacent streams long before the little affair down the Platte, called by courtesy a State Hatchery, was thought of. When Denver anglers catch two- or three-pound trout in the South Platte they should thank Dr. William A. Bell, whose liberality some years ago introduced the fish that are now so common in South Platte water.

—Gordon Land, Esq., March 1888

Fishing As It Should Be

THEY TELL ME there are streams where one, if the planets are in the right conjunction and one carries several pounds of horseshoes and the left hind foot of a graveyard rabbit along with him, and has patience enough, and the fish are hungry, and one has the right kind of bait, he can catch a trout once in a while or maybe two whiles. I do not know—having only the word of fishermen for it. And the word of a fisherman is notoriously no better than a train robber's bond.

So, when I want to go fishing, I don't pay any attention to such information, but dig some worms around the rose bushes in the yard, and hunt a pond somewhere that has a grassy bank and shade trees interpose protection from the ardent rays of a midsummer sun. And there I can lie on the bank and listen

Pure Trout

We believe that the most important factor in the propagation of game fishes in this country today is to have the waters in which they are planted pure. Of what benefit is it to engage in the stocking of waters, which, on account of pollution, will not support the fish? This club is becoming more and more influential each year and is commencing a determined fight against the pollution referred to. We believe that the very best way to begin this fight is to appeal, as we are now doing, to the magazines throughout the country to help. We ask you to help us by using your great influence in the shaping of public opinion, for the benefit of every sportsman throughout the country; for every lover of outdoor life.

–Edward B. Rice, Treasurer of the Angler's Club of New York, August 1909

to the hum of bees in the alfalfa fields, smell the scent of new mown hay and watch the hawks swing on steady wings in airy spirals high above me, keeping an attentive eye on the bobber meanwhile. For, I confess it, I do use a bobber. For what joy, save that of duck shooting, can surpass seeing the concentric circles widening around a bobber and hearing the faint "Kerplunk!" it makes as it goes under. That is fishing as it should be. No whipping of a trout stream to a froth; no getting tangled in waitabit thorns; no barking of shins on razor edged rocks. The fish caught are not many, neither are the trout; but they have one characteristic common to trout: they are all about the size and shape of lead pencils.

–Bryan L. Whitehead, June 1920

The Knack of Trouting

WHY IS IT that one man—or, more likely, one boy—can fish a trout stream and get a string to be proud of, while another man will go over the same ground, perhaps with better tackle and more ardent enthusiasm, and have next to nothing to show for his labor? I used to answer this question by saying that it was just luck, but experience has taught me better. I am now convinced that the secret of successful trout fishing lies in understanding the knack of it—nothing more.

It's hard to top a young boy with a cane pole.

The brook trout is the coyest and most suspicious of all his kind. He must be approached not only with caution, but with knowledge of his habits and disposition—in other words, with science. Caution and science constitute the knack of trouting. The "born" angler inherits an aptitude for acquiring this knack. It is a sort of second nature with him, which a little experience readily calls out and develops. A country boy, whose ancestors have from time immemorial devoted rainy days in summer to fishing, takes to the gentle art quite as deftly as a duck to water. It was just such a boy who demolished my theory about luck as the magic of trouting. I saw him, for the first time, fishing in the locally famous "basin" of Terrill's Brook. The picture itself was worth remembering. Imagine an undersized boy in a gingham shirt, a pair of overalls, one suspender, and a broadbrimmed straw hat. The brook comes roaring down a series of steep, rocky pitches and makes a final leap into the "basin"—the largest trout-pool, without exception, that I ever saw in a mountain brook. On a flat rock at the head of the pool stands the boy—a mere midget down in that sub-cellar of the woods. The ragged banks rise a hundred feet above him on every side; precipitous, bearded with balsams and hemlocks and split into yawning clefts. Only the agile and sure-footed angler can get down to the basin of Terrill's Brook. But, once down there, in the mist and the roar, what an ideal spot for a sweltering day!

There, as I said, I first saw the boy who taught me the knack of trouting. I was on the wooded bank a hundred feet above him; and as I gazed down into that gloomy ravine and saw him outlined against the opposite cliff, my heart leaped with the sudden fancy that it was an elf, a veritable little wild man of the forest, surprised at his sport. But the tattered straw hat, the long bamboo pole, and the pepper-box overflowing with angle-worms soon undeceived me. The little fisherman stood like a statue, his face bent over his rod and concealed by the ample straw hat. I shouted again and again at the top of my voice, but he could not hear. In the roar of the cascade by which he stood, the report of a cannon 20 feet away would have sounded like the pop of a cork from a bottle. Somehow I managed to scramble down to him; and by virtue of that feat we were fast friends at once. He had 67 trout in a lard pail, set in a cool cleft among the rocks; and strung on a forded stick were six big fellows which he had whipped out of the basin—not one of them less than half a pound in weight, and all too large for the lard pail. I had been casting a fly along the brook for five hours, and had captured only three small trout.

Next day the boy and I went fishing together, and I began to learn something about the tricks and the manners of trout. It was a liberal education in angling to watch the way the boy went about his business. He carried, to begin with, a bamboo pole that was at least 20 feet long. "You must keep back out of sight, or you won't get a bite," he remarked. "That whip-stock of yourn is no good for fishin' at long range." I explained the use of the reel and leader in invisible fishing at a distance, but he shook his head. "I've seem 'em try it," he replied, "but it never seemed to work."

In his method of approaching a "hole" he was like a general planning a campaign. He would creep along like a cat, barefooted and crouching, until he came within 25 or 30 feet of it, on the upper side. Then he would straighten up slowly and study the surroundings of the pool and the direction from which the current entered. "Always hide and cast from behind the rough of the riffle," was his rule. If you stood a little on one side of the riffle to cast, his theory was that the trout would see you and would not bite. You must get right in line with that dark ruffling current—hide behind it, as it were—and let your bait come floating down into the pool with the riffle. If necessary, cross the stream, or get into the middle of it, so as to be directly in line with the current. It will hide you more effectively than a stone wall. No trout can see through swift, ruffled water. This was the first invaluable rule which I learned from my "born" fisherman of the blue overalls and solitary suspender:

Flycaster's Tournament

The recently held anglers' tournament in Central Park, New York City, was a most successful affair, though not so largely attended as some others, owing to the unpleasant weather. There were a great many new faces present, showing an increasing interest in the sport. There was an entire absence of any element with "mug hunting" propensities, advertising schemes, or anything else that has caused any unpleasantness in the past. Taken altogether it was the pleasantest and most satisfactory meeting ever held since the organizing of the association. It is the interest of every dealer in fishing tackle to encourage and support all such contests and we expect to see them inaugurated in all parts of the country.

—Editors, July 1888

Hide behind the riffle. It has won me many a goodly trout since then for which in my days of ignorance I would have angled in vain. Nine times out of 10 the eager but inexperienced fisherman will sacrifice his chance of getting a 10-inch trout by fishing down into a likely pool on one side or the other of the ruffling current, where he is in plain sight of every fish in the hole. Get behind the riffle. Let your bait or fly float carelessly down with the current, and if there is a hungry trout in the pool you are sure of a rise.

The reader will observe that I am not saying much about artificial flies and the knack of using them successfully in trouting. This is because I look upon the use of flies in brook-trout fishing as a kind of fad, from which the angler gets little solid satisfaction. An artificial fly is a very uncertain kind of lure; and when trout are rather scarce it hardly pays to waste the necessary time experimenting with it. A trout may take a fly, and he may not. In 99 out of 100 cases he will not. And as for the skill of fly-fishing, I hold that a grasshopper or worm is harder to place just where you want it than a fly, and more effective when it gets there. After you strike your trout, it is all the same in respect to skill, of course, whether you have used live bait or fly. It is just as hard to land a fish hooked with a worm as one hooked with a fly.

—Jack Buckham, May 1908

Flyfishing Fancies

FLYFISHING, IT MAY be seen, is no longer monopolized in its entirety by an august body of trouting purists but is a means of fishing that Sam Jones or Bill Brown can, very successfully, use in picking up a mess of sunnies. In the sense of things, flyfishing is broadening its scope. It has come of age and is attaining to popular favor in a manner that defies contradiction.

Trout fly fishermen deplore this "passing" of a great sport and pastime. At the inception of flyfishing in this country, it is probable that it enjoyed somewhat the dignity of exclusiveness and was participated in solely by men who sported stationery with a coat of arms and who dispensed their wisdom and recounted their experiences from the cozy depths of sleep-provoking chairs in the clubs of the elite. There has been too much snobbery and sniffiness about flyfishing and its peculiar attraction. Where it should have whole-souled joy and all-embracing good fellowship as its pervading sentiment, it has rather been a dry-as-dust performance, repellent instead of inviting to the average angler. Its aloofness from the "mob" has been as empty-headed in its provincial appeal as a volume of the Congressional Record.

—Robert Page Lincoln, May 1931

Trout vs. Bass

OUR ESTEEMED FRIEND E. K. Stedman (which his middle name is Kleber) formerly camped and fished and "writ" in and around Mount Carroll, Illinois, and was then a believer in the superiority of the small-mouth black bass over any and all other fish in the matter of plain and fancy fighting. Then a kindly Fate directed his wandering footsteps across the open country and the Great Divide into a country of swift waters and the swiftwater sort of trout, all mouth and appetite and concentrated scrappiness. And thereupon he experienced a reversal of faith. He yanked the stopper out of his ink bottle, gripped his fountain pen with both hands, and sent *Sports Afield* an interesting article, of which the following may stand as a sample:

"The black bass is a grand, good fish—ever ready for a scrap, game to the last flop, prettily armored, democratic and American—but personally I now think the trout of this Western country afford better sport from the standpoint of the angler—giving one more heart thrills in battle."

And then comes one from Mr. Lew H. Feezer, who had known and loved Mr. Stedman before his lamentable fall from grace, and therefore felt privileged to cuss and abuse the aforesaid Stedman in a friendly way. Harken to the blast of indignation which swept like a simoom across plains and mountains and found the recalcitrant one shivering behind his giant firs and Douglas pines:

"Friend Sted: Little did I think when you left old Mount Carroll, that I should have cause to blush for your ignorance. I'm positively ashamed of you, Kleber. How can you sign your name to such a barefaced lie? You know, deep down in your heart, that no trout ever swam with the life and grit in him that a genuine redeye black bass has. Tie one at each end of a line and see which will kill the other. Your little rainbow fellows are to the black bass what a dogfish is to a salmon. Oh, hush! hush! hush! I'm mad clean through."

—Editors, April 1913

Tail-Water Trout

AMERICAN FISHERMEN have pursued trout across our continent's northern streams and lakes for decades. Now there exists a third dramatic cold-water fishery that has expanded the trout's ranges deep into the South. Just as tackle and techniques differ with lake and stream fishing, so does this new fishery call for specific methods if you wish to meet with reasonable success.

One of the first significant steps in developing this new trout fishing occurred in the early 1940s as the Tennessee Valley Authority lakes were built to control the Tennessee River's floods and to harness the hydroelectrical potential of these waters for public and industrial uses. Perhaps a few farsighted biologists foresaw the advent of ideal environmental conditions for stocking trout, but this was certainly not the motive that inspired the projects in Tennessee as well as in other surrounding states. Later, it was noticed that these tail waters soon became almost void of native warm-water species as cold water was released from the hydroelectric facilities. This situation encouraged experiments and eventually rainbow and brown trout were introduced. But it has taken years to fully understand the new problems, to adopt practical stocking programs, to adjust laws and seasons, and to use the fantastic potential of this infant fishery.

—Dave Whitlock, April 1971

Let's Go Fishin'

RECENTLY I MADE some suggestions for an economic and social tidying-up of our country in preparation for the return of our boys from overseas. As I wrote, I was depressed by the thousand mournful voices chanting daily of "postwar problems" in such powerful terms as recovery, reconstruction, and regeneration.

But in their research efforts in speech and their labors in type, they all concern themselves solely with what we are to do while we are on their promised jobs. Civilization, however, is not going to depend so much on what we do when we are on the job, as what we do in our time off. The moral and spiritual forces do not lose ground while we are pushing "the instrumentalities of production and distribution." Their battle is in our leisure time.

When the guns cease firing, and the gas comes on again, some of us are going fishing. We American men and boys (and some women) are born fishermen—twelve million of us. We have proved it in bygone days by the annual licenses we took out from thrifty state governments.

We have had mostly to postpone the fishing beatitudes for the duration. Many of us are busy at the military front. Some of us on the home front could possibly get a day or a week off, but the fishing holes can only be approached by automobile or motorboats, and a stern government refuses to recognize that fish do not flourish near railway depots.

In the meantime, I suspect that Mother Nature is making the fish bigger and more plentiful by way of preparing to celebrate peace, and our paternal government is doing its duty to solve our postwar problems by running the hatcheries full blast, turning out billions of infant fish and trying to decrease infant mortality.

I have discussed this important subject in years past, but some review and extension of those remarks are not out of place in these days when we are groping for postwar regeneration. Nothing can stop these regenerative forces.

Even the Four Horsemen cannot stop them. War, murrain, famine, pestilence, dictators, or the rise and fall of empires or republics may defeat the game fisherman temporarily, but he always rises again to invade the streams and the sea. More people have gone fishing over more centuries than for any other human recreation.

Sometimes the uninstructed and the people who have bad "isms" scoff at the game fishermen and demand to know how they get that way. It is very, very simple. These regenerative impulses are physical, spiritual, and economic— and they are strong.

The human animal originally came from out-of-doors. When spring begins to move in his bones, he just must get out again. One time, in the spring, our grandmothers used to give us nasty brews from herbs to purify our blood of the winter's corruptions. They knew something was the matter with the boys. They could have saved trouble by giving them a pole, a string, and a hook. Some wise ones (among them my own) did just that.

Moreover, as civilization, cement pavements, office buildings, radios have overwhelmed us, the need for regeneration has increased, and the impulses are even stronger. When all the routines and details and the human bores get on our nerves, we just yearn to go away from here to somewhere else. To go fishing is a sound, a valid, and an accepted reason for such an escape.

It is the chance to wash one's soul with pure air, with the rush of the brook, or with the shimmer of the sun on blue water. It brings meekness and inspiration from the decency of nature, charity toward tackle makers, patience toward fish, a mockery of profits and egos, a quieting of hate, a rejoicing that you do not have to decide a darned thing until next week. And it is discipline in the equality of men—for all men are equal before fish. . . .

Someone propounded the question to me: "Why have all presidents in modern times been fishermen?" It seemed to me a worthy investigation, for the habits of presidents are likely to influence the nation's youth. Some of us had been fishermen from boyhood and required no explanation. But others only became fishermen after entering the White House. In examining this national phenomenon, I concluded that the pneumatic hammering of demands on the president's mind had increased in frequency with the rising tide of economic and international complexity, and he just had to get away somehow, somewhere, and be alone for a few hours once in a while. But there

Mystery Trout

The case of the silver trout has been argued for decades in New Hampshire. Its continued existence is dubious, and some even question whether it ever existed. But the silver did exist— and in great numbers, though its range was extremely limited. It was found only in New Hampshire's Dublin Lake, at the foot of towering Mount Monadnock. It has never been discovered in any other body of water.

The Dublin trout was described and cataloged by naturalist Louis Agassiz in 1884 and named in his honor, *Salvelinus agassizii*. While silver trout numbers steadily declined at the turn of the century, it was still common as late as 1912. From time to time there are rumors of someone catching one of these rare fish, and two years ago a strange "green-and-yellow trout" was taken through the ice. Unfortunately it was not observed by scientists.

—Frances X. Sculley, August 1984

are only two occasions when Americans respect privacy, especially in presidents. Those are prayer and fishing. So that some have taken to fishing.

President Cleveland was both a stream and a sea fisherman from youth. His stiff trout rod is still preserved by a devoted fisherman, and it is recorded that his sea-fishing boatman was chosen for silence. Whether President Coolidge fished in his youth is uncertain. He was a good deal of a fundamentalist in economics, government, and fishing, so he naturally preferred angleworms. But when the flyfishermen of the nation raised their eyebrows in surprise, he took to artificial flies. However, his backcast was so much a common danger that even the Secret Service men kept at a distance until they were summoned to climb trees to retrieve flies.

But I should return to expanding on postwar regeneration and its moral and spiritual values in a gloomy world. Statistics tell us that the gainfully employed have steadily decreased in hours of work during the whole of thirty years. And in shorter hours and longer weekends and holidays, we have devoted more time to making merry and stirring the caldron of evil. Crime has increased. Yet nobody was ever was in jail or plotted a crime when fishing. The increase of crime is among those deprived of those regenerations that impregnate the mind and character of fishermen.

Our standards of material progress include the notion and the hope that we shall still further lessen the daily hours of labor. We also dream of longer annual holidays as scientific discovery and mass production do our production job faster and faster. But when they do the job, they dull the souls of men unless their leisure hours become the period of life's real objective—regeneration by fishing.

Moreover, while we are steadily organizing increased production of leisure time, the production of what to do with it still lags greatly. We do have some great machinery of joy, some of it destructive, some of it synthetic, much of it mass production. We go to chain theaters and movies. We watch somebody else knock a ball over the fence or kick it over the goal post.

I do that and I believe in it. But these forms of organized joy are sadly lacking in the values which surround the fish. We gain none of the lift of soul coming from a return to the solemnity, the calm and inspiration of primitive nature.

Nor is it the fish we get that counts, for they can be had in the market for mere silver. It is the break of the waves in the sun, the joyous rush of the brook, the contemplation of the eternal flow of the stream, the stretch of forest and mountain in their manifestation of the Maker, that soothes our troubles, shames our wickedness, and inspires us to esteem our fellow men—especially other fishermen.

—President Herbert Hoover, June 1944

A Brief History of the Dry Fly

NO SPORT HAS a finer literature than angling, and that dealing with the dry fly features the work of those who expressed themselves extremely well. If a founder and anniversary date can be established, we turn to page 132 of *The Vade-mecum of Fly Fishing for Trout* by G. P. R. Pulman, 1851 edition:

"Let a dry fly be substituted for the wet one, the line switched a few times through the air to throw its superabundant moisture, a judicious cast made just above the rising fish, and the fly allowed to float towards and over them, and the chances are ten to one that it is seized as readily as the living insect. This dry fly, we must remark, should be an imitation of the natural fly on which the fish are feeding."

In view of the facts that insects float and trout feed on the surface, it might seem strange that the wet fly preceded the dry by centuries; however, the deterrent was the matter of making the fly float. Once it was discovered that the imitation could be dried sufficiently in the air by "false casting," to insure buoyancy, the problem was solved. Francis Francis, editor of the famous periodical, the *Field*, reported in 1867 on his work, *A Book of Angling*, that the dry fly was greatly used in southern waters.

The cradle of the dry fly was the Hampshire district of England, the champions of it the members of the Fly Fisher's Club of London. The inefficiency of the wet fly on the free-rising brown trout of the fabulous chalk streams was most apparent. The efficiency and beauties of the dry-fly method won angling hearts.

George Selwyn Marryat was a creative flytier and master angler of the Itchen around Winchester. In the minds of some he is the greatest who ever drew breath. However, he produced no writings and was cut down at the age of 56. Years later another of the hierarchy of anglerdom, Skues, wrote that Marryat was "universally regarded as the prince of fly-fishers, fly-dressers and waterside naturalists." But he left his indelible mark by indirect means. The diadem was passed to a fishing companion, **Frederic M. Halford**, to proclaim the dictum—the effective Marryat approach and fly patterns.

The first of Halford, the prophet's, books under the Marryat influence, *Floating Flies and How to Dress Them*, 1880, formalized procedure and pattern. Great significance was attached to natural drift over the spot of the rise with a well-tied imitation of the natural—form, size, and color being all important.

Anglers funneled into the club quarters after trips to the Test, the Itchen and other chalk streams to compare notes, exchange ideas, and to secure or fabricate flies closely relating to the insect of the moment. Actually their philosophy was to tie so "trout do not look for differences but rather for similarities." Deception had captivated their fancies. The great mind of the originator had brought into being the new approach; the followers made what they considered important changes, but the genius of the originators, Marryat–Halford, remained. . . .

Across the Atlantic there fished a frail little man who angled for a different species of trout in a different type of environment. Theodore Gordon, a native of the state of New York, operated in a rustic setting where the stony fast-dropping streams were inhabited by brook trout. Like Marryat he left no book or articles; however, there was correspondence—salvaged letters to and from Skues. Thus it was that the English dry fly found its way to America to be cast on the Neversink by Gordon. The father of the floating imitation in this country successfully applied his new craft to the slicks, glides, and flats where the rises of brook trout occurred. But there was a second revelation: The hungry trout of the lean freestone waters would snatch at an isolated fly. Even when there was no rise of trout it was practical to fish with the dry fly. Gordon's fishing took him to other New York streams and there is documentary evidence that he sought out and found some limestone water, namely Spring Creek and Big Spring in Pennsylvania.

It was estimated by **Emlyn Gill** that directly prior to the time he produced the first American work on the subject, *Practial Dry Fly Fishing*, 1912, there were less than 100 adherents in the United States and very few fishermen knew the meaning of the term "dry fly." Gill, with two great assets, was well prepared to introduce formally this high form of angling to the wet-fly anglers of his country: He was the possessor of a keen and studious mind, being well read; and he, on occasion, fished with an extremely talented fellow, one **George LaBranche**. Gill had a complaint—half a century ago: there was no available entomological data relative to American aquatic insects.

By comparing English reporting with his own stream observation it was evident that the hatches on the waters he fished were different and less frequent than those on the English chalk streams, yet he could catch trout on the dry fly when there was no rise. In fact he corresponded with the aging Halford about these matters. To him a fly was impressionistic and when there was nothing to imitate, exact imitation is academic. He visualized the water in graph-paper pattern and proceeded to float a fly in the likely places in each block starting with the closest and reaching out from there. Checkerboard casting was his answer to fishing the water well.

The first purist in this country, a dedicated young angler who observed through the sharpest eyes you ever saw, the possessor of an analytical mind and coordinated reflexes, chose to wait until 1922 to produce a compendium of his trout fishing method. George M. L. LaBranche fished the great trout rivers of the East as well as some of the English chalk streams. Favorites were the Broadshead in Pennsylvania, the Neversink and Beaverkill in New York, and the Itchen and Kennett in southern Britain. For good measure he popularized the fishing of the dry fly for Atlantic salmon.

Once and for all time he proved that dry-fly fishing was not simply a passing English fad as at this time was generally regarded in America to be the case. He bridged the fishing-procedure gap between two continents and two environments. The American approach as set forth in *The Dry Fly in Fast Water* was to fish the hatch when there is a rise of trout; but when this does not prevail, and it is most of the time, artificially create a hatch. Obviously trout have hiding places and feeding stations. Hunger and hatches bring them into the open. An undercut rock makes a perfect home and an adjacent line or drift a natural place from which to intercept food. Time and again he would float his favored iron-blue dun over the carefully calculated taking place so that it would appear to the quarry that a hatch is in progress and that it is time to move and partake of it. Involved were individual fish and repetitive flawless casting.

An American version of the Fly Fisher's Club of London came into existence and from it sprang refinement, knowledge, and enthusiasm centering mainly around dry-fly fishing. Residents and nonresidents affiliated with the **Anglers Club of New York**, and 101 Broad Street in the big city became an angler's mecca. The leading light was the late Edward R. Hewitt, the long-time fishing partner of LaBranche. Hewitt, the scientist, was an inventive genius who not only applied his vast store of technical knowledge to angling but planned things so there was ample time and opportunity to fish. Probably never in the history of anglerdom will there again be such renowned trout fishing teams as Halford and Marryat, and Hewitt and LaBranche. Hewitt's definitive work on trout fishing in general, *Telling on the Trout*, was published in 1935.

–Charles K. Fox, Sports Afield Fishing Annual, *1961*

Trout Habits and Habitat

~

"Most anglers spend their lives in

making rules for trout,

and trout spend theirs in breaking them."

—George Aston, 1926

Trout

Family: *Salmonidae*

AUTHORITIES ARE NOT certain how many species or subspecies of trout there are in North America. This is partly because isolated populations vary in color, body form, and other characteristics. Changing conditions have resulted in some species becoming extinct or hybridizing to such an extent that the original groups can no longer be distinguished.

Trout are divided into two groups. First, the chars, including the arctic char, brook, Sunapee, lake, and Dolly Varden trout—all with coloring characteristic of light spots on a darker background. The other group, including the rainbows, cutthroats, and brown trout, has dark spots on a lighter background. All have one or several closely related species. No fewer than eight are closely related to the rainbow, 10 have branched off from the cutthroat stock, and four from the brook trout ancestral form. Several species or subspecies are known to be extinct.

Like the other members of this family, the salmon and whitefish, trout are found over the northern parts of the world, generally north of Latitude 40. They have succeeded in penetrating more southern regions only by taking advantage of high mountain conditions of cool or cold water.

—*From* Sports Afield's Know Your Fish, *1987*

Our American Trout

TROUT ARE DIVIDED into several distinct genera, each of which has special characteristics. Char of the genus *Salvelinus* are named from a word of Gaelic origin meaning red or blood-colored. The term refers to the red bellies of most trout in this genus, which are especially brilliant on breeding males. Most char prefer cold, swift water, but some are anadromous— that is, they descend streams and enter salt water, as does the steelhead of the genus *Salmo.*

Char are easily distinguished by small scales and a boat-shaped vomer—the bony plate that forms the front part of the roof of the mouth. On char, the vomer has teeth only at its end, while on trout of the genus *Salmo*, which includes rainbow, cutthroat, and steelhead varieties, the vomer is flat and well-supplied with teeth. Char found in eastern Canada and the northeastern United States are the most brilliantly colored freshwater fish—yet another distinguishing factor.

The common European char, or Saibling, *Salvelinus Alpinus,* lives in the mountain streams of Europe. The Greenland and Arctic char are closely related to this trout, as is the Dolly Varden, which is said to be a direct descendant of the European char.

The brook trout, *Salvelinus fontinalis,* originally inhabited cold waters from Labrador west to Saskatchewan and southward along the streams of the

Connecticut angler Peter Clarke with a 9-pound Arctic char taken on a No. 8 Royal Wulff.

Alleghenies to Georgia, but it has been widely transplanted and is now found in many streams outside of its original habitat. This trout is distinguished by the vermicular or wormlike markings on its back, which extend into the adipose, dorsal, and caudal fins. It also has many light yellowish spots and red spots ringed in light blue. The pectoral, ventral, and anal fins are red with a white forward edge lined with black. Breeding males have red lines along the sides of the belly that are lined below with black.

The Oquassa trout, *Salvelinus oquassa,* named after Lake Oquassa, is found in this and other lakes of the Rangeley Lakes in Maine. This small, thin trout has blue on its back, with red spots on the sides. Its close relative is the Sunapee, *Salvelinus aureolus,* which, as its name implies, has all the colors of the aurora and is one of the most brilliantly colored chars. The bright colors are particularly brilliant on the breeding male. It is named after Sunapee Lake in New Hampshire and is now found in only a few lakes in the country [see page 41].

To the north we find other closely related chars, among them the exceedingly brilliant red trout, *Salvelinus marstoni,* found only in a few lakes in Quebec. This slender trout has a distinctly forked tail and a rather small head. It is a brownish olive above and red below, covering the entire lower belly and extending onto the lower fins. The red is pink on many specimens, but bright red—even a flaming red-orange—on breeding males. The spots are not numerous, but there are a few red and orange spots on the sides. Closely related and also red-bellied are the Arctic char, *Salvelinus naresi,* of northwestern Canada, some of which run into salt water along the Arctic Coast and Labrador and, at times, into the Gulf of St. Lawrence.

These trout are Canadian representatives of the Arctic char of Europe, as are the Greenland char, or Saibling, and the sea trout, or salter, of Greenland—so-called because it descends regularly to the sea.

It should be noted that most of these trout are commonly referred to as Saibling or char, which can be confusing. They are, after all, closely related and are perhaps subspecies of a single type species—the Arctic char of Europe. Limitations of habitat have no doubt brought about the variations in size and color.

All of the species cited have their original habitat in the eastern and northerly parts of North America, while the trout of the genus *Salmo* have their orginal habitat in the western part. Yet, strangely, it is in the west that we find one of the finest of the chars, the Dolly Varden or bull trout, *Salvelinus malma spectabilis.*

The brightly colored Dolly Varden is gamey and somewhat unusual for most chars, and it can attain considerable size. In some areas, it grows to a length of two and three feet and a weight of between five and 12 pounds. It's not large, as compared to some trout of the genus *Salmo,* but big compared to chars like the Oquassa trout. Olivacious in color with red and orange spots, the Dolly Varden is found in streams west of the Cascade Range, from

Alaska to the upper Sacramento, and in the Colombia River Basin to Idaho and Montana.

Though some char resemble the introduced brown trout of Europe, the latter is a member of the genus *Salmo* and is not a char. It is distinguished from the chars by the black spots on its back, which resemble those found on rainbow and cutthroat trout. It also has red spots on its side, which are lacking in trout of the genus *Salmo*.

Since char prefer cold waters, they die out when timber is cut away, exposing streams and their mossy banks to the hot rays of the sun. Trout streams are kept cold by ice that freezes in the heavy mosses along the streams. When the timber is cut, the sun kills the moss and the ice melts. This has happened to many trout streams that were once abundant with brook trout. Brown trout and rainbow trout have been introduced in their place, since they do better in warmer waters.

—Walter J. Wilwerding, March 1941

Trout and Their Allies

AS PREVIOUSLY MENTIONED, trout are divided into two distinct families, genus *Salmo* and genus *Salvelinus*. The former genus includes the so-called salmon trout, numerous species of cutthroat and rainbow trout, the Atlantic salmon, and the landlocked varieties—the Ouananiche and the Sebago.

There is really no structural difference between the family members that are called trout and those that are called salmon. The steelhead trout of the

A cutthroat gets its name from the bright red or orange slashes on its lower jaws.

West Coast have the same habits as the Atlantic salmon, spending part of their lives in fresh water and part in salt water.

However, a steelhead trout is not a distinct species, but is either a rainbow or cutthroat that has access to the sea. The difference exists in that, when finding access to the sea and apparently to a greater abundance of food, both the rainbow and the cutthroat take on more of the proportions of the salmon. Either the salt water or the food also makes some change in the coloring.

The golden trout is also a member of the genus *Salmo,* as is the brown, which was originally introduced from Germany in 1883.

The landlocked salmon, the Ouananiche and the Sebago, are fresh water varieties of the Atlantic salmon. They do not go to sea, but the Ouananiche is actually not landlocked, since most of the waters it inhabits in Quebec run into the sea. Its cousin, the Sebago, looks more like the Atlantic salmon and is a much heavier fish. The head of the Sebago is larger in proportion to the body than that of the Atlantic Salmon, and it also has more spots, particularly on the head.

The Sebago is the landlocked salmon of Maine, where it is found in four river basins: St. Croix, Sebec, Union, and Presumpscot. From there it has been transplanted into the Adirondacks and other New York lakes. Farther west in the lakes of our middle northern states—Michigan, Wisconsin, and Minnesota—one frequently hears about landlocked salmon, but these landlocked salmon aren't salmon; they're not even trout of the genus *Salmo.* They are lake trout that have been given the name landlocked salmon. This is a common name for lake trout in many northern waters near the Great Lakes.

There need be no confusion as to whether one is catching lake trout or real landlocked salmon. The Sebago landlocked salmon looks much like a small Atlantic salmon, with a similar dark and silvery color and small black spots. The lake trout isn't black spotted. Rather, it's dark and silvery with light spots that can appear whitish or yellowish and, at times, are so thick along the back and sides that they give the fish a reticulated appearance.

The Quebec red trout belongs to the genus *Salvelinus,* which also includes the brook trout, Saibling, and Sunapee, as well as the Oquassa and Dolly Varden; all brightly colored trout, among which the male of the red trout reaches the peak of brilliant coloration during the breeding season.

The grayling of the genus *Thymallus* are closely allied to the trout and salmon. They have the same small adipose fin just forward of the tail and, like the others, prefer cold and swift waters. Long and rather slender with a small head, they have an unusually developed dorsal fin. Besides the European species, there were three species in America: the Arctic or Alaskan grayling and the Montana and Michigan graylings. The Michigan grayling's dorsal was less developed.

We mention the Michigan grayling in the past tense, since, according to reports, it no longer exists. As is often the case with fish and game of a restricted habitat, they can't compete with men and come out a winner. Commercial

A flyfisherman goes after arctic grayling on Alaska's Copper River.

interests usually have first consideration where humans are concerned, so trees are chopped down, causing cold brooks to dry up, and others are filled with the swill from factories. Usually, by the time the State Conservation Department has awakened to the danger, a species has almost vanished. Sometimes they can be brought back, often they cannot. It's a sad thing when a species vanishes, for though man can destroy a species with ease, he cannot recreate it.

The whitefish almost looks out of place among trout, salmon, and grayling, but many naturalists include the whitefish in the salmon family. The whitefish belong to the genus *Coregonus,* which includes the Tulllibee, Bloater, Mooneye Cisco, Lake Herring, and Lake Smelt. All are salmonlike in appearance, having a small, sail-like dorsal fin and a little adipose fin just forward of the tail. They

Mexican Trout

Native trout in Mexico? You'd better believe it. In spite of the fact that northern Mexico's climate is famously arid, our neighbor across the border houses two interesting native trout. The Nelson trout, a subspecies of the rainbow, is found in northern Baja, while the Mexican golden trout is a rare species that was "discovered" and officially described only 25 years ago. This beautiful fish exists in a few streams in the mountains of Sinaloa and is the most southerly, naturally occurring trout in North America.

—Brooks Pangburn, October 1985

have rather large scales as compared to trout and salmon, the caudal fin or tail fin is distinctly forked, and, in the case of the Mooneye Cisco and Lake Smelt, the eyes are rather large.

There are several varieties of whitefish. The common variety has wide distribution and is of considerable commercial importance. A smaller variety, the round whitefish, also called Menominee Whitefish and frost fish, has been widely transplanted as food for salmon and trout.

Whitefish are of course caught in nets commercially, but those who have fished for them with hook and line speak of them highly as game fish.

—Walter J. Wilwerding, April 1941

Rare Natives

THE APPALACHIAN BROOK trout and the redband trout are just two of a surprising number of salmonid races and species which are most often referred to as "rare trout." In almost all cases these trout were historically localized to one geographical region, endemic to a confined watershed—in some cases a single stream or lake system. Most had healthy populations at one time, but today are greatly reduced due to the introduction of hatchery trout into their habitat, poor land management, and overfishing.

The majority of these rare trout are found in western waters, and most belong to one of the beautiful and varied races of the cutthroat trout. Although many might not be well known to the average angler, the rare trout are now, in varying degrees, watched and managed by both state and federal agencies. A few enjoy a "threatened" classificaiton from the U.S. Fish and Wildlife Service. Populations of most, while greatly reduced from former numbers, are stable and in some cases even increasing.

Sorting out North America's salmonid species and races prior to human intrusion is a complex and difficult task. After more than 100 years of man's tampering—in particular, the stocking of trout not native to specific watersheds—the situation is muddled indeed.

Perhaps the foremost expert on North American native trout, and the person who has done much of the sorting, is Dr. Robert J. Behnke of Colorado State University. Behnke is known as a gifted, incisive taxonomist. His work with trout provides a fascinating look at how things must have been at one time. Greatly simplified: In the age of unaltered, pristine trout populations, all watersheds evolved with a well-defined species or race. Many of these races, or strains, were found in only a single stream or lake, while in close proximity would be found yet another race, perhaps very similar, but genetically distinct.

The rare trout that survive today are the remnants of this once highly specialized, eons-in-evolving, order of salmonid. A good example of this is the Lahontan cutthroat trout found in Pyramid Lake, Nevada: This trout once grew larger than perhaps any other North American species. The world record stands at 41 pounds, although larger specimens are rumored to have been caught by Indians. The Lahontan is still found in Nevada, California, and Oregon in good numbers; but the common Lahontan of today is usually a hybrid cutthroat/rainbow instead of a purebred. From 1940 until 1960, in fact, pure Lahontans were thought to have vanished. And while the hybrid Lahontans do reach appreciable sizes, they do not reach the giant proportions of pure Lahontans.

In 1960 Behnke reported four pure Lahontan populations, and since that time more have been found. It is hoped that stock from these finds will provide the nucleus for a new age of pure Lahontans and that fish from this new generation will reach the size of the Lahontan trout of antiquity.

All rare trout are remarkably interesting. Following is a rundown on notable ones found in North America.

>>> *Greenback Cutthroat:* This small, beautiful trout was largely responsible for drawing national attention to the plight of all rare trout when it was declared an endangered species. Today that classification has changed to threatened.

The greenback rarely exceeds 14 inches at full maturity and has the largest spots of any cutthroat. It was once found over a wide area of Colorado, especially near Boulder and Denver, as well as in a small area of Wyoming. Its population was quite large when the settlement of Colorado began, but by 1937 pure greenbacks were thought to be extinct. They have since been rediscovered, and an organization known as the Greenback Recovery Team has made good progress in reestablishing the trout in Colorado. In 1982 anglers were allowed to fish for greenbacks on a catch-and-release basis in some areas of Colorado's Rocky Mountain National Park.

>>> *Appalachian Brook Trout:* Once the only trout found in the southeastern mountains of Virginia, North Carolina, Tennessee, and Georgia, this fish is the smallest race of brook trout. It becomes capable of spawning at four inches, and rarely grows much larger than 12 inches.

Though abundant at one time, this little trout is quite fragile, and its numbers have been greatly reduced. Pure strains can still be found in Virginia, North Carolina, and Tennessee. They are entirely confined to the headwaters of a few remote mountain streams, especially those with natural barriers such as waterfalls. This trout has proved hard to raise in hatcheries, and its existence will depend on wise land management and public concern for its welfare. It disappears almost immediately if other trout are introduced into its habitat.

Golden Trout: A Rare Species

Some fish experts believe rainbows, cutthroats, and goldens are closely related. Yet, unlike other trout, the goldens are loners: They must have the water to themselves.

When goldens are put with brook trout, brookies dominate and the goldens eventually disappear. When placed in waters with rainbows or cutthroats, goldens hybridize, making pure strains obsolete. A mystique surrounds golden trout, partly because of this beauty and rarity, but also because they are most often found in high, remote back-country lakes common to Wyoming, California, and Colorado.

—William H. Sudduth,
September 1990

▶▶▶ *Redband Trout:* The rare redband trout often emerges as a favorite among those who know of it. This trout survives in conditions no other trout can. It does well in water temperatures up to 85°F, yet can also inhabit winter streams that form anchor ice. It faces yearly flash floods and the consequent siltation, and does well in water with high alkaline content. In addition, this trout is one of the few salmonids that can base its diet almost exclusively on other fish, with small desert chubs being preferred forage.

Behnke believes the redband is probably the ancestor of all rainbow trout races. Once thought to be widely distributed over the high desert regions of Idaho, Nevada, Washington, Oregon, and California, today pure redbands are thought to inhabit only a few remote creeks of Oregon's Great Basin region.

▶▶▶ *Alvord Basin Trout:* Perhaps the rarest of North American trout, this strain is known from only two creeks in the Great Basin region. The Alvord Basin trout is a cutthroat, with a maximum size of about 12 inches. Like the redband, it has adapted to harsh desert conditions—water temperatures in midsummer in the two creeks it inhabits can reach nearly 80°F.

The greatest threat to the Alvord Basin trout comes from potential overfishing. The remoteness of its habitat makes enforcement of laws difficult. The trout is easy to catch, but the few people who do seldom, if ever, have any idea what it is.

▶▶▶ *Paiute Trout:* A small cutthroat native to the Silver King Creek watershed of California's Sierra Nevadas, this trout was first described in 1933. The Paiute is the only member of the cutthroat species that is almost totally devoid of spots. At one time it was also an adaptable trout, having switched to clear, cold running streams after the gradual disappearance of the ancient Lake Erie-sized Lahontan Sea.

As with the greenback cutthroat, the Paiute has benefited from large-scale attempts to save it. It is currently found in a few creeks isolated by waterfalls. Pure Paiutes have also been established in several formerly barren creeks in the Silver King Creek watershed.

▶▶▶ *Golden Trout:* It is doubtful that any other trout species has been more romanticized or sought after by anglers than the golden. Brood stock from this fish was captured, reared domestically at an early age of fish propagation, and released in suitable and unsuitable habitat over much of the United States.

Noted for inhabiting water at high elevations, the golden was originally native to a limited region of California's Kern River drainage at an elevation of 10,000 feet. Pure strains still exist within the Kern River drainage, while a similar Mexican golden trout is found in three Pacific drainage river systems in Durango and Sinaloa, Mexico.

▶▶▶ *Rio Grande Cutthroat:* Found in limited areas of Colorado and New

Mexico, the Rio Grande cutthroat is similar, yet separate, from the rare Colorado River cutthroat found in Colorado, Utah, and Wyoming. Both the Rio Grande and the Colorado River cutthroat are very striking. Some specimens have a multitude of heavy black spots that grow thicker down the body past the dorsal fin until the tail appears almost black. Both are also very rare in pure form.

   >>> *Blueback Trout:* The blueback trout, found only in Maine, is officially listed as a form of landlocked arctic char. It inhabits about 10 deep lakes near the Maine/New Hamphire/Quebec border. More than 100 years ago, early settlers in this region netted bluebacks by the thousands for smoking. The Rangeley Lakes system was especially known for this.

Much of the decline in blueback numbers was caused by the introduction of landlocked salmon into their habitat. Today the fish are considered rare only in context to their limited distribution. They still maintain healthy populations in some lakes.

   >>> *Sunapee Trout:* The Sunapee trout is similar to the blueback, and it too is regarded as a landlocked arctic char. The Sunapee was historically found over a wider range than the blueback, inhabiting lakes in New Hampshire, Vermont, and Maine, but was limited to fewer actual lakes.

Much of the attention that has long surrounded the Sunapee originated from the char's best-known habitat, Sunapee Lake in New Hampshire. For many years intensive hatchery programs were formed to restock Sunapee Lake with these char. Unfortunately, predation from lake trout and hybridization with both lake and brook trout have forced the lake's Sunapees into extinction.

A refuge for Sunapee trout was established in the mid-1950s in Tewksbury Pond, New Hampshire, but it is thought that the Sunapee char there are really hybrid fish. At present there are only two known populations of pure Sunapee char, and these are remarkably distant from one another. One is found in Maine's Floods Pond, the other in two lakes in Idaho's Sawtooth Mountains. The Idaho Sunapees came from a 1925 stocking with fish from Sunapee Lake.

   >>> *Apache and Gila Trout:* Both of these southwestern trout owe their recognition to Robert R. Miller of the University of Michigan, who first described them as a totally new species in the 1950s. They had previously been treated as Colorado River cutthroats.

The Apache cutthroat trout, which has the largest dorsal fin of any American trout, was historically native to the headwaters of the Salt River drainage of Arizona. It is currently found in streams on the Fort Apache Indian Reservation. Reservation residents have worked closely with state and federal agencies to assure the trout's preservation. It has also been listed as a threatened species under the Endangered Species Act.

The Gila trout was once found in both Arizona and New Mexico, but its range today is limited to streams in New Mexico's Gila River watershed. One of the main reasons for its decline in numbers over the years has been the introduction of rainbow trout into its original habitat. In 1976 a totally pure population of Gila trout was discovered in an isolated tributary in its former range, and stock from this find is now being utilized for future propagation.

The outlook for most rare trout is bright. Many have been saved from the brink of extinction in the past 15 years and only the Gila trout is still listed as endangered.

Efforts by a few dedicated individuals have contributed largely to this remarkable turn of events. Public concern, interest, and constant vigilance will prove invaluable to assure stability in the coming years. Many of the rare trout are still exceedingly vulnerable—one blunder or disaster could erase much of the work that has been done.

The search for rare trout is still continuing too. The yellowfin trout of Colorado's Twin Lakes is presumed to be extinct. Historically, both the greenback cutthroat and the yellowfin, also a cutthroat, were reported from this region. The greenback is a small trout, while the yellowfin grew to weights of 10 pounds.

Today there are a few yellowfin specimens in scientific collections, a large amount of documentation regarding the trout, and an enigma surrounding whether it still remains today or not. Although doubtful, it's remotely conceivable that an overlooked population still exists.

—Worth Mathewson, February 1984

Rainbow Trout

UNTIL RECENTLY, RAINBOWS were called *Salmo gairdneri* and thought to be a generic relative of the brown trout. New evidence indicates the fish descends from the line of Pacific salmon, the genus *Oncorhynchus* (meaning "hooked snout"), and as of 1990 the rainbow's new scientific name has been *Oncorhynchus mykiss*.

From a fisherman's standpoint, the old genus name, *Salmo*—Latin for "leaping"—fits the rainbow perfectly. When hooked, rainbow trout are among the most acrobatic of freshwater fish. This, plus their often brilliant coloring and eagerness to take a fly or lure, makes them a favorite gamefish.

Although there are many races of rainbow trout, the species can be split into two general divisions: the redband variety—the most dazzling, with yellow and orange lower-body coloring, pronounced spotting, and vivid reddish lateral lines and cheeks—and the so-called "coastal rainbows," which are less flamboyant, having olive, gray, or silvery background colors, with muted spots and paler cheeks and lateral lines.

Rainbows can grow into sizable fish. The sport-tackle record, taken in Alaska, weighed 27 pounds three ounces. Although the average hatchery rainbow measures only 10 or 12 inches, fish up to and over 10 pounds are not uncommon in prime lakes and in the best western and far north rivers.

A steelhead is a rainbow trout that spends part of its life in the ocean or one of the Great Lakes, then returns to its native stream to spawn. Such fish are substantially stronger and typically much larger than normal stream trout. The current steelhead record is 42 pounds 2 ounces, and many over 15 pounds are caught each year.

>>> *Range:* Rainbow trout are native only to the Pacific slope of North America, from Alaska to northern Baja California, but hatchery fish have been introduced throughout the continent. Thirty-nine states have established populations. Rainbows are found in all the Canadian provinces, the Yukon Territory, and in 15 Mexican states. Steelhead occur in West Coast rivers from Northern California to southern Alaska; and extend as far inland as western Alberta and Idaho. Planted strains also exist in the Great Lakes region, frequenting rivers and streams in Michigan, Wisconsin, southern Ontario, and eastern New York.

>>> *Habitat:* Rainbows prefer clear, well-oxygenated water in the 56 - 70°F range, although they are known to survive for short periods in water barely above freezing, or as warm as 83°F.

In streams, rainbows favor fast currents with high riffle-to-pool ratios. Clean gravel areas are necessary for spawning. Freestone streams make prime habitat, with rocky, irregular bottoms that allow copious opportunity for hiding and feeding. Rainbow trout are also common in lakes having similar conditions of water quality and temperature, though they can reproduce only if they have access to a stream.

>>> *Habits:* Rainbows spawn in spring, when the water warms above 40°F (generally from February to June, but in some places as late as July or August). The number of eggs deposited by a female depends on her size: A six-inch fish will carry fewer than 200 eggs; large females may produce as many as 900 eggs per pound. The fertilized eggs incubate for about a month. The hatched fry stay beneath the gravel for two to three weeks, feeding from an attached yolk sac, then emerge to feed freely—or be fed upon. Some rainbows spawn over and over, while others, like Pacific salmon, perish shortly after reproducing.

Bad News Browns

The American angler has become truly endeared to the brown trout. Renowned as a fierce fighter, this European import can grow to impressive size and has bested many fishermen who underestimated its stamina and willpower. The brown feeds largely at dusk and in the dead of night, preferring clear lakes, streams, and rivers with plenty of cover and hiding spots. It takes dry, wet, and streamer flies just as fast as it takes smelt imitations. Surprisingly, large browns have stunned unprepared anglers who were happily catching smaller trout when suddenly the king of the creek hit their fly or small lure. Browns prefer cool water (less than 70°F) and, strangely enough, are related to the pike, both belonging to the *Salmoniformes* order. The brown lays up to 5000 eggs when spawning. This is a lot when compared to the brookie, but small potatoes next to the lake trout, which can deposit 20,000 eggs.

–Bob Newman, March 1995

43

In streams, mature rainbows compete for the best "lies," or holding areas, arranging themselves in a hierarchy. Rainbows feed throughout the day, primarily on underwater and surface insects such as mayflies, stoneflies, and caddisflies; but also on terrestrial insects blown into the water (bees, grasshoppers, ants) and baitfish such as sculpins, dace, and young trout.

In lakes, rainbow trout for the most part abandon their hierarchical stations and, either singly or in groups, hunt for available forage.

—Anthony Acerrano, April 1992

Cutthroat Trout

T HE GENERAL CATEGORY of cutthroat trout (*Oncorhynchus clarki*) encompasses as many as 14 subspecies and a variety of colors, appearances, and habits. The name "cutthroat" derives from the bright red or orange slash that appears on each of the fish's lower jaws, though this can be misleading for identification purposes: Some cutthroats—such as the sea-run coastal variety—may lack the slash marks; while other trout species, such as the Apache, Gila, and redband rainbow, may have them.

The four major subspecies include the coastal cutthroat (*O.c. clarki*), which is silvery with dense dark spots; the west slope cutthroat (*O.c. lewisi*), which is among the brightest and most colorful, with small dark dots on its back and a pale, yellowish lower body that turns bright red and orange during spawning season; the Yellowstone or "interior" cutthroat (*O.c. bouvieri*), which tends to be dull yellow-brown to brassy, often with rosy cheekplates; and the Lahontan cutthroat (*O.c. henshawi*), similar to the Yellowstone cutt in appearance, though often tinted with an olive cast.

Cutthroats vary widely in size, from six-inch mountain creek "natives" to huge lake-dwelling fish that weigh in the double digits. The current all-tackle record is 41 pounds, taken from Pyramid Lake, Nevada.

➤➤➤ *Range:* Coastal cutthroats are the most broadly distributed members of the species, occurring from the Humboldt Bay area of California north to Alaska's Kenai Penninsula; and inland, crest to crest from the Cascade Mountains to the Coast Range, from Oregon to British Columbia. The Yellowstone group of cutthroats exists in the interior Rocky Mountain region west of the Continental Divide, extending to include pockets of the Snake River and southward, in isolated locales, through Utah, Nevada, Colorado, and New Mexico. West slope cutthroats occur principally in western Montana, but extend locally to include parts of Idaho, extreme southeastern British Columbia, and southern Alberta. Lahontan cutthroats were originally fish of the Great Basin, but exist today mainly in remnant

March, 1937

SPORTS AFIELD

and TRAILS of the NORTHWOODS

15¢

W.J.Wilwerding

Fishing, Hunting, Trailer Camping, Trapshooting, Cameras, Dogs
Rotogravure Section——"The Great Outdoors in Pictures"

Rainbow, *Oncorhynchus mykiss*: native to the west coast of North America, now the most widely stocked trout throughout the world.

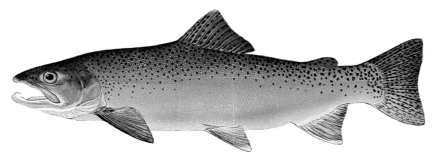

Steelhead, *Oncorhynchus mykiss*: the migratory seagoing form of rainbow trout native to the west coast of North America; also widely stocked in the Great Lakes.

Westslope Cutthroat, *Oncorhynchus clarki lewisi*: native to western Montana, northern Idaho, British Columbia, Alberta, Oregon, Washington, and parts of Wyoming.

Redband Trout, *Oncorhynchus mykiss*: various subspecies of rainbow trout, recognized as redband, that inhabit a few remote creeks of Oregon's Great Basin region and parts of the Sacramento River Basin in California.

California Golden, *Oncorhynchus aquabonita*: native to the tributaries of the South Fork of California's Kern River and introduced to lakes and streams of the Sierras and Rockies.

Mexican Golden, *Oncorhynchus chrysogaster:* lives in the headwaters of Mexico's Rio del Fuerte, Sinaloa, and Culiacan rivers, all tributary to the Gulf of California.

Apache (Arizona trout), *Oncorhynchus gilae apache*: native to the headwaters of Salt River drainage in Arizona.

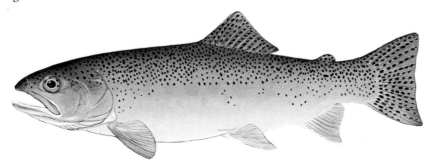

Gila, *Oncorhynchus gilae gilae*: native to the headwaters of the Gila River drainage in New Mexico.

Paiute, *Oncorhynchus clarki seleniris*: native to the headwaters of Silver King Creek and stocked in other small creeks in eastern California.

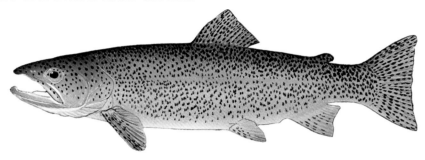

Coastal Cutthroat, *Oncorhynchus clarki clarki*: covers the Pacific shore and islands from Alaska as far south as northern California, and inland to the Cascade mountains in Oregon and to the high headwaters of the Skeena River in British Columbia.

Bonneville Cutthroat, *Oncorhynchus clarki utah*: native to the Bonneville basin, which covers two-thirds of western Utah and includes parts of Nevada, Idaho, and Wyoming.

Snake River Finespot Cutthroat, *Oncorhynchus clarki behnkei*: native to the upper Snake River drainage in Wyoming; named for Colorado State University professor Dr. Robert Behnke.

Yellowstone Cutthroat, *Oncorhynchus clarki bouvieri*: native to the Yellowstone and Snake rivers; stocked extensively throughout the western United States.

Lahontan Cutthroat, *Oncorhynchus clarki henshawi*: native to the Lahotan Basin of Nevada, California, and Oregon.

Rio Grande Cutthroat, *Oncorhynchus clarki virginalis*: native to both Colorado and New Mexico.

Alvord Cutthroat, *Oncorhynchus clarki alvordensis*: native to the Alvord Basin of Nevada and Oregon, it is considered extinct in its pure form. A hybridized population lives in Nevada's Virgin Creek.

Colorado River Cutthroat, *Oncorhynchus clarki pleuriticus*: native to mountain tributaries of the upper Colorado River Basin in Wyoming, Utah, Colorado, and New Mexico.

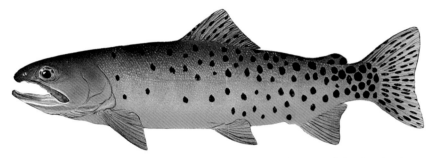

Greenback Cutthroat, *Oncorhynchus clarki stomias*: inhabits headwaters of the South Platte and Arkansas rivers in Colorado. Listed as threatened, this fish has been restored in Colorado through the hard work of concerned anglers and conservation groups such as Trout Unlimited.

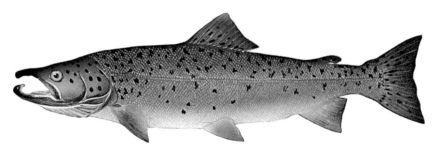

Atlantic (Atlantic salmon), *Salmo salar*: ranges from northern Labrador south to New England.

Ouananiche (Atlantic or Sebago landlocked salmon), *Salmo salar*: found in tributaries of the St. Lawrence River; most commonly found in Newfoundland.

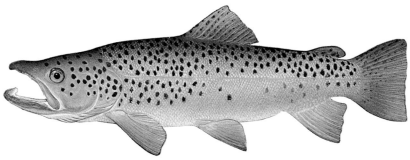

Brown (Non-native), *Salmo trutta*: a European import stocked widely throughout North America.

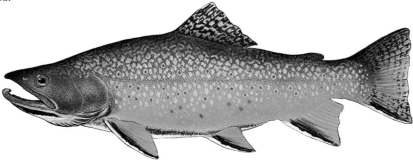

Brook Trout, *Salvelinus fontinalis*: originally distributed from Labrador to Saskatchewan and from Maine to Georgia and South Carolina, west to Minnesota; stocked widely throughout the nation.

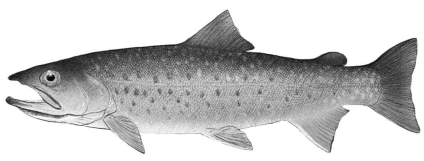

Dolly Varden (Coastal form), *Salvelinus malma*: inhabits rivers from Puget Sound in Washington State to the MacKenzie River in Alaska.

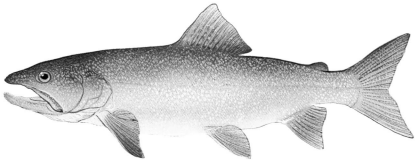

Lake Trout, *Salvelinus namaycush*: native to deep lakes in northern North America.

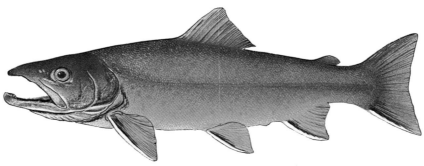

Arctic Char, *Salvelinus alpinus*: distributed around the world in streams tributary to the Arctic Ocean.

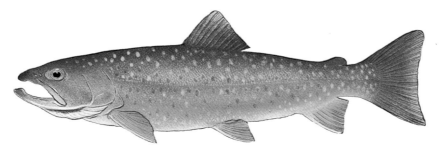

Bull Trout, *Salvelinus confluentus*: native from the Colombia River northward to the headwaters of the Yukon and McKenzie rivers in Canada.

Sunapee (Blueback or Quebec red trout), *Salvelinus alpinus oquassa*: relic Arctic char left over from the last ice age in northern New England and Quebec.

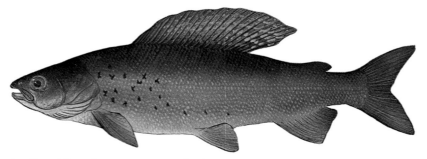

Arctic Grayling, *Thymallus arcticus*: originally found in most cold, clear streams from the Arctic southward to Michigan and Montana.

populations in Nevada, California, and southern Oregon.

▶▶▶ *Habitat:* Coastal fish exist in pristine lakes and well-oxygenated, cool, small- to moderate-sized streams. Where possible, these fish will migrate to sea in spring, spend the summer in nearby marine waters, then return later in the year to fresh water. West slope and Yellowstone cutthroats frequent cool-to-cold mountain lakes, and will also be found in tiny, fast-flowing streams and headwaters, and in larger streams that have comparatively steep gradients and fast, riffly stretches. Lahontan trout show a considerably higher tolerance for warmer, alkaline lake waters, but are also known to inhabit creeks and rivers.

▶▶▶ *Habits:* Most cutthroats are spring spawners—or, more accurately, spawn in springlike conditions (which may occur in July at some altitudes) when the water temperature nears 41°F.

Small cutthroats tend to feed primarily on insects. Upon reaching 12 inches in length, cutts shift toward a more baitfish-oriented diet. West slope trout in lakes, however, appear to be an exception, continuing their focus on insects throughout their lives.

—Anthony Acerrano, April 1992

Brown Trout

THE BROWN TROUT can be absolutely mind-blowing when feeding rhythmically in the surface film for almost invisible insects (a phenomenon historically known as "the angler's curse"), as it must ingest 2000 or 3000 tricos to pass a good burp, while loftier foods float by unmolested. The rainbow will act this way at times, the cutthroat to a lesser extent and, on rare occasions, the brook trout.

Undeniably, those fabled super hatches such as the green drake, giant salmonfly, hendrickson, and Michigan caddis are totally classic in content; the emergences are big, the rising fish often the biggest, and the imitative patterns highly visible at No. 10 up to No. 6. However, these stirring episodes are brief in duration with perhaps a few days or a week of activity.

By contrast, and despite their diminutive size, the *Tricorythidae* and *Caenidae* families of mayflies are choice trout foods throughout the United States, with a period of emergence lasting from June all the way through October. These hatches cannot be avoided on quality, alkaline streams. In addition, other minute insects such as the chironomids or midges (which hatch throughout the winter), numerous caddis, especially the tiny *Hydroptilidae,* many species of beetles, and ants can trigger a feeding orgy. Collectively, these micros, which are fly sizes in the 20s, are the key to some splendid fishing.

Strong Trout

If you've ever wondered how strong a fish really is, consider that water is 780 times as dense as air, and thus moving through it requires much more energy. If you need proof, try hammering a nail below the water's surface. Just swinging the hammer becomes a task. But with a few flicks of its tail and undulations of its body, a fish swims through water at impressive speeds.

—Gerald Almy, April 1983

The brown is considered by many to be the most challenging of all trout.

It was in a stretch of the New Fork River in Wyoming that I caught the best trout I've taken on a No. 20. It occurred during a midge emergence when the browns were on top, rolling in head-and-tail rises for pupae suspended in the surface film. I was float boating that day, and at noon my companion Ted Trueblood and I pulled out to wait for some friends to catch up. I had been rowing the double-ender all morning, so while Ted gathered firewood, I waded below our lunch site. Trout were popping everywhere. I was rigged for fast water with a big hairwing, which didn't interest these fish at all. They just kept rising all around it. I saw some midges beginning to swarm, but there were probably a million pupae in the surface film for every adult taking flight. With shaking fingers, I used up about 10 minutes to retaper my leader. My prize was feeding in midstream. I dropped an Olive Midge a few feet above his station four or five times before the leader showed a little pull, and then I was fast to a brown that evidently had a bonefish ancestor. The trout bolted downstream, well into my backing, while I ran behind shouting for Ted to bring a net.

I never pressure a strong running fish on a gossamer tippet. Instead, I point my rod horizontally and play the trout off the reel against the click, counting on the friction of the line running through water to slow the fish down. This doesn't allow any control if the fish decides to dive into a weedbed or burrow under a stump, but I've found that using the full bend of the rod results in too many snapped tippets. My fish came to the surface, wallowing and threshing, and I finally managed to gentle him into a quiet backwater—at which point I skidded down a clay bank and sat in the New Fork.

"Well that was pretty fancy. What else can you do?" I looked up and there was a grinning Trueblood with the net. The fish circled slowly at my feet. It was the most fun I could have sitting down. New Fork trout are handsome fish, more gold than brown, and this heavily spotted male taped 22 inches: the best I've ever taken on 6X, with a No. 20 fly.

The brown is undeniably the most challenging of all trout no matter where it is found, and while effective techniques run the spectrum of angling disciplines, at times it pays to think small. Indeed, you will have no choice.

–A. J. McClane, February 1984

McClane's Notebook

THE BROOK TROUT was the first species to invade the streams being formed by melting ice in the last Pleistocene epoch of the Appalachians. In her master plan, Nature sent along a companion foodfish, the sculpin, which is also tolerant of extremely cold water. As the ice melted, lakes formed behind barriers on the slopes of mountains. Then, when the water dropped and currents warmed, fishes such as the minnow and sucker began their upstream journeys. In many places, rock slides and impassable falls blocked their entering brook trout habitat in the headwaters. The trout remained in safe havens.

When man (the original Mixmaster) eventually introduced alien brown and rainbow trout to the native, however, a variety of problems began. And in the social fabric of our trout family, the brookie now hangs by a bare thread. Except for certain still-isolated strains, it generally has a shorter life span (five years) than the rainbow (seven years) or the brown trout (10 years). It is much more susceptible to angling and cannot withstand competition from the other species for resting and feeding sites. If you've ever seen a hatchet-faced rainbow nipping the belly of a brook trout in swift, corkscrew attacks, it becomes painfully evident who is boss. The rainbow gets the turbulent, food-rich oxygenated water, while our delicate native gets an inferiority complex.

Brook trout in eastern upland streams reach a climax size of about 10 inches. The largest native I ever caught in the Catskills was exactly 14 inches long, and that was in the 1930s. I have taken stocked fish of greater size, but their only bona fides were a club membership and access to a ton of Trout Chow. During the halcyon era of squaretail fishing in Maine, from the 1880s to the 1920s, five- to seven-year-old brook trout (weighing three-and-one-half to five pounds) were not uncommon. Presumably, some of this genetic stock has survived as the state continues to produce an occasional trophy fish. In Canada, there are even longer-lived brook trout populations such as the Assinica strain, which attains an age of 10 years or more, and weights of nine to 11 pounds. However, our native trout lives in a delicate balance everywhere because of habitat destruction and overfishing. Foam-flecked rivers running through forests where the logger's ax has never echoed do hold trophy-sized fish, yet any of these could be wiped out tomorrow. Fortunately, enlightened resort operators offer their angling on a catch-and-release basis. This is the only hope for the last frontier.

Photographer Dale Spartas with a fat brook trout taken on the Minipi River in Labrador.

The squaretail may jump gracefully through the air on magazine covers, but in reality it usually flops, squirms, and tail-threshes at the surface, seldom becoming airborne. A big brook trout is much more likely to dive for the nearest obstruction in powerful surges. In the thunderous rapids of a river like the Gods or the Broadback, you have your hands full. The squaretail learns his lessons badly, too. He is sometimes seen with a mouthful of rusting flies and broken leaders. I once caught a five-pounder in a small Quebec lake that had a half-dozen hooks in its jaws; if nothing else, the larger fish have needle-sharp teeth and a lack of guile—both points in the brookie's favor.

—A. J. McClane, October 1980

Twelve Lessons for a Trout-Fishing Friend

OUR FISHING EXPERIENCE is filled with hard-earned lessons. Most streamwise knowledge is accumulated after years of trial and error. Following are a few lessons I've learned that sometimes make the difference between an exciting fishing day and an empty creel.

▶▶▶ *One:* My father and his trout-fishing friends introduced me to their sport on a marl-bog creek in Michigan. Learning about the intelligence and spookiness of trout came naturally under these angling experts' patient instruction. But most trout-fishing beginners are less lucky, and usually try trout only after learning basic techniques on easier species. Novices are seldom taught to stalk meadow trout infantry-style, crawling and hiding behind bushes and trees. My father taught me this technique almost 35 years ago. Yet most beginners approach a trout stream without knowing a very basic lesson: Trout are perhaps the craftiest species of all, unless they are fresh from a hatchery, and stalking them successfully means using all the guile of a cat-burglar.

▶▶▶ *Two:* I also find surprising the number of trout fishermen who fail to understand that the nymphs and larvae of aquatic insects are in the water all year. Several seasons ago, I fished Prospect Lake in Colorado Springs all winter. It was the only water open 12 months a year. Along with other bait fishermen, I waded into the icy water, casting my fly in a clockwise pattern and allowing it to sink until my slow handtwist retrieves ticked it back along the bottom. The bait-fishing regulars couldn't believe that I was fishing with wet flies; they were convinced that there weren't any flies around in the winter. But those fish in Prospect Lake were usually full of caddis worms, backswimmers, nymphs of damselflies and dragon flies, beetles and larvae and snails. The regulars just never checked the stomachs of the fish they caught, so they never realized that insect nymphs and larvae thrive in trout water all year, or that flies work anytime the water is clear and the fish are feeding.

▶▶▶ *Three:* When the fish are really rising, the average fisherman often gets frustrated because the trout are boiling but nothing can touch them. Anglers

The ring of the rise, made by a 19-inch cutthroat caught shortly thereafter.

assume the trout aren't taking flies because they're just "playing." But the life of a trout in the river is a precarious balance between calories ingested during feeding and calories expended in the current. It's an existence filled with fear—searching for food while avoiding danger—and the fish are never playing. When the water boils with rising trout, you have a unique opportunity to catch them, if you know what food they're taking and imitate it successfully.

>>> *Four:* The cause-and-effect pattern between aquatic insects and the feeding response of the trout is the key to success, but there are other important variations of this theme. Most fishermen believe that rising trout means surface feeding and dry-fly fishing. Few know that trout often take hatching nymphs and pupae just under the surface. Such fish are taking aquatic insects as they migrate up toward the surface, and their porpoise rolls and swirls cause most fishermen to waste their time with dry flies when a wet fly or nymph is needed.

>>> *Five:* A common error that took me many seasons to correct was observing the hatches in the air and making judgments about their color without actually catching them. One summer 20 years ago, I fished a river with a fine hatch of small *Cheumatopsyche* caddis flies. These insects moved upstream in clouds and the trout brought the current to a boil. The caddis flies look like a straw-colored blizzard in the sun, so I tied pale little imitations for days, hoping to find a fly pattern they would take consistently. I took a few fish each evening, but the results were meager compared to the number of trout rising. Finally I found two caddis flies crawling on my fishing vest. They were a dark mottled brown. Caddis flies usually have darkly mottled forewings and paler wings at the rear, and like most flies in flight, they look pale against the light. I quickly dressed darker imitations and took trout as fast as I could land them and cast again. The good fishing lasted until the hatch ebbed and stopped at the end of the week.

>>> *Six:* Most fishermen have seen trout taking flying ants in their mating swarms when it's impossible to miss the patterns of cause and effect. But few trout fishermen are aware that a trout's constant, unobtrusive rises to ants, leafhoppers, and tiny beetles is a staple of hot-weather activity for the fish. Such feeding is puzzling because terrestrial insects drift flush in the surface film, and although a trout taking them is clearly engaged in surface rises, the fisherman can see nothing on the water. Quiet rises and hot gusty days are two clues that indicate terrestrials on the water, and since these insects are usually small, imitations must be fished on relatively delicate leaders. The silhouettes of ants, leafhoppers, and beetles are all radically different, and make different patterns of light in the surface film. As a result, color, silhouette, and size are equally important.

>>> *Seven:* Another baffling rise of trout occurs when a flight of mating mayflies fills the air. These spinners rise and fall in the rhythm of their mating swarm, dropping their egg sacs or dipping them off in the current. The fish slash and roll at these egg-laying drakes, frustrated with so many flies in the air. Some mating mayflies get into water, but until the egg laying is finished and they begin to fall spent on the current, spinner flights fill the air with insects. But don't put weight in the creel until their mating is over and there are more flies on the water.

>>> *Eight:* Yet another common enigma is a session of midge-pupa feeding on a lake or slow-moving stream. There are times when these tiny insects change from their delicate threadworm stage to millions of tiny pupae breathing under the surface film. The trout range widely in lakes and ponds, sipping the pupae softly by the thousands or nibbling lazily on them in a smooth current. Successful imitations are usually tiny flies dubbed with olive, black, brown, or lead-gray fur ribbed with dark quills and a collar of a few soft hen fibers.

>>> *Nine:* Most fishermen fish their streamers conventionally, casting down and across stream, and letting the current give them life against a rhythmic pumping of the rod. This works well most of the time. But since trout lie facing the current and a streamer is fished downstream, in some pools it's possible that fish see you before you cast to them. In these instances, an upstream streamer is quite effective in tricking a trout into biting.

>>> *Ten:* Most fishermen believe wet flies should sink, and spend a lot of time soaking leaders and flies in soap to take them under. But many kinds of aquatic insects, such as the *Stenonema* mayflies and most *Trichoptera,* drift several feet in the surface film while their nymphs and pupae escape from their nymphal skins. Their life is brief, a matter of seconds in transition to the adult

stage, and they drift helplessly in the current, where they are easy prey for the fish. Old patterns often work best at such times. Flies such as the English March Brown and the slightly younger Hare's Ear are excellent hatching mayflies. Caddis flies are perhaps best imitated by flies such as the Woodcock-and-Green, Partridge-and-Olive, Woodcock-and-Brown, Woodcock-and-Orange, and Grouse-and-Gray.

>>> *Eleven:* There are times when the naturals flutter across the water before they can fly, skittering and skipping and laying eggs, or actually dragging in the current. Fishing a fluttering fly is a technique as ancient as the three-snell leader. Mayflies such as the March Brown and Green Drake often ride the current some distance, and should be given an occasional twitch like a grasshopper. Some caddis flies actually run on the surface when they lay their eggs, and everyone has watched the green inchworms trail in the current at the end of their silken webs. At these times, the twin dry-fly commandments regarding the upstream cast and dragless float should be broken, and a floating fly can be fished downstream.

>>> *Twelve:* The final lesson involves a trout's selective feeding behavior, which is a simple reflex pattern. The cycle of the season is an annual recurrent emergence of insect species, one after another from the river. When a new species appears, it takes some time for trout to get accustomed to seeing it.

An Evening Hatch: Most hatches last anywhere from a few days to a few weeks.

Finally they sample the new insect, find it safe and palatable, and begin taking it regularly. Each hatch can last from a few days to a few weeks. Before a hatch is finished, the reflex patterns of the trout are so focused on a particular species, in terms of its size, configuration, and coloring, that they sometimes ignore other types of insects completely. Catching selctive fish consistently is a matter of matching the hatch—fishing flies that imitate the insects trout are consistently taking.

—Ernest Schwiebert, March 1971

How Trout Live

L ET'S LOOK AT a trout stream. No one needs to be a scientist to study it. The polysyllabic scientific names are unimportant. What really matters is becoming acquainted with what lives there, even if it goes nameless, and the best way to do this is to leave no stone unturned in your research, literally. Step into the stream, pick up as large a rock as you can handle with two hands, and turn it upside down on the bank. Then look at the bottom.

What you see may prove amazing. Not every stone will be the same, but some will be covered with insect life. There will be creepers and crawlers of several kinds, as well as caddis fly larvae in their cases. The caddis cases, made of bits of sand or wood stuck together, are houses for the larvae, and usually are cemented to the stone. Look closely, for the case may so closely resemble the stone that it will be missed if the motion of the larva's head isn't detected. Break open some of the cases. The larvae will differ quite a bit, even on one stone, because there are many kinds of caddis flies, or duns and sedges, as the winged adults are known. A good part of our wet fly fishing is based upon imitating adult caddis flies, because their turned-down wings are better imitated by wet flies than dries. The cased caddis is called "stick bait" in some sections because its house if often made of bits of wood. These larvae protrude their heads and upper body to gather the vegetable food on which they live.

When you catch a trout early in the spring, before the big fly hatches come on the stream, and its nose is raw and sore, you don't have a diseased fish. It has only been grubbing around on the bottom for caddis larvae (which it swallows case and all) and other dwellers under the rocks.

If you want to do a better job of investigation, get someone to help you. Make a net of cheesecloth or wire cloth, rolling in the ends over two sticks to make handles. Station your partner a few feet below the stone you're going to pick up, and have him hold the net close to the bottom. Lift the stone and set it aside for study, then stir up the spot where it rested, and let the current carry any free-moving forms of life down into the net.

A father and son look for nymphs on DePuys Spring Creek near Livingston, Montana.

Once again, you may be surprised. The net will hold stone fly creepers, Mayfly nymphs, waterworms, hellgrammites (which hatch into a huge fly called the Dobson), noncased caddis larvae, and probably a crawfish—or crayfish, depending upon how you pronounce it. This is true even if the stone is lifted in rushing water, for it is simply astonishing how stream life persists even in a white-water torrent. If you wish to take any home for further study, they can be preserved briefly in a bottle of water, but should be transferred soon into alcohol or another preservative.

Before going into what this underwater life means to fly fishing, it is best to list the insects, aquatic and land, encountered on a stream, more or less in the order of their importance as trout food—and, therefore, as insects to be imitated by flies. Thus, it can be seen why some, like the mayflies and caddis flies, deserve more attention than others. The list:

>>> *Mayflies.* Commonly called drakes, these insects hatch all spring and

A hexagina *mayfly, ready for takeoff.*

summer, depending upon the kind. They are most plentiful the first two weeks in June in much of the country.

>>> *Caddis flies.* Called duns or sedges, these flies are probably the most important aquatic insect food for trout in streams of the Great Lakes area. They're common up to the middle of summer.

>>> *Stone flies.* Also known as browns, these flies are most plentiful in spring, but are likely to occur any time, even when snow is on the ground. They're often brown, but can be yellow, green, or other colors.

>>> *True flies.* This group includes flies with only one pair of wings, such as midges, black gnats, cowdungs, crane flies (the big spinners that look like giant mosquitoes), and many others. They are all land insects.

>>> *Alder flies.* These insects resemble caddis flies and are common in the spring.

>>> *Beetles.* Trout feed on both aquatic and land beetles.

>>> *Ants.* Trout usually, but not always, feed on the winged form, which fall into streams during the nuptial flight.

>>> *Caterpillars.* Serving as the land version of the aquatic nymphs and larvae, trout will take this bug, which will eventually turn into a winged insect. The Woolly Worm is a trout fly that imitates fuzzy caterpillars.

By far the most important to the fly fisherman—and especially to the user of dry flies—are the mayflies, which occur nearly everywhere in trout streams. Nearly all of our natural imitation dry fly patterns were tied originally to represent drakes. They are the showiest of flies with large wings and long bodies, two or three very long tails, and 10 segments to the body. The Green Drake, Quill Gordon, Hendrickson, Light Cahill, and March Brown are among the many patterns that imitate them. In the East they are often called "shad flies" because they're most plentiful about the time when shad used to ascend far upstream to spawn, and when the shadbush, or Juneberry, is in bloom, Much of the magic of dry-fly fishing is wrapped up in insect hatches. Usually toward dusk when the hot sun no longer can wilt such fragile insects, the incredible flight of the hatches takes place.

The gray drake hatch begins with a few insects, scarcely noticeable among the others ordinarily seen above the water. Then the slap-slap of feeding fish is heard, and the angler realizes that one of nature's most exciting phenomena is under way. The gray drakes appear by the hundreds, by the thousands, and, it sometimes seems, by the millions, all flying more or less upstream, dipping down to the water, rising again, finally falling into the stream. These are mostly females, laying eggs in the water.

The fish go mad. From the fingerlings up to the giant old cannibals, they gorge themselves on the fat insects. Not just trout, but all fish. Any reasonable facsimile of the natural fly will catch trout, and they will strike at almost anything when on a feeding binge, if they notice your lure at all in the multitude of insects flying above and falling into the stream. This continues until dusk.

And what does all this have to do with the wriggling creatures on the bottom of the rock you have overturned, or in the net spread below it?

Everything. The miracle of the hatch is the miracle of the transformation of the rather ugly little crawler on the stream bottom into the gauzy, ephemeral mayfly (called the gray drake) which lays the eggs. Each aquatic insect has its own particular cycle, but a description of the hatch of the green drake—which is also the gray drake—will lead to an understanding of all hatches. Following is what happens, from egg to insect:

>>> *The egg.* The gray drakes (females) dip up and down above the stream

and lay eggs in the water. The eggs then sift down to the bottom where they hatch into nymphs.

>>> *The nymph.* This particular drake, which is known as *Ephemera guttulata* in the scientists' nomenclature, produces a burrowing nymph. It is more likely to be found in the sand and gravel of the stream bed than clinging to the overturned rock. It is a fragile thing, less than an inch long, creamy yellow in color, and bearing little resemblance to the winged insect it will become. After its full underwater development, it nervously starts to rise and descend in the water until it finally comes completely to the surface. At this stage, trout feed on it, and can be caught on imitation nymphs of greenish yellow color. It is now ready to hatch into the green drake.

>>> *The green drake.*

The nymph floats on top of the water, its back splits, and the winged green drake emerges. In a minute or two, the insect floating

A green drake is greenish-yellow in color, with wings much larger than its body.

on the shell of its former self is sufficently dry to spread its wings and fly to the adjoining stream bank. This is the beginning of the green drake "hatch," a time much respected by trout and trout fishermen, although the activity doesn't equal that of the gray drake hatch which follows. This is the subimago or "dun" stage of the drake's life, and it has still another transformation to undergo.

In this stage, it is greenish yellow in color and large—its wings alone are often bigger than the nymph which produced it. It takes some time for the insect to rise from its shell on the water into the air, and trout often take it during its blundering attempts. An exact imitation is not absolutely necessary, and many good anglers use a bushy bivisible of generally creamy yellow color.

The hatched insect flies to bushes and trees where it clings for several days, moving little, and unafraid. In this it is unusual, for most mayflies go through their complete metamorphosis in a single day. The green drake, however, exists as such until the third or fourth day when the female emerges from her green dress to become the gray drake, and the male changes into a darker form known as the black drake. The male black drake is smaller than the female, and both are smaller than the green drake from which they emerged.

▶▶▶ *The gray drake.* This is the final form of the female. She has lived her life and, after fertilization by the male, she has only one function left—to lay her eggs in the water and then die. This she proceeds to do in the gray drake hatch mentioned. Her ephemeral life done, she falls on the land or into the water to become a "spent wing" fly. The greedy trout gorge on her, and the angler capitalizes on their greediness with imitations such as the White Wulff, the Gray Drake, and almost any large, light-colored fly. The average date of this hatch is June 3, although it may vary two weeks either way.

▶▶▶ *The black drake.* This isn't a very important fly to imitate, since it isn't over the water as much as the egg-laying female. And, incidentally, it is not nearly as dark as its name would indicate, being somewhat cream-colored with dark markings.

There you have the life cycle of a single kind of insect found in trout streams. Not all go through so many changes. Some pass from egg to larva to adult insect of a single form, and have no subimago stage. However, all the foregoing shows the many things that are behind the moment when you put down a dry fly during a hatch and a trout takes it.

Anyone who goes into the subject of stream life more than curiously is going to run into a confusion of terms which will prove puzzling. For example, "duns" can refer to a kind of fly (caddis flies), or to a stage of other flies, such as the dun or subimago stage of the drake just discussed. Also, the green and gray drakes are sometimes called "shad flies," but there is a distinct fly and pattern called the Shad Fly. Each new expert who attempts to systematize trout stream insects only adds to the confusion, and I doubt whether anyone will ever by able to bring order out of this chaos.

This is easily understood when it's realized that streams only a few miles apart can have widely different insect life, and that even hatches of one insect shared by both streams may occur on far different dates. For instance, people who know that their streams contain green and gray drakes may be surprised by my description of clouds of them in the air. Their streams never have such huge hatches. Small hatches, yes; but not waves of insects flying like bombing planes in formation, such as anglers witness on other streams. I too have been startled by the magnitude of caddis-fly hatches in some parts of the country.

The best thing to do is study what you have in your own creeks and ponds, which takes us back to that overturned rock and the net.

The immature forms of caddis, alder, and stone fly found there are next in importance to mayflies when it comes to what the stream has to offer trout in the way of food. If more were available, trout probably would prefer hellgrammites. Hellgrammites look like large, dark centipedes with large pincers on their heads, small ones at their tails, and they hatch into a blundering big fly called the Dobson.

The Dobson is seldom imitated because it is so large, but a natural Dobson fly never gets far on its egg-laying flight before some big trout engulfs it. Repulsive as it may look to humans, the larval hellgrammite form, pincers and everything, is eagerly devoured by all fish. Next time you are on a stream, look

Sports Afield editor Jay Cassell ties on a fly at Turkey Hollow Club in upstate New York. *Pay attention to insect life on a trout stream, and you will learn to catch more fish.*

for the egg masses of Dobson flies. They are the white splotches you see on the downstream side of rocks and logs.

Notice I said the egg masses were on the downstream sides of the rocks and logs. Female Dobson flies instinctively lay their eggs on the downstream side where they will not be affected by high water and debris banging into the upstream side of a rock. It is such small things that make the study of a stream so fascinating. We pass by crawfish, leeches, snails, freshwater shrimp, and brook lampreys (which aren't as destructive as the sea lamprey of recent notoriety) which are of little interst to fly fishermen; but make no mistake about it, they are of considerable interest to the trout and the bait fisherman. If I had to use bait to catch trout, I would use first the hellgrammite and then the small craw-fish in preference to the usual worms.

As for minnows, big trout feed heavily on them, but small trout will not usually take them. All trout prefer to eat insects when they can get them, for their nutritious fatty contents, but big trout must fill their bigger stomachs with substantial things such as crawfish, small fish, hellgrammites, and the like.

Constantly entering the stream, although not part of its life, are land insects. Gusts of wind bat them down on the water, exhaustion from nuptial flights cause them to collapse over streams, and some just blindly wander into creeks or just fall there. Every rain washes them into the trout's domain. Be prepared for such periods of plenty and have imitations of ants, bees, true flies, gnats, and the like in your fly box. Actually, I have never seen a honeybee in a trout stream, but have often noticed drowning specimens of sweat bees. They seem to like warm, sweaty humans and hover around on hot days, scaring those who think they are about to be stung.

I cannot pass by beetles, although they do not enter the fly fisherman's world with any imitations. It seems that black beetles have been present in all of the trout stomachs I have opened. This is especially true early in the season before the big fly hatches come on. Some of these are aquatic beetles, some land dwellers; but I believe that a trout's liking for them accounts for many catches made on dark, almost black, flies.

This is only an introduction to stream life. It is up to you to find out what your favorite trout water contains. Reading water will increase your fishing enjoyment and is much more fun than blindly buying a couple of fly patterns and trusting them to luck, or simply trusting the advice of whoever sells them to you. It may not increase your catch by a single fish, but it certainly should. And if it doesn't, you'll have reward enough discovering an unknown world.

—Bill Wolf, March 1956

Inside a Trout's Brain

TROUT FISHERMEN LOVE to discuss theories. *Don't bother fishing in the rain. Fish won't bite on the day after a full moon. Big fish feed only in the deepest parts of a river. Big fish feed only in the shallows . . . and only after dark.* The list is endless, and often unfounded.

So how can you tell fact from fiction? Perhaps the surest way is to look it up, and the best place to do so is in scientific journals and studies. We picked six areas that are often subject to debate among trout fishermen.

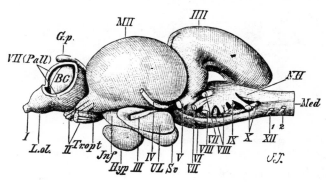

The cerebellum (HH) and optic lobes (MH) help the fish to receive and process information, enabling it to make decisions about whether to strike a prey or not.

Then we went to the science library. Our findings should surprise and enlighten you, as they provide insight into a trout's mind that may improve your fishing success.

1. Unfamiliar Prey: A study on selective predation conducted by fisheries biologist N. H. Ringler suggests that large trout will not immediately attack unfamiliar or exotic prey. Instead, they'll wait several minutes until a steady procession of such prey has passed. Then they will attack without hesitation. (Ringler, N. H., "Selective Predation by Drift-Feeding Brown Trout," *Journal of the Fisheries Research Board of Canada*, no. 36, pp. 392-403, 1979.)

Most anglers cast a few times into a promising pool, and if nothing hits, move on. Ringler's study suggests that it's better to cast repetitively into a given stretch of water for several minutes—especially when you're fishing with an exotic type of offering. Don't make just three or four casts; make 30 or 40. Give the trout ample time to become familiar with your No. 12 Green-Butted Skunk or quarter-ounce Mini-Wobbegong before calling it quits. Remember, in some cases the trout have never seen anything like the offering you're dragging past their noses.

Additional research by Kurt Fausch has also shown that trout immediately spit out almost anything made of plastic, metal, feathers, or fur. ("Trout as Predator," *Trout*, pp. 77-78, edited by J. Stolz and J. Schnell, Stackpole Books, 1991.) Given that, an angler using artificials should set the hook before the trout has a chance to burp. To detect strikes the instant they occur, keep your flyline mended, your monofilament taut, and use a strike indicator when fishing nymphs.

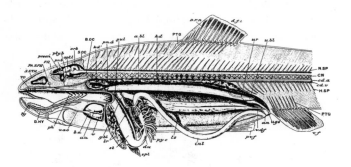

Cutaway of a trout from A Text-Book of Zoology, Vol. II, *by T. Jeffrey Parker and William A. Haswell. The trout also obtains data through its lateral line, or centrum (CN).*

2. Big Lures, Big Trout: Research has put some teeth into this old saying. Two studies submit that the largest trout in a system are those that have been able to make the feeding transition from small prey (nymphs) to large prey such as sculpins, crayfish, minnows, and grasshoppers. (Bannon, E., and N. H. Ringler, "Optimal Prey Size for Stream Resident Brown Trout," *Canadian Journal of Zoology 64,* pp. 704–713, 1986; and Bachman, R. A., "Foraging Behavior of Free-Ranging Wild and Hatchery Brown Trout in a Stream," *Transaction of the American Fisheries Society 113,* pp. 1-32, 1984.) So for trophy trout, use artificials that imitate the largest prey items native to the system in which you are fishing.

3. Invertebrate Drift: Flowing water systems, such as rivers and streams, experience the phenomenon of invertebrate drift. Invertebrates, primarily the sub-adult form of winged insects, leave the stream bottom and drift with the current. Peak drift activity occurs during the hour before sunrise and the hour after sunset. Just why drift occurs is subject to speculation. What is not speculative is that a flyfisherman armed with an assortment of nymphs can catch a lot of trout if he fishes the drift in the early morning and evening.

The classic study in which the nature of invertebrate drift is discussed is T. F. Waters's *Invertebrate Drift—Ecology and Significance to Stream Fishes.* (Symposium of Salmon and Trout in Streams, Institute of Fisheries, the University of British Columbia, paper no. 6452, pp. 121-134, Scientific Journal series, Minnesota Agricultural Experiment Station, 1968.)

4. The Tyndall Effect: Named after John Tyndall, a 19th-century Irish physicist of eclectic scientific tastes, the Tyndall effect refers to the phenomenon in which light rays reflect off tiny particles of matter suspended in the water. This reflected light almost blinds fish, temporarily making it difficult for them to see predators. Large trout, particularly browns, take advantage of this by remaining in deep shade during daylight. From these dark haunts, the predatory trout lie in wait, ready to ambush visually impaired fish swimming in the lighted areas. (Butler, R. L., "Foraging Sites," *Trout*, p. 72.)

5. Trout Vision: Many researchers agree that trout feed primarily by means of visual cues. Furthermore, trout seem to have difficulty detecting baits or lures that are stationary. (Fausch, "Trout as Predator," p. 77.) To counteract this, always impart some motion into your terminal tackle.

Biologists believe that some trout, most notably browns, require little ambient light in order to feed via visual cues. Moonlight, even starlight, is often adequate. (Robinson, F. W., and J. C. Tash, "Feeding by Arizona Trout and Brown Trout at Different Light Intensities," *Environmental Biology of Fishes 4,* no. 4, pp. 363-368, 1979; and Henderson, M. S. and T. G. Northcote, "Visual Prey Detection and Foraging in Synpatric Cutthroat Trout and Dollly Varden," *Canadian Journal of Fisheries and Aquatic Sciences,* no. 42, pp. 785-790, 1985.) So the next time you're fishing at dusk, stay there even after everyone else has called it quits, because nighttime can be the right time when it comes to trout feeding.

6. Color Preference: Trout eyes possess the anatomical structures needed for detecting color. Research suggests that localized trout populations may demonstrate a preference for certain colors of artificial lures. (Ginetz, R. M., and P. A. Larkin, "Choice of Colors of Food Items by Rainbow Trout," *Journal of the Fisheries Research Board of Canada 30,* pp. 229-234, 1973.)

I experienced this phenomenon in southeast Alaska one spring while fishing a stream for cutthroats. They were congregating on the downstream edge of deep pools that held spawning steelhead. Every few seconds, a cutthroat would dart out and snatch a bright orange-red steelhead egg tumbling downstream. Taking the cue, I tried a barbless orange Pixie, designed to imitate the egg sacs of salmon and steelhead, but to no avail. Next I used a red Pixie, but that didn't work either. Exasperated, I tied on a blue Pixie, and that sent the cutthroats into a feeding frenzy.

Blue steelhead eggs? The moral of color preference among trout seems to be that when you select flies or lures that imitate natural prey and the trout refuse to cooperate, try throwing them a red herring. Or a blue egg.

—Bruce Cherry, March 1995

Trout Fishing Tactics

~

"When a trout chooses to prey upon what he thinks

is weaker than himself, the angler ought not to

be blamed for it."

–George Washington Bethune, 1847

Fifteen Tips for More Rainbows

▶▶▶ 1. *Have a Game Plan:* When you get to a stream or lake, don't plow right in and start fishing. Better to study the water from a few yards back first

Methodical fishing nets rewards.

and assess the situation. Try to see where fish might be holding, look for any insect activity, look for rises, look for fish. Map out a game plan before entering the water, then stick to it, fishing the water methodically, one spot at a time, moving slowly upstream (or downstream, if you're fishing nymphs or streamers). Haphazard casting will get you fish, but a methodical, vacuum-cleaner-like approach will get more.

▶▶▶ 2. *Don't Be Undergunned:* During a recent trip to the Blackwater River area in British Columbia, my friend Tim and I were fishing a fast river that was perhaps 50 yards across. Armed with an eight-foot 4-weight graphite flyrod, I was unable to reach many feeding lanes far out in the river, even by double-hauling. Tim, on the other hand, was using a 10-foot rod, also weight 4, and was having no problem punching out 50- to 60-foot casts. He was pulling an impressive number of rainbows out of the fast-water feeding lanes I couldn't reach, and all I could do was fish the marginal waters that were closer in.

The point is: If you're going to fish an unfamiliar piece of water, inquire ahead of time about the fishing conditions. If you're going to fish big water, make sure you take a rod and reel up to the task.

▶▶▶ 3. *Have the Right Flies:* Different offerings work in different parts of the country. In the East, mayfly, caddis, and stonefly imitations all work, depending on the time of year. On the stream, keep your eyes open for signs of hatching insects; if you see dries on the water, check to see if trout are rising to them. If they are, then tie on a suitable imitation. If they're not, turn over streamside rocks and look for nymphs. Gold-ribbed Hare's Ears are always worth a try if you can't find any nymphs. For streamers, the reliable Muddler Minnows will take trout when almost nothing else will.

In the West, Alaska, and the western Canadian provinces, larger rivers filled with glacial runoff call for big and frequently gaudy offerings. Sculpin imitations, Zonkers, and leech imitations, fished down and across, can often draw strikes from big rainbows.

▶▶▶ 4. *If You Miss a Strike, Do Nothing:* Rainbows, particularly those in big waters, have a habit of coming back and striking a fly or streamer a second and even a third time. So if you're stripping in a streamer, and get a strike but no hookup, stop stripping line. Then either let the offering hang where it is or let out a few feet of flyline so the streamer washes back into the strike zone.

▶▶▶ **5.** *Use Spinners:* It's fun at times to experiment with lures such as white curlytail jigs with one-eighth-ounce chartreuse heads, just to see if they work. But if you're serious about getting into some rainbows, you should go with tried-and-true spinners—especially flashy ones—such as Panther Martins, Mepps spinners, and Rooster Tails, in Sizes 0, 1, and 2; or with old reliable spoons such as small Dardevles and Little Cleos. There's a reason those lures have been around for so many years, and it's because they work, especially on rainbows.

Sixteen-inch rainbows like this one are often hooked in fast water with specialized casts.

▶▶▶ **6.** *Know Specialized Casts:* Especially when you're fishing the fast water rainbows love, it pays to know drag-reducing casts such as the "pile cast" and the "S-cast" (see page 100 in "Flyfishing Techniques").

▶▶▶ **7.** *Read the Water:* Rainbows like to hang in certain types of cover, and the more of those cover types you recognize, the more fish you're likely to catch. Seams, where two currents of differing speeds meet, are always likely spots. So are pockets behind boulders, slack-water areas behind logjams, runs under overhanging brush, mouths of feeder creeks, whitewater below riffles and falls, the heads and tails of pools, and along ledges in deep pools.

▶▶▶ **8.** *Wear Camo:* Trout can detect movement as well as shades of color, so I always wear camouflage, tan or dull-colored shirts, jackets, and hats when fishing. Why advertise my presence to the fish by wearing a red hat, white shirt, or bright raincoat? Give yourself an edge: Be dull and you'll catch more fish.

➤➤➤ **9.** *Move Stealthily:* If you make any sudden movements, you're going to spook fish. When approaching a stream, move slowly and quietly. If you see fish rising in a pool, hunch over and move slowly—even crawl—to within casting position. The trick is to get in casting range without being detected.

➤➤➤ **10.** *Fish Close Water First:* While rainbows like to hang in fast water, often out in the middle of a stream, don't overlook the water close to shore. Hidden currents, perhaps not detectable from shore, often run right next to the bank—even a shallow bank. When approaching a stream, flip a few casts right next to shore before getting too close.

➤➤➤ **11.** *Try the Unorthodox:* On another trip to the Blackwater River, I hiked down below a set of falls, looking for new water to fish. After taking a

Fish foam patches below falls, where rainbows seek out food and protection from predators.

few rainbows from right below the falls, I turned around and saw a huge mat of foam floating on the surface, maybe 20 yards below the falls, off in a side current. Just for kicks, I flipped a caddis imitation right into the middle of a 10-foot-square mat—and was rewarded with a smashing hit from what proved to be a 13-inch rainbow. In the next hour, I took 14 fish from under that mat. My guess is that the mat tended to trap insects and other food items, which in turn attracted the rainbows. The overhead canopy also afforded the fish protection from the many bald eagles in the area.

➤➤➤ **12.** *Be Persistent:* When fishing for steelhead on New York's Salmon River, I encountered a situation where the fish simply would not take lures

(Hot Shots), flies (streamers), or bait (minnows). The fish were on their spawning runs. Ultimately my friend David spied a nesting female, with two or three males just downstream of her. Throwing a dead minnow onto a hook, David made about 30 casts to those males. Cast and drift, cast and drift. On the 30th cast one male moved a bit to look at the minnow—he was obviously irritated by it. About 10 casts later, the male couldn't take it anymore, and slashed at the minnow viciously. David reared back and hooked the fish, which promptly headed downstream, with David running after it. It took 10 minutes, but he finally beached a 12-pound steelhead.

>>> 13. *Go Early and Go Late:* In spring, fishing in the middle of the day can be most productive, since that's when fish are most active. As spring fades into summer, however, plan to fish early in the morning and again at dusk. When daytime temperatures rise into the 70s and beyond, the bigger fish in particular will sulk on the bottom—often near a tributary mouth or a spring—until the cooler evening temperatures prevail. The big fish start to move and feed then, because that's when they'll expend as little energy as possible to gather their food. To catch them, get up early and get out on the stream. You can take a nap in the afternoon. Then, when the sun begins to fade on the horizon, fish again until dark. Just before total blackness is the time you might really hit them.

>>> 14. *Troll the Lakes:* While usually found in fast, clear-running streams and rivers, rainbows can also be found in cold, clear-water lakes. In such cases, trolling—with motor or oars—can be deadly. If you're a flyfisherman, knot a No. 8 or 10 black leech pattern on a seven-foot leader and troll through likely areas: off rivermouths, between islands, over dropoffs. If you prefer spinning or baitcasting gear, spoons such as the blue-and-silver KastMaster are hard to beat. Use 6-pound-test line and a snap swivel to prevent line twist. Other good lures for trolling include the jointed, rainbow-finish Rapala; Dardevle spoons; and 5-0'-Diamonds. If you don't get any hits with a moderate trolling speed, troll faster. A quick-moving baitfish imitation, twirling in front of a big rainbow's nose, can bring a lot of strikes.

>>> 15. *Fight the Good Fight:* If you're using fly gear and a rainbow hits, get any slack line you have on the water onto your reel as fast as possible. Do this by holding on to the line with your left hand and reeling like crazy with your right until all of the slack is gone. Once you're fighting that fish from the reel, keep the rod tip high—always—and try to control the fight by keeping the fish away from any fast water or line-tangling structure. As you work the fish in, be prepared for a last-minute dash.

Spinfishermen should use the same fight tactics flyfishermen do, always keeping the rod high and trying to prevent the fish from swimming into

Bass Flies For Big Trout

As trout grow bigger, they require more and larger meals to maintain their strength. After reaching a certain size, they reduce their intake of small insects and begin to prey on small fish, mice, salamanders, snakes, and even birds. For fly anglers, this means that the biggest fish in a stream may no longer be interested in the traditional fur-and-feather imitations of stream insects. Also, big trout grow wary and feed mostly at night or during dark, cloudy days.

A switch to flies designed for bass may be the ticket for these big fish. Hair mice top the list, followed by bulky streamers and frog patterns. At night, a cork popper retrieved noisily across a deep pool may bring a strike.

–Richard A. Bean, December 1985

Netting Tip
Most fish should be netted head first. Since they don't swim backward, any surge will carry them deeper into the net. The only exception is when you are using a treble-hooked lure and the fish is big. In that case, the hooks can snag the net and you can't get the fish inside.
–Gerald Almy, January 1983

structure or worse, getting into fast water downcurrent. If a rainbow does get into fast water, be prepared to run after it downstream.
–Jay Cassell, April 1991

Early-Season Trout

IF THERE'S ONE word that characterizes early-season trout fishing, it's unpredictability—unpredictable weather, stream conditions, and fish.

The most common conditions you'll encounter on early outings are high streams and cold, cloudy weather. I like to carry a thermometer to test the water. When temperatures are less than 48° F, chances are nymphs will entice the most trout. Good early patterns include the Gold-Ribbed Hare's Ear, Stonefly, Bitch Creek, Tellico, Hellgrammite, Hendrickson, and Montana, Sizes 4 to 16, weighted. If the stream's running particularly high and turbulent, use a sinking-tip line, shooting head, or split shot to attain extra depth.

I often work a pair of nymphs, tying one on a short dropper. This lets me probe several levels at once and also see if the trout are showing any pattern preferences. Dead-drift these offerings through deep runs, pools, eddies, and pocket water, making sure the fly nicks the bottom occasionally. That's where most early trout are. With streams running high, it's important to concentrate on finding backwaters, undercut banks, logjams, and rocks that offer the fish access to food but shelter from the main brunt of the current.

The high, murky water does have one important tactical advantage, though: You can move in close without fear of visually spooking fish. And the shorter the nymphing cast, the better. A bright orange strike indicator at the end of the flyline helps you detect subtle takes from lightly pecking fish. Leaders need only be four to six feet, and tippets 1X to 5X.

Streamers take some of the heaviest early-season trout. Top patterns include the Muddler Minnow, Sculpin, Zonker, Marabou Muddler, and Woolly Bugger, Sizes 2 to 10. Cold water temperatures mean a trout's metabolism is slow in early spring, and creeping retrieves that teasingly twitch a pattern past a fish's snout like a crippled minnow generally work best. Cast the streamer across and slightly upstream, let it sink briefly, then work the fly back in six- to 12-inch spurts with plenty of pauses between pulls. Keep the rod tip low to the water and pointed at the fly with all the slack out of the line. This transmits your stripping motions directly to the fly, without letting them dissipate in loose excess line. It also lets you set up firmly when a trout strikes. High-density sink-tip lines or shooting heads keep these flies down near bottom rubble rocks. Streamers are especially good in murky water because their vibrations help trout home in on them.

While bottom–dredging tactics with streamers and nymphs are most reliable for the cold, bank-bulging flows of the new trout season, it's a mistake not to be prepared for other, brighter scenarios—clear, warming water, emerging mayflies, and dimpling trout.

You can rush these ideal conditions a bit in spring by fishing headwaters where snowmelt and rain runoff disperse quickly. Brookies are more common in these headwaters, too, and they'll surface-feed heartily when browns and rainbows still hover lethargically on the bottom.

Even on larger rivers, surface feeding often gets under way earlier than many flyfishermen realize. The smart angler is aware of this and keeps a watchful eye for emerging insects and dimpling trout, even when tradition says good topwater fishing is weeks away.

The midges are among the best producers for early surface action. Most streams have good populations of these minuscule insects, and with a bit of sunlight, hatches can take place even on the coldest of spring days. Trout will often ignore these tiny foods during high-water conditions, but when they do decide to feed on them, it pays to be ready with appropriate-sized flies. Stock both pupa and adult patterns in Sizes 18 to 24, in gray, tan, black, and olive. Deliver on 6X and 7X tippets.

The black caddis is one of several early *Trichoptera* hatches that can entice fish to rise. Stock a selection of downwing patterns in Sizes 14 to 20 in black, gray, and green.

The earliest mayflies to emerge on eastern waters are the Quill Gordons, but more significant and enduring surface sport comes from the three major hatches that follow: Blue-Winged Olives (*Baetis*), Blue Quills (*Paraleptophlebia adoptiva*), and Hendricksons (*Ephemerella subvaria*). This triad of mayflies hatches as early as late March in southern streams and as late as early June in New England and midwestern waters. These hatches often overlap, too, with Blue-Winged Olives or Blue Quills coming off in late morning, Hendricksons taking over in early afternoon, then an exciting spinner fall wrapping up the day's sport just before dusk.

A well-stocked spring trout vest would include a selection of Blue-Winged Olives in Sizes 16 to 20, Blue Quills in Sizes 16 to 18, and Hendricksons and Red Quills (male Hendricksons) in Sizes 12 to 14. Traditional ties will work well in riffly waters, but on calmer stretches or heavily fished streams you'll score better with thorax, parachute, or Comparadun styles of dressing.

Rocky Mountain trout streams may not clear from snowmelt until late June in some areas. But savvy western anglers know that clear, low water and occasionally even rising trout await them if they get to the rivers before spring runoff roils the water. Spring creeks and lakes offer other good options for early trout fishing in the West when most rivers are running high and discolored. Concentrate on the shallow coves and shoal areas in lakes, as they warm up faster than other areas.

Midges, Blue-Winged Olives, and various caddis hatches can offer early surface sport in the West. By June anticipation builds as the watch begins for the famous salmonfly emergence on such rivers as the Snake, Big Hole, Gallatin, Madison, and Yellowstone. Timing this hatch properly can be difficult. But even if you miss the legendary rises it sometimes stirs, take heart, for the salmonfly is the harbinger of a slew of hatches destined to emerge over months to come.

Be flexible, be prepared for extremes, and you'll find early spring one of the grandest times to probe a trout stream.

–Gerald Almy, Fishing Annual, 1987

How to Catch the Fall Hatch

I GLANCED AROUND IN disbelief as my 5-weight rod bucked from the power of yet another heavy brown trout. I was on the no-kill section of the Beaverkill River in eastern New York—one of the most popular stretches of trout water in America—yet there was not another angler in sight. It could have been the weather—blustery and cold, with a light, misting rain. But mostly it was the time of year—late September. Once summer ends, pressure on trout streams drops sharply. On marginal-weather days, some are deserted.

A number of hatches that produce excellent fishing occur during late September, October, and November, however, on both eastern and western streams. Often the cool weather makes it hard for flies to get airborne, drawing trout to the top. The action I experienced was a prime example, with chunky browns slashing at the Slate Drakes (*Isonychia*).

Imitated with a rusty-gray body and gray wings on a Size 12 or 14 hook, the *Isonychia* always entices some of the largest fish in a stream. Late in the day, the spinner fall can also elicit intense rising.

>>> *Prime-Time:* Another prime fall hatch is the Blue-Winged Olive (*Baetis*). Several different species can appear in sizes from 16 to 20, with olive bodies mixed with gray or brown and smoky wings. Like the Slate Drakes, the little Olives seem to hatch best on dark, cloudy days, often during rain showers or even snow flurries. Spring creeks, tailwaters, and other alkaline streams produce the best hatches. Emergers can sometimes score better than duns with this fly; be sure to carry both patterns.

The tiny *Tricorythodes* emerges heavily in summer, but a second generation appears on many streams well into October and November, offering excellent dry-fly fishing. Unlike summer, when the spinner fall is the major event, autumn sees good dun fishing. Stock Sizes 20 to 24, with black bodies and pale, grayish-white wings, both erect and spent. In the west, few hatches are as important as the Pale Morning Dun (*Ephemerella*).

This fly emerges on waters throughout October, hatching over much of the day. Various species require a Size 16 to 20 hook, but all have yellowish-olive bodies with pale-gray wings.

The speckle-bodied *Callibaetis*—Size 14 or 16 hook, brownish-olive body, slate-gray wings—is another excellent Western hatch. Spinner falls can come in morning or evening.

➤➤➤ *Summer Reruns:* Other flies to try include the White Fly (*Ephoron*), cream-colored body and wings, Sizes 12 to 14; *Heptagenia,* grayish-olive with gray wings, Sizes 14 to 16; and *Pseudocloeons,* olive with light-gray wings, Sizes 22 to 24.

Traditional mayfly patterns can work well too. When fishing slower currents or heavily pounded water, switch to parachute, sparkle-dun, no-hackle, and thorax-style ties.

Caddisflies can also hatch well in fall. Carry a few pupa patterns such as the LaFontaine Sparkle Pupa for immature insects and a high-floating pattern such as Al Troth's Elk Hair Caddis, to imitate adults. Sizes 10 to 18 with tan, rust gray, and olive bodies should cover all of these hatches.

Finally, stock a selection of terrestrials such as ants, winged ants, beetles, leafhoppers, grasshoppers, and crickets.

—*Gerald Almy, October 1996*

Trout from Impossible Places

I T WAS BACK in the 1950s when I ran into Ernest Hemingway at the Floridita Bar in Havana, Cuba. I would have settled for a peek from across the room, for having just been in the same place with him, but that chance meeting turned into a clamping handshake and a brief introduction when he noticed me gawking there in my Navy uniform.

You might think this is a strange way to begin a piece on trout fishing, but it was Hemingway who pointed out one of the great frustrations of the sport when he wrote about hooking "big trout in places impossible to land them."

Most trout streams have a number of spots like that, spots that become the favorite lairs for wily old trout. And though they're extremely tough to fish, they can give up some huge trout, and on a fairly regular basis too. All you have to do is adhere to a few basic rules.

Many "impossible" places exist, but the five you are most likely to

Flyfishing Deep

If you want to fish deep with a sinking flyline, use a short leader. Long leaders tend to drift back up toward the surface, keeping your offering well off the bottom.
—Gerald Almy, April 1983

Light Strikes

Flyrodders who use very light leader tippets can set the hook without parting the fragile monofilament by letting go of the flyline before lifting the rod smartly.
—Gerald Almy, January 1983

encounter along a trout stream are logjams, downed trees, bedrock and boulders, pockets of rough water, and sections where dense, overhanging bankside brush leans into the water. Take each as a separate challenge requiring a different approach and often a change in gear.

>>> *Logjams:* These are created primarily in spring and early summer

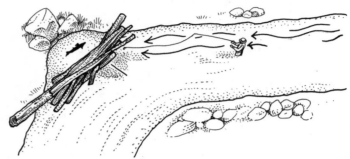

Logjams are lairs for big brown trout. Fish from the upstream side and run your offering deep. If you get a strike, horse the trout out quickly.

when runoff swells creeks and rivers into rampaging courses capable of moving everything from boulders to bridges. Massive logs, even uprooted trees, are carried along like so many sticks. Eventually many of these "sticks" are tossed into chaotic piles along the outside curves of sharp bends.

Logjams are a favorite lair for brown trout. Come across a good logjam, and the odds are that a couple of trophies are hiding in there someplace. If you can get a fly or lure in front of one of these monsters, and if you do get a strike, forget about finesse. Think more about "horsing" it around, which is exactly what the brown trout has in store for you.

Getting a strike, of course, is the first step. Because most logjams are formed at bends, the jumble creates a tangled hood under which trout hide and water action usually carves out a grotto as it undercuts the bank—the grotto itself often a maze of swaying root ends. Large trout remain far back beneath the logs and inside the cave. To do battle with ol' hook jaw, you must run an offering down into the depths and back into the dark reaches. Not just anything will do, either; go with something flashy, wobbly, and definitely meaty.

Three favorites that have done the job for me over the years are dressed and undressed spinners from the Mepps Trouter Kits, any of the midsize Flatfish and weighted streamers such as the Muddler Minnow in Sizes 6 through 10.

To get these offerings into hidden nooks, fish from the upstream side and let the current work the selection for you. As your offering reaches the outer edge of the logjam, start a series of struggling twitches, jerking it forward one step, letting it slip back two. Keep this action up, working it throughout the nooks beneath the logjam.

Strikes by big fish can be surprisingly gentle in these situations. Often they simply clamp down and sit. Watch closely for any sudden slackness in your line. The minute you spot it, set the hook with a firm sideways motion of the rod, which keeps the line down and away from the logs.

Now get that trout out of there in a hurry! This takes a rod with backbone, such as a spinning rod with a medium-heavy action, an open-face reel, and 10-pound-test line. Until the fish is clear, fight your battle with the rod tip held low. Once the fish is away from the logjam, bring the tip up into a more normal fighting position.

>>> *Downed Trees:* Unlike logjams where you must work a fish back out the same way your offering went in, which is against the current, downed trees

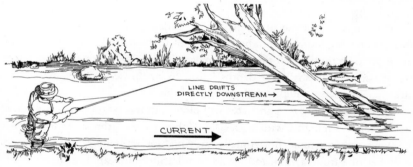

Though it's possible to fish fallen trees from both the up- and downstream sides, the best approach is to cast downstream into the current path running directly under the tree.

lying across current offer two approaches: one from upstream and one from down. The downstream approach is usually the answer, since you have a better chance of getting a strike, and less chance of getting snagged.

Though it's more difficult to get an offering to trout in lies beneath a fallen tree from the downstream side, by laying a fly, nymph, spinner, or lure as close to the swaying branches as possible and on the flow channel showing the deepest water, you'll find that any number of strikes are possible. Just be prepared to react quickly when one comes. As far as offerings are concerned, go to weighted nymphs, wets and streamers, spinners and small lures if trout refuse bulky dry flies.

>>> *Bedrock and Boulders:* Taking trout from areas of exposed bedrock and around boulders presents unique problems. Leader or line abrasion is the main culprit, leading to lost trout in these relatively uncluttered environments where fish rely on darting to and fro, up and down, to escape.

The best approach is from the downstream side. Wade when possible and

Dapping

If you spy a trout ensconced beneath an overhanging bush or against a bank where a traditional cast can't be delivered, try dapping. Sneak slowly up to within rod's reach of the trout on hands and knees, then gently reach out and place the fly onto the water over the fish. Chances are good a slurping take will result.

–Gerald Almy, January 1991

use short casts to work your selections back over seams of bedrock and around the bases of all boulders. On hooking up with a trout, immediately jockey it

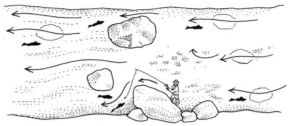

The trick to fishing around boulders is to avoid cutting your line on a jagged edge; do this by placing your selection downstream and moving it into open water when taken.

into the nearest pocket of open water so it cannot cut your line against some jagged edge.

This requires gearing up with heavier leaders and, with spinning tackle, heavier line. A good choice in both cases is 8- to 10-pound-test. When depths are more than three feet, I tie on a spinner, small lure or weighted nymph, wet fly or streamer. In shallower depths I shift to an unweighted fly, nymph, or streamer, or a large, bulky dry fly such as a bivisible.

▶▶▶ *Rough Water:* Rough water will often intimidate you before you even get started. Couple that with aggressive rainbows and cutthroats, which thrive in flows that resemble horizontally moving waterfalls more than they do stretches of a trout stream, and it's no wonder more fish are lost than netted. Hook into a good fish, and you'll soon find yourself scrambling over boulders, stumbling around logs, and splashing right into the middle of the current when necessary and where possible.

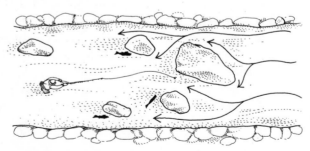

Use short casts or the dapping technique when fishing rough water and wade upstream against the current to avoid spooking trout.

But rough-water sections are great places to find hefty, hard-fighting trout. Landing one is another matter. You must contend not only with the wiliness of the fish themselves, strong currents and abrasive rocks, but with a terrain that makes footing on the bank extremely difficult and wading in the rougher sections downright impossible.

Getting strikes is not much of a problem. Fish the aerated pools below places where water crashes over rocks and tumbles through gaps. Keep casts as short as possible to cut down on line drag to detect strikes. Dapping, simply dangling an offering straight down, is often effective. Dry flies are out. Go with weighted nymphs, wets, and streamers tied on Size 6 through 12 hooks. Spinners are also excellent producers in this water, as are worms.

That's to get a fish on. Keeping it on is the hard part. When possible, do not let it run downstream on you; once it gets some steam, there's no way you'll be able to stop it. Instead, try to keep the fish within the pocket of water where it took your offering. This again requires gearing up with strong 10- to 12-pound-test leaders, or spinning line, and, at minimum, medium-weight rods with enough length to reach over pools and around boulders. Seven-footers are right when spinning, with 8 1/2-foot lengths ideal for flyrods.

If a trout runs and you fail to turn it, your only chance is to give chase. Hold your line and rod tight and high in one hand, using the other for balance. Stay as close to the water's edge as possible. Maintain a taut line, making the fish pull not only against the rod but against the current as well. More often than not, before dashing on, the trout will pause in each pool for a couple of leaps or tumbles, giving you a chance to catch up. Stay with it. If you don't tire, the fish will.

▶▶▶ *Overhanging Bankside Brush:* Such stretches frequently appear to be truly impossible to take trout from. Trout tend to feed on the outer edge of this type of lie. This holds true all season, and especially toward the end of August on through September and October, when water levels drop and fish are forced to feed toward the middle of the stream. At such times it is to the

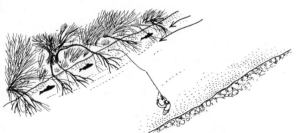

Overhanging brush requires casting across and slightly upstream from the opposite bank. This gives you the leverage you'll need to set the hook and jerk the trout midstream.

angler's advantage to carefully and thoroughly fish these overhung lies.

You must, nevertheless, be geared up and ready for some tough battles. The instant a trout feels the bite of a hook, it will slash into the rootlike limbs

Bright Water Angling

When stream fishing, look for what I call "dancing diamonds"—the small, bobbing wavelets that appear (when the light is right) where fast water meets slow. I have caught some big trout in these turbulent spots.

Food being swept along by a swift current settles to the bottom when it meets slower water. Practically all fish have to do is lie under these patches with their mouths open, making these spots prime locations for large, lazy trout.

If the dancing diamonds are over shallow water, you will do better on overcast days, early and late in the day, and at night. If they are over deeper water, fish may hold there at any time.

–Ed Mendus, April 1995

Scout for Trout

Experienced anglers know that trout, especially wild brookies, are sensitive to water temperature. A neat way to find where trout will be holding during the summer is to scout during a winter cold snap. Look for open water along otherwise frozen streams. Flowing water is usually due to underground springs, which customarily hold at about 52°F, regardless of the season. This is about the optimum temperature for wild brook trout. Pinpoint the springs on a map so you will know the precise locations come spring and summer.

–Steve Springer, February 1995

dangling into the water. If you're not using a heavy 8- to 10-pound leader or line matched with sturdy tackle, and if you don't react instantly to keep that fish from burrowing into the thick stuff, you are going to immediately become hopelessly entangled.

The best approach for this type of cover is from the opposite bank, and across (not down- or upstream) where you are in a position to maneuver a solid fish straight away from the entanglements. From the opposite bank, casting across and slightly upstream, you have the leverage. The minute you set the hook, haul back and jerk the trout into midstream.

▶▶▶ *Beating the Impossible:* In Hemingway's "Big Two-Hearted River," Nick Adams was a young man on a sort of pilgrimage. I like to think that as he grew older, he might have come to look on "impossible" places to take trout as being not so impossible so long as one is properly geared and prepared.

I might have asked Hemingway about that when I met him in Havana, but I wasn't able to get my mouth working in the great writer's presence. However, it's most likely Nick did. I know I have. On a trout stream the impossible only becomes impossible if you let it.

–John Lusk, April 1990

Stormy Weather Means More Trout

TROUT FISHING DURING stormy weather can be nasty business. When the rain starts to drench your old fishing vest or the snow pellets peck at your favorite hat, my advice is to get under cover, build a big fire, and stay put until the storm blows over.

But there's one trouble with this bit of Spanish philosophy—you don't get any trout.

So chances are you'll chuck this advice and do what I do—and maybe turn blue doing it. Since I made a fairly conclusive test on trout-feeding habits during various barometric readings, I have never held much with the theory that trout fishing is normally lousy during a storm.

Sure, I've been skunked during snow and rainstorms, but it has been the exception to the rule. One of my best catches of golden trout came one afternoon while the temperature hovered around 22°F and snow was piling up at four inches an hour.

Golden-trout habits don't follow any particular pattern, you say? Then how about the time a limit of brookies rose to a No. 12 Hare's Ear while the lightning was smashing into the pine trees less than half a mile away? In most cases I have found trout fishing to be better than average during stormy weather.

Don't ask me why this is true. I can't tell you. Fish biologists have all kinds of theories about the effect of atmospheric pressure on the bladders and stomachs of trout. I can only say that the weather has a much greater effect on fishermen than on fish. So if you claim the fishing is poor during storms, it may be that you haven't given it as great a test as you normally would if the weather had been fair. As a general rule, sticking out a storm pays off.

I recall one time at Blue Lake in the granite crags of California's Sierra Nevadas. I had spent a thundery July afternoon tossing my entire assortment of flies at a lake of stubborn rainbows. Four hours had produced nothing, yet I had been there too many times to claim the lake was barren.

At five o'clock the overcast thickened and the cumulus clouds came apart at the seams. I reeled in, crawled under an overhanging rock, and watched the drops spatter the lake. Suddenly the water's surface came alive with trout.

Bending a No. 12 Brown Hackle on a nine-foot leader, I cast out. No takers. I cast again, laying the line down carefully. Still no luck. Working along the west shore I cast again and again with the same results. I kept this up for half an hour trying one fly then another. The trout were absolutely insulting. By this time I was dripping and disgusted. I sat down on a rock right there in the middle of the rain, clamped my teeth together, and thought it over.

The temperature was a sticky 58°F. The rain was coming straight down. I watched the trout leaping out of the water like they were feeding on the raindrops. An occasional rumble of thunder rolled down the canyon. The whole situation was maddening and those buckets of water down my neck didn't smooth my disposition. Sometimes you have to get hit with an eight-pound sledge before you catch on. I got hit five minutes later when I took cover under a white pine near the shoreline.

Climbing a tree in a thunderstorm isn't the sanest thing I've ever done, but it can put trout in the creel. Rod and I went up the tree and out on a limb 10 feet above the water. I let out some line and lightly dabbled a No. 12 Gray Hackle straight down on the surface. A 10-inch rainbow came off the bottom. I nearly fell out of the tree. I missed setting that first one by three seconds, but the next half hour in that tree produced nine beauties.

How did I land those trout while perched on a tree limb 10 feet above the water? It wasn't easy. First I tried keeping a tight line while easing myself off the limb and down on the bank. Most of the time the line would go slack and the rainbow would shake the hook. Finally I wised up and merely played the trout up on the bank before I got out of the tree.

From my pine tree perch I tried Gray Hackles, Hare's Ears, Black Gnats, and Sierra Bight Dots. All patterns seemed to work equally well. But between tree trips I tried the shoreline where the trout were jumping with the same vigor and I drew blanks.

Normally I prefer light tackle when I'm fishing any type of fly, but it presents too great a problem when the wind is blowing 10 to 20 miles an hour. In a situation of this sort I usually stow the spider-web tippets and tie on a seven-foot taper with a four- or five-pound tippet. With a 20-mile-an-hour wind whipping the surface of a mountain lake, you don't have to worry about the trout seeing your line, much less your leader. And with a larger leader you stand a better chance of getting more distance out of your casts.

In windy weather with some rain or snow, my favorite fly is a very wet No. 10 brown Hackle Firefly (fire-orange fluorescent rib on a standard brown Hackle Peacock). Fishing a fly well below the surface is no cinch when the whitecaps obscure the fly. After the cast I usually hold the line lightly between my thumb and fingertips. Then I can strike the trout with this line hand when I feel the hit.

On the retrieve, I use the line hand to slowly pull in about two feet at a time, giving the fly any desired motion I want. Short irregular jerks seem to produce the most consistent results. Don't forget, here you rely entirely on the touch of your fingertips.

Early one summer I took an afternoon solo hike four miles from the end of the road that runs west of Big Pine, California. By three o'clock the clouds were beginning to form over the area, beautiful cottony puffs that result from rising air masses over the mountains. These clouds are exciting to watch unless you object to a good soaking.

By the time I reached the lake some of the cumulus clouds had black bottoms and characteristic anvil tops. Streaks of lightning flashed into the rocks a mile away and the resultant thunder echoes ricocheted across the canyon walls. A perfect day for trout fishing.

Suddenly I realized the trout weren't working the shoreline any more. They had moved out and were dimpling the surface more than 100 feet from the edge. I reeled in and took off my HDH tapered fly rig.

I have another setup on a small single-action reel that I carry for such emergencies. The setup consists of a 20-foot end off of an old HCH double-tapered fly line backed with 100 yards of five-pound monofilament. Put a No. 12 Hare's Ear on the end of seven or eight feet of tapered leader and you're ready for action.

This is old stuff to the seasoned steelhead angler but new and very adaptable to flyfishing in high-altitude lakes. By using the double-pull cast, which means giving the line a strong pull on both the backcast and forward motion, the heavy length of fly line will very easily pull out more than 100 feet of monofilament backing. But you better make sure you have plenty of the monofilament stripped off the reel and coiled on the ground. Otherwise you might see your length of fly line go sailing into the middle of the lake— unattached to the reel.

Whether it's stormy or clear, you won't catch trout unless you can get the fly to them, and this modified shooting line gives you that advantage in a lot of cases. Sure, spinning gear will do it, but dry-fly fishing with a spinning outfit means some type of floating weight such as the plastic bubble. Somehow I can't get used to the idea of using weights with dry flies, so I stick to the shooting outfit.

It paid off during this thunderstorm. Thirty minutes of those 110- to 125-foot casts and I had seven brookies and a full creel.

[Editor's note: Fishing in a lightning storm increases your chances of getting struck, so you might regard this piece with historical—not practical—interest. See "Flyrod Lightning," page 267.]

–Tom Henderson, June 1954

Trout of the Last Wild Places

IN 1859 FRANK FORESTER wrote that brook trout were "one of the most beautiful creatures in form, color and motion that can be imagined." Henry David Thoreau likened them to "the fairest flowers," and in recent times Ernest Schwiebert has referred to brook trout as "the Aphrodite of the hemlocks."

Well, brookies are pretty fish, and during the autumn spawning rush they can be lustful little devils as well, slashing over gravelly riffles in serious mating fervor—so maybe a comparison to the love-and-beauty goddess isn't completely overblown.

In any case, the aesthetic aspect of brook trout angling has long been part of its tradition. Brookies tend to run small in most places, often less than 10 inches, and even the larger specimens are comparatively unglamorous fighters. They jump in magazine photographs but seldom in life, and ounce for ounce they are probably less spunky than pond bluegills. They can sometimes (by no means always) be embarrassingly easy to catch. Rainbows and browns grow larger, and they fight harder and more spectacularly.

>>> *Why, When, and Where:* So why would anyone fish for brookies? Partly because, like legendary mountain peaks, "they're there," but more because of that fine and insistent aesthetic tradition. One fishes for brook trout as much to be in contact with beauty as for any other reason. There is the beauty of the fish itself, as the trout writers attest, and there is also the allure of its environs, for brookies have pristine aquatic needs and thrive only in places that have been largely preserved from the more ravaging onslaughts of progress.

Brookies occupy a wide range of general habitats—tiny creeks, midsize

Worm Tip

One of the best ways to take trout is to place a single garden worm on a No. 8 or 10 hook, add one or two split-shot a foot up the line, and drift the offering through pools and deep runs. Keep your rod tip high and let the worm tumble down naturally in the flow, setting the hook when you feel a tap on the line.

–Gerald Almy, July 1987

Lake Trout Logic

With planning and patience, you can take deep-running lake trout on light tackle. First, look for birds. A gull or two on the water may mean lake trout 100 feet below. Second, I've found dozens of three-inch rainbow smelt in very large fish, proving you don't need a big lure with heavy flashers to attract them. Third, trolling is the best tactic. The trick is to move slowly. A great boat for laker trolling is a gently paddled canoe. Fourth, the best time to troll this slowly is on a still day, around dawn. Fifth, fish deep. In most places at most times, lakers hold deeper than 50 feet. Use 6-pound line and a rapidly sinking lure that suggests a minnow. (I use a white, quarter-ounce twister-tail jig.) Run your lure to the bottom and raise it a couple turns. Ease your boat through an area where birds have settled, keeping your rod and line as perpendicular as possible.

–John Swinton, August 1990

streams, large rivers, ponds, mountain lakes—but their specific habitat requirements are more demanding: cold water (preferably 55° to 66°F) that's clean and unsilted, with minimal competition from other trout species. In streams, they like to position themselves next to cover (rocks, logs, boulders, overhangs, sunken brush), with the largest fish staking out the best territories—especially the deeper, still-water areas such as pools and beaver-dam ponds. In lakes, these fish cruise individually or in schools and can often be seen and cast to in the shallows—an exciting, quick-draw form of angling.

>>> *Fly Tackle Ideals:* According to Forester, the ideal brook trout rod "should be 12 feet long and as pliant, almost, as a coach-whip, equally bending from the butt to the tip." (This reminds us that some progress actually is progressive.) My favorite brook trout rods include an 8 1/2-foot 2-weight and a nine-foot 4-weight, both built from comparatively flexible graphite blanks. These are not soft but not overly stiff either (30 to 35 ppm, for those of you who count modulus ratings), with medium to fast actions. I also use a 6-foot 9-inch 4-weight for brookies, but only in places where streamside trees make a longer rod uncomfortable. (A longer flyrod actually lets you have more fun with small fish and is more efficient for casting and line control.)

In currents and where the fish are gullible, I use a standard weight-forward flyline and a seven-foot leader, with the tippet diameter gauged more to the size of the fly than to the wariness of the fish. In still water, however, where brook trout can be exceedingly wary, I'll often use 12 or more feet of leader with long tippets, narrowing down to 7X or 8X if necessary.

>>> *Ultralight Fun:* I've also had much brook trout fun over the years with ultralight spin rods. My "mini" outfit for small fish and fine fishing consists of a four-foot slow-action, soft graphite rod with palm-sized reel and spools of 2- and 4-pound-test line. This rig is fun even with eight-inch brookies, and the demands of flipping a tiny spinner into cup-sized pockets of bankside cover make it interesting angling as well. For larger lake and beaver-pond fish (more than 12 inches and up to several pounds), I move to a five-foot, fast-action, stiff (though not wholly inflexible) graphite rod with ultralight reel and 4-pound line, keeping a spare spool of 6-pound line on hand just in case.

–Anthony Acerrano, July 1994

Double Up with Nymphs

FISHING A SECOND, or indicator, fly is a common practice among experienced nymph fishermen. Many use a piece of colored yarn or plastic at the tip of the flyline, but equally effective is a dropper fly tied well up on the leader.

The dropper fly should be an easily seen small fly. Usually it's a small dry fly with a white wing for maximum visibility and minimal interference when casting a nymph, but I have found it more productive to use either an unweighted nymph in light color or a small wet fly as a dropper. Often the dropper will draw as many strikes from fish as the main fly.

Double duty: Indicator flies attract trout and also alert you to their presence.

If you have never tried this, you'll be surprised at how often the indicator draws as much attention from the trout as your main fly.

It wasn't too many years ago that the accepted, practiced flyfishing technique involved casting a set of three or four wet flies—and the equipment wasn't even as good back then.

—James W. Frantz, November 1988

Lakes: Top to Bottom

HERE'S THE INSIDE dope on catching fish: Cast where they eat. Casting anywhere else may gratify your appetite for grace or accuracy, but it won't catch many fish.

This is so obvious that stating it in print may seem churlish, but the fact is that most of the time fishermen cast in the wrong places. If that were not the case, they'd wear out their arms hauling in fish.

Nowhere is this more true than in ponds and lakes, where fish-holding hotspots are hardest to find. In rills, brooks, streams, and rivers, where the flow of the current is easy to read, anyone can figure out that the fish will be holding under the cutbanks, next to midstream boulders where the current causes eddies that trap things, and near the cover of fallen trees and debris.

But in lakes and ponds the still surface reveals little about what is going on beneath, and the spots where fish feed are much more difficult to identify.

In the cool waters where trout thrive, they are rarely lazy. The urge to eat is largely activated by the presence of food. When food appears where it can be eaten without the expenditure of much energy, trout eat. Your ability to catch trout, therefore, requires knowing where trout go to eat what.

In lakes and ponds, food is concentrated in five basic areas: (1) spots where incoming flows enter; (2) at the outflow of the body of water; (3) around springholes; (4) in the shoreline shallows; and (5) in shallow-water areas created by either reefs or sandbars.

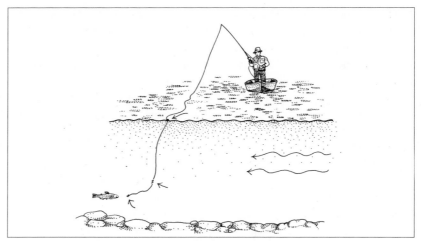

Trout are frequently found near incoming currents in lakes and ponds. These currents transport insects into still water, where trout can feed while expending little energy.

Incoming flows, whether trickles or full-fledged rivers, carry a heavy supply of insect life. Larvae, nymphs, emerging insects, terrestrial insects that just happened to fall into the water, all ride the incoming flow into the still-water pond or lake. Small fish gather at the entry point to sort through the current-born feast. Big fish gather there, too, to feed on small fish and insect matter.

If heavy fish are eating insects floating on the surface here, their rushing about will result in splashes and rings that reveal their location. The fish can be taken by casting flies or minnow-shaped lures to those spots. When no surface disturbance indicates the presence of fish, assume that big fish are present but staying deep. Deep-running lures and weighted streamer and bucktail flies are useful then.

Outflows concentrate fish for similar reasons; insects hatching in the lake are sucked into the outflow and borne by the current to fish gathering there to harvest an easy meal. The biggest fish will lie where eddies cause floating matter to pause. When small fish are seen taking this matter, you can bet that bigger fish will be coming by from time to time to prey on them.

Springholes are the great secret fishing spots in all lakes and ponds. Areas in the immediate vicinity of springholes contain more oxygen than stagnating surroundings. This results in the growth of the vegetation types that are of greatest importance to aquatic insects.

When water temperatures rise, trout seek the cool springholes and feed on the insect life that gathers there. The big fish typically swim upward from the bottom of the lake in spirals through the vegetation, dislodging nymphs clinging to the leaves and eating those that are easiest to catch.

Upon reaching the surface, the trout roll and dive to the bottom to repeat the procedure. Anglers seeing the rings of rolling fish often mistake them for ones feeding on the surface; they then cast floating flies and wonder why they don't get strikes.

Instead of a floating fly, you need a sinking line and a meaty-looking nymph. Cast to where the fish rose and let the line sink until it reaches the weeds growing near the bottom. (You'll know you are deep enough when you bring up vegetation. Count the seconds required to get the fly that deep, and cut two off that amount of time on subsequent casts.)

Springholes can sometimes be located by trolling at slow speed, dragging deep-running leech imitations and lures or weighted minnow-shaped flies.

Shoreline shallows get the most attention from pond and lake fishermen, but a lot of these fishermen may not have figured out why. Shoreline shallows undergo the greatest temperature change hour by hour and day by day. Wind stacks warm surface water against the far shore, raising the air temperature by several degrees. The angle of the sun changes hour by hour, and its radiant heat penetrates the shallow water and warms the lake bottom there first.

Due to the overhanging branches of shrubs and trees, shoreline shallows are rich in leaf litter and decaying wood. Aquatic insects lay their eggs in these food-rich shallows, and the varying water temperatures here are the cause of sporadic hatches.

The temperature changes are most pronounced early in the morning and late in the afternoon, and hatches are frequent then. Fish of all sizes are drawn into shoreline shallows during twilight hours to indulge in the insect feast. And of course, the bigger fish eat the smaller ones when given the chance.

Flycasting and spincasting tackle is equally effective during these conditions. If the hatches are heavy, the chances of taking a big fish are often best if the angler uses flies and lures simulating small fish rather than trying to match the hatch. One tiny artificial fly floating on the water's surface among hundreds of authentics doesn't have much of a chance of being noticed.

Reefs and sandbars draw fish for some of the same reasons. The shallow waters undergo periodic temperature changes, drawing both crustaceans and insects—two dependable food sources that attract fish.

Again, lures and flies that simulate small fish are most effective. When the wind rises, wave action disturbs insects and crustaceans that have taken refuge around sandbars and reefs, causing them to seek out new hiding places.

Fish know this and will go to these spots to chase down easy meals, regardless of the time of day. Casting or trolling around reefs and sandbars on windy days can provide good fishing when all else fails.

—Jerome B. Robinson, April 1989

Great Bait

Natural bait is deadly for taking trout, but don't confine yourself to the standards—worms, salmon eggs, etc. Try offerings such as small live minnows, hellgrammites, large mayfly nymphs, caterpillars, grasshoppers, and crickets. Fish them on fine-wire hooks, with just a tiny split-shot or two for weight and 2- or 4-pound-test line.

—Gerald Almy, January 1992

Driftfishing

When driftboat fishing for trout, concentrate on the first 12 to 24 inches next to land. Here the shoreline provides escape from the current, ambush points, and food. It's almost always where the biggest trout hang out. After your fly pulls a few feet, false-cast and deliver it to the next stretch.

—Gerald Almy, July 1994

Winter Trout Action

MOST TROUT FISHERMEN used to consider winter a time for tying flies beside a crackling fire. Lately, however, more and more anglers are discovering that winter fishing action will warm the insides every bit as well. And states are responding by offering special extended seasons, often with reduced limits or no-kill restrictions. Before discussing the flies that work best for cold-weather trout, though, let's clarify a few important points:

➤➤➤ *Expectations:* Don't go out planning to hook 20 or 30 trout, as you might on a hot summer day. Their metabolisms are working slower this time of year. They need less food and digest it more laboriously. They strike less often and don't range as far to seek meals. If I fool five or six fish in winter, I consider it a good day. A dozen is outstanding.

➤➤➤ *Preparation:* Don't go out in a light sweater expecting to be warm enough to withstand the bitter temperatures and the wind, rain, sleet, and snow that might greet you. Dress about the way you would for a duck hunt.

Where to go is another important consideration. Not all trout streams fish well when it's cold. Call a game warden, fish biologist, or local fly shop to save wasted effort. Two of your best bets are tailwaters and spring creeks. Both of these types of water have fairly constant year-round temperatures, making their trout more eager to strike. If there are no such waters near your home, freestone streams can still yield action—you just have to plan your trips more carefully.

➤➤➤ *Proper Timing:* And that brings up the final ingredient needed for a successful winter outing—proper timing. It can make or break any trip, but is particularly important on freestone streams. The temperature at which trout start feeding is usually around 37° to 42°F. The breaking point varies from stream to stream, but more significant than the precise mercury reading is the direction the temperature is heading. Fish may feed heavily in water only in the low 40s if it has been much lower than that and has suddenly risen during a warming trend or on a sunny day.

The peak temperature, just before the mercury starts to drop off, will yield the best action. Thus it's important not to get out at the crack of dawn. Sleep in, and hit the water at midmorning. Start fishing, but expect your best action from lunch time until four o'clock. Avoid going out after a cold front has blown through. The fish will likely be off their feed.

➤➤➤ *What to Use:* The best flies for winter trout vary with location, but several have proven so outstanding that they belong in every angler's box. Streamers are a good starting point. Black-and-white Zonkers, Sculpins, and Grey Ghosts are effective, but the overwhelming favorite is the Woolly Bugger.

Black and olive are the two top colors. Size 6 is good for Western waters and larger Eastern rivers; otherwise go with Size 8 or 10. The main thing to remember is to keep streamers deep, right along bottom rubble, and work them slowly with short spurts of four to 12 inches.

Nymphs are also very effective. Gordon Rose, an expert guide on the Bighorn, says his favorite patterns for Western rivers include the Golden Stonefly, Size 10 to 12; Pheasant Tail, Size 18 to 20; Red Midge Larva, Size 16 to 18; Orange Scud, Size 14 to 16; and Gordie's Worm, Size 8. Says Rose, "The Golden Stone is my all-time favorite winter nymph on all Western freestone-type streams that have stoneflies. The Scud, Midge Larva, and Pheasant Tail are best in waters that evidence some type of spring-creek-like conditions."

These patterns also score well on many Eastern waters in winter. Other nymphs include a Black Stonefly, Size 6 to 8; Hare's Ear, Size 10 to 16; and a Size 16 to 18 grayish-tan Cress Bug for fish spotted burrowing in watercress and elodea on spring creeks. On streams with spawning steelhead, stock egg flies in Sizes 6 to 8. Fish these patterns on a tight line, feeling for takes or using a strike indicator. Several small split-shot are often required to take the fly deep where it should nick along the bottom and draw the most action.

Dry-fly action in cold weather is never dependable, but when it happens, it's a great tonic for a raw winter day. Common hatches include black stoneflies and caddis, Size 14 to 18; Blue-Winged Olives, Size 16 to 20; and various midges. One of the best patterns for the latter flies is a Griffith Gnat, Size 18 to 22. Look for winter trout rising in midafternoon during warming trends, often when skies are overcast. The fish will usually be in back eddies, side sloughs, or long, slow pools rather than fast areas.

—Gerald Almy, November 1991

Winter Trout Simplified

BRYAN DUNN IS the 48-year-old assistant superintendent of schools for the Bozeman, Montana, school district. But when he's not marshaling school policy, he's fishing—summer and winter. Over the years, Dunn has found that three rules keep him in winter trout:

1. Fish Over Fish: Dunn says that 99 percent of the water in a typical trout stream is barren of fish in the winter. One percent of the remaining water holds 100 percent of the trout, so finding that water is the key.

2. Fish Deep: Trout will be found in deep pools, Dunn says, usually those shaped like a bathtub. Typically the fish will hold just below the lip of the chute that feeds the pool, sheltered from the current but in a position to pick up food as it washes over their heads.

Easy Eggs

Bits of brightly colored yarn are excellent egg imitations and are a deadly driftfishing lure for steelhead and salmon. Flyfishermen use them with fast-sinking flylines. Inexpensive cards of flourescent gift-wrapping yarn are available in department and discount stores. Also check for pom-poms—inexpensive little round balls of acrylic yarn that are ideal as egg simulators. Pom-poms come in one-quarter, one-half, three-quarters, and one-inch sizes in many bright colors. They don't need to be tied on— just slipped on over the hook for a quick and easy yarn egg.

–Deke Meyer, June 1987

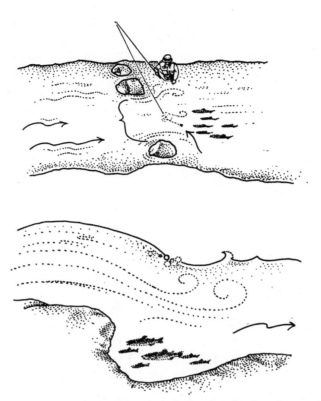

Winter trout gather at the heads of deep, bathtub-shaped pools where they are sheltered from the current but still in a position to feed. Fish over these pools for the best action.

3. Detect Strikes: Dunn believes that because of their slow metabolisms, winter trout will rarely move more than six or eight inches to intercept a drifting nymph, and will generally move less than that. Therefore, a precise drift is critical. Dunn uses a floating line and says that nearly imperceptible strikes make strike indicators a big help. Because he's found fish in the same places over and over again, he sometimes sets the hook as his fly bottoms out in the holding area of a pool, even though his indicator hasn't moved.

–Dave Carty, February 1991

How to Read a Trout Stream

IS ANY ONE SPOT on any given trout stream better than another? Quite frankly, no. The myth that one section is better than another rises out of the mists of "preference" water. Fred likes to fish riffles; Don, pools; and maybe some old expert revels in long stretches of sedate water. But up from those pools, riffles, and runs might be a canyon where the stream thunders across boulders. And up from that are the headwaters.

Throughout them all are trout, and anglers who limit themselves to one or two types of water never fully understand what any given trout stream has to offer. For those who accept the challenge of different environments found along a trout stream's course, this guide will get you started toward that total experience.

Conditions vary from trout stream to trout stream across the country, but you generally find six distinct environments for trout on each: headwaters, creek, canyon, meadow, river, and farmland. Sometimes they are in combination, as in meadow and river; one, or two, as in canyon and/or farmland, may be missing. Regardless, by understanding the complete makeup of a typical stream having all six environments, you can easily adapt to those with fewer.

1. Headwaters: In one form or another, headwaters give birth to all trout rivers. The majority rise up in high elevations, often above timberline, or in far-northern regions, and are, for the most part, accessible only through hiking or horseback. As such, headwaters are truly the last frontiers for anglers seeking adventure, solitude, and wild trout, and no angler wanting to fully experience what a trout stream has to offer should pass up the chance to fish at least one— especially since a surprising number can be hiked to, and returned from, in a single day over well-marked trails.

Headwaters are generally small streams, often with wide-open grassy banks, sand and gravel bars, and exposed bedrock creating series of runs, pools, riffles, and broken water. Look for trout in all of these spots. Because of the environment, short growing seasons, and Spartan supplies of forage, the trout—mostly brookies and cutthroats—seldom are over 10 inches in size. Don't be surprised if you tie into a trophy, however, especially if you're fishing on the downstream side of a high-country lake.

If a lot of trout are present, you can be fairly bold in your approach; if numbers are less visible, a situation that lessens competition for available food and increases the trout's overall wariness, you must take a more cautious approach by keeping a low profile and remaining at least one rod-length back from the water.

2. Creeks: Headwaters become creek environments where brushy banks make casting (even with spinning tackle) downright aggravating at times. Because of that brush, though, it's along creek sections where you find some of the best and most varied fish populations on any trout stream, with brookies, cutthroats, rainbows, and browns all likely to be present when they inhabit that fishery. Average size will run from six to 14 inches, but larger fish are possible. I've taken two- and three-pound rainbows and browns from such places, and have seen five-pounders caught on occasion.

Night Trout

Many streams come to life in the dark. Since in heavily fished waters fish spend a good part of their day spooked, they feed in the dark, unhindered. Also, aquatic insect movement increases during summer nights. Trout become aware of this movement and take advantage of it.

The low-light vision of trout is very good, and they have no trouble seeing a swimming lure or drifting fly in the dark. Studies on brown trout have shown that on a starlit, moonless night they can clearly see drifting insects smaller than a Size 26 fly, and that they actively feed on them.

The best season for night trout fishing is in the summer months during the first hour or two after sunset. For safety reasons, it's best to fish with a friend and in areas with which you are thoroughly familiar.

Wetfly and nymph patterns are good choices for the flycaster while spoons, jigs, and salmon eggs work well with spinning gear.
–Robert Drew, August 1988

Scout Frozen Streams

This winter take a leisurely walk along your favorite ribbon of fishing water, making notes as to where the spring holes are—places where the stream is not frozen over. During hot summer days these are the coolest spots in the stream and may offer you the hottest angling action. Fish seek out springs. When all other holes fail to produce, holes with springs should prove to be far better.

–Joe Parry, October 1985

Creek flows are a series of long, broken-water runs separated by fast-water pools. Some undercut banks are present, but for the most part, trout are found by rocks in the creekbed.

Where brush thins you can fish from the bank, but most often your only approach is to wade up the middle of the creek, casting upstream, or across, to lies around rocks and beneath overhanging entanglements.

3. Canyons: Most trout streams have at least one narrow canyon section somewhere along their course. Though the canyon may be low-walled or steep-sided, long or short, timbered or open, one thing you can bet on is that it's strewn with boulders, creating a rough-water environment not for the faint of heart. But such places hold some of the most brilliantly marked, hard-fighting trout (usually rainbows and cutthroats) you'll find anywhere.

The best way into steep-sided canyons when no trail is available is to pick your way upstream by entering at the lower end; for low-walled canyons having solid footing into them, work your way down wherever you feel comfortable. In either case, travel light. Wear hiking boots to get in and out, and surefooted wading shoes for fishing. (Use your own judgment; some canyon stretches have banks, and flows, that lend themselves to hip or chest waders; some you cannot wade at all.) Also, it's a good idea to wear a combination vest and life preserver.

This is rough-water fishing and, because of the turbulence, be bold in your approach, using short casts directly into pools and swirling backflows found around every boulder. Work each thoroughly. If offerings don't come close to a lie, trout will seldom chase them far.

4. Meadows: These sections are the great confounders. With all that slow-moving water meandering back and forth across grassy, often brushless, meadows, you pounce on them with great enthusiasm, only to discover they're not nearly as easy to fish from as you thought. In fact, meadow environments, like some famous Eastern limestone creeks, demand exacting presentations, approaches, and fly and lure selection.

The reason is twofold: First, water, varying in depth from a few inches to several feet, is still moving across silty bottoms and alongside deeply undercut banks, affording trout an unbroken view of anglers, presentations, line fall, and offerings. Second, most trout that inhabit meadow stretches are browns. Brown trout are wary as it is, but in meadow flows they become downright paranoid.

Stay well back from the water, even kneeling during presentations. Position yourself downstream from where you want to cast. Use the longest, lightest leader, or line, you can handle fish on, taking into consideration that browns in rich meadow environments often reach weights of two pounds or more.

The best places are just out from undercut banks, but where aquatic vegetation fills one of the runs, fish the open pockets. Also, where riffles separate long runs, try them first before working the smoother water. Don't overlook adjacent beaver ponds, either.

5. Rivers: These environments contain all the flows recognized as "classic": riffles changing into long smooth runs; broken-water stretches; deep pools; converging currents; sweeping bends; and water moving smoothly around exposed rocks and over bedrock shelves, all occurring where banks, though often timbered, are fairly free of brush. For the most part, wading is restricted only by depth, as currents are moderate.

On any given trout stream, river environments receive the most fishing pressure. This is also where you'll find sections set aside for catch and release and/or use of artificial flies and lure only. Where no special regulations are in effect, resident trout numbers are often supplemented through stocking.

To fish river sections, pay attention to where various flows converge, especially at the heads of long runs of smooth surface water where faster currents enter, at places where you find undercut banks, and in stretches containing exposed rocks and slow- to medium-slow-moving water.

6. Farmlands: Land this far down is usually privately owned. Access can be a problem, except where game and fish departments have landowner agreements that open access to anglers. Where no agreement is in place, it's up to you to get permission to fish that stretch. It's worth the effort. Farmland environments are where you find the largest trout, usually browns.

Trout streams in farmland environments flow at moderate rates in medium-to-deep channels, with banks generally well-defined and undercut, and where the best lies, and biggest trout, are found. Be particularly watchful for where undercutting has toppled trees into the flows, as the root systems of these trees are prime spots for huge browns.

Such is the nature of many trout streams, where separate environments with different, distinct characters make up the whole.

—John D. Lusk, April 1993

Floatfishing Tactics

I F ANYTHING IS more delightful than joy riding a wild river full of bends and gushes and slick-topped pools, it's riding a river and fishing at the same time. I've floatfished for more than 20 years, on some of the finest waters in North America, and I can't get enough of it, still excited by the first push into the current.

Launching a floatboat, you know you're in for a good ride at the very least, and, more often than not, a great day of fishing. Generally speaking, a float-trip lets you experience the best a river has to offer. A few hours will take you past more good water than you could reach in several arduous days of wading, opening up the most inaccessible, and therefore least fished, stretches and holes. Invariably, I make the largest catch of the season, as well as the highest

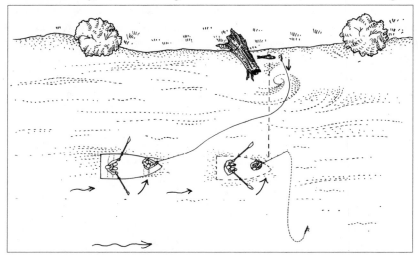

Floatfishing allows you to reach more water faster, including the least-fished areas.

fish-per-day catches, from a floatboat. This is true not only with trout but with most river-dwelling gamefish.

Such fine rewards do require that you know what you'll be facing. Floatfishing a river is different from ordinary wading and casting. For one thing, it can be extremely demanding. Things tend to happen at double-speed. The boat zips along, a good cut bank or current cushion appears, so you prepare to cast; but if you aren't quick enough, or if you miss on the first throw, there are seldom second chances. Unsuitable tackle or an inept approach can quickly turn your anticipated joy into frustration and even (I've seen it more than a few times) rod-slamming misery.

>>> *Tackle Craft:* Flyfishermen must be able to cast the line and the fly quickly and on target, with minimum false-casting and preparation. And since there is usually at least one other person on board, both line and hook must stay well above head-level. (Floatfishing guides are especially appreciative of this.) These stipulations point to a long, strong rod. Eight-and-a-half feet is the minimum; 9 to 9 1/2 feet is better. The rod should be graphite, high-modulus (stiff), preferably in a power-designed taper (encompassing a beefed-up butt section).

For trout, the best all-around floatfishing rod is a 6-weight, particularly on

Western rivers. A typical day of fishing will include pitching thumb-sized Woolly Buggers against the bank, deep-drifting a large weighted nymph, casting No. 16 parachute dries, and maybe even finessing a few midges here and there. This requires flytackle with some range.

Another option is to bring two rods: the powerful 6-weight and a standard-taper nine-foot 5-weight. The 6-weight will be your standard boat rod; but you may want to switch to the lighter 5 when using smaller flies, or for those times during the day when you beach the boat and wade-fish prime sections of water. Be sure to keep the spare rod prerigged, so it's ready to grab and go in a moment.

In a flatboat, you can be casting to the bank 40 feet away, and the next minute, because of a bend or a shifting midstream flow, be 70 feet out. Moments later you're in tight again, only 20 feet from the target. Such ever-changing conditions can create a line-handling nightmare—a constant mess of flyline knotting on itself or wrapping around your shoe, catching on boat struts—and frantic bouts of reeling. A multiplier-style flyreel (which has a faster retrieve ratio) will make it much easier to zip extra slack back onto the spool without having to crank your wrist numb.

>>> *Casts Ashore:* In waters that are at all swift, the prime directive is to look for and cast to targets ahead of the boat, not directly across from it. This gives your fly or lure a chance to settle and work in the fish zone before the drift of the boat causes drag or forces you to pick up or retrieve. Anglers casting directly across-stream spend most of the day fishing behind themselves, continually hurrying to fight the flow and to control the fly or lure, which is rarely where it should be for very long.

On a typical float, especially but not only for trout, a lot of time is spent casting to bankside water, particularly undercuts. Most fishermen believe a fly or lure should be cast right up tight against the bank. Sometimes this is the correct approach. Spinners or weighted streamers, because they sink quickly, are often most productive when thrown as close to the undercut as possible. Fish lying under the bank will see the sinking fly or lure immediately. But the fish's view of a topwater lure or dry fly that lands tight in may be obstructed by the overhanging undercut (or cover); and I've found I generally catch more fish by letting surface offerings land a few inches away from the bank.

My experiences have also shown that trout don't always lie tight to even classic undercuts, sometimes preferring to hold in feeding lanes a few feet out (often just at the edge of a faster current). Flycasting right into the bank not only puts the fly past the fish, it tends to line-spook them as well. The lesson is to figure out where the fish actually are, if necessary making experimental, even unorthodox, casts to find them.

—Anthony Acerrano, February 1996

Big Browns

Fall is a great time to take jumbo browns in streams. Look to the mouths of tributaries and farther upstream if there is sufficient water. Use big streamers and bushy nymphs to take these fish that are preparing to spawn.
—Gerald Almy, November 1995

4

Flyfishing Techniques

~

"How expert the trout fisherman was expected to be
in the old days is told very graphically by the late David Foster,
when he says that casting a fly into a floating walnut shell
at a distance of not less than 36 feet 'betokens a fair
degree of proficiency and precision in casting.'"

–Sports Afield *Editorial, February 1908*

<<< *A bent rod and a tight line on the lower Madison outside of
Yellowstone Park.*—**Photo by R. Valentine Atkinson**

Better Flycasting in Minutes

>>> *Rhythm vs. Strength:* Flycasting is an act of timing and precision, not of brute strength. Think of a flyrod as a lever, not a bullwhip. If you hear your rod whipping the air or feel as though you're getting too little result from too much effort: Slow down. Relax. Concentrate on a smooth movement of the rod, back and forth, on the same horizontal plane. Begin with a short line—40 feet, say—and don't stretch it until that length feels comfortable.

>>> *Mechanics:* Remember, your line follows the rod tip. If the rod tip dips low, the line moves in that direction (opening up the casting loop, losing momentum). On the backcast, your wrist is kept locked to prevent the rod tip from dropping. This allows the flyline to unfurl straight behind the rod. "Don't break your wrist on the backcast" is a common warning to beginners. But—and this is very important—remember the same logic on the forward cast. Don't drop the rod tip too far, or too soon. A forward cast should be pushed ahead, with the reel, not the rod tip, leading the rod.

Anglers who regularly suffer from tailing loops (loops that "close" and tangle on themselves) should take particular heed of their forward-cast mechanics and the position of the rod tip. A common mistake is to throw the rod forward, rather than push it. Also, don't accelerate too soon. After the line straightens on the backcast, begin a smooth forward push with the rod butt and reel ahead of the tip. Accelerate your stroke after the rod reaches the 12 o'clock position. Then stop the stroke around the 1:30 or 2:00 point. Don't overmuscle; let the rod do the work.

>>> *More Distance:* Learn to widen the arcs of your casting stroke. There's no reason to keep your elbow and arm tucked close to your side. For extra distance, curve-cast torque, or to throw into a wind, maintain good step-by-step mechanics but let your arm drift farther back on the backcast. This effectively lengthens the stroke and provides more time and space for line acceleration and rod loading.

—Anthony Acerrano, January 1991

Five Vital Flycasts

LET'S SAY YOUR basic casting stroke is in pretty good shape. You know when and how to power the back and forward casts. You can even shoot a good length of flyline. Loops are looking tight. The line stretches out straight as a Nebraska highway onto the lawn or water. Possibly you've been flyfishing for some time now, maybe even years, but all you really know is the basic forward cast presentation.

If so, it's time to learn some vital casting techniques without which no one can be a truly effective flyfisherman, especially on moving water. This amounts to a virtual guarantee: If you master and apply these casts, you'll catch more fish. Try them and see.

>>> *Roll Cast:* A familiar cast, yet only a small percentage of flyfishermen

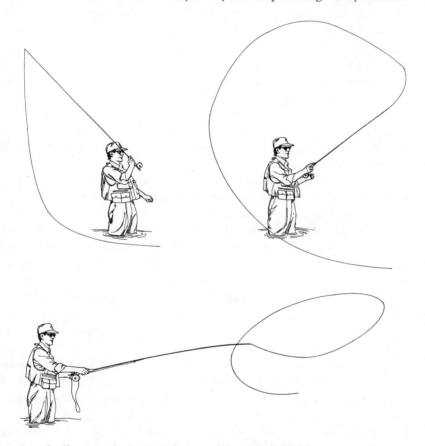

A good roll cast results in an oval, outward-thrusting forward loop; use a roll cast when there's no room for a traditional backcast, or when there's a strong rear wind.

seem to execute it properly, with true efficiency and forward-directed energy. In practical fishing situations the roll cast is valuable for: (1) casting when there's no room for a traditional backcast; (2) making rapid or repeat casts without false-casting (for example, when you're working a bank while wading or drifting, or when nymphing a riffle upstream with short casts); (3) when a strong rear wind makes a normal backcast difficult or impossible;

and (4) picking up an extended flyline in preparation for a backcast.

Try to practice the roll cast on a pool or calm surface, because a certain amount of line resistance—which is tough to get on grass—is necessary for proper execution.

To begin, make a normal cast of about 30 feet. (In a fishing situation you can simply shake the line out through the guides or jiggle slack into the current.) Hold the line tight by hooking and clamping it with the forefinger of your rod hand. Now lift the rod up and back at an even pace, so that the line will be pulled directly toward you. With your rod hand at about head height, stop when the rod is at the 11 o'clock position. Lean the rod away from your body, causing the line to hang slightly outside and behind the rod tip. (This cast works best when the line is fully extended.) You should use a slight backward pull to begin the motion, then push forward and down on the rod forcefully. This motion will cause the line to roll out smoothly when you deliver the fly.

To help you clearly understand the precise forward motion, expert casting instructor Mel Krieger suggests that you imagine a wooden block in front of your waist. The proper hand/rod movement mimics the exact motion of chopping a hatchet tip into that block: a slight up-and-back pull, a forceful arc downward, and finally an abrupt stop when the block is hit. This movement is very important for a good roll cast, in that it transfers the energy onto an outward path, rather than directly down onto the water, which creates a slack and inefficient casting loop. Lefty Kreh, one of the country's most respected flycasting authorities, compares the motion to driving a nail into a board with a hammer. It's basically the same concept—use whichever works best.

A good roll cast results in an oval, outward-thrusting forward loop; a poor roll cast has a "high" circular loop that dissipates forward energy. The latter case results from bringing the rod too far back and/or powering the forward stroke too early.

A useful variation: Once you get the basic roll cast down, practice executing it "off-shoulder" as well—that is, to the side opposite your casting hand. This makes for much easier pickups and casting when the flyline has drifted to your left side (assuming you're right-handed), or when a right-to-left crosswind threatens to tangle a rod-side cast by blowing the line into the rod's path. It can also be a very useful cast when you are fishing with one or two other persons in a boat.

▶▶▶ *Reach Cast:* It's depressing to think of all the years I fished without knowing, or thinking of, this simple cast. As far as I know, it was named, or at least popularized, by the whizbang angling team of Doug Swisher and Carl

The reach cast is best used when you need to make a drag-free float to a fish that's either directly across from you in a strong current, or across-and-down.

Richards. As Swisher/Richards have explained in their essential book, *Fly Fishing Strategy*, the reach cast is the best way to get a drag-free float when casting directly across stream or across-and-down.

Let's say you have a trout rising across stream in a reasonably strong current. A straight-line cast to the target would result in immediate drag as the intervening current pulls and bellies the flyline. The dragging fly would put down, or at the very least fail to interest, the fish. An S-cast [see next page] would be an improvement, giving you several inches or a foot of drag-free float before one of the S's became straightened and drag ensued. Ideally, you should cast in such a way that the main body of the flyline alights above (that is, upstream of) the fly, so that the fly and line can float down to the fish without any drag whatever. This is precisely the effect of a reach cast.

Execution is easy with practice. For a left-reach cast (used when a right-handed caster is presenting to a left-right current), begin a forward cast as usual, using a fairly open loop (versus an extremely tight one), pointing at the target—in this case, several feet above the ring of the rise. In one motion, as the line begins to unfurl, sweep the rod across your body, with the tip pointing left at about a 45-degree angle. When the cast ends, you'll be extended as far left as possible, with the rod tip low. The fly will have landed directly on target, but the rod tip will have directed, and deposited, the body of the line above the fly, providing a nice drag-free float over the fish.

For right-to-left currents, a right-handed caster would use the right-reach presentation, utilizing the same basic stroke, this time sweeping and leaning the rod and line to the right. Take care not to overpower the forward cast. Remember, this is a sweeping rather than a sharp and crisp delivery.

➤➤➤ *S-Cast:* To get drag-free drifts while fishing upstream, or in up-and-

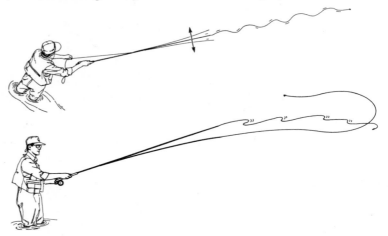

The S-Cast gives you slack on an upstream presentation. You can either wiggle the line in midcast (top) or stop it short on a normal cast to make S's on the water.

across or direct downstream situations, try the S-cast, also known as the serpentine or wiggle cast, so called because of the shape the line describes when it hits the water—a snakelike meander of S's. While the current works to straighten out the S's, your fly gains extra moments of drag-free float—with luck, enough to entice a strike.

The S-cast is easy to learn and takes only a little practice. Make a forward cast as usual, aiming a few feet beyond your target, then wriggle the rod tip as the line begins to unfurl. You'll soon learn how to create large or small S's, many or few, depending on your needs at the time.

A variation of this presentation is even more simple: Make a good tight-looped forward cast straight over your target, again shooting beyond it by several feet. As the flyline unfurls near the end of your forward stroke, stop the rod suddenly. The outward-accelerating line will jerk back in the air and fall in meanders on the water. You can exaggerate the result by not only stopping the rod tip but also tugging back on it slightly; and you can increase even that effect by simultaneously hauling (pulling) on the line with your left hand just as the line straightens in the air. Experiment until you can control both the amount and the placement of slack line on the water.

➤➤➤ *Off-Shoulder Cast:* World-champion flycaster Steve Rajeff showed me

When crosswinds are too strong for a normal cast, try casting your line off your opposite shoulder. This cast is also useful when you are boat fishing in close quarters.

Casting at Night

Casting a trout fly on a black night can pose problems. One solution lies in marking your flyline so you know the exact distance past the tiptop of the rod. Take the measurements in the daytime, and then either make a nail knot with monofilament around the flyline at the precise spot, or wrap it with dental floss. When your fingers feel this projection, you know you're ready to make the cast.

–Gerald Almy, May 1983

the finer points of this cast while tarpon fishing off Islamorada Key, strengthening my belief that it's an essential tactic for dealing with a variety of wind, boat, and current situations.

The basic idea is to vary your normal rod position so that the flyline casts over your "off" shoulder, the one opposite your rod side. This can be lifesaving in a rod-side crosswind. The off-shoulder cast is also useful for: (1) keeping your hook and line safely away from a partner or guide when you're boat fishing in cramped quarters; (2) keeping your backcast clear of rod-side obstacles without having to change position; and (3) getting the best angle on across or down-and-across drifts when fishing an "opposite" current—for example, a left-to-right flow if you're right-handed.

The more typical approach to all of these situations is a "turn-around" cast, in which you basically turn away from your target to falsecast and present the fly on what is actually a "dropped" backcast. This works but can be awkward and imprecise. The off-shoulder cast is better.

To execute the cast, keep your rod hand and reel on the normal side, but tilt the rod so that the tip moves back and forth over your opposite shoulder. Keep the reel at about forehead level throughout the casting stroke (if your backcast height allows), raising your elbow but keeping your forearm in front of your shoulder, and as nearly vertical as possible to maintain an even back-and-forth rod movement without dropping the rod tip or depending

How to Weight a Nymph

Flyfishermen who want to work a nymph right on bottom in deep water typically add some lead, either splitshot, fuse wire, or twist-ons, to the leader about a foot above the fly. This is a very effective way to fish nymphs, but it can cost you a lot of flies as you hang up on the bottom. (If you're not hanging up, you're probably not fishing deep enough.)

A good way to save flies is to put your weight at the tip of the leader, above a small knot so it doesn't slip off, and attach the nymph to a dropper a foot or so up the leader. When you hang up, you'll break off the weight and not the fly. This rig also gives you a more direct connection between the rod tip and the fly, which makes detecting those delicate strikes a bit easier.

–John Gierach, August 1987

entirely on your wrist for stroke and strength. This procedure will probably feel strange to you at first, so practice on the lawn before going fishing.

➤➤➤ *Curve Cast:* These casts, once you master them, are fish casts, because they can put your fly into places, and into prolonged drag-free drifts, that straight-line or even slack-line fishermen simply cannot duplicate. Let's say you approach a fallen, partially submerged tree trunk from downstream. To run a fly drag-free along the edge of the trunk, a straight-up caster would have to drop the flyline right over the fish he hopes to catch; or he'd be forced to move to an across-stream position and settle for shorter effective drifts. But if you can throw a good curve cast, you can throw your line directly upstream, parallel to but well away from the fish-holding edge of the trunk. The fly will then whisk around and drop right next to the bark. The leader and line tip will float above—so fish see the fly only. If you make the cast properly, the drift will be a long one and your chances for a take are excellent.

This is one example of 100 possibilities. A curve cast will also let you drop a dry fly around bass corners, into stump nooks and weed crannies, into undercut banks and so on.

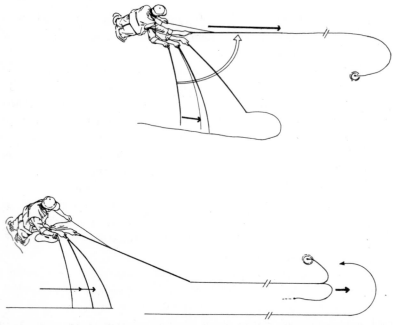

To make a right-handed curve (above), start with a wide, underpowered cast, then drop the rod tip before the loop can fully open. To make a curve that swings to the left (below), make a tight, slightly overpowered forward cast, then stop it suddenly.

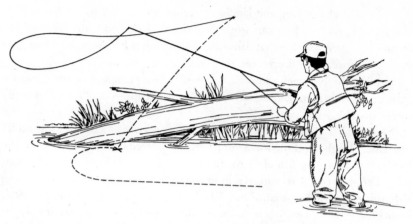

Another way to make a right curve is to simply use an underpowered delivery throughout.

If you're right-handed and want to throw a curve to the left, all you need to do is cant your rod so that it's horizontal or on a 45-degree angle to the water, and deliver a tight-looped, overpowered forward cast. Stop the rod tip suddenly just before the loop straightens, and the line tip, leader, and fly will swing around, falling to the water in curve. For more curve, pull back slightly with your casting hand or tug with your line hand just as the loop opens.

Throwing a right-handed curve is more difficult. One approach is to make a wide-looped, underpowered forward cast, dropping the rod tip before the loop can fully open. The unopened loop will fall to the water in a right-facing curve. This works but is difficult to control precisely, especially in a wind. My preference is to use an off-shoulder casting position to make what is essentially a back-handed, left-side cast, canting the rod low to the water and hyperaccelerating a tight loop as described before.

—*Anthony Acerrano, April 1991*

How Not to Break Your Rod

WE WERE HAVING great fun catching large steelhead on flies. My partner, Chris, was casting from the stern. A steelhead in the 12-pound range slammed his fly and he lifted the rod sharply overhead, straight up, to set the hook. The fish surged and the rod cracked like old wood. Choice words were spoken. This was the first day of a week-long trip, and though I still had my 9-weight rod, neither of us had brought backups.

We did, however, have plenty of spinning tackle on hand, which Chris made good use of. Periodically I'd turn my flyrod over to him. On the last day of the trip, after hooking and landing a record steelhead, I gave Chris the 9-weight and watched him cast from the bow deck. A good fish followed the fly and hit. Chris struck—that damnable straight-up hookset move of his—and the rod popped like a firecracker. Broken clean in two places.

Landing the big steelhead on a fragmented rod proved interesting, but we managed it. Chris looked at me with a seasick expression. "Jeez, I'm really sorry," he said.

➤➤➤ *Straight Up:* Since the trip was practically over and the rod was under warranty, I laughed off the incident. Later, I wondered if his style of setting the hook (and of playing fish close to the boat) didn't contribute to the fact that he had popped two first-class flyrods in a few days. His habit—a common one, I've noticed—of hook-setting and fish-fighting with an upthrusting, vertical, high hold places an excessive strain on the blank, particularly on the upper third or tip section. This positioning doesn't guarantee a broken rod, but it adds significant stress that can contribute to breakage—especially with the modern generation of stiff, comparatively brittle graphite sticks.

All fishing rods have a span of flex that begins at the tip and extends to some degree down the blank. Fast-action rods flex most actively in the upper third; slower actions flex well down into the butt section (just above the handle or grip). The more flexible the rod, the more widely it distributes stress, which in turn minimizes the likelihood of breakage at a single point. What's not commonly understood is that the way you position a rod can affect its ability to distribute, and handle, a load.

An extreme example: Once a few years ago in Alaska, after catching dozens of 10- to 12-pound sockeye salmon on a 6-weight flyrod, I tried to skate in a spent fish by gripping the rod with my free hand just under the tipsection ferrule, then pulling back. The rod that had performed well for days snapped instantly. Why? Because by clamping down below the tip section, I eliminated the lower half of the rod and put all the strain on the slender tip, which was never designed to bear such a load. Dumb, but a lesson fully learned.

➤➤➤ *The Weak Link:* Similarly, Chris uses a harsh, straight-up lift of the rod and arm when a fish is struggling near the boat. This move puts abrupt, intense strain on the upper third of the rod, its weakest part. In effect, the motion shortens the rod and takes the stronger butt section largely out of play. It's far wiser and more effective to use the whole rod and its entire range of flex. Whether on a hook-set or when fighting a fish, favor a slightly upward but mostly sideways motion. Not only does this put less strain on the rod, it also puts more pressure on the fish.

A week after the steelhead trip, Chris phoned to say there was another, probably more contributory reason the first rod broke. His strike motion may have been one cause of the breakage, but he had also inadvertently put the tip from his 6-weight rod of the same make and construction into the 9-weight case. The tip sections looked identical and he had mixed them up. Careful pre-trip tackle inspection would have caught this error—another valuable lesson.

And we've both finally learned to always pack a backup for the main rod(s) when on a major expedition. If our one remaining 9-weight had snapped on the second day instead of the last, we would have missed out on all that tremendous flyfishing.

—Anthony Acerrano, November 1996

The Art of the Dead Drift

TAKING A BIG TROUT on a dry fly is one of the most exciting challenges in flyfishing. Exciting because you see the fish feeding and can tell it's a big one; because of the anticipation you feel as you ease into casting position; because you see the take. On the other hand it's challenging because big fish are usually in places where presentation is difficult; and because big fish are overly sensitive to drag.

But taking big trout on top is not impossible. With proper equipment and an understanding of only a handful of casting and presentation tactics, the dry-fly fisherman can take big trout from waters the world over. In fact, if the naturals are actively moving on the surface, dry-fly fishing can almost be too easy.

Most organisms do not move about on the surface, but instead drift along at the mercy of the currents; where the currents go, the organisms go. Thus, to be successful under most conditions, the fisherman must be able to present his imitation on a drag-free float. And because a straight line lying across several currents of different speeds can only promote drag, he must learn to throw slack line. The three foundation, slack-line techniques for dry-fly fishing are the puddle cast, the parachute mend, and the reach mend. Knowing these will put the flyfisherman a long way toward getting his offering in front of his quarry. The physical condition of line and leader is also important. The dry-fly angler should use a high-floating line and a soft, flexible leader to help get that natural drift which fools even the biggest trout in the toughest situations.

Fishing the fly upstream to achieve a dead drift dates back to at least the middle of the 17th century. But it was W. C. Stewart's 1857 book *Practical Angler* that firmly established upstream angling as a preferred tactic. He developed his technique not for dries, but for soft-hackle wet flies. He wrote so persuasively about the upstream dead drift, however, that it quickly became the darling of the flyfishing community. The newly evolving cult of dry-fly purists, lead chiefly by F. M. Halford, seized upon the method. So firmly

Selective Situations

Much has been written about the need for exact imitations when fishing over selective trout. Everybody knows that if you don't have the precise Size 16 Pale Moon-Winged No Hackle when the *Paraleptophlebia hafelegenius* are hatching, you might as well sit on the bank and take a snooze. It's not always true. You can do a lot with the patterns you have. What you need when trout are selective is a more exact silhouette of the natural insect. Clipping the hackles off the bottom of the caddis or mayfly dressings you always carry will lower the body of the fly into the surface film. The fly not only looks more natural to the trout but also has the appearance of being in trouble on the water. And an insect, or its imitation, that is in trouble on the water is more likely to get in trouble with trout.

–Dave Hughes, February 1988

did they hold to the precepts of the upstream tactic that it became dogma. This was unfortunate, because the concept is dead drift, not upstream angling. True, an upstream approach is effective, but in some instances the angler is better served by fishing the dry fly down.

Because the fly reaches the trout's window before the leader, downstream dry-fly fishing is especially good in spring creeks and similar waters where the fish are leader shy or where the surface is flat and the water very clear. It's also the presentation of choice when casting to a fish feeding far back in the tail of a pool. An upstream cast here would drop the fly on the slow water of the pool while the line would drop the fly on the riffle water downstream, creating instant drag. Although a puddle cast could be used for such fishing, I prefer the parachute mend because it introduces controllable slack.

There are also situations in which neither a downstream nor an upstream approach can be effected; only an across-stream effort will work. In this case the angler should use the reach mend to eliminate drag. The reach mend can also be combined with the parachute mend to position the line precisely as needed. Make a normal cast and pull the rod back while simultaneously tipping it out to the side. Sometimes it's just what the doctor ordered. Mike Allen, a New Zealand friend, met my plane the last time I went to that country, and promptly told me that he had found an impossible fish for me. We chatted excitedly as we headed to the spot. Positioned back under the uprooted stump of a fallen tree and just upstream of a fence that sagged into the water, the fish was indeed impossible to reach with an upstream or straight-across presentation, and I couldn't wade close enough to use a standard downstream parachute mend. But Mike hadn't anticipated that I would combine techniques. Using a parachute mend and then reaching it out and across the currents as far as possible, I was able to position the line the same way I would have placed it had I waded across stream. The fly dropped in the correct current lane and ran, drag-free, back under the overhang, right into the mouth of a 26-inch brown.

The heart of dry-fly angling is the drag-free float. Don't just cast your fly the moment you see a fish. Analyze the situation and select the tackle and the tactic that will allow the fly to float over the fish without drag. And be ready, because you're going to get a lot more rises than you ever have before.

Here's how to master these important casts and mends (see also Anthony Acerrano's explanation in "Five Vital Flycasts" on pages 96–103):

>>> *The Puddle Cast:* The puddle cast [also called an "S-Cast"] is an all-around presentation tactic for the dry fly. It works in slow water, fast water, pocket water, upstream, downstream, across stream, with big flies and with small flies. And it's easy to learn. Aim the line high on the forward cast. As

soon as the line begins to extend, smoothly but quickly lower the rod tip to the water. Don't jerk the rod tip down and don't wait unitl the line has fully extended and is starting to fall; the line should continue to extend after the rod tip has been lowered. Because the rod tip is at the surface and the line is aimed high, it will now fall back upon itself, creating slack as a series of S-curves. Aiming horizontally will puddle just the front few feet of the line and the leader; the remaining portion of the line will be straight. Aiming 30 degrees or more above the horizontal will puddle the entire line.

This cast is especially good for up-and-across-stream presentation. Such an angle usually drops the line across several current speeds, and without slack, drag would occur.

➤➤➤ *The Parachute Mend:* When trying to introduce slack into a downstream presentation, use the parachute mend. Unlike the puddle cast, in which slack is dumped onto the water and left to itself, the parachute mend produces slack that can be controlled at all times. Make a normal forward cast. As the line begins to extend, pull the rod back until it's vertical. Don't jerk it back. The idea is to draw the line toward you, not to make a backcast. When the line drops into the water, it will be hanging straight down from the rod tip. As the fly drifts downstream, lower the rod tip to feed out slack.

Normally the parachute mend is used for casting slightly across as well as down. Thus debris kicked up by the angler's feet will not drift downstream to the fish and put it on alert. In addition, if the fish refuses the fly, the angler can let it drift past the feeding position and then, by moving the rod to the side, skate the fly out and away from the fish's feeding lane before recasting.

On rivers such as the Henry's Fork, the fish can be very picky and will not move more than an inch or two right or left to take the fly. No matter how good you are with a flyrod, it's impossible to cast the fly into such a narrow feeding lane every time. In this case, fish down and slightly across with the parachute mend. Cast four to five feet above the fish and beyond its feeding lane. Keep the rod vertical and permit the currents to drag the fly back toward you until it's perfectly placed in the lane, then drop the rod tip and allow the fly to drift down to the fish. It works like a charm.

➤➤➤ *The Reach Mend:* The reach mend [or cast] is the most important and useful mend the flyfisherman can know. Like the parachute mend, it introduces controllable slack. Once learned, it becomes an integral and often unconscious part of fly presentation. It would be worth the effort to learn even if it were difficult to master, but it can be perfected with only a few minutes' practice. Make a standard forward cast. As the line begins to extend, tip the rod out to the side. That's all there is to it. The fly will go straight to the target, and the line will fall to the side. Reach the rod to the side immediately after making the forward cast, and the entire line and leader will be mended. Make the reach after the line is partially extended, and only the rear part will be mended.

—*Gary Borger, June 1989*

Tips for Longer Flycasts

1. Lower your grip: The strongest part of the flyrod is the lowest part of the butt section. Instead of holding the rod by the grip, slide your hand down to just above the reel. Those extra inches of leverage will add five to 10 feet of distance.

2. Turn the rod: Once the final forward cast is launched, instead of holding the rod with the guides facing down, rotate the rod 90 degrees to the side. As the flyline shoots through the guides, the up-and-down line vibration increases friction between the speeding line and the rod shaft, slowing the line. If you turn the rod to the side, the up-and-down vibration doesn't hit the rod. Reducing friction adds five to 10 feet of distance.

3. Raise the trajectory: When firing the final forward cast, extend your arm, holding it at a 15-degree angle to the water's surface. Gravity tries to pull the flyline down; by extending your rod arm upward, you establish a higher trajectory, which will add five to 10 feet to your cast.

In a normal grip the thumb is on top and the hand is on the cork grip. In a Distance Grip, the thumb is on top but the hand is down close to the reel, below the cork grip.

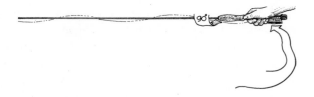

In a standard rod position, the flyline vibrates up and down, hitting the rod shaft. Turning the rod 90 degrees to the side keeps the vibrating line from hitting the shaft.

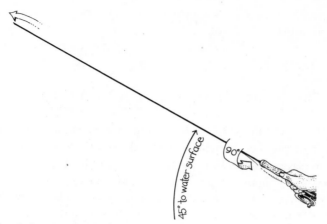

Establish a high trajectory cast by extending your arm and holding the rod at about a 45 degree angle to the water. Don't worry, gravity will pull down the line.

—Deke Meyer, August 1994

How to Avoid Snags

NOW YOU'VE DONE it. You just looped most of your tippet over a bankside willow limb the diameter of your thumb. The water over there is too deep to wade, and in any case you'd rather not spook the fish in the area. What do you do?

What you don't do is yank on the line. When it's obvious a cast is headed for the rough, the instinctive reaction is to immediately jerk it back—which is fine if the line is still in the air and clear of obstructions. But once line or leader touches a limb, low-hanging wire, or strand of fencing, a yank on the line will wrap the leader tightly around the very object you had hoped to avoid. Instead, drop the tip of your rod to lessen tension on the line, and retrive the line and leader slowly until it clears the snag.

When dead-drifting nymphs and other wet flies under root wads or similar bankside tangles, you'll have fewer problems if your leader and fly are drifting just off bottom. Perhaps because the constant abrasion of silt and sand wears away obstructions immediately above the streambed, nymphs drifted just off bottom seem to hang up less often than those drifting a foot or more up. You'll catch more trout, too, since your fly will be that much closer to where the trout live.

Despite these precautions, you're bound to hang up once in a while. Should you wade to the snag and free your line? Many fishermen slosh through prime

Timing Your Fly

When flyfishing for trout in a lake, you must determine the depth at which to fish a nymph or wet fly. Wear your watch on the inside of your wrist, where you can easily monitor it. After casting with a sink-tip or sinking line, note the time the fly hits the water and approximately how much line is out. When a fish strikes, again note the time. If trout are feeding selectively on a particular species of aquatic insect, they often do so at the same general level. By casting out the same amount of line and monitoring your watch on each cast, you'll be prepared for the next strike.

—Robert H. Jones, January 1995

water to retrieve snagged flies as a matter of course. But is one fly really worth the cost in scared fish? It's your call. If you must have it back, why not break the tippet and retrieve the fly after you've fished the water below the snag?
—Dave Carty, March 1991

The Finer Points of Playing Fish

I N MOST DIFFICULT endeavors the worthy participant should first learn the rules, then learn when to break them. This is never more true than when playing fish on light tackle. (Ordinary tackle becomes light tackle when the fish you hook is bigger than you anticipated.)

The accepted rules are: keep the rod tip up; keep the line tight except to give the fish slack when he jumps; keep the fish moving to tire him out; and, finally, bring the fish to shallow water or surface for the capture by netting, tailing, breaching, gaffing, or whatever.

There are good reasons for all of these rules. Keeping the rod tip up means that the fish is working against a springy resistance, to prevent him from getting a solid pressure that will break the line or leader. A tight line keeps a steady pressure on the fish and thus tires him out. Giving slack when the fish jumps keeps the line from coming tight with a solid jolt against the tackle. If you stay downstream of the fish, it means that the fish is not only fighting the tackle but the speed of the current as well. Bringing the fish to shallow water moves him to a position where he can maneuver only laterally and cannot go under a net. . . .

Let's look at the rules more closely. The high rod does give a fine playing cushion, but when the fish pulls the line out at that high angle the drag of pulling the line through the guides is increased greatly. If a fish is being played on a very light leader, the extra drag of a high-held rod may be just enough to break it. If the angler wants to tire the fish quickly, he will want him to run far, expending the maximum energy on the run. The high rod may slow the fish down and discourage the long, tiring drive. Pointing the rod at a running fish gives the least resistance and is the best procedure with light tackle.

It is worth considering here that success is determined by the length of time it takes to subdue a fish with given tackle. It's like driving a car. The driver in a race seeks the maximum speed he can make without losing control. Similarly, the angler wants to be able to exert the maximum safe pressure without breaking his gear. Those who are most skillful bring their fish in with a minimum of time—a special advantage if the fish is to be released. A quick capture will leave him with a reservoir of strength for speedy recuperation.

Slack is not the demon danger it is reputed to be when a fish is being played on a fly or a simple hook, because neither of them has any appreciable weight. They cannot be shaken free by the fish or rubbed off since they are on the inside of a fish's mouth. The fly or hook will only fall out if there has been so much hard pulling that it has worn a hole big enough for the hook to slide back out. It is something that rarely occurs until late in a fight and where hard, sudden pressures have been used. . . .

There are some times when it's impossible to give fish slack, however. That's true when the fish is swimming fast enough to stay under tension from the drag of the line, like a [large trout] running downstream or a tuna that never stops but swims until he breaks free or dies.

Your playing strategy should be to get the first wildness out of the fish before he realizes he's in real trouble. If you've set the hook, make sure your tackle is in order and your position good while you give line, then play the fish on a very gentle pressure. He'll fuss a little and make a few short runs or easy leaps, but he won't give you the problems a completely fresh fish that's frantic with fear will give you. After that first short period of gentle playing, he'll be somewhat accustomed to the tackle and just a little out of breath. Then when you increase the pressure toward the tackle's maximum he won't be so surprised. He won't run or leap with maximum speed and wildness.

How, then, should the angler play the fish? As if it were hooked lightly, which it may be, or as if it were hooked well, which it may be, or as if it were hooked well, which it may not be? I choose the latter for these reasons:

If I assume the hook hold is good and play the fish accordingly, I will use maximum tackle strength for each maneuver and bring the fish in as swiftly as possible. If I act as if the hook hold is not a good one and baby the fish, I will have him on much longer (perhaps needlessly) and may lose him simply because of the accidents that can happen in the longer time required. If the fish is poorly hooked, the chances are he'll be lost anyway. Only if I can see that the hook hold is poor when the fish comes close at the end of the fight do I become gentle where I could be strong. When a hook pulls out I do not fault myself. If I break a leader or line I do.

If you can bring a big fish in before he gets his second wind, you may save quite a bit of time. Some fish will fight with a frenzy that brings them to momentary exhaustion in a relatively short time. If they are not captured then, they get a second wind and can settle down to a long, dogged fight that can go on for a long time if the tackle is very light and conditions difficult.

One of the best tricks in the book is to give slack when a fish swims into a snag. To try to hold him usually means broken tackle and a lost fish. If you let the fish swim into the snag and then give him only an occasional twitch or no pressure at all, sometimes he'll come out the same way he went in.

The time of the strike is one of the two most important times in playing a fish. When a fish is first hooked the angler's coordination must be at its peak. It is all too easy to hold the strike a fraction of a second too long. This lets a fish start to move at his fastest speed against a solid pressure. A quick pull is far better than a prolonged one. Several strikes, one after the other, tend to upset the fish, like digging spurs into a bronco. It's exciting but it certainly doesn't help in playing the fish.

The basic concepts of playing a fish are the same regardless of the tackle involved, but there are advantages and disadvantages to the various types. Long and limber flyrods give the best possible shock cushion, but there's a lot of resistance when the thick flyline must be pulled through the water. Flyrods have more guides than shorter plug spinning rods and thus generate more friction-drag when the line is pulled through them. The single-action reels used in most flyfishing are more difficult to reel swiftly than are the multiplying reels used in most casting and trolling. Getting to the right position quickly becomes more important for a flyfisherman than for a troller or baitcaster, if he's fighting a fish of the same capability.

When it comes to following the rule and bringing a fish to shallow water for capture, the shore or wading fisherman has a better alternative—if he's able to use it. That is to capture the fish in deep water, say two or three feet, instead of six to eight inches. Look at it this way: a big fish is terrified of shallow water. He'll fight to the last of his strength to avoid being pulled into it. This takes time and, at any moment while the fish is in those desperate throes, an error or accident may free him.

The alternative is to wade out (or, if in a boat, work deep) holding the net steady at depth. The trick is to get the fish used to the net. All movements must be very slow and deliberate. The fish should think of your legs as immobile tree trunks and of the net and the rest of your body as something very slow moving and not dangerous. Then it can be coaxed or pulled gently into position.

Should a fish always be given slack when he jumps, as the rule says? No. There are times when moderate pressure and a rod cushion are better than slack. That is true when a fish is hooked on a lure that has appreciable weight. If instead of slack there's some tension on the line and spring in the rod, it will cushion the shock without giving a real jolt to the tackle.

Which side of the mouth did you hook your fish on? It's important to remember. The strategy is to play the fish right up to safe tackle strength on the side you hooked and relax the pressure a bit when playing him from the opposite side. Pulling the hook back against the way it went in, especially with long-shanked hooks, develops leverages that can free a hook in short order. Many a good fish is lost when this back pressure works a hole around the hook.

Tackle gives the angler a connection, no matter how delicate, with the fish he is playing. Through it he can read the fish's feelings and his capabilities. Sometimes I think I can almost feel their heartbeats and judge how tired they are, how likely they are to run or jump and, if so, how far or how high. I know from where they derive their strength (some fish depend on speed, others on power) and I've learned to sense how they tire. If you can make a fish use his fins in an unusual manner, you can tire the muscles that move them.

If you can convince the fish you're playing that his cause is lost, he'll give up easily. When you've led him to believe he's about to be free and then he finds that he isn't, you can break his spirit. Fish behave differently. Each one is a separate problem. Then too, there is much difference in the capability of different anglers to play fish. Where one requires an hour to bring in a fish, a skillful angler may well do it in 15 minutes using the same tackle. But whatever your skill, to play each fish as perfectly as possible is both exciting and rewarding.

—Lee Wulff, December 1978

Early-Season Trout Secrets

SINCE TROUT FEED on flies all winter, they are still bottom feeding on flies in those uncertain half-winter half-spring days of early season. And when trout are feeding they can be caught with the right tackle and tactics.

Most early-season feeding is near the bottom—no surprise to the accomplished bait fisherman who frequents trout water in the first weeks of the season—and most of their feeding is concentrated on nymph and larval insect-forms. Flies imitating these forms must be fished where the fish are feeding on them; the early-season answer is slow and deep.

Most seasons enforce that rule and begin with high water and cold weather, and the deep-nymph technique is the answer, but some seasons serve up good weather and good water; then the fishing is like midsummer and several important insect forms can trigger selective feeding. Most fishing then is with normal nymphs and pupa imitations and wet flies. Silk fly lines and nylon floating fly lines fish these early-season flies at the proper levels, depending upon the insect hatches and the feeding of the fish.

Perhaps the most versatile early-season nymph is the unweighted Gray Nymph with the muskrat-fur body in several hook sizes. Selective trout have fallen to it in many situations: big versions have been taken by big trout feeding on everything from big stone fly nymphs to mouse-colored salamanders, normal sizes have simulated everything from mayfly nymphs to shrimps and sow bugs, and the minute sizes have worked for the minuscule nymphs and midge forms.

The big muskrat-bodied nymphs fished with the slow bottom retrieve have taken big browns for me on the Namekagon in Wisconsin, the Beaverkill in the Catskills, and the Little South Pere Marquette in Michigan. Big brooks were taken on them in Henry Lake in Idaho and in Jackson Hole. The normal sizes have produced trout under all conditions in all seasons, fished with everything from the fast quick-pull retrieve to hanging motionless in the surface film of weed-bordered ponds. The minute sizes are best fished just under the surface with a slow retrieve or hanging in the surface film or floating dead-drift in the current. Selective feeding in early season in high lakes and beaver ponds usually occurs near the surface and concentrates on a multiplicity of minute insect forms.

The back swimmers are often active early in the year when other insects are still dormant and their thicketlike weed cover is down. Since they are moving about exposed in the cold water, many of them are picked up by foraging fish in the early season. Their imitations have produced good catches for me on trout ponds. When fishing these imitations, try to enliven them with a quick, darting retrieve suggestive of naturals.

Caddis and midge pupal forms are often an important facet of early-season surface and subsurface feeding. The caddis imitations should be fished with the now-classic Leisenring lift-retrieve: presentation should permit the cast to drift deep before the slow rhythmic retrieve is started, simulating the slow emergence-drift of the pupal forms toward the surface. Since the trout are following the emerging pupae from the bottom to the surface, momentum sometimes carries them above the surface as they take the pupal forms or miss them when hatching occurs and the adult caddis flies escape. Midge pupae drift motionless in the current or hang in the lake-calm surface film. Midge pupa feeding is quiet in character with the trout rolling softly under the surface film; and such feeding is concentrated in the quiet pools and wind-sheltered water. Midge feeding is widespread and nerve-shattering because rises are everywhere and the fish are selective, and imitation requires fine tackle and minute flies. The so-called winter feeding is often aimed at minuscule midge forms.

Minnow feeding makes up another major part of winter and early-season activity, and minnow imitations are an invaluable part of the first-week fly box. Three patterns have proved useful in my fishing: the Golden Dace is a versatile all-season pattern on waters having the stripe-sided dace in good numbers, the Marabou Shiner suggests the multiplicity of small silver-colored minnow species, and the Brown Stickleback simulates a number of small brown-mottled minnows with good success. The unweighted, sparsely bodied Fledermaus can serve as a reasonable creek-sucker and chub imitation when fished with the quick, darting rhythmic retrieve so effective for the big minnow-imitative patterns.

So much for hoarfrost and high water.

Conditions can sometimes dovetail to produce fly hatches in the first weeks of the season, and with reasonable clear water there can be midday surface feeding. Then the homage-paying dry-fly purist who refuses to fish anything but his conventional patterns can have more than the satisfaction of repeating ritual and tradition. Some six major insect species have produced significant dry-fly fishing for me in the first weeks of the season: Gordon Quill, mayflies, Hendrickson hatches, dark Capnia stone flies, early brown stone flies, little back caddis flies, iron blue dun hatches, and Baetis olives. Each of these adult forms has nymph or pupa counterparts that are important before and during the hatch, when the nymphs and pupae lose their natural caution and move above rather restlessly in anticipation of the hour for emergence.

The first major hatches are usually the little black and early brown stone flies. Surface feeding sometimes results when they are present, but experience indicates that the wet-fly imitations are most useful. Emergence occurs in shallow water along the edges of the faster runs. Imitations should be fished deaddrift in the current. The little black Chimarrha caddis is also a swift-water insect and can be seen swarming at midday in early season. Trout sometimes feed on them then, holding below the swarms and feeding on those that fall into the current or jumping into the swarms and taking the little caddis flies in midair. Both stone flies and caddis flies are often present when the brittle branch-rattling trees are barren and snow lies along the stream.

The first dry-fly hatches are usually those of the famous Gordon Quill group: these hatches are often enigmatic, for some seasons find bad weather and high water and scattered hatches, and still have sporadic but good surface feeding; others offer good weather and water and relatively heavy hatches with poor response by the trout. My own stream notes record several days when the mayflies were so numerous that one could collect them from the current in amazing numbers, yet few rises were observed. Perhaps the trout had not begun looking for surface food after the long winter months of bottom feeding and were picking up the subsurface forms while letting the adult duns escape.

The Gordon Quill species group emerges from the nymphal shuck while still on the bottom, so many insects are taken straggle-winged and struggling toward the surface. Rising to the surface is accomplished with gases which gather under the loosening membranes and cause the embryonic mayflies to drift buoyantly toward the surface. The rough-bodied Emerging Gordon Quill pattern holds air bubbles in its dubbing and catches the light in its gold-tinsel

Get Wet

If you find your creel getting lighter and lighter as the trout season progresses, forget you're a purist. Forget how pretty those mayfly imitations look riding high on the water—and how dry. The novice flyfisherman will be brainwashed by the countless texts on mayfly imitations. But there is much more variety in nymphs and wet flies, thereby allowing the beginner a better opportunity for success should he not choose an exact match from his fly book. And they usually hatch all season long, as opposed to specific times. A down-wing beneath the surface catches trout when the dry, high-riding fly won't draw the slightest glance. Mayfly imitations are effective, but only at certain times. Even though mayflies will catch trout, the fisherman who is stocked with a good supply of caddis imitations will outfish the one waiting for the mayfly hatch.

–Joe Parry, July 1995

ribbing, suggesting the partially hatched naturals perfectly when fished over feeding fish in a dead-drift current swing.

Hendrickson hatches come later and after the uncertain appetite-whetting Gordon Quills; the trout are looking for surface food and feed heavily on them. Like the Gordon Quills, the Hendricksons are an afternoon hatch: both begin with a few specimens coming off in late morning, but the adults really come off the water after lunch. The Gordon Quills start coming down from 1:30 until 3:00, and the Hendricksons reach peak activity between 2:30 and 4:00. Nymph forms are active on the bottom before the adults appear and imitations of immature forms begin working in midmorning.

Two species of minute mayflies may also play some role in early-season surface activity: the small iron blue duns and the minute olives. Both begin emerging late in the morning and are present sporadically until dark. Trout sometimes feed on these smaller species in anticipation of the larger Gordon Quills and Hendricksons, and resume feeding on them after the juicier insect hatches are over in the late afternoon. The slate-colored iron blues are larger than the minute Baetis olives, but the olives are more numerous and many-brooded: their life cycle is short and they will appear again two to three times each season.

These several insect hatches can set off surface feeding when the early-season weather is good, and the water is near normal in clarity and level. But such seasons are rather rare.

But the dedicated flyfisherman need not despair: winterlike conditions can be conquered without resorting to other methods, with flies fished slow and deep.

—Ernest Schwiebert, March 1961

Trout Fishing Simplified

VERY SMALL, BRUSHY streams often have a surprising number of very large trout for the simple reason that they're pretty safe there, since it's difficult to fish such places successfully. Spinning won't do, for there's no room to work the lure without its hanging on the brush. So how would you go about catching some of them?

By "dapping," a method pretty common in Ireland but rarely heard of elsewhere. It's done merely by dropping a dry fly straight down from the rod tip so that it, but practically none of the leader, touches the water. Larger live flies on tiny hooks are also used.

Here's an improvement on the Irish way that I worked out: Have you ever seen a fly bobbing up and down a few inches above the water, occasionally dropping lower to touch it? It's said that it's a female laying an egg at each touch. Try using the same movement with your dry fly—not overdoing it. I found that this sometimes murders 'em in a small, brushy stream when just floating the fly produces little or no result. The movement must draw more attention to the fly, as well as making it seem more lifelike.

Naturally, to do well with dapping on a small, brushy stream you must do extremely careful stalking, and keep out of sight.

Some time back an article in *Sports Afield* described Irish dapping as done with long poles, not rods, but in the parts of Ireland where I saw it practiced it was invariably done with regular fly rods. Still, in many places a very long pole (a pole means a crude thing, generally without guides or reel) would no doubt be better for dapping than a rod.

However, if I were a judge, and a man were brought before me for suing a pole for trout, I'd give him 90 days for the first offense, longer if he proved a repeater. (For calling a rod a pole, I'd give a person only 10 days.)
—*Jason Lucas, April 1959*

The Wet Fly in Fast Water

WET-FLY FISHING IS not the simple, cards-on-the-table endeavor that casting the dry fly to a rising trout can often be. With the wet fly, you are always working in three dimensions; you have to work only in two dimensions with the dry fly. This poses a number of problems which simply do not exist for dry-fly fishermen. It is essential to present the sunken lure at almost the exact depth where the trout are feeding. Fine leaders help to sink the fly, and they are, in my opinion, even more important in wet-fly fishing than in dry, since a heavy leader can easily be seen. The trout can see the sunken lure from below, and also from the side. He can swim up and look your offering over, and he usually does, except in the heaviest broken water.

Learning when to set the hook when you can see neither your fly nor the "rising" trout takes years of time and practice. There are times, of course, when the taking fish can be seen perfectly by the angler, as when a pair of wet flies are fished across the surface of fast heavy water. Then the trout literally hook themselves. I remember fishing the head of the Klamath River in northern California many years ago, when a pair of gray wet flies skipped across the riffles resulted in one explosion after another, with the fish almost always hooking themselves solidly. I saw another demonstration nearly 30 years later, one day when Harry Darbee was with me on the Delaware River about a mile above Kellam's Bridge. We came down the heavy, deep water going slow and easy, and casting big streamers in front of us. Harry was making 70-foot casts with the 10-foot salmon rod he uses, and having no luck at all. Then he changed to a pair of No. 6 wet flies. I saw him work those flies across and down, across and down, for cast after cast. Then he shortened the line and skipped the flies over a break behind a boulder that nosed above the water. There was a bright flash, the rod tip went down, and a fine rainbow went into his dance.

Brown, brook, and rainbow trout tend to differ markedly in their reactions to the attractor type of wet fly (a lure that imitated some kind of small bright minnow in a general way rather than imitating any specific form of natural stream life). But all species of trout will take a wet fly with the form and color of the natural, if it's fished with a natural motion by a delicate rod and wrist action, or fished with a "dead float" and almost no motion at all.

–George Gordon, April 1961

Flies That Bind

SEVERAL YEARS AGO I taught a young man the basics of fly-casting in our backyard. His main problem was a bad habit of bending his wrist back too far on backcasts, causing his line to slap the ground. No matter how hard he concentrated, he would unconsciously make the same error, so I went in the house and found a piece of heavy string. I had him lift his forearm

Casting with an overly bent wrist—which causes the line to slap the ground—is a common flyfishing mistake. All you need to solve the problem is a short piece of string.

upright and hold the rod tip in the 1 o'clock position. I tied a loop around his wrist and the reel seat to restrict his backcast. The improvement was immediate.

Two years later, I saw the young man in his canoe, flycasting with casual grace and rhythm. Padding my own canoe closer, I saw a piece of string tied from his wrist to the reel seat. "It's the same one," he admitted. "If I don't use it, I'm forever slapping the water behind me." Then he smiled and said, "Some people drink, some people smoke, and I'm addicted to a piece of string."

–Robert H. Jones, November 1994

Scissors on the Stream

EVERY FLYFISHERMEN HAS his favorite flies, ones that he uses more than any others. Those flies that we have the most faith in are usually fished with more hope, more determination, and for longer periods. And,

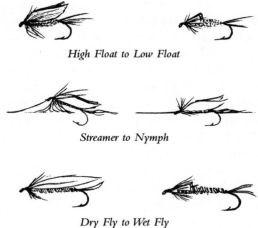

High Float to Low Float

Streamer to Nymph

Dry Fly to Wet Fly

Dry Fly to Nymph

Wet Fly to Nymph

because we give them the best chance, these favorites catch most of our fish. We use our other flies only when conditions are poor and our preferred flies

Cosmetic Fly Flotant

Dry-fly fishing is a lot easier when the fly is treated with a flotant— such as unscented Albolene liquefying skin cleanser. Rub a little of this cream into a fly with your fingertips, and it will float very well. I use a small plastic jar with a good screw cap that holds about half an ounce. The cap must be tightly secured during the summer because heat causes the product to liquefy, and it can leak if the cover is loose. One standard jar (purchased at a pharmacy) will provide enough flotant for your entire fishing club.

–Herb Buch, September 1987

Fishing with a Loaded Rod

When learning how to cast with a flyrod, try to do so on the water instead of on grass or dirt. The drag of the water on the flyline will help load the rod during the pickup, which in turn will get your backcast off to a good start. And letting the line straighten out behind you on the back-cast helps load the rod for an easy forward cast. If you don't load the rod, your leader and possibly the flyline will collapse in midair, sometimes falling all around you. With prac-tice, though, you'll be able to feel the tug on the rod as the line turns over and straightens. Anglers who cast artificial lures with spinning or baitcasting rigs should also load the rod instead of merely slinging the lure out. In this case, loading the rod with the lure takes only a split second and can be accomplished with wrist action.

–A. D. Livingston, October 1995

have already failed. We don't really give them a fair shake. If we fished our doubtfuls instead of our favorites in the best fishing times, we might change our views of which flies are best.

Fishermen have always taken great pleasure in the artistic design of their flies. The fancy expressions of the flytiers' art reached a peak in the late '20s and early '30s, and such designs are still prominent today. Flytiers or their agents had searched the world over to find feathers of the perfect color, texture, and length to make the fantastic designs they believed trout and salmon demanded. The tying was absolutely perfect. No cut or broken fiber ends were permitted on a fly.

At that time of great complexity, Ed Hewitt's spiders and bivisibles and the hairwing Wulff series came along to start the American revolution in dry flies. Fish liked the unconventional and simple flies. Though the spiders and bivisibles have faded a bit from their early popularity, both patterns are as good today as they were then. Spiders and bivisibles also have a special value to the angler who knows how to trim them on the stream.

The artistry of the flytier has always dictated that the ends of any hackle or feather fiber on a fly should be natural, never trimmed. Soft, fine ends give more life and wet-fly action than stiff blunt ends. Carefully matched ends move more softly in the water and spread more smoothly on the surface. I always tie every fly with care to match the natural fiber ends. But on the stream, where it really counts, I've changed my habits a bit and will do there what I never do at the flytying table.

Though almost every flyfisherman carries a nail clipper for cutting and trimming chores, from the very beginning I have carried a small pair of scissors. In fact, I even built a place to carry scissors into the first flyfishing vest. Of the few anglers who carry scissors with them today, still fewer use them for trimming flies on the stream. Only recently has fly trimming come into serious use. Few anglers used to consider that the things hackle and other fibers imitate, such as insect legs, do not taper down to infinity but have blunt ends. Nor did they realize that if some of the fibers are allowed to keep their complete delicate taper, others on the same fly can be cut with impunity.

One of the flies on which I have long used a pair of scissors is the spider. It's one of my ace-in-the-hole flies. When a small insect is hatching and trout are taking it occasionally but not regularly, I often put on a No. 16, No. 18, or even a No. 20 spider. While fishing the Red Rock River last season, I started with a complete spider, Size 18. In a few minutes I fooled one of the occasional risers and caught him. When no others would take that fly, I cut off the hackles on its lower half. With the fly in that condition, floating at hook level with the bushy fibers in the air, I caught another. Then no more action. So I cut off all the top fibers, leaving a few coming out on each side.

The fly then floated like a spentwing (with very long and practically invisible wings). I caught another trout and, again, the action tapered off. I cut off all the remaining hackles and ended up with nothing but the thread wrapping and a lot of very short fibers sticking out at the head. I caught two more with that fly, which was a pretty fair representation of a tiny nymph. Finally, I put that fly in my "very small nymph" box for use at another time.

Spiders are the easiest flies to tie. If you tie your own, you can make up to 30 an hour. They're good flies to cut up and experiment with.

The bivisible is also an easy fly to tie and then trim. It was so-named by Hewitt because he put a few turns of white hackle behind the eye of the hook for good visibility on the water. Behind the white hackle, Hewitt then tied multiple turns of whatever hackle the fly was named for—brown hackles for the brown bivisible, ginger hackle for the ginger bivisible, and so on.

The bivisible can be trimmed to almost any conceivable shape. You can shape it into a bee or an ant, a spentwing or a caterpillar. The greatest fun of having and using flies is to innovate with them when ordinary patterns don't work. Whether or not you tie your own flies, trimming can spell the difference between catching and not catching fish.

Taking away some hackle, for example, will make a fly float lower on the surface. This can make it much more attractive to the fish. Cutting away the wings can make the fly resemble an emerging insect instead of one that has already emerged. Reducing both the hackle and wings can change a dry or wet fly into a nymph. Careful trimming of the hackle, on the top and bottom, will turn a normal dry fly into a spentwing. The possibilities are limitless.

Another tool that fishermen should always have on hand is the felt-tip marker. I first used such a marker to change the tone and color of small flies when I was trying to fool some wise fish in Armstrong's Spring Creek in Montana. That was back in 1964, while I was making a TV film. A lot was riding on our ability to catch fish for the cameras. So I changed my pale watery dun into something darker, and was then able to take enough fish for the cameras.

Changing color or shade can be very effective. Though it's better to carry a full complement of flies, streamside coloring can be a sensible last resort.

Just as a scissors can only make flies smaller, so can the felt-tip marker only make light flies brighter and darker. If you must limit your flies to only a few, be sure to include a number of larger, light-colored ones that will be most susceptible to change.

–Lee Wulff, June 1979

The Doublehaul

A N AURA OF MYSTERY and confusion surrounds the doublehaul cast. Anglers who don't know it seem anxious to learn what they perceive is a difficult, complicated technique, one that will suddenly give them the power to throw an entire flyline effortlessly.

Actually, doublehauling is pretty easy. It's basically the same as regular casting, with the addition of two well-timed yanks on the line. A "haul" is simply a pull on the line with your line hand. To single-haul, begin your backcast as usual. Exactly at the moment you begin your backward power snap, tug downward on the line, pulling no more than 15 or 20 inches. If you've timed it correctly, matching the power snap with the pull, you'll feel the line jump backward with unusual speed, loading the rod.

The first step in a doublehaul is to pull down on the line at the exact moment that you begin your backward power snap. Pull no more than 15 or 20 inches of line, and if you've timed it correctly, you'll feel the line jump backward with unusual speed and power.

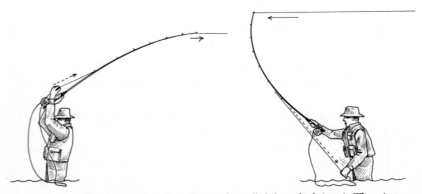

As the cast unfurls backward, feed the line you've pulled down back into it. Then, just as the line straightens out behind you, pull down crisply on the line, without too much muscle.

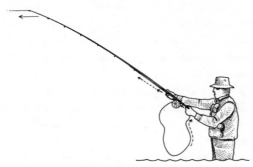

To complete the doublehaul, let the slack line shoot out through your line-hand (which you should make into an "O" with your thumb and index finger), and your cast will be significantly longer and more powerful than a regular cast.

You've just done half of a doublehaul. If you do nothing more than that and simply finish the cast as you normally would, you'll still have an improved cast: more line speed and rod-loading efficiency for less expenditure of muscle.

To finish the doublehaul you need to do two more things. First as the backcast unfurls, you must "feed" the hauled line back into it. Do this by simply letting the line hand-drift (not jerk) back up toward the reel. Then initiate the forward cast as you usually would, bringing both the rod and the line hand (which is now near the reel) forward. Just as you begin the power snap (usually as the rod appears in your peripheral vision, not sooner), haul again on the line. Don't rip it as if you were reefing a loose sail. Just a nice, crisp tug. And don't exert any more muscle into the cast than you normally would. Finish the cast and let the slack line shoot out through your line-hand O-ring.

That's a doublehaul. Here are the keys: (1) Throughout the cast, both hands start and stop together. (2) The line hand should stay near the rod hand throughout the cast, except during the actual hauls. (3) Use sharp, short hauls, no more than 20 inches, often less. Long sweeping pulls aren't necessary and will hamper the cast. (4) Aim for timing, control, and ease of performance. Don't overpower.

—Anthony Acerrano, March 1994

The Rise of the Caddis

THE ST. VRAIN RIVER in Northern Colorado is a typical caddis river. Its bottom is covered with the distinctive rock and stick cases of the caddis larva, sometimes so thickly that the bottom itself is all the free roamers, which do not build cases. They are usually cream in color with a greenish to brown cast and are sometimes called rock worms.

On the Level

Many anglers have a natural tendency to keep the rod tip high when using a subsurface deaddrift technique. This results in too much line between the tip and the fly. The more slack in the line, the longer the delay time when setting the hook. A subsurface

A high tip on a dead drift (above) results in too much slack between the tip and the fly. A level tip (below) enables you to respond more quickly.

dead-drift presentation is most productive with the use of short casts and a level rod tip. This way, you'll be able to respond quickly and with less effort to a subtle take. If, however, you wish to imitate an emerger swimming off the bottom toward the surface, it is permissible to lift the rod tip up during the drift.

—*Gene Trump, May 1992*

The free-roaming larva doesn't swim. It crawls along the bottom looking for food and, when it is dislodged, drifts helplessly until it can grab onto something. Imitations consequently should be fished very deep and on a dead drift. Larva imitations work well in deep runs, where action is slow, and can be excellent during periods of high water, when more than the usual number of larvae are adrift in the current.

As with most other aquatic insects, caddis are most available to the trout during emergence. After the larva has transformed into a pupa, it leaves the streambed and swims quickly to the surface, where it casts off its pupal husk and becomes airborne.

A caddis pupa is easily the buggiest-looking creature in a trout stream. Its body is deeply segmented, its wings are held along its sides, and its gangly legs below and long antenna above trail out past the end of the body. No one has described its appearance better than Don Roberts who, in his book *Flyfishing Still Waters*, compared a caddis pupa to a wet cat.

Although some caddis pupae are bright green, most are one shade or another of muddy brown or olive. They range from hook sizes of about No. 22 all the way up to some real bombers that can be tied on No. 6 or No. 8 hooks. Regardless of size, their basic shape remains the same.

Many drab classic wet flies, such as the Alder, leadwing Coachman, and Cow Dung, make good caddis-pupa imitations; there also are a number of more realistic patterns available. When all is said and done, however, there's no better all-round caddis-pupa imitation than the simple Soft Hackle.

Trout rising to caddis are easy to spot. The insects are bumbling, erratic fliers—unlike mayflies—and a trout has to work pretty hard to catch one.

As the pupa rises quickly to the surface, the trout has to dash after it without hesitation. Chances are he'll range farther from a specific feeding lane than he would for mayflies or midges. Since the insect becomes airborne almost the instant it reaches the surface, you're likely to see more boils (fish taking just under the surface) than classic rise forms of trout taking right off the top.

Although some feeding is done on adult insects during a hatch, most trout take caddis underwater before they emerge into the winged stage. Sometimes you'll even see trout coming out of the water, which is a sure sign of caddis. Many of these fish are after the winged insects, but a fair number of them are taking just under the surface and are carried out by the momentum of that last burst of speed. A dry fly will produce during a caddis hatch, but you'll usually do better with a wet fly.

Trout tend to be less finicky about fly patterns during a caddis hatch because they have less time to study each insect before taking. These fish are predators and are attracted as much by the movements of their prey as by its appearance. Although some fishermen strive for highly realistic fly patterns, all you really need is a fly that's close to the right size and color.

A few years ago, I was fishing the olive caddis hatch on the Arkansas River. The rise was in full swing and I'd left my nymph box back at the cabin. All I had with me were dry flies. I worked a No. 12 Adams for about 20 minutes and got only one or two short strikes so, in desperation, I squeezed it wet and fished it under the surface. Bingo. I started taking fish. The Adams was the right size but the wrong color and shape. The fish didn't mind.

A mayfly's wings are held upright (above), while caddis wings are folded along the body.

When fishing a caddis pupa, it's critical to give it the proper action. The easiest way to do this is to use the time-honored wet-fly cast. Cast the fly across the current and let the flow belly the line out downstream. This pulls the fly across the current and creates a fair simulation of a rising pupa. You may want to cast upstream a little and mend the line a few times to let the fly sink deeper before it starts to move; in either case, you'll get most of your strikes just as the fly starts to swing.

An effective variation of this method is the Leisenring Lift. Cast the fly well upstream of a working fish and let it sink deep. When the fly nears the fish, lift if off bottom so that it rises in front of the waiting trout. This is best done by stripping in line with the left hand and raising the rod tip steadily with the right hand. Make sure you don't raise the tip so high that there's no leverage left to set the hook.

It's best to use a weighted fly when working this method. In very deep and/or fast water, you may even have to put some split-shot on the leader to get the fly deep enough. This technique copies the behavior of the caddis pupa almost exactly and can be mastered with very little practice.

It's been proved time and again that the bigger a trout grows, the less inclined it is to feed on top. Even when a hatch is going on and fish are feeding so close to the top that you can see their swirls and wakes, the larger fish are likely to be down deep taking pupae coming off the bottom.

Ed Engle, an outdoor writer from Manitou Springs, Colorado, taught me how to fish flies deep a few years ago on the South Platte River. I'd been taking trout with dry flies, but Ed was outfishing me so much that I asked him to show me what he was doing. The 10- to 12-inch trout I'd been taking near the top became 16- and 18-inchers once I got my fly closer to bottom. My dry-fly snobbery disappeared.

The caddis completes it life cycle by returning to the stream, mating, and then laying its eggs on the water. The adult females buzz erratically over the surface, plopping down here and there to deposit their eggs. Trout taking egg-laying caddis have to move fast and hit hard. When all this is taking place, the dry fly can be deadly.

Adult caddisflies are drably colored, usually gray to brown to muddy olive. Robust insects with short bodies, four mottled wings, and long antennae, they are imitated by a number of standard fly patterns. The Adams, first tied by Len Halliday to imitate the caddisflies on the Boardman River in Michigan, is an all-time favorite. It's followed closely by the Irresistible and the Humpy, both tied with deer hair. Bivisibles or palmer-tied flies such as Leonard Wright's Fluttering Caddis work well too.

Fishing the caddis dry fly involves breaking most of the classic rules of presentation. First, the dead drift is out. A dry fly floating calmly in the current won't catch the trout's eye as a caddis; it has to be worked, pulled twitched, and otherwise made to look alive. There are a number of systems for making a dry fly act as a caddis, but generally speaking, each situation will require a slightly different approach. In good flows the drag of the current on line and leader may do some of the work for you. In calmer waters you'll probably have to use the rod tip to make the fly bounce a little.

Another tactic that breaks with tradition is the placement of the fly. The old masters tell us to cast the fly well upstream of a feeding trout and let it drift down to him, but you can sometimes entice a trout to strike if you drop your caddis right on his nose. Remember, he's on the lookout for buzzing, bouncing insects; when something lands right in front of him, he'll sometimes go for it automatically.

Tradition also tells us that the fly should settle on the water "like thistle down," but the egg-laying caddis is capable of hitting the surface hard enough to leave small rings on the water. If your fly hits the surface a little harder than usual, you may attract a trout rather than scare him the way you might if he were feeding on the more sedate mayflies. Again, remember it's an insect you're imitating. A touch that's too light is always preferable to one that's too heavy.

When fishing for trout that are rising to adult caddisflies, you have a wide leeway in your selection of a fly pattern. Matching the size, color, and general outline of the naturals is always a good place to start. When you consider the presentation methods involved, however, it's better to use a simple bivisible or palmer-hackled fly with lots of stiff, high-quality hackle than a more realistic one that won't stand up to much twitching and pulling.

Probably the best thing about caddisflies is their predictability. On the St. Vrain River, where I do most of my fishing, the hatches and egg-laying flights come off like clockwork every evening from late June, when the runoff subsides, until the weather turns cold.

Of course, it's not always the same insect that's hatching. There have been 14 species of caddis identified on this river alone and, although I try all kinds of fly patterns, I can fish them all successfully with an Adams or Soft Hackle.

Now, I don't want you to think that the caddis is the final solution. For instance, there's a time, along about the middle of July, when the big tan caddis are on the water in droves but the trout start going for little rusty spinners. But then that's another story.

—John Gierach, May 1980

Striking It Rich

GREAT TACKLE, HOT lures, canny retrieve techniques, trophy waters—all of these things mean very little if you fail to get a solid hook-set when a fish takes. Occasionally, gamefish strike hard and hook themselves, and there are times when you need only haul back on the rod, however artlessly, to get the job done. But more often than not, knowing precisely how and when to set a hook can mean the difference between catching many fish and catching few or none at all.

Consider, for example, the line strike in flyfishing. Whenever you need to set a hook quickly—as when nymphing, and the takes are typically light and fast—you'll connect with many more trout by jerking back sharply with your line hand, while simultaneously, but very slightly, lifting the rod tip. This delivers ample force to the hook point in half the time it takes to haul the rod tip up and back in standard fashion, and it makes a break-off less likely because the strike is controlled rather than excessive.

You can also combine a line-strike with a normal lifted-rod strike whenever you want to add controlled force to a hook-set. This is more reliable than the multistrike approach used by some, where the rod is jerked back, dropped, and jerked back again, sometimes three or four times, to bury the hook points. This tactic is inefficient and prone to causing "slack intervals" that strong fish can surge against, possibly snapping the line. Striking over and over can also widen the hook point's channel of penetration, actually making it easier for the hook to dislodge.

The slip-strike is another important technique for flyfishermen. It achieves the opposite effect of the multistrike, setting the hook lightly and gently without straining or breaking a light tippet. Lift the rod tip as for a normal strike, while at the same time allowing slack flyline to slip through the forefinger of your rod hand. The outgoing line mitigates some of the upward force of the rod and the result is a quick hook-set that is firm but gentle. With practice you can regulate the exact amount of force, whether very light or just under breaking strength, to an amazing degree. I like the slip-strike for midge fishing and nymphing with tiny flies and very light (6X to 8X) tippets, or whenever I'm using a rod that's powerful enough to exert more strike-force than my tippet can safely hold.

Even the standard lift strike deserves closer attention. Many flyfishermen make the mistake of lifting not just the rod tip but the entire rod as high into the air as they can reach. This is an excessive, wasted motion that actually delivers less force to the hook point, while also being more prone to creating after-strike slack. The rod tip needs to move first, with the body of the rod following or levering.

The direction of pull can be straight up and back for comparatively light or easy hook-sets, as when a fish takes while moving straight away or is directly below in a current. It's usually better, however, for the direction of pull to be off to one side—preferably the side opposite the fish's position or direction of movement. The snap or pull done sideways and slightly up will generate the most hook-setting power, especially if aided by a coordinateed twisting of the hips and torso so that you strike with your whole body, not with just your arms. Of course, the power of this strike must be suited to your tippet and quarry. There's no need to hit this hard on a 12-inch rainbow, for instance, even if your leader can stand it.

—Anthony Acerrano, May 1995

How to Tackle a Heavyweight

WHEN HOOKED INTO a big one, anglers tend to make either of two mistakes. Some reel too hard, as if overeager to get the trophy to the net. Possibly out of sheer adrenaline rush, they lurch back against the rod and try to horse or plankship the fish with brute strength. Broken lines, even shattered rods, are common consequences.

Others become timid. Afraid to put any pressure on the fish, they simply hang on, hoping to outlast it. Unfortunately, it doesn't work that way. As renowned trophy fisherman Stu Apte notes, "With a big fish, there aren't any stalemates. Either you're gaining line or the fish is." Your hand must be alternately light and firm, balanced to the fish's display. When a heavyweight runs, jumps, or bulldogs, meet it with just enough resistance—the most you can get away with without risking the line's strength. When the fish stops or tires, it's your turn to be aggressive. Draw the rod back, reel the slack as you bring it forward again, pump it back or off to one side, angled away from the fish, wearing down the fish bit by bit.

—Anthony Acerrano, October 1995

5

Flies and Flytying

~

"And regarding Flies:

here you will find [the angler] very obstinate

and at times pugnacious."

—Claude King, Editor-in-Chief, October 1909

<<< *A menacing stonefly by professional flytier Al Niemiec.*—**Photo by Richard V. Procopio**

What Trout-Fly Patterns Are Best?

L ET'S TAKE AN imaginary chap who's called Herbert Smith. Herb has been flyfishing for trout for years with fair success, but he isn't up in the expert class and admits it. Now let's have him enter the lounge of some imaginary fishing resort. Back in one corner are a dozen of the country's leading fly anglers in a very solemn discussion. Some sort of expert anglers' convention got them together.

Here, says Herb to himself, is my chance to get the real lowdown on the fine points of this fly-fishing business. He strolls up pretending not to notice them, sits down behind an open newspaper, and strains his ears to catch their words of piscatorial wisdom. What does he hear?

Nothing but fly patterns. They're showing each other their fly boxes, and each seems able to name thousands of patterns offhand. Herb gathers from their casual remarks that, of course, they all tie their own flies. They wouldn't consider themselves real trout fishermen if they didn't.

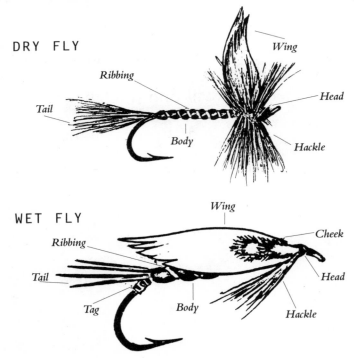

DRY FLY — Wing, Ribbing, Head, Tail, Body, Hackle

WET FLY — Wing, Ribbing, Cheek, Tail, Head, Tag, Body, Hackle

NYMPH

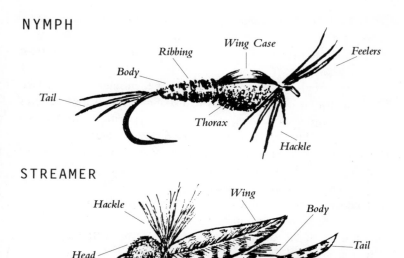

STREAMER

Nymph Know-How

Fishing a nymph on a dead drift is arguably the most difficlut method of flyfishing to master, but it may also be the most consistently productive. The recent popularity and wide-spread use of strike indicators have made this type of fishing easier to learn—but even with these, the average fisherman will probably miss more strikes than he has hookups. By the time the angler detects the take and sets the hook the fish has had enough time to realize his folly and eject the imitation. While hard-bodied nymphs make for more realistic imitations (at least to the human eye), an artificial nymph tied with wool, mohair, or a similar material will often give you the extra time you need to make a hookup. That's because the fibers get stuck in the fish's teeth, making it more difficult to spit out.
–Bernard L. Kurley, August 1994

Despair comes over Herb. It would take him 20 years of study to learn fly patterns as well as they know them, and he hasn't time or fishing opportunities enough for that. So the only question seems to be whether he should give up the sport or be satisfied to remain a dub all his life. He gets up his courage and speaks to the mighty anglers.

"Gentlemen, pardon me for interupting, but do I have to know fly patterns as well as you to have any real success catching trout?"

They turn and stare at him in consternation. And suddenly they break out in a roar of laughter.

"Heck," says the noted Henry X. Pert, "you don't have to know anything about patterns to be as good a trout-fly fisherman as anybody else. You'll probably get more trout if you don't know them, because instead of wasting a lot of time changing flies you'll keep your fly out where a trout can take it."

Herb puts a hand to his brow. "But your deep discussion of patterns . . . ?"

"Oh, that. It's only a little game fly fishermen have to amuse themselves. You know, like arguing which came first, the chicken or the egg. Doesn't mean a thing."

Herb gulps. "Well, anyhow, don't I have to learn to tie my own flies?"

They all chuckle, and the famous Ira Walton III answers: "Tying flies is a nice hobby—for anybody that likes to tie flies. But it won't help you catch one more trout, any more than making your own lures would help you catch more bass."

Flytying Tips For Beginners

One of the biggest mistakes a beginning flytier makes is to attempt to tie a different pattern each time. Try this instead: Lay out half a dozen hooks the same size and the materials needed to tie six flies in the same pattern. Instead of tying a Size 8 Woolly Worm, a Size 6 Mickey Finn, and a Size 10 Royal Coachman, tie six Size 8 Woolly Worms. You will be surprised at how much easier and faster it is to tie the sixth than it was the first, and at how much better it came out.

-B. L. Kurley, June 1992

This, after their ponderous debate about patterns, is getting Herb pretty dizzy, but after a moment's thought he comes up with another question.

"How many patterns does one really need to be successful in trout fishing?"

Ah, now he's stirred up an argument. Most of them agree on six. That seems, for some reason, to be the favorite maximum number of patterns thought necessary; almost no leading angler or angling writer holds that one needs seven or more. But no two of them agree on what those six should be, and that's what the argument is about. Finally Ira Walton turns to Herb and says the fact that they don't agree proves that it doesn't make much difference what they are—just get six that are pretty different from each other.

The rest nod reluctant agreement. Henry X. Pert hadn't joined the last argument; he just stood there grinning.

"Who," he inquires, "is the greatest investigator of trout-fly matters this country has ever produced?"

No disagreement there, of course; it's the late Edward Ringwood Hewitt. He wrote some profound books on the subject, but since he didn't write for magazines it seems that only top-notch anglers are familiar with his work. He was born the year after Lincoln died and caught fish eaten by Wilhelm I of Germany, and Bismarck, which would make him seem a historical character—but in an account of an interview with him in the March 1956 issue of *Sports Afield*, he was still very active mentally and physically in spite of having recently broken a leg while fishing. He was right up to the minute, able to show far younger anglers where they were going wrong in their latest fishing theories.

"How many dry-fly patterns," Henry asks, "does Hewitt say one needs to catch all possible trout?"

"One," Ira admits reluctantly. "He mentions a medium brown, but implies that it doesn't matter much what the color is."

"And what natural fly should it imitate?"

"Why, it's the bivisible he invented, which isn't supposed to represent anything but some hackles tied around a hook. Some one solid color the trout can see, but always with white in front so the user can see it easily too. Bivisible, equally visible to man and fish."

Poor Herb mops his brow. All he'd ever heard or read regarding trout flies seemed to be tumbling about his ears.

"Do you mean to say," he asks, "that just a little tuft of hackles, representing nothing, will get as many trout as all my nice patterns?"

"Hush!" warned Ira hastily, glancing around. "We don't want that to leak out any more than we can help. It takes about 30 years of constant fishing for anybody to find it out for himself. Why, if it got to be common knowledge it would ruin the sport, make it unpopular. When somebody failed to catch trout, he couldn't blame it on not having the right fly—he'd have to admit that it was because he didn't fish right. That would be awful!"

Herb's head sank until it was what one might call hanging; no longer could he meet their eyes or get a word out. So he couldn't blame his catching none that day, while Tom Follingsbee got plenty of fine ones, on Tom's having the right pattern while he didn't. He'd have to admit that Tom was the better fisherman.

"Pardon me, gentlemen," he muttered and staggered off to the bar for a double Scotch. So we'll have to continue this discussion without Herb, and hope he doesn't get too tight.

If he'd gone on with it, they'd all have told him—and so would Edward Ringwood Hewitt if he'd been there—that while the value of patterns is at least highly questionable, every last trout angler of any experience would agree that a matter of extreme importance indeed, at most times, is the size of the fly.

Then, you may ask, how about the times when you yourself were catching nothing until you changed patterns, and suddenly began to catch lots? Might have been that they suddenly started rising then. But it's more likely that it was the size of the fly that did the trick.

You may think you have me there, since sometimes both the fly that works and the one that doesn't are, say, Size 12. Trouble is that you're talking about hook sizes, and I'm talking about fly sizes. On a Size 12 hook you may have either a skimpy little nymph consisting of a few strands of something twisted on tight, or a great, big spider. At a given time, either may be just exactly what the trout want, and the other just exactly what they don't want.

So I think few really experienced anglers will disagree with me when I say that for catching trout, it's far better to have flies all one color, but various overall sizes (which will mean some different hook sizes too), than to have 1,000 patterns all the same size.

But, provided the fly is roughly the right size for the time, by far the most important thing of all is to learn how to fish for trout with flies. That is, where to find trout and how to present the fly.

This, too, isn't nearly as complicated as some try to make it seem. It's chiefly a matter of studying feeding habits just a little, knowing where to look for them and using your head. The way not to catch trout is to rely on switching patterns instead of learning how to fish.

How many patterns do I personally think useful? Three—one mainly black, one mainly white, and one of some neutral shade in between; it makes no difference what they're called.

Do I myself stick to those three colors? Goodness, no! That would be no fun at all. But I really think I catch almost as many trout on them as I would if I stuck to those three colors, or to Hewitt's one color; that is, if you'll count only when I'm fishing, giving me time out for all my fly-changing. After all, I get a lot of fun from monkeying around with all those patterns, and that's what I'm out for—fun. If I just wanted dead trout I could buy them frozen.

—Jason Lucas, September 1957

Spring Ties

CONDITIONS ON TROUT streams in spring can range from shirt-sleeve weather and low, clear water to arctic blasts, sleet, and roiling rivers. The key to coping with these variables is to stock a wide variety of patterns and be adaptable.

▶▶▶ *Believe in Streamers:* These are workhorse patterns. When no fish are showing, tie one on and chances are, you can pound up a few trout.

When rivers flow clear and low, opt for a thinly dressed pattern designed to imitate dace or shiners, such as the Clouser Minnow, Black-Nosed Dace, olive or black Marabou, Matuka, and Zonker, Sizes 4 to 8.

If waters are high and stained, choose a bulkier pattern such as a Sculpin or Marabou Muddler. These push more water, allowing fish to locate them by sound and vibration as well as sight. Tie them weighted in Sizes 2 to 6. A hybrid streamer pattern that's good for both low and high waters is the Woolly Bugger in black, olive or brown, Sizes 4 to 8, or variations such as the Crystal Bugger or Bead Head Bugger.

Use a tapered leader of 4 to 8 feet testing 4 to 6 pounds at the tippet, a floating or sink-tip line and a 5- to 7-weight rod. Cast across or slightly upstream, allow the fly to sink, then begin a slow, twitching retrieve.

▶▶▶ *Get Down with Nymphs:* Imitations of immature aquatic insects are often even more productive than streamers. Check with local tackleshops to see which patterns produce best on the specific waters you fish. Also watch for heavy hatches and choose a pattern that duplicates the nymph or pupa of the insect emerging. As a rule, though, you can't go wrong with the Hare's Ear, Zug Bug, Bitch Creek Nymph, Stonefly, Pheasant Tail, LaFontaine Sparkle Pupa, and a few bead head patterns that get deep quickly, such as the Bead Head Caddis Larva and Pupa. If you're fishing tailwaters, add a few San Juan or Gordie's worms to your collection. For spring creeks, be sure to include sowbug and scud patterns in 14s and 16s. Slightly weighted versions are all right, but you'll get a more natural action if you use unweighted ones and crimp split-shot on the leader when needed.

Use a 4- to 6-weight rod, floating line, and leader of 7 to 10 feet. Fasten a strike indicator just below where the leader joins the line.

Sparkle Pupa.

Bitch Creek nymph.

The most productive way to fish nymphs in the early spring, when streams are running high, is two at a time. One way to do this is to leave a tag end of the tippet blood knot longer than usual and attach a second nymph to it. Or you can simply rig up one nymph, then tie an extra length of tippet material (about 12 to 20 inches) through the eye of the first fly and attach a second offering to that.

Use nymphs to probe backwaters off the main current, deep pools, runs, undercut banks, rocks, eddies, logjams, and bridges. And a short line is important for both good fly control and a quick hook-set.

➤➤➤ *The Dry Look:* When water temperatures reach the upper 40s trout will begin feeding on the surface. By the time it reaches the 50s, steady rising is the norm during the warmest part of the day.

Midges will stir up some of the earliest feeding activity. First find long slick stretches of water or sloughs off the main current. Then search for the tiny dimples of chironomid-feeding fish. Try using a pattern such as a midge pupa, a Palomino, a Serendipity or a Griffith's Gnat, Sizes 18 to 24, on a 2- to 5-weight rod with a 10- to 14-foot leader that tapers to a 7X tippet.

Pretty soon the caddisflies are likely to follow. Black, tan, and olive will match the most common species, in Sizes 12 to 18. Effective styles include the Elk Hair Caddis by Al Troth, the CDC Caddis, the Goddard Caddis, and Stimulator.

Mayflies generate some of the most frenzied surface feeding early in the year. Quill Gordons can provide a few days of early suface fishing if you hit

Reduced Elk Hair Caddis

The Elk Hair Caddis, one of the most successful trout dry flies, is tied with hackle ribbed with fine wire. The hackle improves flotation in rough water, while the wire reinforces the hackle stem, making the fly last longer.

The Reduced Elk Hair Caddis eliminates the hackle and wire, resulting in a caddis imitation that sits flush on the surface. Besides being quicker and less expensive to tie, the reduced version is deadly on calmer stretches of water. Particularly in larger flies, elk hair is an advantage because it is a tough material and offers superior flotation. When used in smaller flies, however, the stiffness of the elk hair wing tends to pop the fly out of the fish's mouth. For Size 16 and smaller Elk Hair Caddis, tying a deer hair wing often makes the fly more effective.

–Deke Meyer, September 1992

A stimulator (top) is great for a caddis hatch; a Blue Quill (bottom) works for mayflies.

them right. More important are the Blue Quill and Blue-Winged Olive. Stock Blue Quills in Sizes 16 and 18; Olives in 16, 18, and 20. Experiment with different styles, but it's hard to beat a Thorax, Comparadun, or Sparkle Dun.
—*Gerald Almy, March 1995*

Streamer Magic

STATISTICALLY, A STREAMER fly will take more large trout than any other kind of fly, simply because most big fish eat little fish. However, it isn't your everyday or everywhere reliable method for taking trout consistently. Follow an electrofishing crew doing a stream census, as I have done on many occasions, and you'll realize that on a per mile basis in most U.S. rivers, big trout are mighty scarce. To define big, let's say a fish over three pounds in the East or over five pounds in the West. I faithfully wade streams every season that probably don't even hold more than one or two such trout. In streams, insects are the dominant food form and the nymph or dry fly is prerequisite—the appearance of a streamer will often send the fish running for cover. However, angling wouldn't be very much fun if is was predictable.

I recall a summer afternoon on the Saranac River in New York when the trout were feeding steadily on midges, ordinarily a selective performance, yet we caught numerous risers on a little Blacknose Dace bucktail. The same gentleman who told me to try that, Ray Neidig, also advised swimming a Mickey Finn whenever rising water began to pearl in a heavy rain, a tip that has paid off on many wet days. All streamer-fly specialists have a bag of tricks, but there is often more logic than magic in their origins.

The Missouri is probably the best-known river for this kind of fishing. It produces trout of 10 pounds or more, and there have been reported scuba sighting of browns in the 20- to 30-pound class below Toston Dam. But let's get down to some streamer and bucktail basics.

There are more than 200 species of true minnows in North American water. This includes the shiners, dace, and chub, and at least 200 additional species that belong in other families such as the darters, killifishes, silversides, and sculpins that are considered minnows in an angling sense. Although many baitfish, especially the widely abudndant shiners, can be described as olivaceous dorsally and silvery to white on the ventral surface, most of them become very colorful during their spring to summer breeding period. At that time they acquire splashes of rose, lavender, orange, and yellow. Others such as the bleeding shiner, warpaint shiner, and fire shiner have bright red markings throughout the year. The seemingly implausible colors in many streamer patterns often find a counterpart in nature. Conversely, simple barred-rock hackle wings closely simulate the body markings of all killifishes, while a badger hackle wing, with its pronounced dark lateral stripe, could represent almost the entire shiner genus.

There are plenty of tying materials that will suggest, if not imitate, the naturals. In any one river system there is always a dominant forage species that trout consume with some frequency; a familiar example is the mottled sculpin or bullhead found in Rocky Mountain streams, which has inspired so many Muddler patterns, or the abundance of darters in the southeast hill country. What's important for the angler to know about sculpins and darters is that they find protection by lying quietly between stones, then hop or dart erratically along bottom when feeding or disturbed. They do not swim freely like the true minnows. This is the basis for two generally effective techniques with streamers—the swimming retrieve and bottom bouncing. They have a corollary worth noting, too. The free swimmers are mostly silvery in color while the bottom dwellers are camouflaged, dark in color.

Under normal water conditions, with a floating line, the fly is cast across or slightly upstream. As it drifts with the current, a regular movement of rod and hand gives it a pulsing motion spaced at short intervals to simulate a minnow struggling in the flow. Don't be in a hurry to lift for a new cast. Even after the line has made its full swing, let the fly rise and fall in the current for at least five or six seconds. A helpless minnow is tantalizing to big trout. The important thing to remember is that you should hold your rod tip close to the surface during a retrieve—almost in the water. This eliminates that critical few feet of slack between the tip and surface and accomplishes two things. It permits you to give the streamer a positive swimming action when stripping with your line hand and, equally important, you will feel the strike in your fingers, and can tighten instantly. Streamer flies draw a very high ratio of missed strikes in running water because of the slack factor as the trout is now attacking its food as opposed to accepting a drifting insect.

The other technique is to get a deep swim with a fast-sinking line. Some anglers prefer high-density shooting heads with monofilament running line, but this has no advantage except on the largest rivers. The weight of the line should be matched to the depth of the water you're fishing. A No. 7 or No. 8 weight-forward fast sinker will serve most purposes. This demands a short leader of three or 3 1/2 feet because precious seconds elapse while the sinking line is pulling the fly down, and the longer the leader the greater the delay. The standard nine-foot leader will buoy a fly near the surface even when your line is fully submerged. The angle of your cast must be judged against current velocity, but normally you will aim diagonally upstream, then delay drag by mending line until the fly has settled near bottom. As in a swimming retrieve, the rod should be pointed at the water and the fly worked with your line hand. It takes practice and a delicate sense of touch to steer a streamer at the correct level in foot-long hops, but once this is mastered you will be able to cover the deepest pools effectively.

During the summer streamers are generally more productive at night. Big browns are especially cautious about chasing minnows in bright sunlight. In the protective cloak of dark, or in roily water after a rain, they will cruise the shallows looking for baitfish. As a result, daylight feeding of this kind is unusual. Yet on various occasions I've hooked small trout on a dry fly and, while the fish splashed wildly at the surface, had a dark shadow shoot out from under a ledge or cutbank and grab our mutual victim before I had sense enough to slack off. Once I stood eyeball to eyeball with a big Delaware River brown that held my little trout crosswise in his jaws as though daring me to pull it loose. Trout are keenly predator conscious, but as they grow into double figures the need for vertebrate food is essential to their survival. I once watched an angler dress an 8 1/2-pound Gods River brook trout, out of which he pulled a partially digested burbot or "ling" that weighed almost two pounds. It's a wonder that the trout had the stomach to pounce on a wobbling spoon, no less ingest a fresh-water cod of that size.

There are times when a streamer fly fished right in the surface will score consistently. It would be a mistake to regard all patterns as baitfish imitations. Sparsely tied dark dressings on No. 8 to No. 12 hooks fished with fine tippets do a very good job of simulating many nymphs. Apply a little silicone flotant to a small Muddler, for example, and you can drift or skim it on the surface as a grasshopper, stonefly, or dragonfly imitation. And there are undoubtedly situations where a topwater streamer not only suggests a baitfish, but is just what a diffident trout is looking for.

SPORTS

April
1938

NOW
15¢ ★ AFIELD

and TRAILS of the NORTHWOODS

America's Oldest Monthly Outdoor Magazine – Established 1887

Dry Flies

Adams: Sizes 10-22

Blue-Winged Olive: Sizes 14-22

Light Cahill: Sizes 10-20

Royal Coachman: Sizes 12-16

Mosquito: Sizes 12-18

Light Hendrickson: Sizes 12-16

Dark Hendrickson: Sizes 12-16

Red Quill: Sizes 12-16

Pale Evening Dun: Sizes 14-20

March Brown: Sizes 12-14

Gray Fox: Sizes 12-16

Quill Gordon: Sizes 12-16

Blue Dun: Sizes 12-20

Black Gnat: Sizes 12-18

Irresistible: Sizes 12-16

Henryville Special: Sizes 12-18

Griffith's Gnat: Sizes 16-20

Eastern Green Drake: Sizes 8-10

Schroeder's Parachute Caddis:
Sizes 12–16

Schroeder's Hare's Ear Parachute:
Sizes 12–16

Sulphur Parachute: Sizes 14–20

Adams Parachute: Sizes 14–20

Blue-Winged Olive Parachute:
Sizes 14–20

Glow-In Dark Parachute: Sizes 14–18

Light Cahill Thorax: Sizes 14–20

Pale Morning Dun Thorax:
Sizes 16–22

Hendrickson Thorax: Sizes 14–16

Trico Thorax: Sizes 20–24

Spring Creek Dun: Sizes 12–18

Extended Body Comparadun:
Sizes 12–18

Quick-Sight Spinner: Sizes 14–18

Spinner: Sizes 16–20

Sparkle Wing Trico: Sizes 18–24

Travis Para Midge: Sizes 16–22

Troutsman Hex: Size 6

**Travis Extended Body Green
Drake:** Sizes 10–14

Streamers

Royal Coachman Bucktail:
Sizes 6-12

Mickey Finn: Sizes 6-12

Gray Ghost: Sizes 6-12

Black Nose Dace: Sizes 6-10

Matuka: Sizes 6-8

Girdle Bugger: Sizes 4-10

Black Marabou Leech: Sizes 6-10

Marabou Muddler: Sizes 4-8

Cone Head Marabou Muddler:
Sizes 2-8

Zonker: Sizes 4-8

Mini Muddler: Sizes 10-12

Muddler: Sizes 2-12

Cone Head Muddler Minnow:
Sizes 2-8

Woolhead Sculpin: Sizes 4-8

Bead Head Leech: Sizes 4-8

Bead Head Minnow: Sizes 6-10

Woolly Bugger: Sizes 4-12

Cone Head Woolly Bugger:
Sizes 2-12

Krystal Bugger: Sizes 4-12

Bead Head Woolly Bugger:
Sizes 4-10

Travis Bead-A-Bugger: Sizes 4-12

Woolly Bomber: Sizes 4-10

Nymphs & Wets

Hare's Ear: Sizes 10-16

Pheasant Tail: Sizes 12-18

Hendrickson: Sizes 12-14

Flashback Adams: Sizes 10-18

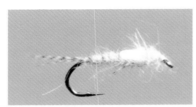
Travis Floating Nymph: Sizes 14-20

Stauffer Midge: Sizes 12-18

Sparkle Prince: Sizes 10-14

Serendipity: Sizes 14-18

Bead Head Emerging Caddis:
Sizes 12-16

La Fontaine Sparkle Pupa:
Sizes 12-16

Bead Body Scud: Sizes 10-14

Bighorn Scud: Sizes 12-16

Sowbug: Sizes 12-18

Wiggle Damsel: Sizes 10-12

Bead Head Caddis Larva:
Sizes 14-18

Lepage's Bead Head Mayfly: Sizes
12-18

Bead Head Rabbit Emerger: Sizes
12-18

Golden Nugget: Sizes 12-16

Gead Head Brassie: Sizes 12-18

Peacock Bead Head: Sizes 12-18

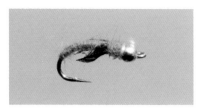

Bead Head Caddis Pupa: Sizes 12-18

Gold-Ribbed Hare's Ear: Sizes 10-14

March Brown Wet: Sizes 12-14

Lepage's Brassear: Sizes 14-20

Breadcrust: Sizes 10-16

Buckskin Nymph: Sizes 14-20

Disco Midge: Sizes 16-22

Brassie: Sizes 14-20

Tellico: Sizes 6-12

Early Black Stone: Sizes 10-12

Zug Bug: Sizes 10-18

Prince, weighted: Sizes 8-16

Case Caddis: Sizes 10-12

Sparkle Stonefly: Sizes 8-12

Sparkle Black Stone: Sizes 6-10

Marabou Dragon: Sizes 8-10

Montana: Sizes 8–14

Travis Golden Stone Nymph:
Sizes 4–12

Fastwater Nymph: Sizes 4–10

Woolly Worm: Sizes 6–12

Vernille San Juan Worm: Sizes 8–14

Golden Stone: Sizes 6–8

Blinn's Ugly Stone: Sizes 4–10

Halfback Nymph: Sizes 8–16

Travis Bead Head Swimming
Damsel: Sizes 10–14

Marabou Damsel: Sizes 8–12

Whitlock's Hellgrammite: Sizes 6–8

Yuk Bug: Sizes 4–10

Stonefly Bugger: Sizes 6–10

Bitch Creek: Sizes 4–8

Jeff's Hex: Sizes 4–8

Hornberg Wet: Sizes 8–12

Kauffman's Stone: Sizes 2–10

Crayfish: Sizes 4–6

I have a number of favorite streamer flies. For general trout fishing I stock basic bucktails in two- and three-color combinations, mostly Keith Fulsher's Thunder Creek series that suggests many shiners, dace, and darters. In feather wings, I'm partial to the Nine-Three, Black Ghost, Gray Ghost, and Supervisor. In a fluffy stork-feather wing, I use the White Marabou for clear water and the Black Marabou in roily water. For a breather-wing, get the Dar, Spruce, and Chappie patterns. For western trout fishing, Dave Whitlock's Sculpin and Multicolored Marabou are the two deadliest designs I know of for deep fishing. Throw in a Mickey Finn and a Muddler Minnow and you are pattern prepared. These flies should be stocked in a good range of sizes, from No. 12 in the simpler dressings to a No. 1/0. Trophy hunters often go to 3/0 on western rivers.

—A. J. McClane, September 1979

A Fly for All Seasons

FISHING WITH AN artificial nymph is the basic method of trout angling. The nymph will catch fish 365 days of the year—not always the largest and not always the most, but it will take them consistently. Equally important is the method of nymphing because it teaches beginners everything they must know about trout habits and habitat. Nymph fishing can be successful in the coldest or hottest weather, in dead-calm water or a raging torrent, and from the surface to the very bottom of those secret places where great trout hide.

Nymph fishing is old and its development has quite a history, but it did not become popular in America until about 1930. In the half-century since, the totemization of G. E. M. Skues's *Minor Tactics of the Chalk Stream* has certainly inspired those who fish and those who write about it. For any angling writer, it is a rare privilege not only to describe his country and time but to give perspective of the sport. Skues succeeded in doing this, but in a strangely delayed way.

It's hard to believe now, but once upon a time nymph was a dirty word. In the formal establishment of 1910, Skues was considered a heretic "dabbler in unworthy excesses" by many of his peers. Gentlemen belonged to the Houghton Club, marinated their Stilton in 150-year-old port, and fished with floating patterns. It has never been clear to me why a fly that is sunken, presumably the inferior condition in which artificials originated in the first place, would become the villain in morality play. Some idea of where the nymph existed by 1936 can be found in a little 55-page book, *Tying American Trout Lures*, by Reuban R. Cross. Rube, the sage of Shin Creek, was a master craftsman, yet all he had to say about nymphs covered 4 1/2 pages and concerned

Flypaper Fishing

Want to know the exact types and sizes of the insects currently hatching along your favorite trout stream? Hang some old-fashioned flypaper from a streamside tree limb in mid-afternoon and inspect it the next morning. The strategy may sound primitive, but unless the weather changes drastically overnight, you'll be all set to match the hatch.

—John Swinton, May 1995

A Little Yarn

Many nymph fly patterns are weighted with lead fuse wire wrapped around the hook shank. To ensure a quick and deeper-sinking fly, some tiers use large-diameter lead, or double-wrap one layer over the other. This does create a deep-sinking nymph, but the step up from the hook shank to lead underbody makes dubbing the body over the lead much more difficult. A solution to this problem is to use a very soft yarn, such as Super Fluff or Glo-Bug yarn, to overwrap the lead wire. Use the softest yarn you can find to avoid excessively fat bodies, and choose colors that match fairly well with the dubbing material. The yarn makes a transitional ramp from the diameter of the hook shank to the diameter of the lead wraps, and you'll have no problem at all dubbing a nice, smoothly tapered body.

—Gene A. Trump, February 1991

four patterns: the Guinea Nymph, the Black-and-White Nymph (grub), the Olive Wood-duck Nymph, and the Carrot-and-Black Nymph.

I learned the fundamentals of nymphing back in the 1930s. The only popular American patterns, then purveyed by William Mills & Son, were the flat-bodied, lacquered creations of Edward Ringwood Hewitt—a design also claimed by John Alden Knight, although I can't imagine why. These nymphs came like licorice sticks in three color combinations: black with a gray belly, black with an orange belly, and black with a yellow belly. I seldom caught many trout with these, so, like everybody else who took fishng seriously, I tied my own.

It was April of 1936 when I caught my first big trout. The weather was cold and snowy and the river was running high. I was fishing a home-tied nymph by casting upstream and letting it sink close to my bank—which was no trick with a waterlogged silk line. I caught quite a number of trout that morning before getting stuck in the bottom, and when that brown finally came thumping to life it was the biggest thrill a 14-year-old boy could ever have. The trout was too big for my landing net, and after getting the head stuck in its meshes I remember wrestling my prize into a snowbank. I walked home by way of the lumberyard, the butcher shop, the drugstore, and the ill-named Palace Hotel, making sure everybody in town saw my fish. It weighed in at 7 pounds 2 ounces—not an adult trophy for the East Branch of the Delaware in those days, since fresh mounts in double figures to 15 pounds or more hung on every saloon wall.

When I dressed the trout, some of the nymphs that filled its belly were still alive; its digestion rate had almost slowed to a halt in the near-freezing water. What fascinated me was the fact that the fish had continued to feed. Although big trout are often caught on bucktails or streamers, in very cold weather a nymph will outfish a minnow-like fly simply because the trout doesn't have to chase it through heavy currents. A nymph can be fished absolutely dead and catch fish, while a bucktail cannot; a nymph can also be fished alive when the accepted food form is otherwise dead. This is the ultimate conundrum.

I had some fabulous fishing in 1978 at Henry's Lake in Idaho. This particular lake is known for its voluminous mini-mayfly hatches where even the best dry-fly man can spook trout with a No. 22 on a 7X tippet. The naturals look like dandruff. There is some action at the beginning of an emergence, and you can hook three, maybe four, nice fish. But the real sport occurs when the gulpers (fish of four, five, and six pounds) appear after rafts of spent mayflies are floating on the water. The fish cruise in a leisurely fashion, often porpoising in plain sight as they take ephemeral minutae out of the surface film. With countless thousands of naturals windrowed to a small area, the most perfect imitation is lost in sheer numbers.

After spending a futile morning casting at repetitve risers and hooking exactly three trout, Tom McNally provided the solution. McNally, who is an expert angler in every sense of the word and chronicles his adventures for the *Chicago Tribune*, learned nymphing fundamentals as a lad on the hard-fished streams of Maryland. In this case, he chose a No. 10 fuzzy-bodied brown nymph and worked it across the surface in a hand-twist retrieve.

Using this combination, we began hooking rainbows and browns in the 2 1/2- to 4-pound class fairly consistently. Many simply popped our tippets, and we lost several large ones in the lake's numerous weed beds. This method of outfoxing the gulpers was no fluke. Tom and I visited that lake regularly through September and into aspen-yellow October. On any morning when the water was mirror calm his method paid off.

I enjoy writing about the joys of nymph fishing. It reminds me of Rube Cross. When I mentioned his book earlier, I had to go scrambling through my library to check the title. I remembered the volume had a brown cover, but I had forgotton that he wrote an inscription inside the year I caught my first big trout, an inscription that deserves to appear in print. The author is anonymous, yet the words reflect to some degree the transcendental joy of angling:

> To my young friend
> I dreamed,
> that I again my native hills had found,
> the mossy rocks, the valley, and the
> stream that used to hold me captive
> to its sound.
> And that I was a boy again.
> (Anonymous)
> Reuben R. Cross
> Jan. 3, 1937

—A. J. McClane, March 1979

The Red-Hot San Juan Worm

WOULD A FLYFISHERMAN stoop to fishing a worm? Well, most wouldn't go back to digging red wrigglers out of the compost heap. But what about an artificial fly that imitates a worm? One that's lighter than most nymphs and can be fished on a delicate rod and long, fine leader?

Now you're getting closer. Indeed, many would fish such an offering, and one of the hottest flies to hit the stream in recent years is just that—a strikingly realistic worm imitation called the San Juan Worm.

Actually, it's worth pausing here to consider exactly what this devastating pattern does imitate. Novices assume it strictly duplicates a common garden earthworm. In truth, it does mimic these rather well, and particularly after a rain, some terrestrial earthworms, wrigglers, and nightcrawlers do find their way into rivers where they're consumed by trout.

But the San Juan's similarity to earthworms is largely coincidental. The original flies were tied to duplicate midge larvae and scuds with their thin profile and the curved back of the English bait-style hooks used. Soon the patterns were enlarged and tied to duplicate not the land-dwelling worms but aquatic worms that exist in many streams, particularly tailwaters like the San Juan in New Mexico and Bighorn in Montana. Pull out a bog of weeds in one of these rivers, and you'll see the reddish-pinkish worms wriggling about and understand why a fly imitating them is so effective.

But the San Juan Worm doesn't just imitate different food forms realistically. It also presents a nice clean silhouette to trout and, because it is dressed in such a sparse manner, the fly is able to sink rapidly into the strike zone.

➤➤➤ *Fishing the Worm Flies:* When aquatic worms break loose from weedbeds, they wiggle slightly but for the most part do not swim strongly in the heavy river current. The best presentation is thus a free-floating, or dead-drift, delivery. Cast upstream and slightly across, and allow the fly to float down naturally with the current.

San Juan worms were originally tied to duplicate midge larvae, not earthworms.

You can use any rod from a 4 to 7 weight for this, but optimum would be a 5- or 6-weight, 9-foot rod with a floating double taper or weight forward line. Add a 9-foot leader with a 3X to 5X tippet, then crimp a Size B or BB split-shot to the leader 16 to 20 inches above the fly.

Though not vital, a piece of colorful yarn or plastic foam for a strike indicator does make fishing this and other nymphs easier and more productive. It should be fastened on the leader just below where it joins the flyline, or slightly closer to the fly in shallow water. You want the indicator to stay on or within a few inches of the surface to help you detect strikes and also determine when the line needs mending.

➤➤➤ *The Patterns:* The traditional San Juan fly is tied on an English bait-style hook with a humpback shank, with floss wrapped around the hook and ribbing added. Due to anglers' concern that trout were being injured because of the difficulty of removing this type of curved hook, however, several alternative versions were concocted. The one I find most effective and durable is the Gordie's Worm devised by well-known guide Gordon Rose of the Bighorn.

I know Rose's version of the worm works because in two days on the river with him I took more than 50 fish using this pattern, while also spending much of the time trying other nymphs and dries. The fly is also rugged, sometimes accounting for dozens of fish before becoming mangled.

–Gerald Almy, October 1991

Terrestrial Tips

ALTHOUGH AQUATIC INSECTS have long dominated the philosophy of flyfishing for trout, anglers are now beginning to appreciate the role terrestrials can play in making the experience complete. Some even believe that terrestrials are more interesting to tie and fish, likely because the appearances and habits of these insects are more varied than those of their streamborn counterparts.

While space does not permit a complete listing of the innumerable land-born insects and their appropriate imitations, it's safe to say that the following three types have proved consistently reliable.

➤➤➤ *Ants.* Trout have a particular fondness for ants, probably because they are both prolific and hardy; that is, there are lots of ants available despite extremes of weather. Look under stones along a streambank, soon after the snow melts off, for example, and you'll find ants busy at work. They will still be at it during the final days before snow comes again.

A foam ant is a simple fly to tie.

Ant imitations can be dressed in many styles, most of which are available from retail tiers. The two most popular shades among experienced flyfishermen are black and cinnamon, probably because these are the colors of the most abundant species in nature. To tie an effective ant is as simple as winding a small ball of black fur or polydubbing near the rear of a hook, followed by a couple of turns of black hackle, clipped top and bottom, in the center, and

Color-Code Flies

If you fish nymphs or other wet flies, you have probably tied some with weight added to the hook in order to get down deeper or more quickly. In a crowded fly box, it is difficult to keep flies separated by pattern, let alone by those that are weighted or unweighted.

A simple way to make stream-side fly selection quick and easy is to tie your nymphs using different thread colors. Color coding can also be used to indicate normal weighting or extraheavy weighting.

A good code is black for unweighted flies, red for normal and yellow for extraheavy weight. If the thread color is likely to affect the appearance of the finished fly, use color on the head only.

–James W. Frantz, December 1988

Mount Your Flies

An inexpensive yet attractive display for our favorite fly patterns can easily be made with a decoupage board (available in craft or hobby stores) and stick-on cork dots (sold in hardware departments and used to keep flowerpots or vases from scratching furniture).

The self-adhesive dots can be stacked on top of one another—a stack of four will give you ample clearance for the hackles of most dry flies—and then arranged on the decoupage board in any fashion you desire. Allow plenty of room between cork stacks for the flies and press the dots on firmly. Once the cork is secured, you can give the display a bit of color and class by applying wood stain, varnish, or any other finish.

–Gene Trump, June 1991

then a second, slightly smaller ball of dubbing near the hook eye. These ants can be greased for dry-fly fishing or left untreated to absorb water for wet-fly fishing.

Ants are effective throughout the season, though periods outside major emergences of other insects understandably have the edge. Ant imitations are best presented to trout near streambanks, but fishing ants in center stream can also pay off. Being poor swimmers, ants are carried by the whims of currents and may be encountered by trout virtually anywhere the water goes.

The dead drift is unquestionably the most effective method for fishing ants dry. When several dead-drift presentations fail to induce a rise, however, a slight twitch can sometimes awaken the quarry. When resorting to the twitch, remember to transmit the action only to the fly. If the tippet is allowed to disturb the surface, even the most unsophisticated trout is apt to be put down.

Ants fished wet are also most effective on the dead drift, as they imitate helpless insects that have been swamped by the currents. When fished below the surface, ants tend to be most useful in broken water where naturals are likely to be overcome by water turbulence.

Although large ants (up to No. 10 hooks) are common, trout seem to favor smaller imitations (Sizes 16 to 22), perhaps because smaller imitations can't be given critical inspection by the fish. The best condition in which to fish them is during a wind that's apt to blow significant numbers of naturals from the banks onto the water.

➤➤➤ *Hoppers.* The availability of grasshoppers to trout varies widely by region and anglers can help themselves by pinpointing optimum hopper periods in the areas they intend to fish. Dozens of hopper imitations are currently popular, the best two probably being the Letort Hopper and Dave's Hopper. Both are made of buoyant deer hair, are reasonably easy to dress, and can be bought in a wide range of sizes from most tackleshops.

The famous Dave's Hopper.

Hopper imitations are best fished near spots where naturals fall into the water. A typical location would be a run six to 10 feet out from shore along a stream with grassy banks. Hoppers are usually fished like dry flies; that is, dead drift across stream, across and slightly upstream, or on a loose line across and downstream. While leading fish by several feet can work well, you do even better by dropping your hopper either a few inches upstream of a feeding station or right over a trout's nose. It's important to provide for long downstream drifts with such presentations, as trout often turn and follow hoppers 15 feet before taking them.

Imitation hoppers sometimes undergo careful scrutiny by trout, and the angler must consider the pros and cons before deciding to enhance the action of his fly by moving it in any way. Take extreme care to avoid leader drag that may put trout down. Toward that end, the smallest possible tippet diameter is recommended.

>>> *Beetles.* Hundreds of species of bugs comprise the beetle category. Perhaps the best-known beetle fly pattern is the Jassid, which unfortunately is tied with a jungle cock wing. Because jungle cock cannot be imported and existing supplies are virtually exhausted, the Jassid has become all but impossible to tie commercially. Excellent substitute patterns are available, however, with equally attractive wings fashioned from ruffed grouse or hen pheasant feathers. These alternatives work no less well than the originals, and perhaps even better in large sizes.

A black foam beetle.

Walt Dette of Roscoe, New York, has featured a beetle pattern that has proved effective across the country for 40 years. The fly is begun by tying in a clump of deer hair, dyed brown or black, just forward of the bend of the hook. Peacock herl is wound as a body, and the deer hair is then drawn over the top of the body to form a cased wing. Excess deer hair is clipped square near the hook eye to represent a head, and the top of the wing is lacquered for gloss and durability.

Beetle imitations will take trout throughout the season, though periods when naturals are plentiful should prove best. Because most beetles can fly, it's not necessary for imitations to be fished on any particular part of a stream. If given just one cast, however, I would probably place the beetle in a small side eddy under an overhanging tree where beetles congregate. Beetles are best fished dry, but permitting them to sink as if overcome by currents also works well. A floating beetle's silhouette is very important, and anglers must be sure their flies float low on the surface, preferably with only the cased wing out of the surface film. Initial presentations should be dead drift, leading trout by several feet. If that fails, try progressively shorter leads until, finally, the beetle is slapped right on the trout's nose. Twitching the rod tip should be employed only as a last resort.

—*Art Lee, August 1980*

Getting Antsy

I F FORCED TO select one dry-fly pattern for trout fishing in August across the entire country, the ant would be hard to top. These ubiquitous insects are almost always found in trout streams. Some stumble in, others are blown by wind or washed in by rain showers. They quickly become trout food.

While good aquatic hatches still come off occasionally on our better streams, they usually last only an hour or two a day. Ants, on the other hand, erratically dribble in all day long. And while summer is a peak time for fishing them, ants can produce any time from spring through fall on freestone and limestone streams, tiny beaver ponds, and sprawling lakes.

Whether they offer a special taste appeal or are simply a calorie-rich food, trout consume ants of all sizes and colors. Imitations can range from Sizes 8 to 22, and effective hues include black, brown, russet, tan, or even hot orange— a color that's particularly easy to see. If you don't want to carry such a broad range of sizes, narrow your selection down to Sizes 12 to 18.

▶▶▶ *Patterns to Success:* Whatever style you select, it should have a strongly accentuated thin waist, since this is the physiological feature trout key in on.

▶▶▶ *Sinking Ant.* Ants float remarkably well and most are sipped in by trout when on the surface. But wet patterns do catch lots of fish. They're especially good for freestone mountain streams and brook trout. Tie with a floss or thread body, lacquered heavily to produce a hard ant that sinks fast. Black. Sizes 12 to 16.

▶▶▶ *Fur Ant.* This is the classic ant fly developed by Bob McCaffety in the early 1930s. Two humps of fur separated by a thin waist made with several wraps of hackle. Black, brown. Sizes 14 to 18.

A black fur ant is most effective in the summer, but it can be fished year round.

▶▶▶ *Foam Ant.* Closed-cell foam is a great tying material that floats well and does not require dressing. It has a bit of weight, too, making it nice for splatting onto the water. Black, brown. Sizes 12 to 16.

▶▶▶ *Legged Ant.* This is a fly I developed in the 1970s. Use two oval humps of dubbed rabbit or synthetic fur for the abdomen and head of the fly, separated by a thin waist with three or four bent deer or caribou hairs tied in forlegs.

A legged ant, best used in black, orange, or brown.

The individual hair strands make a more prominent and realistic representation of legs than hackle. A good choice for supercritical fish in difficult spring creeks. Black, orange, brown. Sizes 12 to 18.

▶▶▶ *McMurray Ant:* This fly was invented by Ed Sutryn of McMurray, Pennsylvania, in 1965. It's a pattern so unique that Sutryn patented it.

The McMurray ant invented by Ed Sutryn.

The fly is constructed of two pieces of cork or balsa threaded on a section of monofilament that is attached to a hook, with the hackle wound between the body sections for legs. This fly works best in black and brown. Sizes 10 to 18.

▶▶▶ *Winged Ant:* When ants swarm in the air on mating flights they often

Winged ants can create a feeding frenzy in summer months.

fall to the water in huge numbers and incite ravenous feeding. Tie fur patterns in black, brown, or tan, with hackle tip, polypropylene, or CDC (cul de canard) wings. Sizes 14 to 20.

—Gerald Almy, August 1995

Tighter Deer-hair Wings

When tying off a deer-hair wing, most tiers wrap the thread over the hair in one spot, then trim the hair. That method works, but the hair can work loose and come off the fly. A better method is to wrap the thread through little clumps of the hair as you tie it down with thread. Then the hair, bound in several spots, will hold more securely.
—Deke Meyer, September 1991

When no trout are rising, don't hesitate to fish ants blind in likely holding areas. Especially good are riffles, pocket water, tails of pools, and areas near shore where a tree or brush leans over the water. Long leaders are helpful, and tippets should run 5- to 7X. If a trout is hanging in an area that's hard to reach, try tying on a cork or foam pattern and splatting it gently onto the water, to the side and slightly behind the fish's location. The noise alerts them to a potential meal and they often come cruising over to inspect— and, usually, to eat.

—Gerald Almy, August 1995

Search Flies

ALL FLYFISHERMEN would agree that there's nothing like a good hatch, that eruption of insects and trout that roils the water and the blood. But like an intense thing, hatches are usually short-lived, spanned by long periods of comparative inactivity. In fact, most hours astream are spent facing plain water . . . riffled, seamed, boulder-specked, becalmed . . . but by all surface appearances, troutless. At such times the only way to find fish is to hunt for them; one of the best ways to do this is to use search flies.

Search flies, to define them, are generally flies that have proven effective on a variety of water types throughout the country. These are old (and sometimes new) reliables that will catch browns in the Beaverkill, rainbows on the Bow, and cutthroats on the Green or Flathead. They will catch fish early in the morning, or at midday when the heat is at full bloom—any time when there's no substantial hatch in action, no fish visibly breaking the surface film (or tailing beneath it). Search flies work on riffles and runs, against undercut banks and midstream logs, in pocket water, and in the lane where two disparate flows meet. Search flies may be large and gaudy, impressionistic, imitating nothing specifically but much generally; or they may be realistic, mimicking the more ubiquitous aquatic insects.

One category of search flies is the attractor group. These tend to be the larger types—Size 8 to 14—and are minimally representative of actual insects. Some favorites in the dry fly are the Brown Bivisible, Hairwing Royal Wulff (or Coachman), Goofus Bug, and Ugly Rudamus. What exactly these bushy, ungainly flies represent to trout is anybody's guess. But trout tend to like these patterns, especially in broken currents, and often rise to them eagerly when no native insects are in sight.

Another category of dry search flies includes the realistic patterns, those that attempt to imitate certain abundant and common insects. The Adams is a good example. As a mayfly pattern it's effective nearly anywhere (though the fisherman may have to experiment with sizes). For a general caddis imitation try an Elk Hair Caddis or Henryville Special. These more realistic search flies are especially suited to calmer, more unbroken waters (pools or gentle runs in spring creeks); places where the larger, gaudier attractor patterns might alarm more fish than they lure. Other realistic flies are more regionally oriented. I've found, for example, that black-and-yellow bee patterns, made from high-floating deerhair, are good search flies for the summer trout streams of Wisconsin and Michigan; I've not had much luck with them in the West, however.

The main benefit of search flies is the sheer fun of using them. Most are large and easy to see, and easy to keep afloat. You cast them to likely water and follow the drift, making sure there's no unwanted drag, mending when necessary, using reach and/or curve casts to maximize the drag-free float. Trout often rise with reckless abandon to the big attractors, and that's more fun. Sometimes, however, especially when the water is slow or the day bright, the fish will move up to the fly but pull away at the last moment. This is unnerving at first, but to your advantage in the long run. Remember, these are search flies; their job is to hunt trout when none are visible. So if an attractor pattern teases but fails to hook a fish, you've at least confirmed the whereabouts of a target.

Less visually interesting but still enjoyable and productive are underwater search flies. There are many possibilities here—too many to list. In the West a favorite example is the Woolly Bugger, which can be fished against the banks (tossed in close and twitched back) or weighted and used to plumb the deeper runs and riffles. Another is the Woolly Worm, especially in lime green, which can imitate all kinds of stream fodder, and which all trout find alluring when drifted near the surface, twitched in pocket water, or bounced in runs.

One of the best flies ever invented is the Muddler Minnow, which in the original brown design can imitate a sculpin, a stonefly, and, more vaguely, a grasshopper and perhaps even a caddis. Variations in the basic pattern—in color and materials, especially marabou—give this fly an incredible range and effectiveness. Muddlers are fun to fish, too, because it's hard to fish them incorrectly. If they float, they can be pitched like dry flies, fished without drag. If they sink, they can be twitched broadside to the current like streamers; if they sink deeply, they can be free-floated, tumbled along like nymphs.

–Anthony Acerrano, June 1988

Meet the Beetles

TERRESTRIALS—PATTERNS THAT imitate land insects—have been inaccurately labeled as summer flies by many anglers. And that's unfortunate, because they can actually provide superb fishing starting in April or May in most regions.

Land insects manage to stumble, jump, and get blown by wind or washed by rain into streams and lakes countless times every day. When they do, they quickly become trout food. Ants, crickets, true bugs, leafhoppers, bees, caterpillars, and a variety of other insects become significant items in the diet of trout as soon as fish begin rising in spring, and they remain so through repeated frosts in autumn.

Few land insects, though, are as important to trout as beetles. Well over 300,000 species of beetles have been identified, making *Coleoptera* the largest order in the animal kingdom.

A foam beetle can solicit strikes if it hits the water with a slight "splat."

I once caught a trout on Yellow Creek in Pennsylvania that had at least seven different species of beetles in its stomach, ranging from match-head-size to some as big as a thumbnail. For angling purposes flies ranging from Size 8 to 20 will match the most common species.

➤➤➤ *Fishing the Beetle:* Two methods can be effective for fishing beetles. If you see fish rising delicately to small foods, tie on a Size 16 to 20 beetle, cast above the fish, and let the pattern drift in traditional dry-fly fashion with a drag-free float.

For pounding up fish that aren't rising, prospecting likely holding lies, or casting to fish lying tight against the bank, try a different approach. I developed the sound cast for this type of fishing 20 years ago, and it still produces well today. Use a heavy fly such as a cork, foam, or deer-hair beetle, Size 8 to 14, and cast it with an overpowered forward stroke so the fly lands with a slight splat. It can hit to the side or slightly behind where the fish is hovering but should not be presented above it.

The gentle plop of the fly alerts the fish that an insect has tumbled in from land. More often than not it will whirl around, speed to the source of the sound, and sip in your fraud. Having the fly land to the side or behind takes the trout by surprise and elicits an instinctive strike before its sense of caution and wariness takes over.

—Gerald Almy, May 1994

Blue-Winged Olives

WHEN MY MIND drifts back to memorable hatches I've fished, none compare with the tiny Blue-Winged Olive or Baetis mayflies. There were days when the Olives emerged so strongly and fish rose so heartily that trout fishing dreams became reality. I even fished a tremendous grayling rise once on a plunging northern Saskatchewan river where the smoky-winged Olives emerged by the thousands on a cold, gray, shower-swept day.

And that's another thing: They often emerge heaviest and draw the strongest feeding from trout when the air is leaden and showers spit from the sky or late winter snowflakes rush sideways through the air.

A Blue-Winged Olive (top) and a Blue-Winged Olive emerger. Olives are especially effective in the spring, but look for a hatch to occur during any month.

Spring is an excellent time to find Olives on the water, but they can emerge any month. Often they overshadow more heralded hatches, such as Quill Gordons or Hendricksons.

You can find Baetis on neutral pH streams, but they do best in alkaline waters. Spring creeks and tailwaters are prime; areas with vegetation and shallow gravel runs are also good.

Sizes of the various members of this genus can range from 4mm to 10mm, matched by hook Sizes 14 to 24. The most common sizes are 16 to 20.

Midafternoon is best for Olives. Look for hatches as the water nears 50°F.

Nymphs of Baetis are slender and quite active. Imitations of them can be effective shortly before a hatch or during its early stages. A Pheasant Tail pattern works well. Once duns start popping out, switch to emergers. As the hatch progresses, switch to full dun patterns with erect wings. A traditional pattern may work, but I've had better results with parachute, comparadun, thorax, and no-hackle dressings. The bodies of these flies can range from intense olive to a dark grayish brown. You can tie a variety of colors to match these or simply blend all three fur colors into an amalgam that works well for all Baetis hatches. Wings should be medium to dark gray.

Nymph and dun fishing may last several hours, but spinner falls can also provide good fishing. Use a rusty brown colored body with gray clipped hackles or polyproylene wings to imitate these mating insects, which return between late afternoon and early evening. At times a subsurface pattern such as a Blue Dun wet fly produces during spinner falls. Use a 10- to 14-foot leader tapering to 5 to 7X tippet and a 2- to 5-weight rod.

—Gerald Almy, April 1994

Flytying Material as Close as Your Pet

Hair obtained from your pet cat or dog can be excellent flytying material. Next time Tabby or Fido is snoozing on the porch, quietly sneak up and cut a snip of fur with scissors. Tie this sample and see if it meets your expectations. If it works, you will now have a source of hackle; just don't get too enthusiastic or you'll end up with a very funny-looking pet! Another source is the mane or tail hair from horses and cattle; this coarser and thicker hair is great for tying on jigs.

—Thomas C. Tabor, June 1993

Dry-Fly Indicator

When trout are feeding on small, dark flies on the surface, you should offer them an artificial similar in size and color. The problem, particularly around dusk, is seeing the nearly invisible offering and detecting when a strike comes. My solution is to borrow a technique from nymph fishermen and tie a small tuft of white or fluorescent orange polypropylene yarn to the leader.

Using a 2-pound monofilament tippet material, knot a two-inch piece of the bright poly yarn to the leader above the first blood or barrel knot connection. Then cut the yarn back to about half-inch total length and apply a dab of flotant to the yarn. By watching the ruft of highly visible yarn rather than the hard-to-see fly, you'll easily spot movement signaling you to strike. Casting will not be greatly affected by the small bit of yarn.

—Robert Drew, August 1991

Hit the Hendrickson Hatch

THE EARLIEST SURFACE fishing often centers on midges and tiny Baetis flies. It's a welcome sight to find a few stray heads sipping in these insects, but if you want to see a river at its ultimate with every trout in a frenzy, be on a good stretch of water this spring when the Hendricksons emerge.

Ephemerella subvaria stimulates some of the best surface fishing of the year on eastern and midwestern streams. They are big flies that quickly fill a trout's belly, and they can hatch in incredible numbers early in the season.

Use a Hendrickson Thorax (top) or a Red Quill (bottom) to imitate Hendrickson duns.

From mid-April to early May, when water temperatures reach 50 to 55°F, look for nymph activity from noon to 1:00 P.M., and hatching between 2:00 and 4:00 P.M. Toward evening, spinner-falls occasionally stimulate a brief but impressive feeding binge.

For duns, you can imitate the reddish-brown color of the male or the yellow-tannish-olive hue of the female, Size 12 or 14. Good styles are the Thorax, Parachute, Sparkle Dun, and Comparadun, though in riffly sections Art Flick's Red Quill and Roy Steenrod's Hendrickson patterns still produce. For spinners, tie a clipped hackle or a polypropylene down-wing pattern with a brown body. Use a 4- to 6X tippet on a 10- to 12-foot leader, and get set for some of the greatest dry-flyfishing of the year.

—Gerald Almy, April 1995

Fit to Be Tied

EXPERTS CAN ARGUE for hours over the merits of No-hackle versus Parachute or Thorax versus Sparkle Dun patterns. But all these intricacies can leave the less experienced angler a bit befuddled. What if you just want a dozen proven fish-catchers that will fool trout on streams throughout the country? Here are my picks.

Streamers:

>>> *Wooly Bugger.* Tied with a chenille body overlaid with palmered hackle and a marabou tail, the Woolly Bugger is about as multipurpose a fly as you can get. Worked at the proper depth with the right rod movement, it represents a myriad of creatures trout feed on—dace, tiny catfish, sculpins, crayfish, leeches, or large nymphs. Stock weighted and unweighted versions, and fish them down and across with subtle twitches or dead-drift with an upstream delivery. Black/olive and black; Sizes 2 to 8.

>>> *Zonker.* This flashy fly tied with a Mylar body and a thin strip of rabbit hide and fur on the top is a hot ticket for trout. When fish are in minnow-feeding mode, use Zonkers with snappy 12-inch strips of line, keeping the rod tip low to the water. Pearl, olive, black; Sizes 2 to 8.

Nymphs:

>>> *Gold-Ribbed Hare's Ear.* The most popular-selling nymph of all time, the Hare's Ear well represents the immature life state of many insects. The dull grayish-brown fur is highlighted by a touch of gold ribbing that gives it flash and a natural segmented look. Fish weighted with a strike indicator in deep water, or grease your leader down to the last few inches and use as an emerging nymph rising to the surface film. Sizes 10 to 16.

>>> *Bead-Head Pheasant Tail.* No other innovation in nymph tying has had more impact in the last decade than adding a small metal bead at the head of the pattern. The solid brass bead gets the fly down fast and gives it a metallic sparkle as it drifts along the bottom. Sizes 12 to 18.

>>> *Bitch Creek Nymph.* This great stonefly pattern pounds up big fish on western waters and large eastern rivers. The white rubber legs and antennae add a quivering motion to the fly when it's twitched lightly. Sizes 4 to 8.

>>> *San Juan Worm.* In its most basic form, this simple fly consists of a piece of chenille tied on a hook so it extends out both the front and back. Dead-drift it through runs, pockets, and pool tailouts. Deadly in tailwaters. Red or maroon; Sizes 8 to 12.

Dries:

>>> *Adams.* The gray body, brown and grizzly hackle, and grizzly-tip wings imitate a myriad of mayfly species. If you can't match the hatch, tie on an appropriate-sized Adams and you'll usually catch at least a few fish. It's also good with the bottom hackle clipped flat during spinner falls or in parachute version for finicky slick-water risers. Sizes 12 to 20.

>>> *Blue-Winged Olive.* No other mayfly pattern seems to stir as much consistent rising from big trout. The Blue-Winged Olive imitates both the

important Baetis species as well as the tiny pseudocloeons. Especially good on overcast and drizzly days. Sizes 16 to 24.

➤➤➤ *Elk Hair Caddis.* Most flyfishermen consider this to be the best all-around caddis pattern. Tied with a dubbed body, palmered hackle, and elk hair wing, it floats like a cork and gives a perfect silhouette of a caddis. It's also good for selective trout when tied without the hackle. Olive, tan, gray; Sizes 12 to 20.

➤➤➤ *Ant.* Whether it's tied with fur, foam, balsa, or cork, the main criteria are a thin, pinched-in waist and two distinct humps front and back to represent the head and the abdomen. Black is best, but also stock cinnamon and hot orange; Sizes 12 to 22.

➤➤➤ *Beetle.* Drop a foam, deer hair, or cork beetle just behind and to the side of a shore-hugging trout with a tiny splat and you can enjoy some amazing fishing from April through October. Black; Sizes 10 to 18.

➤➤➤ *Hopper.* Use any number of patterns, including the Letort, Dave's, Joe's, Henry's Fork, or MacHopper. It's also good on eastern streams, though a black cricket is often more productive. Sizes 8 to 16.

—Gerald Almy, March 1997

Matching Fly to Tippet

ONE OF THE old-fashioned ways to decide what fly size to use for a particular tippet is to multiply the tippet size by four and use a fly of that size or one step larger or smaller. For a 6X tippet, sizes 24, 22, and 26 would be the traditionally recommended flies.

Unfortunately, this calculating technique and the published charts found in most fly-fishing books were compiled when the strength and quality of tippet materials was far below today's standards. Also, most of those earlier flies imitated mayflies, which tend to twist light, fine leader tippets.

Many of today's popular fly patterns imitate terrestrial insects and caddis flies, which generally lack the projecting wings that twist fine tippets. These two factors often make it possible to use far lighter tippets with a given size fly than is normally recommended by the published charts. The converse is also true: you can use much larger flies on lighter tippets than is traditionally suggested.

The table below suggests tippet and fly sizes adapted to today's strong, thin-diameter leader material. Of course, the final test is in the twist. If you tie a No. 14 fly on a 7X tippet and it twists the leader, you have two recourses: cut back to a heavier tippet or go to a smaller fly. For most fishing situations and patterns, however, this chart is a valuable guide.

Tippet Size	Diameter	Fly Size
4X	*.007*	*6, 8, 10, 12*
5X	**.006**	**6, 8, 10, 12, 14**
6X	*.005*	*10, 12, 14, 16, 18*
7X	**.004**	**14, 16, 18, 20, 22, 24**
8X	*.003*	*18, 20, 22, 24, 26, 28*

—Gerald Almy, April 1983

The Tiniest Hatch

AN EARLY SPRING SNOW shower didn't affect the regular head-to-tail porpoising rises of the trout at all. In fact, the overcast skies and light snow seemed to encourage them. When the rises had started an hour earlier, I'd overheard a nearby angler grumble.

"Might as well head home. They're on the little stuff now," he said. Twenty minutes later he was gone.

The "little stuff" he was talking about were tiny insects called midges, and he wasn't the first early season flyfisherman I've seen leave the river in disgust when trout were rising to them.

Midges are small and it does take a little practice to get used to fishing flies a quarter of an inch or less in length, but it beats heading home. Besides, in many parts of the country the season's first rising trout will be coming up to midges.

Midges hatch year-round, and what they lack in size they make up for in numbers. A particularly rich trout stream may have as many as 50,000 midges per square meter! Even the largest trout can't resist a food source so abundant.

Anglers used to call any tiny insect a "midge," but in recent years the term has become more specific, referring to tiny two-winged aquatic insects of the order *Diptera*. Midges are found in waters across the United States and commonly range in length from three to eight millimeters. An exception is the "giant" midges that grow as large as one inch and are found in some western lakes and reservoirs.

Biologists call the midge's development a "complete metamorphosis," which means there is an egg, larval, pupal, and adult stage. Trout feed heavily on every stage except the tiny egg.

Midge larvae are wormlike in appearance. Trout often root around beds of aquatic vegetation or "vacuum" silty or muddy bottoms in slow-moving water in search of them. Although midge larvae are most often found crawling along the streambed or lakebottom, they also get caught up in the stream's drift,

Leave Room for Tying the Head

When tying a fly, novices often forget to leave enough room to tie the head. Develop the habit of starting the thread a little way back from the hookeye. The bare spot on the hook will act as a reminder to leave room for the head.
—Deke Meyer, December 1989

where trout pick them off. At times large numbers are found drifting downstream and are highly vulnerable to trout.

Trout feeding on midge larvae are best caught using standard dead-drift nymphing techniques. Weight should be attached to the leader about six to 12 inches above the larva imitation. A brightly colored floating strike indicator is then attached farther up the leader. The nymphing rig is cast upstream and allowed to bounce along bottom in a natural fashion with the current. Any hesitation or unusual movement of the strike indicator signals a strike.

Flies tied to imitate midge larvae should highlight the larva's segmentation, color, and size. Most larvae can be imitated in a No. 16 to 22 hook size. Common colors are white, olive, gray, bright red, and brown.

The most exciting midge fishing occurs when the larvae mature to pupae and finally emerge as adult midges. Pupae of the most common family of trout stream midges, the *Chironomidae*, have distinct heads, thoraxes, and gills. A pupa matures in about a week and then swims to the water's surface, where the flying adult midge emerges. Trout feed heavily on the midges throughout this final transformation.

On the stream you'll know a midge hatch is imminent when you see trout flashing and darting around underwater as they chase the pupae swimming to the surface. This is a good time to switch to a pupa imitation with a soft-hackle or flashy sparkle yarn husk. At the beginning of the hatch a midge pupa can be effectively fished with dead-drift nymphing techniques. A two-fly dropper system using a larva imitation with a pupa imitation on the point is deadly.

When the trout begin rising to the surface, it's best to switch to dry-fly tactics. The key is to determine whether the trout are taking midge pupae or actually feeding on midge adults. Take a few minutes to observe the hatched adults as they float downstream. In many cases you'll note that the trout ignore them. That means they're taking pupae. It's not uncommon for trout to concentrate on pupae for much of the hatch. Adult midge imitations are often most effective toward the end of the hatch.

Fishing midge pupae imitations is similar to fishing standard, larger dry-fly patterns, except the fly will be too small to see. If you grease the entire leader (not the fly) with a paste floatant, you will be able to watch the floating leader for strikes. When it moves unnaturally, set the hook—gently. Striking too hard, whether you're nymphing or fishing on the water's surface, will break the delicate 6X and 7X tippets necessary for midging. Many anglers simply lift the rod tip, which is enough to allow a small hook to penetrate.

You'll find that midging trout tend to hold to very tight feeding lanes.

Your casts must be accurately placed about a foot upstream from the rising trout. Midging trout also have definite feeding rhythms; try to time your cast to coincide with the rises. Your success will increase dramatically the closer you can position yourself to the rising trout. Shorter casts mean less line on the water, greater accuracy, and the ability to see your fly more clearly on the water.

New-generation rods designed for lightweight flylines have improved midge fishermen's chances of landing larger trout on delicate terminal tackle. But even with the high-tech advances, remember that you may still have to give line to a trout on its first run or two to protect the tippet. Tippets in the 6X and 7X range should be a minimum of three feet long. The extra length allows the tippet to stretch, which significantly increases its strength.

Getting all this down does take a little work. Expect to break off some trout until you get used to the light terminal tackle. Figure to make a lot of casts until you learn the timing of the rises. Accept the occasional exasperation when midging trout turn picky and don't want anything in your flybox. Just remember that trout rise to midges year-round. Eventually you'll start catching trout on the days when other fishermen go home because the little stuff is on.

—Ed Engle, February 1992

A Midge Fisherman's Fly Box

THE KEYS TO successful midge fly patterns are simplicity and variety. Some of the best patterns are little more than thread and a hackle. Carry a variety of colors and sizes of flies that imitate the larval, pupal, and adult midge phases. Here are a few proven midge fly patterns for each phase of the midge's life cycle.

➤➤➤ *Midge Larva.* These imitations can be as simple as a little fur, thread, or even copper wire wrapped around the hook (remember that larva are wormlike). Red, olive, white, yellow, and gray are good colors. Successful patterns include the following:

South Platte Brassie: Hook No. 16 to 22. Copper wire (small gauge) wrapped over hook shank. Muskrat thorax optional.

South Platte Brassie.

Miracle Nymph: Hook No. 18 to 24. White silk body, copper wire rib.

Miracle Nymph.

Red Midge Larva: Hook No. 16 to 22. Body of bright red thread or dyed red fur. Rib with small-gauge wire.

Red Midge Larva.

➤➤➤ *Midge Pupa.* The pupa in an active stage. It swims to the water's surface and then hangs there as the adult midge struggles from the pupal shuck. Marabou, sparkle yarn, or peacock herl captures the movement and flash of the pupa on its way to the surface. Pupal color varies, but gray, black, olive, or yellow is often successful.

Green Machine: Hook No. 18 to 24. Body chartreuse silk, silver rib. Peacock herl collar.

Green Machine.

➤➤➤ *Adults.* There are two types of midge adults: those that have emerged but are still trailing the pupal shuck, and fully emerged adults. Fly patterns that include a thin trailing shuck of polypropylene yarn or soft partridge feathers can be deadly. Bright red, orange, or yellow thread-bodied dry flies with a simple hackle sometimes work.

Kimball's Emerger: Hook No. 20 to 26. Tie black thorax on front half of hook. White polypropylene yarn is pulled over top of thorax to form a humped wing case. Tail is partridge tied long to represent trailing shuck.

Kimball's Emerger.

Griffith's Gnat: Hook No. 18 to 26. Peacock herl body. Grizzly hackle tied palmer-style through body.

Griffith's Gnat.

No-Name Midge: Hook No. 20 to 26. Body is muskrat fur. Grizzly hackle.

No-Name Midge.

—Ed Engle, February 1992

Spring Trout High and Dry

LOOK OUT THERE. It's cold. It's wet. Maybe it's snowing . . . and the trout are rising. Not just here and there—everywhere. Finally, the fish are on the move, provoked by the tan multitudes crawling along the banks and the bushes and down the neck of your sweater: caddisflies.

Better get to fishing. This won't last long. But while it does, the annual spring caddis hatch can provide the best dry-fly fishing of the year. If any hatch brings large fish to the surface, this one will; the downside (isn't there always a downside?) is that there are few hatches quite so dependent upon the weather.

➤➤➤ *Timing Is Everything.* Caddisflies aren't the first flies to hatch each spring—midges, for instance, hatch year-round—but they're often the most noticeable flies after a winter spent fishing midge imitations over lethargic browns. Depending on the area, some caddis hatches may begin as early as March, and some as late as May. Some peter out after only a few days, and some last until mid-summer.

Hitting the hatch just right usually means staying one step ahead of the weather. Warm afternoons may bring the bugs out earlier than usual but increase runoff, while cool weather may delay the hatch but keep flows fishable, if not crystal-clear. Around my neck of the woods (southwestern Montana), the traditional beginning of the spring caddis hatch is Mother's Day, or right around the second week of May. Unfortunately, spring runoff,

Flies That Float Longer

Usually dry-fly fishermen dress their flies with flotant just before they cast them to a fish. A few false-casts are considered sufficient to dry the fly, but that is not really enough. The fly is only partially dried and will not float nearly as well as it could.

The time to dress a dry fly is when you are tying it, while it's still in the vise. Rub paste flotant into the body dubbing before winding the dubbing onto the hook. A fly dressed this way will float three to four times as long as one dressed just before it hits the water.

If you prefer a liquid flotant to a paste, soak the fly after it's tied and dry it before it goes into your fly box.

If you buy your flies instead of tying them, you can still treat them with paste or liquid flotant. Just let them dry thoroughly before you fish them.

—Dave Hughes, August 1987

which also begins around Mother's Day, invariably dumps a mountain of mud into the Yellowstone and other big rivers in the area, quickly obliterating the fishing, if not the hatch itself. Yet those willing to dance around snow squalls and marginal water can usually squeeze a few days or even weeks of fishing before the rivers are completely blown out. Generally speaking, once flows are chocolate-covered, fishing is a lost cause. But as long as there's a foot or two of visibility, you'll still be able to take trout.

Although most anglers fish nymphs while waiting for a hatch to commence, caddis dries sometimes produce as well between hatches as during them, particularly on small streams. One effective technique is to wade slowly along the bank, casting a dry upstream and toward the bank as you go. Caddisflies swarm on bankside willows and brush, and the trout will be accustomed to picking off stragglers that drop into the water.

➤➤➤ *The Caddis Shuffle.* After congregating in the bushes along the bank, female caddisflies return to the river and flutter above the surface as they lay eggs. Trout take them with hard, splashy rises—the classic "slashing" rises we've all read about.

Dead-drifted dries will certainly draw strikes in the midst of a hatch, but when the action slows, try skittering your fly to add realism. To accomplish this, quarter your cast downstream, using a curve cast or mending the line in such a way that the leader extends upstream, above the fly. As you pattern drifts within range of a trout's sight window, twitch it once or twice, no more than an inch or so each time. A spun-deer-hair pattern, like the Goddard caddis, works best.

Left to Right: Elk Hair Caddis, Goddard Caddis, CDC (Cul de Canard) Caddis.

Although there are dozens of caddis patterns, a few common flies in a few common sizes will work nearly anywhere. Caddisflies come in four shades: light tan, slate, black, and olive. Flies tied on No. 12, 14, and 16 hooks will match most hatches, with No. 14 perhaps the most common. The Goddard Caddis, mentioned above, is a fine all-around fly for heavy water, as is the classic Elk Hair Caddis, which may use wings dyed to match the color of local bugs. A Henryville Caddis or a similar pattern with slate wings will also work when a darker pattern is called for. Although they're not really caddis patterns, many experienced anglers also keep a supply of Humpy or Double Humpy patterns on hand. Both will pass for caddisflies, and their upright wings provide a bit more versatility during heavy hatches.

>>> *Can It Be Good?* You bet it can. A common complaint—which is hard to believe if you've never experienced a full-contact, no-holds-barred spring caddis hatch—is that, during the hatch, the overwhelming number of bugs on the water make spotting an imitation impossible.

Under such daunting conditions, almost anything you try will be more miss than hit, but a few tricks may help. First, be there just as the hatch begins. When the hatch is building, you'll find fewer insects on the water and more receptive trout. Second, make a strike indicator with a tuft of yarn tied several feet up the leader. Rub the yarn between your fingers to form a ball and grease it thoroughly. When you see a rise anywhere near your indicator, strike. Third, tie your patterns with fluorescent orange wings of some sort. Orange Antron Body Wool can be layered over a standard elk-hair caddis wing. The visibility of even a tiny tuft of orange is startling. Fourth, switch to a different, larger pattern—perhaps a Humpy or Royal Wulff. Fifth, add a two-inch dropper and nymph to a buoyant dry. When the dry twitches, strike.

—Dave Carty, April 1994

How to Pick the Right Fly

THE PROBLEM OF knowing when to use what fly is one of the most baffling an angler has to solve. There are times when it is easy. When a good hatch is coming off and you can see the trout taking the floating insects, then a dry fly is obviously the answer. But for every time this has happened there will be many others when the solution is far more difficult.

>>> *When to Use Nymphs.* Whenever trout break the surface, apparently rising, but there are no insects on it, they are probably feeding on nymphs. An artificial nymph is the best bet to catch them.

Even when a good hatch of mayflies is coming off, the trout sometimes feed on the rising nymphs in preference to the adult flies. They frequently catch nymphs barely beneath the surface and the breaks they make are hard to tell from actual rises. This is called "bulging."

Usually if you watch closely you can see that bulging trout arch partly out of the water, something like a porpoise. Part of their backs and their dorsal fins often show. Occasionally, you can see their tails as they turn down.

These signs are not infallible, however. I have seen trout taking floating insects much the same way. At other times it was impossible to distinguish the breaks made by nymph-feeding trout from genuine rises.

One time on the Teton River we started fishing while a terrific hatch of small blue-dun mayflies was coming off. There were millions of them and the trout were dimpling the water like hail. Naturally, our first thought was a dry fly. We tried three or four apiece—as I recall, I used a No. 16 Blue Dun, a No. 18 Iron Blue Dun, a No. 14 Quill Gordon, and some other small, dark fly.

Finally, it dawned on us that the trout couldn't possibly be taking floating insects. If they were we surely would have had at least one strike.

We put on small nymphs and began to catch trout as soon as we discovered how to fish them. They had to drift in a natural-looking way, no more than an inch or two beneath the surface. A greased line, a leader greased except for the last 30 inches, and a nymph fished like a dry fly was the solution. Even though the trout broke water only 10 to 15 feet away, nothing indicated that they were not actually rising. The tip-off was that we could not take them on dry flies.

It is a fortunate thing for the angler that trout don't feed like people. One man may go into a restaurant and order a steak. The next may want chicken, and so on. But when you discover that one trout is eating a particular mayfly, you can be sure that all the others are, too. Furthermore, the odds are 100 to one that the trout will continue to do so until conditions change. Then they will all begin to take something else.

➤➤➤ *When to Use Streamers.* One morning I began fishing a stream near the Vermont-New York line shortly after it was light enough to see. By mid-morning I still had caught nothing. There had been a shower during the night. The water was up a few inches and slightly discolored, but it certainly was neither too high nor too muddy for good fishing with either wet or dry flies. I didn't see a trout rise, however, and not a single one hit any of my wet flies.

Finally, while I was standing on a gravel bar near the tail of a pool wondering what to try next, I saw a trout chase a minnow out into water only a few inches deep.

That was the clue I needed. I put on a No. 8 Marabou streamer and had terrific sport for the rest of the day. I think every trout that saw it struck, and I would have had three or four times the legal limit if I had not released all but a couple of the best ones. I've had good fishing with a streamer several times since under similar conditions, and I owe it all to that chance observation.

Previously, I had thought that bucktails and streamers were early spring flies and that they had outlived their usefulness by the time the streams went down in early summer. Actually, they occasionally are even more effective in July or August. Sometimes a slight increase of water starts the trout chasing minnows. At other times they don't need any excuse at all. I have taken trout on streamers when the water was just about as low and warm as it ever gets. Possibly a halt in insect activity at this time causes the trout to look for other food.

>>> *When to Use Dries.* Dry flies, which I consider the easiest of all to fish, are also the most fun. Ordinarily, deciding when to use one is no problem. You fish dry when the trout are taking floating insects. When a big hatch of one particular kind is coming off, it usually is the best bet to attempt to match it. When trout are feeding on a wide variety, you can imitate any of their foods or occasionally catch them on something entirely different.

There is another condition under which dry flies are often successful. Sometimes when the water is clear, reasonably low, and neither hot nor extremely cold, a dry fly provides the best way to catch trout, even though there is no sign of surface feeding. I have had good sport many times when the only rises I saw all day were to my own fly. One particular instance stands out in memory.

Ernest Anderson and I began fishing the St. Maries River in northern Idaho when the dawn mists were rising from the water. We both tied on dry flies, more, I think, because we liked to use them than from any logical reason. Not a trout rose while we were assembling our tackle, nor did we see any surface activity all day. Yet we had wonderful sport and we kept four trout apiece, none of which was smaller than 16 inches.

The amazing thing was this: Every trout we caught was gorged with crawfish. They were so full that their bellies were lumpy. Still they took our dry flies. Possibly a floating insect struck them as a nice tidbit for dessert.

When a stream looks as though a dry fly should work but no trout are rising, suggestive patterns that resemble nothing in particular are at their best. In the East, I have had good luck with various spiders, especially a Badger Spider. It is a taking fly. Farther west I have usually done better with a Brown Bivisible, Gray Hackle, or Royal Coachman—although all of these flies work very well clear across the country.

—*Ted Trueblood,* Sports Afield Fishing Annual, *1954*

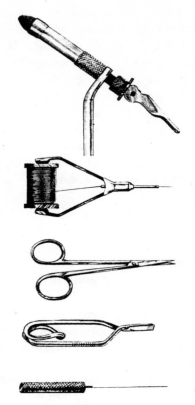

Flytying

Learn to tie your own flies and you will not only become a better flyfisherman—you will have more fun.

Getting Started Flytying

FLYTYING EXTENDS THE pleasure of flyfishing. While I'm wrapping the tail, dubbing the body, and winding the hackle, trout rise to the Adams clamped in my vise. Yet there are more reasons for tying than winter dreams; there are subtle and compelling reasons. Flies are pleasant to hold. They make excellent gifts, attractive displays, and they take trout. Tying broadens your understanding of the world of insects. That, in turn, makes you a better angler, allowing you to match the insect hatch more closely and handle angling conditions more effectively. A pattern may be weighted for heavy water or tied sparsely for reluctant trout. A tier can also create his own patterns.

Furthermore, despite the initial cost of equipment and materials, tying can save you money in the long run. The typical dry fly, such as the Adams, costs about $1.25 retail. According to *The Metz Book of Tackle* by Eric Leiser, the commonly used No. 2 generic grizzly cape has 662 hackles ranging from Sizes 10 to 28. If the neck costs about $35, then the average hackle costs about 5 cents. And there are still 190 usable hackles left on the cape. The total cost of making an Adams might then be calculated as follows: Figure that two dry-fly hackles cost about 10 cents; one dry-fly hook is 4.7 cents; fur dubbing is 1.2 cents; and two hackle tip wings and tail fibers are 10 cents each. The total cost is thus 25.9 cents per fly.

A nymph pattern with a dubbed body, wet-fly hook, hackle fiber tail, and wing case can cost as little as 8 cents. If you tie just simple patterns with modest equipment, you can really save money. For example, I regard myself as an average angler who fishes spring creeks, freestone rivers, and lakes. In four vest-sized boxes, I tote 916 flies, including dries, wets, nymphs, and streamers. When you consider that the average angler probably carries more than 50 flies in his vest, tying becomes thrift. However, many serious tiers who experiment with tools and materials find more pleasure in tying than just saving money. Simply, tying your own flies is the most practical method of filling your fly boxes with the imitations that trout take in the waters you fish.

Flytying is the wrapping of thread over various materials, such as furs and feathers, to bind them to the backbone of a hook. Through size, shape, and color, the flies imitate the various foods—the mayfly, caddis, stonefly, midge, dragonfly, damselfly, shrimp, grasshopper, ant, and small fish—that trout feed upon. A fly pattern usually consists of several parts: the tail, the body, the wings, and the hackle. If the pattern is a dry fly, the tail and hackle, which respectively represent the tail and legs of the insect, support the pattern on the water surface. Thus it imitates those insects adrift on the currents. Other patterns, such as nymphs, streamers, and shrimp, represent creatures that move beneath the surface. The tier can imitate not only the various insects and crustaceans, but also the various stages of some insects, such as the larva, nymph, dun (the newly hatched mayfly), and adult.

▶▶▶ *Tools:* The beginning tier may be confused over what seems to be a bewildering array of tying tools. Fortunately, only a modest collection is necessary: a tying vise, fine-tipped scissors, hackle pliers, thread, and bobbin.

Stronger Herl Bodies

Many effective trout flies use peacock as the body material, just as many Atlantic salmon flies incorporate ostrich herl. These materials have a somewhat weak stem, however, and often break during wrapping or when fished. Twisting three or four strands of herl with round or oval tinsel will make the herl much stronger.

–Deke Meyer, May 1992

Double Whip Finish Saves Flies

Most flytiers finish the fly with a five- or six-wrap whip finish. A better system is to use two sets of three wraps and two separate whip finishes. Following heavy casting, it's time to sharpen the hook and check the condition of the fly. With the separate whip finish approach, often just the top has frayed and come unraveled. Instead of being thrown away, the fly should be saved and another head whip finished later. The is especially true with durable flies such as Wulffs, Humpies, and Muddlers.

–Deke Meyer, March 1987

The purpose of the vise is to hold the hook securely while the materials are wrapped onto the hook shank. The hook must not move during tying. Features to look for in a vise include maximum hook hold with minimal adjustments. I prefer a pedestal vise, one with a weighted base. The base avoids C-clamp mounting problems, and allows me to tilt the vise during tying. A nonglare, matte finish eases eyestrain during long hours of tying. On any vise the knurling should be clean and precise. The threads should be fine and adequately deep to prevent backoff. The finish should be durable. Chromed jaws are not usually recommended because they reflect light and flake at the edge when under pressure. Vises, both domestic and imported, may range from $25 to more than $200.

A vise that clamps to a table is often not as sturdy as a free-standing vise.

Tying scissors should have a smooth shear action, fine tips for close cutting, large finger loops for comfort, and a short length (about 4 1/2 inches) for control. An adjustable screw pivot allows tightening of the blades. Those scissors with serrated edges are excellent for cutting synthetics and deer hair. The serrations trap the fibers in the closing V so the material is cut rather than pushed away. No single pair of scissors should do all the cutting; coarse materials such as moose mane and tinsels require heavier shears for yeoman duty. This will prolong the life of the more expensive and delicate tying scissors. There are many fine scissors on the tying market, with prices ranging from about $12 to $25. It makes sense to buy the best pair you can afford.

Hackle pliers, a spring clip used to hold the hackle during winding, must have smooth, well-matched jaws that hold firmly without slipping or cutting the tender hackle tip. Some tiers prefer heavy tackle pliers for spinning dubbing. To spin dubbing, place the fur or hair in a thread loop and attach the heavy hackle pliers to the end. Spin the pliers and wrap the resulting "chenilled" strand on for a fly body. All pliers should have adequate weight to hold while "on the dangle" and be large enough for comfort yet compact enough for maneuvering. Hackle pliers cost about $6.

The most popular tying threads, Size 3/0 for hooks, are available in many colors. Many tiers use only one color—black. In most patterns the head is the only place that shows the thread color. However, a light color, such as cream, allows the tier to match more closely the color of pale insects. Most beginners tie with the heavier 3/0 and later with the finer 6/0 as they develop a lighter hand and tying prowess. Thread comes on either the standard spool or the small, sewing machine minibobbin. A thread bobbin reduces waste and maintains constant tying tension. Bobbins, either standard or the minispool, appear in a variety of lengths and cost from $4 to $8.

Other tools, such as a hair stacker for aligning fiber tips and a whip for tying the final knot, increase tying ability. Both tools have become common among tiers. To some, the nonessential tools—such as dubbing wax, a dubbing spinner, head cement, a small file, a bobbin threader, and a material clip—become essential as their tying skills improve.

>>> *Materials:* Only a limited selection of tying materials is required to create a variety of patterns. The furs and feathers used come from food byproducts and game animals and birds. Initially, the beginner should limit the purchase of materials. It is best, perhaps, to select a particular pattern and buy only those materials needed to tie it. Once the pattern is perfected, the tier may advance to other patterns and materials. In this manner, the materials accumulate over time. Substitutions may usually be made for materials that a tier lacks.

The first problem that a beginner confronts is the price of quality dry-fly hackle. The generic hackles on the market cost about $35 to $65 each. There is really no substitute for them, either. The roosters have been bred to produce a hackle feather that has stiff fibers and a lack of webbing. (Webbing absorbs water and causes the fly to sink.) Some flyshops offer quality half-capes—cut lengthwise to include the complete size range—to decrease hackle cost. The beginner may also purchase a quality cream or white cape and dye a few hackles to match various patterns. This way, a number of colors may be produced from a single cape. From tying materials come the textures, the shapes, and the colors that trout try to eat. Tail material may be elk hair, moose mane, hackle fibers, or calf tail hairs; body material comes from fur, yarn, floss, chenille, or tinsel. Wings are often made from strips of duck wing, duck body feathers, hackle tips, or calf tail hairs. Dry-fly hackles come from rooster necks; soft wet-fly hackles, from hen body feathers. Remember that almost any material, natural or synthetic, can be used. Experimenting is part of tying. The following materials may be regarded as basic for trout patterns:

1. Brown, dun, cream, and grizzly dry-fly hackles (tails and dry hackle).
2. Hen body feathers (wings, nymph legs, and soft hackles).
3. Eyed peacock tail feathers (bodies).
4. Deer, moose, and elk body hair
5. Grouse, pheasant, and duck body feathers (bodies, legs, and wet hackles).
6. Duck and goose wing feathers (wings).

7. Fine and medium gold and silver wire and Mylar tinsel (ribbing).

8. Black, brown, green, and olive floss and chenille (bodies and underbodies).

9. Pheasant tail (bodies and legs).

10. Natural dubbing furs, such as wool, rabbit, and hare, in colors including cream, tan, brown, black, olive, pink, green, and gray (bodies).

11. Polypropylene and Antron yarn and dubbing (bodies and yarn wings).

12. White calf tail (tails and wings).

13. White, gray, black, brown, and green marabou feathers (bodies and wings).

14. Wood-duck breast feathers (wings).

15. In various colors, prewaxed Danville 6/0 thread (for hooks 14 and smaller) and prewaxed Monobond 3/0 (for larger hooks and hair spinning).

16. Hooks come in a variety of sizes and bends, with the hook number getting larger as the hook becomes smaller. Hence, a Size 20 is small and a Size 10 is large. Each hook size can also vary in shank length and shank weight, indicated by an X rating. A Size 12 hook that is 2X long has the same length shank as the larger, standard Size 10 hook. A Size 12 hook with a 2X stout shank (2X heavy) would have the same heavy wire as a standard Size 10 hook. The popular Mustad 94840 and 94842 and the Partridge E6A and E4A make excellent dry-fly hooks, while Mustad 3906 and Partridge G34 are good for nymphs and wet flies. The most common fly sizes in the West range from 10 through 18. Tiers use various VMC and Tiemco hooks as well. Beginners often start with larger hooks before progressing to the smaller ones.

Some books claim that the tyro tier should begin with inexpensive feathers. Poor-quality feathers only produce poor-quality flies, however, and the tier will quickly become discouraged. Only an experienced tier is able to derive success from inferior materials. Buy the best materials and tools you can afford. There are many ways to learn tying skills: Attend classes at local flyshops, join flyfishing clubs, visit regional and national conclaves of the Federation of Fly Fishers or Trout Unlimited, read various flyfishing books, and rent flytying videos. If you can tie a knot, you can tie a fly.

>>> *Learning to Tie:* Flytying is simple. Place the hook securely in the vise jaws. The thread spirals around the shank and locks on, then laps over tail fibers to hold them down. Wrap in the wing butts and erect them. The thread then passes to the rear to dub the body forward, and a hackle spins behind and in front of the wings to create legs. A whip finisher wraps a tight head, and the thread is snipped. The fly, a typical dry pattern, floats upon the water supported by the wisps of tail and the stiff, radiating hackle barbs. This procedure, illustrated by the popular Adams, produces hundreds of patterns. Only the color and materials change. To tie one pattern well is to tie all patterns well.

With attention you can avoid fundamental errors such as mounting the tail and body too far forward, catching the thread on the hook point, unevenly stacking fibers, using the wrong size thread for a particular pattern, or failing to keep the working thread ahead of the tying point. Remember: Tying styles vary . . . and much of the pleasure in tying comes from sharing your methods and materials with others. Through tying you come to know the beauty of fur and feather; you learn more about the insect world; you become, finally, a better angler. Tying is discovery.

—Darrel Martin, May 1988

The Basic Flytying Procedure

TYING IS SIMPLY wrapping thread over various materials so they adhere to a hook. Generally, only two knots are used: a friction wrap and a head knot. A friction wrap winds the thread back onto itself to lock it in and provides a foundation for the materials. A head knot usually whips the thread over itself several times, and then the underthread pulls the whole head tight. The mechanical whip finisher accomplishes the same operation: It wraps one thread over itself several times so that the underthread may be pulled taut, securing the knot. The typical sequence in tying a standard dry fly, such as the Adams, begins with selecting materials. You'll need the following:

> **Hook:** *Mustad 94840, Size 12 to 16.*
> **Thread:** *Waxed, black or gray 6/0.*
> **Wings:** *Matched and divided grizzly hackle tips.*
> **Tail:** *Mixed grizzly and brown hackle fibers.*
> **Body:** *Natural-gray muskrat fur.*
> **Hackle:** *Mixed grizzly and brown hackles.*

1. Clamp hook in vise, with the shank horizontal. The barb (if there is one) and point may fracture if buried in the vise jaws, so leave them exposed and learn to tie around them. To facilitate working around the point, tie with a short length of thread.

2. To mount the thread, the taut end, held in the left hand, is nearly vertical. The thread wraps clockwise (when viewed from the hookeye) around the shank and overlaps the first wrap. Continue to spiral down the shank with several wraps, thereby locking the loose end. Trim excess underthread. Notice that the weight of the thread and bobbin allows it to hang while maintaining tension. Wrap a thread foundation for the wings, which will prevent them from twisting or rotating out of position.

Tie on a Girdle

The Girdle Bug, or Rubber Legs, is an effective imitation of a stonefly nymph that takes trout in cold-water streams. (The name Girdle Bug may have originated because the leg material, "living rubber," was used for making girdles and other stretch-fit garments.)

The classic pattern, tied on a long-shanked hook, calls for a simple black chenille body with white rubber hackle used for legs, tail, and antennae, all tied in with black thread. The rubber hackle has an enticing wiggle even with no action provided by the angler.

The same wiggle makes rubber-legged surface bugs effective for bluegills. In lakes and ponds, most strikes take place while the lure is sinking instead of on a retrieve. The slower the bug sinks, the better, at least when the bluegills are in relatively shallow water. I tie a little deer hair on top of the bug to slow the fall rate. I also paint white eyes on the head so the blugill can tell which end is which.

—A. D. Livingston, July 1994

3. Measure and match two grizzly hackle tips so that, when mounted, their lengths equal the hook shank length. Select hackle tips that have dense, bold barring and rounded tips. If you mount the tips "convex to convex," the wings will arch gracefully. Mount the hackle tips, pointing to the right, with authority. Pinched between the thumb and index finger of the left hand, the wings are placed one-fourth the shank distance from the eye. The lateral pressure of the thumb and index finger prevents the hackle wings from twisting. The thread passes between the thumb and the hackle butt, loops over the butt, and passes down between the butt and index finger. Wrap over the hackle stems several times to secure them. After practice, this, like most tying techniques, becomes easy. The wings should neither move nor rotate during mounting. Wings mounted in this manner resist wind pressure and maintain an erect stance.

4. Next, wrap the thread to the rear of the shank, directly above the barb point, for tail placement. Mix several stiff grizzly and brown hackle fibers. Cut off any soft webbing at the base and align the natural tips with a hair stacker. Remove the hackle fibers from the hair stacker; measure them along the shank so that their extended length beyond the tail mounting point is equal to the shank length. Position them and wrap them on with several firm thread wraps.

5. Add medium-gray muskrat fur for the body (dubbing). Mount the dubbing on the tying thread with thumb and forefinger. Rotate the dubbing in a single direction until it adheres to the thread. Keeping the thread taut, wrap the dubbed body to about one millimeter behind the wings. The body should have a gentle taper from tail to wing.

6. After the body is completed, pass the thread forward and bead the thread in front of the wings to correctly cock them.

7. Although only one hackle is essential, mount two—one grizzly, one brown. For correct proportions, the hackle barb, the fiber that extends from the stem, should be three-quarters the hook shank length. The two hackle stems are tied in along the foreside of the shank, with the dull side of the hackle facing the tier. Wrap the stem ends firmly and cut excess. Clip hackle pliers to both ends and bend them sharply so that their dull sides face the eye of the hook. Wrap the hackles several turns behind the wings and several turns in front. Each successive turn of hackle collar lies just in front of the previous wrap. Lap the thread over the hackle ends several times and cut excess. Use a half-hitch tool or whip finisher to tie off the head. Some tiers may wish to place a drop of cement on the head.

8. The completed Adams—done, with practice, in less than 10 minutes.
-Darrel Martin, May 1988

A Flytier's Helper

A S FLYTIERS STRIVE for efficiency, both beginners and advanced "brothers of the art" at one time or another purchase a set of hackle guards. When used with a whip-finisher, these thin metal discs help create a small, neat head, with virtually no hackle trapped underneath. A set of three will cover most hook sizes from No. 28 to No. 2/0; that is about the extent of their coverage. The center hole on the largest hackle guard is too small to accommodate No. 3/0 hooks, and others have a large ringed eye that encourages a dense build-up of larger thread and bulky material ends at the head.

A simple but effective guard can be added to the trio by using an empty foam plastic thread spool. With a razor blade or very sharp knife, make a clean, straight cut completely through to the center hole. This slit allows the tying thread to pass to the middle hole as it would with a standard hackle guard.

Unlike conventional guards, held in place by a small sinker or other weight attached to a string, no weight is needed since the homemade guard is secured by the hackle itself. Simply push the guard back until some of the hackle protrudes throughout the center hole.

Mine has remained on my flytying desk for years now, and has proved invaluable when tying large streamers, hair bugs, or any pattern that utilizes a front hackle in the dressing.

—Paul E. Shell, July 1983

The Versatile Hornberg

T HE HORNBERG IS a fly pattern developed in Wisconsin, but its popularity has never seemed to catch on west of there. Any flyfisher, regardless of where he lives, who has overlooked the Hornberg would probably benefit from having a few in his fly box. Made from readily available materials, it can be fished as a dry fly, wet fly, or streamer.

In Sizes 12 through 16, the Hornberg is an excellent attractor dry fly, and some anglers feel it is a good match for a caddis or stonefly. Once it becomes soaked and will no longer float, you can fish it effectively as a wet fly. On a Size 8 or 10 long-shanked hook, the Hornberg will take on the overall appearance of a streamer and does more than an adequate job of imitating baitfish.

The construction is simple: an underbody of yellow yarn, two mallard breast or flank feathers for wings and a grizzly hackle. The original pattern also called for a jungle cock shoulder, but because of its scarcity, it is rarely used in today's patterns. You can substitute either imitation jungle cock eyes or the light-tipped body feathers from a starling.

—*Anthony J. Route, December 1989*

A. J. McClane's Favorite Nymph Patterns

FOLLOWING ARE FOUR old favorites that have taken many fine fish over the years. They suggest subaquatic food forms in general, and except on those occasions when fish are truly selective, one or another will usually produce if worked at the right depth.

>>> *Strawman Nymph*

Hook: Regular or 2XL in sizes to suit.
Tail: A few strands of gray mallard or wood-duck flank.
Body: Deer hair spun on hook thinly and clipped in a taper from tail to head, ribbed with pale yellow floss silk. May be tied without hackle or, if desired, a turn or two of partridge hackle may be added.

>>> *Hare's Ear Nymph*

Hook: Regular shank, Sizes 6 to 16.
Tail: Brown hackle.
Body: Dubbed very rough with fur from European hare's ear, mixed with fur from the hare's face, ribbed with oval gold tinsel.
Thorax: Tied very full with wing pad from gray goose or duck tied over.
Legs: Dubbing from thorax picked out long and fuzzy; this represents the nymph legs.

A Hare's Ear Nymph is one of the most effective flies ever tied.

>>> *Leadwinged Coachman Nymph*

Hook: Sizes 6 to 12 2XL.
Tail: Dark brown hackle fibers.
Body: Bronze peacock herl ribbed with fine black silk.
Hackle: Dark rusty brown.
Wing pads: Small dark black duck upper wing covert feathers (cut to shape).
Head: Brown lacquer.

>>> *Iron Blue Nymph*

Hook: Regular shank Sizes 14 to 16.
Tail: Cream or gray hackle wisps.
Body: Bluish muskrat fur ribbed with gold wire.
Thorax: Bluish muskrat, no rib.
Hackle: Grayish cream.
Head: Clear lacquer over tying silk.

—A. J. McClane, March 1979

Gee, Your Hackle Looks Terrific

IF YOU'RE NOT HAPPY with the current colors available for flytying hackles, or if you'd just like to experiment with colors of your own, try using hair coloring. While you're unlikely to find any in yellow or chartreuse, you can easily turn a cream-colored neck into a dark auburn in a few simple steps.

>>> 1. Loose feathers are difficult to dye, so use necks (or capes) and saddle patches with the feathers still attached to the skin. Caution: The use of human hair coloring to dye feathers is not an exact science. I recommend using less expensive imported necks for the first try. This will give you an idea of what color change to expect, without risking high-priced feathers.

>>> 2. The darker the feather you start with, the darker the final results. So if you plan to dye a cream-colored neck dark auburn, the final color will not be as dark as if you had started with a ginger-colored feather. You can achieve more darkening by letting the feathers dry out and reapplying the hair color, but you may lose some of the tint. Experimentation is still the key.

>>> 3. The feathers must be thoroughly cleaned for the dye to take. Liquid dishwashing detergent works well. Be sure to rinse all of the soap out of the feathers before moving on to the next step. Then simply follow the product instructions. This amounts to mixing the color and applying it, waiting the specified time, and then shampooing and conditioning the dyed feathers. Be aware of the product warnings, and be sure to use plastic gloves to keep from dyeing your hands. Do not be alarmed if the color appears unacceptably dark when first applied. The final color is always much lighter.

There are a number of commercial products available in blond, black, auburn, and brown. I use Colorsilk from Revlon because it's moderately priced and offers a nice range of colors. I've also tried other brands with similar results, but when it comes to dyeing feathers, I'm not sure if the brand makes any difference.

—Gene Trump, May 1995

Fur File

My good friend Rocky Baker has an inexpensive system for keeping dubbing material neat and organized. He uses a typical three-ring binder with pocket-type photo album pages. The clear-plastic pockets work well for storing packages of synthetic or fur dubbing materials.

Replacement pages for photo albums come in a number of sizes. Unless you want to use a photo album, buy replacement pages with three holes in the sides. You'll need a large-capacity three-ring binder to hold the pages, since dubbing takes up much more room than photos. Use the pocket access opening to insert and organize the dubbing according to color, fur type, synthetic type, or any system you'd like. With this method of storage, locating desired dubbing material is as easy as turning pages in a book.

—Gene Trump, May 1992

<<< Dave Lenihan hikes into a remote pond in Northeastern California with a float tube in tow.
—Photo by R. Valentine Atkinson

[6]

Rods, Reels, and Other Equipment

~

"A trout is known mainly by hearsay.
It lives on anything not included
in a fisherman's equipment."

–H. I. Phillips, 1925

A Flyrod for Every Occasion

EVERY FLYFISHERMAN HAS an unreasoning view of flyrods; and I am no different. Generally, we are united in the belief that all rod design has been progressive and that the ideas about flyrods in the past were so bad it's amazing people were able to fish at all. This is based in American fashion on the belief that angling is progressive and chiefly concerned with efficiency. "I stepped into the water," a flyfisherman was recently heard to say, "and proceeded to empty the pool." We, his listeners, were bowled over by the picture of efficiency: trout stream as modern toilet. Now I understand this hyperbole is part of the fun; humor based on the idea that we're trying to be efficient.

Aren't we? I don't think bamboo rods, for example, are as efficient as glass and graphite. But I do like the smell of varnish when I open the rod tube. I had a graphite tarpon rod whose hook keeper wouldn't take anything larger than a No. 10 dry-fly hook, an understandable mistake when you realize it wasn't made by a fisherman but someone who looked with equal interest upon golf shafts, riding crops, and umbrella handles. Yet I dearly love graphite for helping me put some poetry in my loop and for relieving the tennis elbow I acquired, not from tennis, but from steer roping.

Anglers have begun to crave conformity. This has not always been the case. Now some of us crave leadership, someone to tell us whether we should have a fast-action rod or one that loads with less line. Fast was the answer until recently; but slower, softer rods have claimed the moral high ground.

The evaluation of rods is completely subjective. The dream is of the perfect rod, but there is no such thing. A flyrod has to meet too many criteria and many are contradictory. Take a rod for western rivers that must make delicate presentations in high wind. Is the rod matched to the fish, the fly being cast, or the weather conditions? And the rod needed for casting large streamers on western rivers in the fall is as big as some people use for tarpon. But the fish haven't gotten any bigger since August. A 5-weight easily handles the sparsely dressed flies we use on bright sand bottoms for tarpon, but it would never land the fish. The perfect distance for a trout rod to load is probably around 25 feet. But who wants to try out a rod down at the fly shop with 25 feet of line? And no rod casts nicely with split-shot, though some tolerate it better than others. In a perfect world, fishing with split-shot on the leader wouldn't be flyfishing at all. Neither would monofilament nymphing and maybe even shooting heads. Lee Wulff said that the fish is entitled to the sanctuary of deep water. That's where most of us used to set the bar in trout fishing. We fished on top and tried to devise ways of catching big fish that way, fishing at night, fishing with greater stealth, hunting remote places that rarely saw an angler.

So many rods are now designed for micro-niches, extreme line sizes, weird lengths. It's a pleasure to use some of these rods when the conditions for which they were designed are perfect, but it's useful to remember that conditions are rarely perfect in angling. Long ago, when I started flyfishing, the standard trout rod was an HCH, a 6-weight, 8 to 8 1/2 feet long. After four decades of evolution in material and ideas, I've concluded that this is still the case, especially considering what it takes to make an all-day rod in most places. The rod might have grown to nine feet. A full day in one of my local rivers might require going through five sizes of dry flies and three of wet. The wind will range from 0 to 40 miles per hour. A 5-weight rod isn't enough; a 7 is too much.

In my view, flyrods have some mysterious ergonomic range of length that is hard to explain. The same is true of hammer handles, tennis racquets, golf clubs: The variations in length are surprisingly small. A trout rod significantly under eight feet is too short, and significantly over nine too long. If it is too short, it leaves too much line on the water for good drag control and speeds up the casting cycle. Too long and the rod becomes a handful in the stand and helps produce tailing loops. I had a 10-foot summer steelhead rod that I loved until the wind came up; and then I wanted to swap it with someone unsuspecting enough to daydream too much about line control, just as I had. A rod better have a great reason for being more than nine feet or less than eight. Nine is a wonderful length for a trout/tarpon/billfish rod. It's a length the human body likes. Just today I got out an old favorite, a 7 1/2-foot trout rod, and fished half a day with it. I hadn't used anything shorter than 8 1/2 for so long that I was unpleasantly surprised to discover the extra drag problems the lower angle between rod, line, and water produced, not to mention the hurried casting cycle. The speeding technology of flyrods has finally just emphasized some basic truths. Even in the days when bamboo was king, light and fast were the ideals, sometimes called "dry-fly action." Prescribing a rod as having a "wet-fly action" was tantamount to admitting that it was a clunker.

I know that I'm not going to stop anyone out there from acquiring a bunch of overly specific niche rods. I'm probably not even going to stop myself. I haven't so far. The dream of flyfishing is one of simplicity, and most pursue it in the same way—by acquiring a blizzard of flies and gear in the belief that they're casting a wide net and that, at some point, they will get rid of all but the few perfect items and angle with the dreamed-of simplicity. But for most, the pile grows until death brings it to a stop. If flyfishing weren't still more or less esoteric, yard sales would never recover.

The biggest problem with flyrods is that you must not only meet all the physical criteria for the fishing you do but that you must also "love" the rod. For example, I have a 6-weight rod that is far and away the best trout rod I

Reel Seat Insurance

A reel seat locking ring that works loose is a potentially heart-breaking situation. If your reel becomes loose—or even falls out—while you are playing a large fish, you could end up with a damaged reel or a broken or bent line guide. Or worse yet, you might lose the reel in midstream or heavy surf, not to mention the fish.

A quick and easy remedy is to apply a small dab of clear silicone seal to the threads behind the reel seat ring. The silicone will keep the ring in place indefinitely, and it is easily removed.

–Robert Drew, June 1988

The Fly Box King

The first Richard Wheatley fly boxes (which is nearly to say, the first commercially produced fly boxes) were tin, with black japanned exteriors, white enameled insides, and metal clips to hold flies. The year was 1890.

A typical, commercially produced fly box.

By the turn of the century aluminum was the choice material and a satin finish was developed—the formula is still used on a number of boxes Wheatley uses today. The famous Wheatley "compartment box" for dry flies was designed in 1908. Though material and construction refinements have been made, one thing hasn't changed: The interior compartment fittings are still assembled by hand, and the finished boxes are still works of craft.

—Anthony Acerrano,
February 1990

have ever owned. It is fast, light, and has the quickest damping stroke imaginable. It was designed by probably the greatest flycaster of all time. It is also cheerily built with porous cork in the handles, disco guide wraps, and decal graphics that give the codes that distinguish this product from other recreational products by the same company. I'm going to have to work at loving this, the best trout rod I've ever had. I'm going to have to almost wear it out. Its ultra-modern decor is going to have to sink into history and become sort of campy. I may have to break it. I may have to defend myself with it during a holdup or use it to stand off a bear. Right now it's a kind of yuppy artifact with less soul than a paper clip. It casts a thousand times better than the beautiful old Garrison I have that takes the same line.

I think we can work it out, but this great new rod is made of materials that are part of a rapidly evolving technology. My rod may be obsolete by Thanksgiving. I may be given cause to worry that the modulus of elasticity of my new rod may be trailing others. I'm actually capable of thinking about petty things like that. I kind of like it. The other day, I put this soulless wand away for the day and, instead, fished with that fine old bamboo I've had for several decades. By comparison, the beautiful wooden shaft with individualized handwork and matchless aesthetics was a dog to cast. Someone compared the classic action of a bamboo rod to a cow pulling its foot out of deep mud. This one was better than that, but compared to the disco rod with the cheesy graphics and porous grip, it was pretty much of a dog.

Gough Thomas, the English gun writer, warns against the vice of "poly-gunning," which means using too many guns and becoming master of none. I could point out that this same malady afflicts anglers; but what's the use? We'll always have too many rods. But back to my topic: A trout fisherman can do it all with a nine-foot for a 6-weight line.

A nine-foot for an 8-weight line will cover most of the rest. If the angler is a fisher of riverine salmonids, those two rods will cover it all. The 8-weight will do perfectly for bonefishing and small tarpon. I have seen tarpon over 125 pounds landed on 8-weights. It's an ideal snook and redfish rod. For repetitive casting as demanded in steelhead and salmon fishing, it's as much as most of us want to cast all day long. Plenty of people use 6-weight rods for steelhead.

I know, nobody's listening. But this is very good advice. Is it because I have about 20 flyrods? Let's see what my excuses are.

>>> I have an eight-foot Garrison for a size 6 line. I keep this and use still it because it's full of fishing memories. It was owned for years in the middle of its life by my former brother-in-law. I had to buy it back from him and he did well in the transaction. I also my remember consultations with the builder and the giddiness of those years when there were relatively so few of us flyfishing.

>>> I have a six-foot three-inch Bob Summers "Midge" because it reminds me of my original flyshop, Paul Young's, where Bob originally did his beautiful work. It also reminds me of the follies of A. J. McClane and Arnold Gingrich and Lee Wulff when they were promoting these impractical flea rods, suggesting that even the very great are prone to foolishness.

>>> I have a 4-weight nine-foot Light Line Sage that is, to me, so far the most exquisite use of graphite I'm familiar with in a spring-creek-type rod. With it, I caught my best public-water dry-fly trout last June, after 45 years on the job: a 25 1/2-inch male brown on a Size 20 pale morning dun from Silver Creek near Ketchum, Idaho. I think this rod kept me from breaking the 6X tippet and the avalanche of grief that would have followed the loss of that fish.

>>> I have an 8 1/2-foot Winston for a No. 5 line. I have followed this rod throughout its evolution of materials. This one is of IM6 graphite. To me it is the 5-weight trout rod against which all others are measured, although the Scott of the same size is right in there. These are the best rods for the small freestone rivers that I fish. I do most of my trout fishing with this versatile rod.

>>> I have a 7 1/2-foot bamboo rod for a 5 line built by John Long, a gift from a builder I've never met. A fine piece of work and an extremely pleasant small-stream rod.

>>> I have a 7 1/2-foot Payne, a two piece, for a 5 line because I always wanted a Payne and even named the hero of one of my novels after this maker. I consider Payne to be the finest cane-rod builder of all time. When you pick this rod up, you can tell everything you need to know: It's startlingly good.

>>> Now the rod I discussed earlier: a nine-foot 6-weight Loomis GLX, a tremendous flyrod, designed by Steve Rajeff and otherwise a thoroughly impersonal artifact. The guides are single-footed; there is glitter thread in the windings; the reel seat is air-weight spun nylon. It's the flyrod as pure idea. It tracks perfectly and dampens perfectly; the action seems to progress through infinity without ever hitting bottom. You forget about the rod and think about the line. I don't think it weighs three ounces. I can fish big western rivers for 10-hour days and never feel I brought the wrong rod.

>>> I have an eight-foot nine-inch Russ Peak Zenith for a 7 line. Russ Peak understood what could be done with glass better than anyone. He was the *ne plus ultra* rodmaker in the '70s when I was fishing 200 days a year; so there is sentimental value. By today's standards, it's a deliberate rod that requires the angler to recalibrate his timing somewhat. When I fish it, usually on the Yellowstone in the fall, I quickly fall back into its rhythms. It is perfectly built.

>>> I have an eight-foot nine-inch Winston cane rod for a 7 that goes best with a Wulff 7/8, was built by the great Glenn Brackett, and was a gift of the Winston Rod Company. I enjoy fishing it enormously. It's entirely in the

spirit of the West Coast glory days in steelheading when Winston and Powell were kings. I can accept the extra weight of the rod because of the time between casts in steelheading. It is a great roll casting or single-handed spey casting rod.

>>> I just traded for a nine-foot two-piece Payne light salmon for an 8 line. It has a detachable fighting butt, ferrule plugs, and weighs the same as a 13-weight billfish rod. What will I do with it? I'll come up with something.

>>> The 8-weights and the age of excess: A Sage eight-foot nine-inch for an 8 line, an outstanding, wind-penetrating bonefish rod, doesn't seem to be good for anything else I do. A Sage 9-foot for an 8-weight, the 890 RPL, as much of a classic as the old Fenwick FF85. A Loomis four-piece nine-foot for an 8, an outstanding travel rod designed by Steve Rajeff and Mel Krieger— the only rod I know of better in the multipiece than in the two-piece.

>>> A nine-foot for a 10-line Winston graphite, my faithful permit rod. Somewhat sluggish by current standards, it absorbs the vagaries of big, heavy permit flies better than stiffer rods. It's a good all-around striped bass rod too.

>>> A nine-foot for an 11-weight Sage built for me as a gift by George Anderson. I use a 12-weight line on this rod. It's adequate for big tarpon, used carefully, which will not wear me out on active days the way the 12 does. It is simply built, no fighting grip, and is full of happy memories. I couldn't replace this rod, though the 12s and 13s are nicer after the fish is hooked.

I'll leave out my three spey rods. I have some good single-handed steelhead and salmon rods but may never go back to them: The speys just work too well.

I subject the reader to this inventory for two reasons. First, I myself love to read this sort of thing, sniffing around the author's tackle room; and second, to suggest that there is something at work here that has nothing to do with necessity but rather with the elaboration of the dream that is fishing.

—Thomas McGuane, February 1996

Practical vs. Perfect

SOME MAY OBJECT that this is getting beyond the realistic concerns of ordinary angling. Possibly, but flyrodding is also complex on the home front. You own a generalist 6-weight rod for trout, but one day a friend calls up and says, "Let's fish Suzy Spring Creek in the morning." Like most spring creeks, this one is clear and gentle, full of trout that spook quickly from the slightest disturbance. Come morning, your friend rigs up his 8 1/2-foot 2-weight; attaches a 12-foot 7X leader; knots on a No. 28 sparkle nymph, and quickly begins laying into fish. You, meanwhile, flog away with your 6-weight. Every time the heavy line smacks the water, three or four trout scatter for cover. When you finally do blunder into a fish—a 12-incher—it isn't much fun on the big 6-weight. That same fish on your buddy's 2-weight is excellent sport—which is why, next day, you're at the flyshop, waggling 2-weights and wondering how you lived so long without one.

Practically speaking, it's fair to say that if you're concentrating mainly on trout, the only rod that is truly necessary is a nine-foot 5 weight. With it, you can toss hefty Woolly Buggers into big rivers or lay small dry flies over slick lies. When used carefully, this rod will even prove adequate on small creeks.

On the other hand, I own 1-, 2-, 3-, 4-, 5-, 6-, and 7-weight "trout rods," and I believe I need every one of them. (I probably could part with the 1-weight—at gunpoint, over tears—and still go on with life.) There are times when, for instance, a 2-weight is too light but a 4-weight is perfect, if for no other reason than the 4-weight lets me cast a much wider range of flies, yet is light enough for small-water casting and fish-playing. To further complicate matters, sometimes I need a seven-foot 4-weight (for overhanging brush on small streams and no room to wave a long rod); or a nine-foot 4-weight (for small lakes and smallish trout, but not a lot of casting room). Thus a serious fisherman needs rods not only of varying line weights, but also of different lengths within each weight class.

—Anthony Acerrano, April 1995

The Recycled Flyrod

FLYRODS SEEM TO have a knack for getting broken, particularly by getting slammed in doors and car trunks. But all is not lost, especially when the break occurs near the end of the tip section. I have two such rods that were recycled to fish again.

I owned a nice little four-piece pack rod that was a 5-weight flyrod in its first life. After a 3 1/2-pound smallmouth helped me break it in two places, I resurrected the rod as a three-piece boat rod. I trimmed the break with a fine-toothed hacksaw and replaced the snake guides with baitcasting guides. Then I removed the butt cap and extended the handle behind the reel seat about six inches by gluing a piece of fiberglass from another broken rod into the butt section. After replacing the tip, I had a very functional boat rod for 8- to 15-pound-test line.

Another former flyrod, an 8 1/2-foot 6-weight, lost six inches at the tip. I replaced the snake guides with single-foot spinning guides and installed another butt extender. This left me with a perfect jig rod that easily throws quarter- and one-ounce lures and is a joy to fish with—which took some of the sting out of the mishap.

—Fred Everson, August 1995

Struck Ferrule

For fishing-rod ferrules that stubbornly refuse to part no matter what, try some Liquid Wrench. Available in automotive and hardware stores, this product is specifically formulated to loosen items frozen together by rust, corrosion, old grease, etc. Just spray a little around the male ferrule and let it drip down. It takes only a few minutes for the liquid to penetrate. Wipe both ferrules clean after pulling them apart.

—Laurent E. Beaucage, February 1985

Dry-Fly Atomizers

As every dry-fly angler who has done much wading will know, sooner or later, you're going to take a tumble. This is an accepted occupational hazard. When a dousing occurs, it is important that equipment be thoroughly dried as soon as possible. This is especially true of dry flies. Failure to do so can result in rusted hooks, and it doesn't take much corrosion to ruin flies tied on tiny hooks.

As protection against rust, try to find an old perfume atomizer, or buy a new one. Fill it with liquid flotant and give your flies a good spraying.

Doing this after every outing will guarantee both longevity and maximum buoyancy of the flies, and they'll be ready to be fished when you are next casting flies at streamside.

–Jim Casada, October 1986

Today's All-Around Trout Rod

MY FIRST ALL-AROUND trout rod, 8 1/2 feet of thick tubular fiberglass, was the envy of pole-vaulters everywhere. It threw a 7-weight flyline and, back in the 1960s, was considered a reasonable piece of equipment for all manner of trout water. It was also a heavy, gangly rod and a fatiguing one to cast all day, especially in a wind.

Graphite refinements in the '70s brought us longer, stronger, lighter flyrods. Interestingly, though, except for rod weight, the basic dimensions of an all-purpose outfit changed very little. One top company, for instance, offered as its generalist trout rod an eight-foot three-inch graphite matched to 7-weight line The theory was that this rig could cast everything from small dries to large streamers and weighted nymphs; supposedly it had power in reserve to subdue the largest brown while serving adequately on steelhead as well.

Now we have the lightest, strongest graphite rods ever, with studiously engineered tapers that force a revision of all-rounder conventions. Consider:

➤➤➤ *7 Weight* is still useful for fishing large rivers with large flies, using long casts for heavy fish, but no longer a true all-purpose weight. It's unnecessarily heavy for most situations, and the bulky line falls hard on small-to-midrange streams or spring creeks, often spooking fish.

➤➤➤ *6 Weight* is perhaps the true all-round number these days, especially when combined with a strong, light nine-foot rod such as a G Loomis IMX, Sage Graphite III RPL, or Orvis HLS. For even more adaptability, choose a "travel" model that breaks down into three or four pieces for easy carrying and transport. (These will cast every bit as well as the two-piecers.) With a 6-weight outfit you can cast near or far, equipped with small or large flies, and subdue any trout that swims. The nine-foot length allows for easy and effective line handling and comfortable casting, even from a float tube or driftboat.

➤➤➤ *5 Weight* is the perfect generalist tool if your trouting is confined to midsize streams and creeks and you seldom use large streamers or heavily weighted nymphs. The line is heavy enough to provide crisp turnover on long casts with the general range of dry-fly, nymph, and small streamer patterns; but it's light enough to allow for delicate spring creek presentations. Also, the light rod matches pleasantly with the tussle of average-size fish. Stay with a nine-foot length for casting and line-control efficiency.

➤➤➤ *4 Weight* is too light to have all-round capability. Distance casts are limited, especially in a wind. Fly size and weight are also restricted. The 4 weight is a fine, pleasurable rig for small streams, medium-to-small flies, and casts less than 40 feet; but by no means is it the only rod to own.

–Anthony Acerrano, November 1990

Restoring Old Bamboo Rods

HANDMADE BAMBOO FLYRODS dominated the market for more than 100 years prior to the early 1940s. Then other materials better adapted to machine production came into general use and the bamboo rod gradually passed from the fishing scene. Although bamboo rods are still being made, their prices, unfortunately, are beyond the average angler's budget.

Many vitage bamboo rods are gathering dust. Most would require work to restore, but it's well worth the effort—if not for fishing, for their antique value.

Handmade bamboo flyrods were hot items prior to the 1940s.

All early bamboo rods were handmade. Rods bearing the names of famous rodmakers could warrant restoration depending, of course, on their condition: Gillum, Winston, Thomas, Leonard, Phillipson, Payne, Edwards Dickerson, Garrison, Granger, Orvis, and Powell. These rodmakers frequently engraved their names on the reel seats or autographed the rod shaft.

Rod shafts were made in four, six, and eight strips of bamboo, tapered, beveled, and glued into tubular shapes. Restoration is enjoyable and fairly easy.

Helpful information on rodmaking history as well as restoration techniques can be found in the following books available at most public libraries: *The Care and Repair of Fishing Tackle,* by Mel Marshall; *Classic Rods and Rodmakers,* by Martin J. Keane; and *The American Sporting Collector's Handbook,* by Allen J. Liu.

—Arthur J. Swartz, August 1984

What's Your Action?

ACTION DENOTES WHERE and how a rod bends under a load. This curvature is rated in terms of speed. An ultrafast-action rod bends mainly in the upper fourth of its blank. Fast action engages the upper third of the blank. Moderate (sometimes called medium) action bends at the midpoint (half of the blank); and slow action flexes the entire shaft, from butt to tip.

Action is often confused or wrongly integrated with other terms by fishing experts and rod manufacturers, which adds to potential misunderstandings. For instance, someone might refer to a "stiff action." But stiffness is the rod's resistance to bending, a concept separate from action. Stiff rods resist bending more than soft rods; but when they do bend, it's with a consistent curvature, and the description of that curvature is the action. Moreover, the action of a stiff rod can be identical to the action of a soft rod. So telling someone to select a "stiff-action" rod is telling him precisely nothing.

The same is true of an often-encountered designation, the "heavy-action" rod (or "medium" or "light-action"), which doesn't exist. The term "heavy" can be used to designate a rod's strength, which is its ability to withstand pull without breaking. But heavy can also simply describe weight—the thickness of the blank, for instance—or power, which again relates to stiffness under a load. (A heavy-power rod may bend at the same point in the blank as does a medium-power rod, only it will bend less per given load). None of these usages, however, has anything to do with the correct concept of rod action.

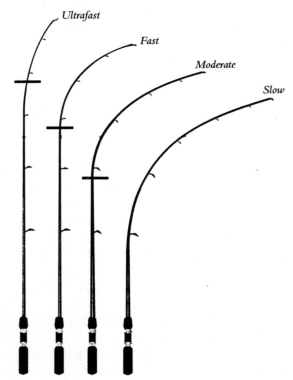

Action is determined by where and how a rod bends under a load. From left to right: ultrafast-, fast-, moderate- (or meduim-), and slow-action rods.

A wrong action is one that impedes your ability to make proper presentations, to feel the lure and/or to detect strikes, to set the hook as needed, and to play the fish successfully. If you think about the implications of those criteria, it becomes clear that, in general, fast- to ultrafast-action rods are more desirable than slow ones. Faster actions transfer vibrations well (given equivalent rod materials and stiffness), which means you can better register lure vibrations, contact with bottom, and light takes. Faster actions also let you strike more quickly and forcibly, since less of the rod needs to bend to send your energy down the line. (A slower-action rod has more length to flex, which means more delay in sending power to the hook.) For the same reason, faster actions are helpful when you need to jerk lures free of fouling weeds or when you must move a strong fish quickly away from cover.

Slower actions have their place too, of course, and are often preferred in softer rods, where the combined effect is a gentler, smoother cast motion and hook-set. Examples: when casting live bait that might—with a stiffer, faster rod—be torn from the hook; when angling for soft-mouthed species; or when using ultralight lines that a stiffer, faster rod might snap either on the strike or when playing a fish.

—Anthony Acerrano, February 1994

Understanding Action Terminology

TRADITIONAL ASCRIPTIONS OF dry-fly (fast) and wet-fly (slow) actions have little use today. Top-grade modern graphite flyrods tend to have "progressive" tapers, which means the action varies with the load placed on the rod. Such rods can be used with equal efficacy for dries, wets, nymphs, or streamers.

Modulus or stiffness ratings enter into action dynamics here because a stiffer rod bends less and will use less of the progressive taper than will a softer rod for a given length of line. Very stiff (high-modulus) rods tend, then, to effect faster actions on short casts. This means a less giving rod, one that throws tighter loops and, for poor casters, more tailing loops and tangles. Softer rods utilize more of the taper and have slower (usually moderate) actions, which many beginners find easier to handle. The difference in difficulty is probably exaggerated and should not concern anyone who plans to get formal casting instruction. Moderate-action rods tend to feel smoother on the cast, which some casters enjoy. Faster rods seem crisp and powerful and throw tight loops easily. Avoid very slow, soft rods, which are usually cheaply made and are poor fishing tools, ineffectual to fish and cast.

Dampening (also called damping) is another important term and concept. Pick up a rod and give it a brief, sharp waggle. Just as when you cast, the tip bends backward, then forward. When you stop applying pressure, the tip will continue to move, or vibrate, before coming to a stop. A good rod dampens the movement almost instantly; a poor rod—like a worn-out shock absorber—takes longer. When choosing a new rod, remember to keep in mind that casting distance and accuracy, hook setting, lure action, and fish-fighting ability can be impaired by a rod with poor dampening ability.

—Anthony Acerrano, February 1994

Spool Storage

This simple gadget stores and dispenses monofilament lines and is easy to make. Find the center on a spare piece of wood 1x2 inches or 1x4 inches. Length determines the number of spools. Drill 1/4-inch holes on a slight angle (about 85 degrees) every five inches. Insert 1/4-inch dowels that have been cut five or six inches in length. If the dowel rods are snug enough, no glue is needed.

Drill a hole in the top and bottom of the back board so you can mount it vertically in a place of your choice, or clamp it to a vertical support for temporary placement.

The efficiency of this gadget lies in the angle of the spools to the board. Sufficient friction between the edge of the spool and the board prevents the spool from running wild—when you stop winding line on your reel, the spool stops turning. Tape holds the mono end.

—Jack Olson, June 1983

Extendable Rod Case

WHILE HARDLY THINGS of beauty, rod cases I've made from lengths of PVC sewer pipe have withstood all but the worst abuse.

Required are a length of pipe, two end caps, a 1x10 inch length of belt leather or nylon webbing, and a piece of two-inch-thick soft foam rubber about six inches square. Use white or light green sewer pipe so you can print your name and address on the side.

Cut the tube four inches longer than the longest rod or section normally carried. Saw off the flared end, but don't discard it.

Cut the foam rubber to fit inside the tube. Smear contact cement inside the

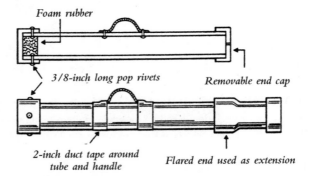

Foam rubber

3/8-inch long pop rivets

Removable end cap

2-inch duct tape around tube and handle

Flared end used as extension

The sawed-off flared end of a PVC sewer pipe can be used as an end cap to extend your makeshift rod case, allowing you to carry rods of all sizes.

permanent end cap to secure the foam rubber, then place it on the tube. Drill four equally spaced 1/4-inch diameter holes around the end cap and tube and secure with 3/8-inch-long Pop Rivets. Drill a 1/32-inch-diameter hole in the center of the removable end cap to facilitate installation and removal.

Load all rods you expect to carry into the tube, then install the end cap. Determine the tube's point of balance and measure four inches to each side of that point. Remove the rods and fasten each of the handle ends on the marks with two pop rivets. Make three wraps of two-inch-wide duct tape completely around the tube and handle ends for added strength. Duct tape is also used to secure the removable end cap.

Remember that flared end you sawed off? Keep it for times when a longer rod must be carried. Fit the flared end over the tube, tape it securely, and place the cap over the extended end. The case won't balance while being carried by the handle, but this is a minor inconvenience considering all of its advantages.

—Robert H. Jones, July 1990

Homemade Rod-Winding Supports

B UILDING A NEW fishing rod, or rebuilding an old one, is a lot easier if you have some sort of support to roll the blank on as you wind the thread over the guide's feet. A rod-winding support can range from the simplest V-notched cardboard box to an elaborate contraption with rubber-lined ball-bearing wheels.

To handle any size rod, I've found that two independent supports work best, and they are easily and inexpensively made.

You will need two one-pound coffee cans; two hardwood slats 12 inches long, one-half inch thick, and 1 1/2 inches wide; two sets of plastic or rubber bumpers; a container; plaster of paris; ballast—wheel weights, gravel, etc; and some one-inch screws.

First saw a V-shaped notch into one end of both slats. Make it wide and

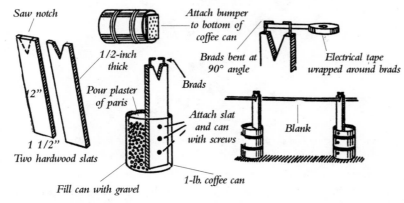

Homemade support: Saw V-shaped notches into two hardwood slats; stand each slat into a coffee can, screw into place; add ballast to each can; pour enough plaster of paris to cover ballast and fill can to rim; mount plastic bumpers to cans to prevent sliding.

deep enough to accommodate the biggest rod you will work on, and leave a quarter inch of wood on one side of each notch. Stand the slats up inside the coffee cans, with the widest side against the can. Screw in place. Add ballast— two to three pounds—to each can. Mix enough plaster of paris to cover the ballast and fill the cans to the rim. After it has set, mount the plastic bumpers onto the bottom of the cans to prevent sliding and protect the table's surface.

For a nice finishing touch, install a couple of brads into the top of the slats next to the notches. These prevent the blank from lifting out of the supports.

The supports work well with winding tools that affix to a blank, and are extremely flexible in regard to blank size and guide spacing.

—Fred Everson, June 1991

Fish Measure

For most anglers, a small, retractable metal tape measure secured to their vest or kept in a tackle box is adequate for measuring fish. Anglers rarely give them a second thought—until they start catching big fish.

With a 36-inch tape it is difficult to measure fish that go beyond 30 inches. You are continually stretching the tape to its limit, and the retractor part gets in the way and into the water. Bending the tape to get a girth figure isn't easy, and usually isn't very accurate.

The solution is to use a cloth measuring tape—the kind found in fabric stores. Cloth tapes have several advantages over retractable tapes. Available in plastic that isn't affected by water, they come in 60-inch lengths, so you can measure the biggest salmon or steelhead. You can cut the tapes anywhere, if you don't need something that long. And girth measurements are much more accurate and easier to take.

–Anonymous, March 1990

The Well-Stocked Vest

MY FIRST FISHING "vest" was actually a shirt—an Army-surplus model with extra pockets sewn in to hold my fly boxes and everything else I needed for a day astream. While it served me well during my teenage years, it was ultimately replaced with a full-fledged fishing vest. And though I've worn out quite a few vests since then, each has quickly been replaced with a new one, for there is no more practical piece of gear than a quality vest.

If you doubt the need for a vest, try fishing without one and just picking out what you'll need for the day. Inevitably, something—usually something crucial—will be left behind. And if it isn't, the chaos caused by not having each item in its proper pocket where it is instantly accessible is most unnerving.

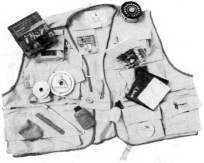

A fishing vest keeps crucial gear organized and close at hand.

Vests, then, actually serve a dual purpose: They allow us to store and carry our gear, and they let us categorize it so we don't have to waste time searching for items when they're needed. Organize your vest's contents however you wish, but do organize them. Once you establish where a certain box of flies goes, always put it back in the same place, so you'll know instantly where to retrieve it the next time you're waist-deep in a stream, surrounded by rising fish and desperately in need of those patterns.

If you're ready to purchase a vest or already have one and are ready to stuff it, here are some suggestions on a basic selection of flies and ancillary gear that will help you cope with most fishing situations. Some anglers pride themselves on being specialists—fishing exclusively with dries, nymphs, or streamers. But if you want a chance at good fishing in any situation, stock a selection of wet flies, nymphs, dry flies, and streamers, then use the variety that best suits the conditions at hand.

Wet flies are available in hundreds of patterns. A few good ones to start with are the Black Gnat, Partridge Peacock, and a black or olive Woolly Worm or

Woolly Bugger, Sizes 8 to 16. For streamers, a basic selection that will perform well on most streams includes a Sculpin, Marabou Muddler, Zonker, and Black-Nosed Dace, Sizes 4 to 10, on long-shank hooks. With nymphs, you can't go wrong stocking Gold-Ribbed Hare's Ears, stonefly imitations, March Browns, and Scuds, Sizes 6 to 16. And for dry flies, make sure you include a variety of imitations for mayflies, caddis, and terrestrials. The Adams imitates numerous mayflies and is an excellent searching pattern. Add a Light Cahill or Pale Morning Dun to imitate light-colored mayflies and a Blue-Winged Olive in a sparkle dun or comparadun style for three mayfly patterns that will cover most hatches. Many patterns imitate caddisflies well, but few can outperform Al Troth's Elk Hair Caddis tied in olive, gray, and tan versions. Finally, include four terrestrials—ants, beetles, hoppers, and crickets. Grasshoppers and crickets work well in Sizes 6 to 14; the dries listed above are most useful in Sizes 12 through 18.

Chances are you'll want to stock some locally popular patterns too. Ask for advice at a flyshop if you're unfamiliar with a certain area.

Besides flies, you'll need a number of accessories. Clippers for cutting leader material should be tied to a string attached to your vest, but kept in a pocket out of the way so they don't tangle in your flyline. A good flotant is crucial for fishing dries. Paste and gel types generally work better than sprays.

Special wallets are handy for storing extra tapered leaders. You'll also want spare spools of material kept in a specific pocket and arranged by diameter so you can find the line test you want quickly. Tippet Sizes 2X to 6X cover virtually all trout situations.

Leaders can curl severely after being stored on a reel, so it's wise to stash a small piece of leather or rubber; to straighten your line, simply pull it through.

A hook-sharpening stone or file should also be in every vest, and split-shot or twist-on leads are handy for fishing nymphs and streamers in fast, deep water. Strike indicators make nymphing easier. A water thermometer is another useful tool, as is a small mesh net for catching and examining trout foods floating in the water. No trout fisherman should go without a pair of forceps for removing flies from a fish's mouth. Polarized sunglasses are vital for cutting glare and allowing you to spot fish in the stream. A small flashlight should also be in every vest, for night fishing.

Other items that can make for a more enjoyable day on the stream include suntan lotion, insect repellent, headnet, butane lighter, toilet paper, collapsible wading staff, line cleaner, lunch or a snack to eat while on the stream, and raingear. The bulkier items fit in the back pocket of most vests. Finally, it never hurts to attach a landing net to the ring on the back of your vest, just in case.

–Gerald Almy, January 1988

Keeping It Together

Some two-piece fishing rods tend to separate after a few hours of fishing. The angler tends to notice only after an especially vigorous cast sends half of the rod soaring like a javelin toward the horizon. Hopefully, the lure on the end of the line will jam in the rod tip, facilitating a retrieve. However, if the lure snags or the line breaks, the angler is left holding a useless tick. Prevent this problem by firmly assembling the rod, being careful to align the guides. Then apply a thin, 3-inch strip of plastic tape (in a color that contrasts with the rod) across the joined ferrule, parallel with the length. Place the tape on the top so you can see it when you fish. Cut the tape crosswise where it straddles the ferrule, so half will be left on the tip section and half on the butt. Now a quick glance will let you know whether the halves of the rod are drifting apart.

—*Mark Cerulli, July 1995*

How to Survive the Breakdown Blues

THE SOUND OF a good rod snapping is one of the ugliest noises on the planet. You don't just hear a rod break; you feel it—a jolt of surprise and dismay. This is especially true when you're playing a trophy-sized fish.

On a recent trip to Alaska I felt a good ($400) flyrod go pop as I was fighting a 15-pound silver salmon. As I drew the fish in with no more force than I'd applied a dozen times in the previous few days, the rod simply snapped in half. The precise shear of the graphite—smooth and clean, as though sliced with a razor—indicated an internal structural flaw, an accident waiting to happen. I knew the company would make good on its warranty (which it did), so money wasn't the issue. The issue was being 400 floatplane miles from the nearest outpost, in the midst of a fresh salmon run, with a flyrod that could not be put back together. Luckily I had a couple of spare rods back at camp. I lost a few hours of fishing but was back in business later that afternoon. Without the spare, however, the entire trip could have been in jeopardy.

▸▸▸ *Preventing Pain:* There's the first lesson: On any outing that's even slightly expeditionary, carry spare tackle. Rods can break, reels can jam. Entire outfits can fall overboard or be lost in transit. It's far easier to set aside a split rod or gear-jammed reel than it is to attempt field repairs.

Another way to prevent trouble is to inspect your gear carefully before you leave home. Drags should function smoothly; handles, bails, levelwinds, release buttons, and antireverse mechanisms should all be operating without pause or hitch. Rods should be given a quick once-over to ensure that the guides are smooth, unbroken, and tightly wrapped down, and the rod blank itself should be examined for splits and cracks. Even a small indentation or fracture in a graphite rod can lead to breakage if the right amount of stress is applied.

It's also smart to carry a field-repair kit: a spare tip-top and rod guides, duct tape, superglue, a spool of rodbuilder's thread, light sandpaper or an emery board, small (jeweler's) screwdrivers, needle-nosed pliers, a single-edged razor blade, a toothbrush, cleaning solvent, and thin, high-speed reel oil.

▸▸▸ *Rod Repairs:* Probably the most common rod problem is a broken or fractured tip. If the break occurs in the last six inches or so, the best remedy is simply to cut the rod below the break, dot the new "tip" with superglue, and put on a new tip-top guide. If you lack replacement guides, use the original. Pull out the old material with pliers and widen the guide's base aperture to fit the new, thicker shaft. (In a real jam, you can fashion a makeshift tip-top or snake-style guide by bending a paper clip or bit of wire into shape and securing it tightly to the blank with duct tape and/or a thread wrapping.) The result will be a slightly stiffer but completely functional rod.

Guides that break loose from the blank can be reattached with a simple wrap of duct tape. Better still, and more permanent, is a thread wrap, which is also good for temporarily splinting parallel fractures in the rod blank.

>>> *Reel Problem:* Sticky drags lead to broken lines and lost fish. If the problem is caused simply by a buildup of gunk, take the drag apparatus apart and clean everything with solvent and a toothbrush. Apply a light coat of oil if appropriate (check the reel's manual for specific maintenance guidelines).

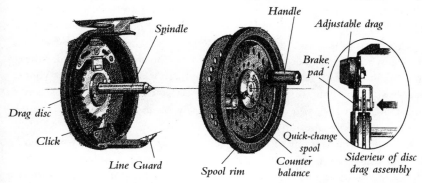

Sometimes solving a sticky drag problem is as easy as disassembling and cleaning the drag apparatus with solvent and a toothbrush; above, a Scientific Anglers "System Two" reel.

With spinning reels, perhaps the major breakdown area is the bail, or, more specifically, the bail-return spring. This is what allows the bail to pop back over the spool when you crank the handle to begin line retrieval after a cast. When the spring wears out, the bail will no longer flip back into place, and the result can be frustrating. I keep backup springs (which can be ordered from the manufacturer and are easy to replace with a screwdriver) in my repair kit.

—Anthony Acerrano, May 1994

Long Live the Long Rod

T HE MOST OVERRATED piece of fishing equipment in America today is the short fly rod. It is the least effective, least comfortable, and least sporting angling tool ever invented. I know it's risky to knock another man's woman, dog, or favorite rod, but a close look at the evidence will only confirm my position.

At first glance it may seem that the choice between a short or long rod for stream fishing is simply a matter of whim. After all, it is less visible, and a fairly skilled caster can lay out 60 or 70 feet of line with a tiny rod—more than enough distance for most trout stream situations. But, keeping out of sight of the fish is only a small part of the game. What is important is the ability to

Hook Your Foot, Not Your Guide

Never put a hook into the eye of a guide. Metal ones can be scratched and brittle ceramic ones can be broken. Damaged eyes translate into damaged line and lost fish. If you must secure a hook to a guide, use the foot.

–Danny Hicks, April 1996

present the right fly in a way that deceives the trout, and then to hook those you've fooled. This is what separates the anglers from the casters. And it is exactly here that the stubby rod shortchanges you.

A short rod leaves far too much line on the water while you're fishing out the average cast. Every extra foot is a crippling disadvantage, whether you're presenting a dry fly, wet fly, nymph, streamer, or (forgive me, Federation of Fly-Fishers) live bait.

Suppose, for example, you're casting to a fish 30 feet away. With a six-foot rod, tip held high, you'll probably still leave 18 feet of line and leader on the water when you make your presentation. (A bit more when fishing upstream, a bit less when working downstream.) With a 10-foot rod, casting under the same conditions, only about 10 feet of terminal tackle—perhaps just your leader—would be lying on the surface. Judge for yourself which presentation is most likely to give you a badly dragging fly or an underwater fly that's moving unnaturally and out of control.

Admittedly, the amount of line on the water isn't a critical factor when fishing a still-water pond or lake. But on streams with braiding currents, tongues of fast water, and unpredictable eddies, more line on the water often increases the likelihood for an unappetizing presentation of your fly.

It is also much easier to hook a fish when most of your line is off the water: You're in more intimate touch with your fly and you don't have to guess at how hard to tug to straighten out the esses in your line, overcome the friction of water, and set the hook. More than 90 percent of trout are lost at the strike. Examine the circumstances the next time you leave your fly in a fish; the problem usually is too much line on the water when the take occurs.

It took me years to learn these simple fly-fishing facts of life. The truth started to sink in only about a dozen years ago when I was fishing in the mountains of Southern France. I was using a snappy, eight-food rod (certainly a sensible length by Eastern U.S. standards), but I wasn't catching many fish and almost no really good ones. This was slow, clear limestone water, heavily fished by vacationers and constantly harvested by a group of professional fishermen who supplied the local hotels. Any fish that had run this gauntlet and grown to decent size was as thoroughly trained as an astronaut.

The professionals finally showed me their secret—which they regarded more as common sense than as an ingenious technique. They'd learned that, in this clear, slick water, they couldn't approach the fish from upstream. Neither could they give the trout a look at their leader. So they cast upstream to a rising or observed fish, but with a variation of the conventional method. They'd drop their fly—usually a sparsely dressed wet pattern on a light hook—just downstream of the trout's tail so the leader wouldn't pass over his head. When the tiny ripples from the fly's entry passed over the trout's nose, he would usually turn around to see what sort of insect had fallen into the water behind him. If the stunt was pulled off perfectly, all the trout would see now was the artificial sinking slowly down-current.

Any line splash or drag meant instant failure, and I began to see why these experts used long rods—10 to 10 1/2 feet long, in fact. "With a rod of three meters (nine feet 10 inches) you are just beginning to fish," they told me.

I finally learned how to execute this presentation with occasional success after days of practice. But my eight-foot rod, even though it could throw 70 to 80 feet of line with ease, was a big handicap.

Fishermen I saw in the Pyrenees on the Spanish border had taken this theory one step further. They used rods 12 to 14 feet long on those tumbling mountain streams and these kept so much line off the water there wasn't even a word for "drag" in their local *patois*. They would simply swing their fly (or more often maggot) directly up-current and let it drift back naturally, keeping in touch by raising the rod tip. They neither added nor took in line. And they took in trout with unbelievable regularity.

The implications of all this to the dry-fly man, with his almost paranoid fear of drag, are enormous. The perfect presentation of his fly has to be one dapped on the surface with no leader at all touching the water. This is true whether the offering is to be made dead-drift with the natural flow of the current or simply bounced on the surface like an egg-laying insect.

I proved this to my satisfaction several years ago after a neighbor had been given an ancient and enormous English flyrod. This awesome wand was a full 20 feet long, made of a solid wood called greenheart, and must have weighed more than three pounds. However, it had a light, flexible tip, having been built when single strands of horsehair were used as leader tippets.

I found some pretext to borrow this rod for a couple of hours and, after I'd rigged it with a light line and fine leader, I headed for a nearby river. Once I got the hang of it, I could dap a fly on the surface 30 to 35 feet away and make it dance and hop there with no leader at all touching the water. Smart, overfished trout nearly herniated themselves to grab my fly. If I'd continued to use that rod, the State Conservation Department would have named me Public Enemy No. 1. However, my friend soon retired the rod to his collector's case and perhaps that was just as well. After two hours with that wagon tongue, I felt as if I'd slipped every disk in my back.

With all this talk about comfort and convenience, you may ask how I can say "comfort" after that 20-footer nearly put me in bed under traction. And doesn't a long rod have to punish the angler more than a short one? Well, yes and no.

Rod Handle Repair

When readying your flyfishing gear for trout season, double-check the grip on your rod. Pits and crevices appear naturally in cork grips on most fishing rods. If there are some that are bothersome, if not downright irritating and worrisome to your fingers or thumb, get rid of them. Use epoxy glue to fill and level all pits and holes, then set the rod aside until the glue hardens.

The "potholes" will no longer be a source of annoyance while fishing long hours on the stream.

—Don Shiner, February 1986

In the first place, sheer lightness in a rod doesn't necessarily mean less effort. The difference between a two-ounce rod and a longer five-ounce model, compared to the angler's total weight on the scales, is negligible. So rest assured that the longer, slightly heavier rod won't weigh you down.

I have fished with many superb casters who said they reveled in the lightness of their short rods. But how they huffed and puffed and sweated. They were using both arms, both shoulders, and their back to make those long casts with toy tackle. Double-hauling may be the ultimate technique for tournament casting, but it's about as placid a way to enjoy a summer evening as alligator wrestling.

The point is, ask not what you can do for the rod, but rather what the rod can do for you. With a long rod, a small arm or wrist movement will take any reasonable length of line off the water for the backcast because there really isn't that much line clutched by surface tension. The line goes back over your head, straightens out, and bends the rod backwards. Now a minimal effort forward with forearm, wrist, or both, and the rod snaps back, propelling the line forward. What could be easier than that? The rod has done most of the work for you. Your hand has moved a foot or so with very little exertion instead of moving three feet or so and bringing shoulder and back muscles into play.

My experiences in France were not the only reason why my rods became longer about a dozen years ago. At approximately that time, I read an article in an outdoor magazine extolling the joys of mini-rod fishing. The author honestly admitted that he did, at first, have trouble avoiding drag with his shorter rod, but that he had solved this problem by holding the rod high above his head as he fished out every cast. Thus this six-footer, he claimed, was every bit as effective as an 8 or 8 1/2 footer and (get this), because his rod weighed only 1 3/4 ounces, it was far less fatiguing to fish with. Anyone who subscribes to that theory should now hold his right arm fully extended over his head for two or three minutes and tell me how it feels. I can't recall seeing any more articles from this man, and I can only assume that acute bursitis has prevented him from taking even a pencil in hand.

If a 20-footer can break your back and a six-footer gives you too much drag and too much work, what should be the length of an efficient and comfortable fly rod? A lot depends on your physical makeup and your style of fishing. If you're a continuous and compulsive false caster who likes to fish pocket water upstream, where the effective float is a foot or less, any rod over eight feet might put your arm in a sling. If, on the other hand, your style is more deliberate and you spend most of your time on slower water where you may take less than 10 casts per minute instead of nearly 100, you could probably handle a 10-footer with ease for a whole day's fishing.

And don't be misled by the "bush-rod" addicts. They argue that you get hung up too often fishing small, overgrown streams if you use anything longer than a five-footer. But the fact is, you'll get hung up a lot with a very short rod, too, because any form of true casting here will put your fly and leader in the branches. A long-line presentation is seldom an effective way to fish a string of small potholes, anyway. Drag is instantaneous and disastrous with a lot of line out on this type of water. Here, you're far better off with the long rod, flipping or swinging your fly to the chosen spot while you make the extra effort to conceal yourself.

Use as long a rod as you comfortably can. I have been fishing for the past several years with an 8 1/2-foot bamboo that weighs 4 1/2 ounces. I am now going through a trial marriage with a 9 1/2-foot glass rod that weighs about the same. This liaison has been so enjoyable that I'm now searching for a 10-footer with the same qualities.

On salmon rivers where I make only four of five casts per minute, my favorite wet-fly rod is a 10 1/2-footer that works beautifully with a medium weight No. 6 line. But I'll admit that I have to drop back to an 8 1/2-foot stick for dry-fly fishing. I just can't false cast that often with the long rod—although that 10 1/2-footer is the most effortless wet-fly rod I've ever hefted. And let me repeat: I find all these rods, both trout and salmon models, comfortable for a full-day's fishing.

In case you're interested, the man who wields these monster rods bears no resemblance to King Kong. I don't even tip the scales at 140 pounds with chest waders, spare reels, and enough assorted fly boxes to drown me if I fell into deep water.

I'll have to admit, though, there's one disadvantage to long flyrods—and it's a beauty. When you've finally hooked a fish, the long rod makes the fish stronger: The extra length gives the fish greater leverage against your hand.

Isn't this precisely what the short-rod people are espousing? That fish are now smaller and tamer so we must use tackle that magnifies the quarry? But aren't they actually doing just the opposite?

There are only two basic ways to measure a rod's ability to glorify the struggles of a fish. One is the weight or force it takes to bend the rod properly. This factor is usually printed on the rod, just in front of the cork grip, in terms of the weight of line it takes to bring out its action. I've seen a lot of six-foot rods that call for a No. 6 or No. 7 line to make them work properly. This means that it takes between 160 and 185 grains to flex it to its optimum.

But there's still another factor that makes one rod more sporting than another for playing a fish. That's the leverage against your hand. With a fly-rod—which must be considered a simple lever once a fish is hooked—the fulcrum is where the hand holds the rod. You don't need an M.I.T. degree to see that the mechanical advantage is approximately 66.66+ percent greater in favor of the fish and against the sportsman with a 10-foot rod than it is with a six-footer.

Despite this elementary fact, I am often accused of derricking small fish out of the water with a whacking great salmon rod. Fault my reasoning if you can: I'm convinced the shoe is on the other foot. I maintain that short-rodders aren't only selling themselves short on presentation and overexercising themselves needlessly, but grinding down small fish with mechanically superior weapons, as well.

Going back to 18-foot poles might be a bit too much. But do try a new nine- or 10-footer. If a ribbon-clerk like me can swing one all day long, you may be able to handle one like a conductor's baton.

Can't I, after all this, find at least one kind thing to say about our new short flyrods? Well, yes. Perhaps this.

I am reminded of the country sage's defense of bad breath. "It's mighty unpleasant, but it sure beats no breath at all." Same goes for short flyrods. They beat handlines, or no rods at all.

—Leonard M. Wright, Jr., February 1974

Superlight Flyrods

IF YOU HAVEN'T TRIED the modern graphite rods designed for a 1-, 2-, 3-, or 4-weight line, you're missing out on one of the more pleasant angling surprises of the decade. These rods, if used properly, can open up a whole new world of flyfishing pleasure.

>>> *Applications and Limitations:* Let's make it clear from the start that these light graphite rods, in varying degree, are specialty rods. That is, they're not designed for all-round, all-encompassing use as is, for instance, a standard 5- or 6-weight outfit. Each light rod has limitations and favored applications; the lighter the rod/line class, the narrower the application. A realistic appraisal must include the following:

In general, light-line flyrods, especially short ones, are not generous to awkward or unskilled casters. These are not rods for beginners.

Rods of 1 or 2 weight are best matched with flies no larger, and preferably smaller, than No. 14. I've gone to No. 12s with 3-weight outfits. You can push these sizes some, of course, depending on your ability and the wind conditions, but it's an effort. These light lines just don't generate the pull of standard-weight lines, and cannot turn over much of the bulk at the end of a cast. Four-weight lines are closer to standard and offer a little more leeway.

Getting a good "turnover" of the fly on a light-line outfit means you'll also have to pay attention to your leader matchup. A proper taper is required to transfer the light line's comparatively meager energy efficiently so the fly can be laid out as desired. In sum, the light-line flyrodder must be a little sharper at all points of craft than the angler with the standard gear.

These qualifications aside, the key word in light-line, light-rod use is fun. Pick up one of these rods (which weigh a mere 1 1/2 to 3 ounces, averaging around 2 1/2), and it virtually leaps to life in your hand. Casting, assuming you are not expecting more from the rod than it can deliver, is delightful.

Using these rods, you're permeated with a sense of delicacy. The lines make the barest dent when they fall into the water, letting you fish small streams, spring creeks, pools, and still-water ponds with an appropriate soft touch.

Perhaps fun becomes most noticeable once you've hooked a trout. The fish you take on light-line rods seem spunkier, heavier, and tougher because you're giving them a chance to show their stuff.

>>> *Grading the Line Weights:* To illustrate how the differing line weights vary in performance and application, I took four light-line rods—a 1, 2, 3 and 4 weight—out for dry-land testing. To keep variations in rod design, stiffness, length, and overall construction to a minimum, I chose four rods from the same company, Orvis. Gusting crosswinds of 15 to 20 mph added realism and an important dimension to the testing.

I began with an eight-foot Western Midge rod for a 4-weight line. This 2 7/8-ounce rod is one of my favorites in its line class because it loads easily with a short line but also has the spunk to throw 70 feet of forward-taper if necessary. The comparatively soft (medium) action makes both casting and fish-fighting a pleasure.

A 4-weight line casts very close to normal; that is, the wind caused little more problem than it would with a standard 5-weight outfit, and turnover on the No. 14 fly was efficient. When I was throwing crosswind, the forward cast settled with minimal wind drift. I also found it painless to put a 40-foot cast directly into the wind, using a tight loop to drop the fly where I desired.

Switching to the 3-weight Western Tippet (an eight-foot three-inch, 2 3/4-ounce rod) showed a clear line of demarcation: At 3 weight, you're truly getting into light-line dimensions, and the limitations begin to show. The rod did not load as crisply on short casts, and on longer throws, the weaker tug for line-shoots was noticeable. To work a long line, more rod acceleration was necessary. Maximum practical distance was about 60 feet. (That's more than adequate, however, for most stream situations.) The 3-weight line also showed an obvious difference in wind drift, being shunted six to eight feet while unfurling out of a tight loop on the forward drop. Casting into the wind

Safeguard Your Gears

Sheepskin cases are great for storing spare spools, but the shearling tends to rub off the protective silicone lubricants that gears and spindle bases need for prolonged reel life. A quick remedy is to cover the inside padding of the case with Scotch tape, which is slick so it doesn't absorb the reel lube. Or cement a circle of slick plastic to Velcro. Those little fibers grab the case lining and hold tight.
–Deke Meyer, April 1984

meant a shorter line, a vise-tight loop, and extra snap to turn over the fly. But it could be done up to 35 feet, probably longer had I pushed it.

The Western Two (8 1/2 feet, 2 5/8 ounces) drifted 10 or more feet in the crosswind on a 50-foot cast, which was close to the limit. (I threw one 55 feet on a double-haul just to see if I could, carefully pacing off the cast to avoid optimistic guesswork.) Throwing into the wind was difficult and not much fun, but workable up to 25 feet. Casting with the wind, however, I found I could make 50-foot casts without undue strain.

The One Weight (7 1/2 feet, 1 3/8 ounces) in such conditions has the feel of casting without line. Wind drift was prohibitive, casting into the gust essentially pointless. This, remember, is not to refute the value of 1 weights, which can be splendid fun, but to illustrate how limitations of application increase proportionally with decreases in line weight.

In terms of advice to new light-line flyrodders, this test can help put things into perspective. If you want the fun of light lines and rods for the widest possible application, begin with a 3 or 4 weight, the latter if you want to use flies larger than Size 14 and cast 50 feet or more. Two-weight rods, and especially 1 weights, can be delightful but are clearly more specialized.

>>> *Length Logic:* Rod length is an important part of light-line fishing. It's common to assume that light-line fishing means short-rod fishing, but this isn't necessarily the case. In fact, the reverse is often true: A comparatively long rod will serve better in nearly every way.

To make sense of length logic, consider how a rod works. Think of the rod as a bendable lever. If you apply force to the base of the lever, that force is transferred to the tip, which then exerts a measure of work or a load—the amount, for example, that you can pull or lift. The longer the rod, the less pressure you can put on a fish. Conversely, the longer a rod, the more pressure a fish can put on you, and the more torque you feel from the fish's fight.

So a long light-line rod will usually give you more fish-fighting enjoyment than a short rod. Longer rods also provide more line control in casting, fly manipulation, and mending—and over a broad range of distances. (Short rods handle line effectively only on short casts.) Generally, this means you'll have more fun and control using long light-line rods (eight to 8 1/2 for these line weights) when conditions allow it.

Does this mean shorter rods should be avoided? Not at all. Shorter rods—those less than eight feet—can be wonderful trouting tools if matched to the right circumstances, such as small, brushy creeks.

As a general rule, though: Choose as long a rod as you can use effectively in a given condition for maximum sport and line control.

—Anthony Acerrano, June 1990

Equipment for Midge Fishermen

IT TAKES A little practice as well as the proper equipment to get used to fishing flies a quarter of an inch or less in length. Gear up and practice with the following equipment, however, and you will be glad you didn't head home.

>>> *Flyrods:* Flyrods in the 1- to 5-line-weight categories are best for midging. The rod should be capable of making delicate and accurate casts at the short to medium casting distances most often encountered by midge fishermen. Softer rods with medium to medium-fast actions cast with the most delicacy. The softer rod action also helps protect fragile tippets. Rod length depends on where the rod will be used. Shallow, brushy creeks are best fished with shorter rods, while larger rivers that require the line to be mended are best fished with longer rods.

It's important to separate midging rods into two line-weight categories. The 1- to 3-weight rods should be considered highly specialized tools. They are a joy to fish when conditions are right, but a little wind can make casting the ultralight lines next to impossible. The 4- to 5-weight rods are the better choice for all-around midging chores.

Advances in technology over the past five years have created an explosion of graphite rods in light line weights. The best way to choose a midging rod is to decide which length and line weight rod will most suit the conditions where you intend to fish. Then test-cast as many rods as you can. Choose the rod that feels best to you.

Many fishermen consider bamboo the best material for midge rods. Bamboo rods in lighter line weights tend to load more quickly than graphite rods and are capable of superbly delicate casts.

>>> *Reels:* Choose a flyreel that balances your flyrod. Superlight rods require lightweight reels. A number of different drag systems are available. The smoother the drag system, the less chance of breaking delicate tippets when playing a fish. Reels with exposed-spool rims can be palmed to provide additional drag control.

As a general rule, reels weighing 4 1/2 ounces or less are best. Most of these will have diameters of 3 1/2 inches or less. Very-small-diameter superlightweight reels may cause flylines to kink and become unmanageable over time.

Much like light-line graphite rods, flyreels have undergone tremendous growth over the years. The array of models and reels to choose from is mind-boggling. In many cases it's wise to buy a reel from the same company that makes the rod.

Pillbox For Midges

Foam-type dry-fly boxes are fine for large flies, but the tiny hooks of midge patterns don't stick well in the porous foam and will easily fall loose. Plastic compartmentalized boxes work fine for normal-sized flies but are often too large to efficiently keep itty-bitty flies. Vest-pocket space is a precious commodity, so it makes no sense to use a box that fills one pocket just to house 30 midge patterns.

The answer to this little problem may be found at a corner pharmacy. A daily pill box makes a dandy midge box. On the type I use, the entire top comes off for easy filling. It's about the size of a cigarette pack, so it fits in a shirt pocket. Not only does it hold a good number of flies, but it floats—a big plus.

–Gene A. Trump, September 1990

➤➤➤ *Flylines, Leaders, and Tippets:* Double-taper floating flylines are best for midge fishing. If your rod isn't loading properly at short casting distances, try a flyline one weight heavier.

Many midge fishermen use the tapered knotted or knotless monofilament leaders familiar to most flyfishermen. As a rule, midgers prefer long leaders in 10- to 15-foot lengths to lessen the chance of spooking trout. Braided leaders, which are machine-made from many tiny filaments, are also popular. A braided leader can make casting easier and presentations more delicate. Braided leader also stretches when a fish has been hooked, which protects tippets.

The tippet is the final link of monofilament between the leader and the fly. Midge fishermen use 6X, 7X, or 8X tippets, which are the smallest diameters available. Recent advances in technology have greatly improved the pound-test ratings of these ultrafine tippets.

—Ed Engle, February 1992

Spring Fantasies

THERE'S A MOMENT in late winter when it's suddenly time to start thinking about fishing season. For me it's usually toward the end of February, with a week or so left in the last small game hunting seasons and then, believe it or not, only a month or six weeks until trout fishing starts. With any luck, that is. In Colorado we don't have a closed fishing season, so we don't have an opening day.

We also have a few rivers that stay open more or less all year, so if you just can't stand it anymore, you can slog through a snowbank, fish in 34°F water, and maybe even catch a few cold trout. In fact, most of the fishermen I know own a pair of monster insulated chest waders for just that purpose, though we still think of "fishing season" more in terms of April days that are merely chilly.

➤➤➤ *Fly Review:* I tie most of my own trout flies, and over the years I've developed a winter ritual: I go through all my flyboxes and get rid of any fly I can't remember catching a fish on. Most of these are patterns I decided to try that didn't pan out for one reason or another. I have to dump them to make room for the next batch of flies. (Okay, I don't actually dump them. I usually give them to friends who then go out and catch fish with them, which is a little frustrating.) I figure that after another 20 or 30 years of this I'll have the ultimate fly selection.

I do the same thing with gadgets: If I can't remember the last time I used one, I toss it in the desk drawer that's already two-thirds full of other gizmos that didn't work. Actually, I'm developing a kind of sales resistance to gadgets, if only because a lot of the new ones are modern versions of the ones I already tried a decade ago.

As long as the fishing vest remains half empty, I go through everything else in it to make sure it's there or to replace it if it's empty, worn out or lost. This is also a good time to toss out sandwich wrappers and snarls of monofilament and to shake the sand out of the pockets.

I resist any temptation to do a major reorganization of the vest because I did that once and it was catastrophic. By now, everything in my vest has its own place—even if it's not always the most convenient—and I found that if I move something like the bug repellent from one pocket to another, I might as well just throw it in the river because either way I'll never find it again.

Now is the time to inspect your lines, clean them well, and think about whether or not they've got another season in them. If there's any question, you probably need a new line.

I'm talking about flylines. I think all your monofilament should be replaced with fresh stuff every season. Mono can get weak and brittle with time and exposure, and you don't want to be that fisherman that every guide talks about: the one with the new waders and expensive rod and reel who broke off all his big fish because he was too cheap to spend a few bucks on some new spools of tippet material.

>>> *Leaks:* Patching waders is another ritual, and I've determined that there are two distinct kinds of leaks: the injury leak and the wear leak.

The injury leak is the hole that got poked in your waders with, say, a sharp stick in a beaver dam or maybe a run-in with some barbed wire. These things are unavoidable and, in fact, if you don't get them every now and then you're probably not fishing enough.

Wear leaks are more ominous. I usually get them in the feet where the material is compressed and grinds against sand that gets in even if I remember to wear my gravel guards; and also between the knees where the material rubs when I walk.

How many times you patch your waders before you break down and get a new pair is a personal choice, and I've seen people go to great lengths.

My old friend A. K. Best once kept a pair of canvas chest waders alive and more or less waterproof for the better part of a decade. He said later he did it because he was broke for 10 years and because he wanted to prove some kind of point, although he can't remember what it was now. Anyway, he finally got tired of it and of people asking me, "Who's your friend in the clown suit?" (By the way, the best wader patch material is pieces cut from your last pair of waders, so if you do get new ones, don't throw the old ones out.)

Found Fly Boxes

Some of the best fly boxes are containers we normally throw away. A Sucrets box is a fine one. A Milk Duds container makes a distinct fly box. Even a tiny Anacin tin will carry three dozen of your tiniest flies. Why would you want them rattling around in a large fly box?

To hold your flies in these found fly boxes, use foam packing cut to the shape of the box with scissors or a razor blade. On the smallest boxes, cover the inside of both the bottom and top. On larger ones, cut strips and stagger them so the flies in the top nestle between those in the bottom.

To hold the foam in the boxes, stick it down with double-stick tape. If you want something a bit sturdier, glue the foam to the box with a five-minute epoxy.

–Dave Hughes, June 1990

Bugs in the Soup

One of the more useful pieces of equipment a stream flyfisherman can wear is a nylon-mesh soup strainer hanging down his back from a cord. Ignoring all jeers and gibes about the size of the fish you are expecting to catch, use the strainer to sample the broth you dislodge while moving downstream—no angler ever got skunked who imitated the largest and most abundant aquatic food form in any river or stream at any given point in time.

–Bob Scammell, August 1991

Soup strainers help determine what type of offering to use.

>>> *Temptations:* I'm sure it's just a coincidence, but about the time I'm getting geared up for the fishing season, the spring tackle catalogs start to arrive in the mail: all that neat stuff pictured in color on glossy paper, modeled by handsome young people with perfect hair—except maybe for the guy showing off the XXXL-size waders.

I have to be careful because I'm a tackle freak from way back, but then I've learned the hard way that how much gear you have is a delicate balance. Just enough will help you catch fish, but too much gets in the way.

If you need something, you should probably get it, and you might as well go ahead and get a good one. In the long run, the good one will cost less than the two or three cheap ones you're likely to wear out in the same amount of time.

On the other hand, if you weren't casting as well as you'd have liked to last season, take a deep breath and ask yourself: "Do I really need a new rod, or do I just need casting lessons?"

–John Gierach, February 1997

Gadgets and Gear for Trout

TROUT FISHING GEAR doesn't have to be expensive to be effective. Here are 10 items that will fit easily into your pocket, but won't put a dent in your wallet. And they'll help you catch more trout.

>>> *Stream Thermometer.* Trout tolerate only a narrow range of water temperatures. Each species has its own comfort zone. In water above or below the tolerance range, the likelihood of finding trout is greatly diminished. Water temperatures along a fairly short section of stream can differ markedly, particularly in the immediate vicinity of springs and feeder creeks. Trout may be abundant at one location, but nonexistent at another location less than 100 feet away. Concentrate your efforts on those areas within your quarry's temperature tolerance range.

>>> *Aquatic Insect Net.* Trout feed heavily upon aquatic invertebrates. Use a small seine net in an eddy or pool with minimal current to capture a sampling of these invertebrates. Sink the arms of the seine into the streambed until the mesh just touches bottom. Walk slowly upstream for 50 feet, then turn around and walk back down. The insects should stay hooked in the mesh. (Note: Don't turn over rocks or dislodge gravel and vegetation. Such actions are unnecessary and may adversely affect delicate stream ecosystems.) The net can also be used by sticking the ends into the streambottom and leaving it for a few minutes, letting insects wash into it from upstream. Or, by crossing the arms at the bottom, it becomes a dipnet.

>>> *Aquatic Insect Identification Guidebook.* Once you've captured a few aquatic insects, use *Trout Stream Insects* to identify your catch. This bantamweight hardcover booklet by Dick Pobst is indispensable. Detailed color photos of stream insects in various stages of their life cycles make identification relatively simple. Once you identify the invertebrates, follow Pobst's recommendations for selecting artificials that most closely match the naturals.

>>> *Strike Indicators.* Detecting a strike when fishing nymphs is difficult under the best of circumstances. Improve the odds by using a strike indicator. A strike indicator is a brightly colored gizmo that attaches to the leader above a nymph or wet fly. The gentlest strike will cause the indicator to dip below the water's surface. Several types of strike indicators are available. I recommend the fluorescent bobber-type.

>>> *Clear Plastic Bubbles.* For lake fishing, use spinning gear and tie a fly (wet or dry) four feet below a plastic bubble. Filling the bubble with water will add weight and increase casting distance. Retrieve slowly. The trailing fly should create a V-wake behind the bubble. For high-country lakes, this is the most effective trout system I have ever used.

>>> *Sunglasses with Polarizing Lenses.* Polarizing lenses cut through reflected glare to reveal whatever lies beneath the surface of the water. Not only will fish that are otherwise invisible to the naked eye suddenly materialize, but the polarizing effect will also reveal submerged logs, undercut banks, and boulders— all favored haunts of trophy trout.

>>> *Hook Sharpener.* How often have you felt a strike, tried to set the hook, and then reeled in your lure, minus the trout? As often as not, dull hooks are to blame. Every time you tie on a lure or a fly, even if it's brand new and just came out of the box, sharpen the hooks. The niftiest hook sharpener I have used is smaller than a ballpoint pen and has a V-shaped hook disgorger at one end.

>>> *Knot Guidebook.* How often have you felt a strike, set the hook, and then reeled in, minus trout and minus lure? Not to worry. *The Waterproof Vest Pocket Knot Booklet* from Orvis will show you, in clear detail, how to tie many important fishing knots and when to use each one.

>>> *Steel Wool.* Spinner blades and spoons become tarnished and dull after they have been used and then put away wet. These lures are designed to imitate the flashing movements of baitfish and fry. When they lose their sparkle, they lose their effectiveness. Carry a piece of steel wool and polish your tarnished lures before offering them to the trout.

>>> *Fingernail Polish.* Some days, nothing goes right. If you try every lure and fly in our tacklebox without success, it's time to get radical. Using ordinary fingernail polish, paint dots, stripes, or hieroglyphics on a spinner blade or spoon. Paint the head and tail of your wet fly or nymph. The most

productive color I've ever used was a fluorescent chartreuse with platinum sparkles. I bought a small bottle from a retired belly dancer, who spends her summers nymphing along the Upper Madison. That particlar bottle of polish ran dry several years ago, but bright red seems to work just about as well.
    —Bruce Cherry, April 1993

A Handle on Handles

SPINNING AND BAITCASTING rods have been greatly improved by the advent of blank-through handles. The main rod shaft (the blank) forms the core the handle is built around, improving the "feel" for a lure's vibrations or a fish's delicate take.

Fighting butts append to the rear of a rod handle, providing extra leverage for hook setting, distance casting, and fish fighting. At one time used mostly on big-game flyrods, they are now common on baitcasting and spinning rods.

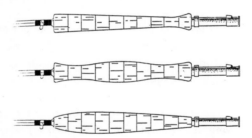

Typical handles: the Gordon (top), Full Wells (middle), and Philippe Cigar (bottom) are three of the more common flyrod grips.

Flyrod grips come in several styles and shapes. The diagrams illustrate those most commonly found on modern rods.
    —Anthony Acerrano, October 1991

From Bottom to Topwater

THE INTERCHANGEABLE shooting-head system is very effective for deep-water presentation of flies. Sinking heads are cut to various lengths to allow for depth and speed of current. With a loop-to-loop setup, the heads are easily replaced on the running line, allowing for a multitude of subsurface situations without replacing the entire flyline. As a result, the system has become the mainstay of many fall-salmon and winter-steelhead fly anglers.

As an addition to the sinking system, the wise flyfisherman will also carry an interchangeable head of dry line. Discarded floating line can be cut down to a 10- to 15-foot length and coiled for storage with the sinking heads. With the same loop system, the setup also allows for topwater presentations. This setup is quite handy if the fall-salmon/steelhead angler wishes to cover shallow riffles or comes across some rising trout and wants to change to floating flies.

—Gene Trump, December 1993

Smoother Guide Wrap Transistion

PERHAPS THE MOST trying problem you'll encounter when tying guides onto a fishing rod is winding thread smoothly from the rod blank to the guide foot. Carefully tapering the guide feet with a mill file prior to installation helps, but thread gaps often persist anyway.

One method of dealing with the problem is to lead the wrap up the guide foot with the tag end of the thread left from the beginning of the winding. As you begin to

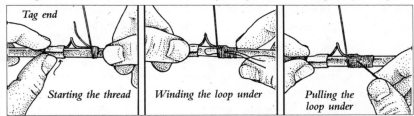

Tag end

Starting the thread | *Winding the loop under* | *Pulling the loop under*

To simplify winding thread from your rod blank to the guide foot, lead the thread up the guide foot with the tag end left from the start of the winding. Align the end with the center of the guide foot, cut, wind a few more turns, and tie in a finish loop.

wrap the guide, align the end of the thread with the center of the guide foot. It will help bridge the tiny gap that exists between the guide and the rod blank, making for a smoother, gap-free transition.

I generally cut the tag end even with the wrap once it comes up over the tapered area of the guide foot. Then wind a few more turns and neatly tie in the finish loop, which is used to pull the other end of the thread beneath the wrap in order to finish it.

—Fred Everson, August 1989

Field-Testing Flyreels

HOW MUCH FLYREEL does a trout fisherman need? That's a necessary question for today's flyfishermen, many of whom look at the bewildering display of new products with nothing less than intimidation. One might ask, Do I really need a $400 hand-machined work of art to successfully land trout?

Ferrule Protection

Ferrules on rods collect dirt and foreign particles that contribute to rapid wear. A ferrule plug can be made for the hollow female ferrule to help keep it clean. The plug can be all wood, or have a wood top and center with cork covering the shaft that goes into the ferrule. For very small ferrules, a wood-and-cork-covered brass welding rod works well. Adding a loop of string helps to prevent losing the plug.
—Deke Meyer, February 1985

Or can I get by with the $30 cheapies? What's the best value for my money? How much flyreel do I really need?

Traditionally, a flyreel was thought to be little more than a storage wheel for line. For many trout fishermen, such is still the case—a reel functions mainly as a way to hold and smoothly release flyline and a reasonable amount of backing. Those who fish small streams or who angle primarily for smallish hatchery trout do not require a reel with high-tech disc drag and 150-yard backing capacity. I think of a friend with a fine little trout stream running through his ranch who admitted one day that after 20 years of catching rainbows and brookies up to 17 inches, he has never had a fish get into his backing—a fact he realized while changing flylines, when he discovered that the 50 yards of ancient Dacron backing was, after two decades, yellowed and brittle, and worthless.

My own theory is that a fisherman, like a Boy Scout, should always be prepared. Moreover, he should always be an optimist. So even on small streams I like to have fresh backing on a reel I can trust to perform smoothly, just in case a large trout should sip my fly and take off for the nearest big river. But I don't kid myself that a small-water reel need be anything sophisticated. In fact, to be honest, trout fishing in general (with a few exceptions to be discussed later) rarely requires the kind of ultrafine reel necessary to a bonefish, steelhead, or salmon man. A "good" trout reel meets the following criteria:

1. It should be light enough to balance with the rod and not cause unnecessary fatigue during a day of casting.

2. Its line capacity must be adequate for the water and fish. Again, for creeks and small trout, this need not be much. Ten-inch brookies or foot-long rainbows will not get into your backing unless you're doing something very wrong. On the other hand, big browns and rainbows in larger rivers and lakes, especially wild trout in the West or muscular Alaskan leopard trout, may make fast, long runs. Here it's wise to err on the side of too much backing rather than too little.

3. A good flyreel should have reliably solid construction. No wobbles, in other words. More on this in a moment.

4. The reel must offer the potential for a quick and painless spool change in case you need to switch to a sink-tip line, or back to a floater or deep sinker, and so on.

5. The drag must be stiff enough to keep the spool from overrunning itself when you strip out line, and it should operate smoothly when stressed by a fish. An exposed rim for applying manual drag is essential, since it's probably more important than the actual "drag" device found in the reel.

6. Last, the reel should not cost more than it's worth.

> > > *Construction.* The finest modern flyreels are machined from high-tech aluminum bar stock, which is incredibly strong for its weight. The spool and sideplates are finished with great care and are anodized against corrosion. Spools are counterbalanced for maximum efficiency, and are usually perforated to get rid of unneccessary metal and achieve the lightest possible finished reel. The

craftsmanship and precision here match those of Swiss clocks, and the prices reflect it. Reels of this caliber begin at a low-end price range of about $120 and average closer to $200, with the finest going for $350 or more; spare spools generally cost more than half the price of the reel itself. Not cheap, but for those who despair of such prices, it should be pointed out that a trout fisherman needs such a reel no more than a lawyer needs a Mercedes to drive to the office. The top-end reels (for trout fishing) are luxuries pure and simple. For those who appreciate the finer things, and are willing to pay for them, the top-end reels are a delight to own. Their quality, durability, and beauty are undeniable.

Midrange reels are usually diecast of good but not necessarily highest-end metals. Strength comparisons between machined and die-cast metals reveal the gap in quality—with the machined aluminum being in some cases nearly four times stronger (86 psi tensile strength for the machined versus 23K psi for the die-cast). The differences in weight and appearance are obvious, but reels in this price range are normally durable and quite serviceable in every respect.

Low-priced reels are formed from cheaper materials such as stamped metals or graphite composites. Many of these have what are called "rim-and-post" connections, in which the sideplates are held together by screw-locked metal posts. Unfortunately, these screws have a way of loosening, causing wobbles, lost screws, and general unease. Also, rim-and-post reels tend to be heavy for their line capacities, partly because they're made of essentially low strength-per-weight materials. Though thousands of anglers have used this type of reel for years, and for the most part happily, my experiences have led me to prefer solid-frame reels over the rim-and-post models, which in all probability will soon become relics of the past.

Reels made largely or partly of graphite may not have the aesthetic appeal of aluminum or metal designs, but there is no disputing over the fact that graphite-composite reels are extremely light, tremendously durable, and inexpensive. Some of the best lower-priced flyreels I've tested are made partially or primarily of graphite composite, which may prove to be much more popular in the future.

▶▶▶ *Drags.* Despite all the talk about drags—"smooth-as-silk drags," "hard-working drags," "tough drags that wear down fish"—the subject of spool brakes is fairly simple when applied to trout-weight flyreels. There are two basic types of drag systems. The more common is variously named a "clicker" or "click" or "pawl-and-spring" or "ratchet-and-pawl" design. The pawl is normally a wedge-shaped piece of steel or plastic that engages a ratchetor gear to provide a clicking noise and a modest amount of tension (drag) on the spool. Generally, a leaf-spring exerts force on the base of the pawl, and this force may be adjustable via a side knob on the reel. Obviously, the more force against the pawl, the more tension created and the more drag you receive. The shape of the pawl allows you to reel in the line without much resistance; but when the spool direction is reversed (as when a fish runs), the pawl engages fully, providing a louder click and increased level of drag. The better "click" drag reels have two pawls instead of one, for added tension.

You may be surprised to learn that the ratchet-and-pawl system is found on 98 percent of today's flyreels, including some of the most expensive ones. It's sobering to open up a $200 reel and find a drag device nearly identical to that in an $80 model, and it's instructive as well, because it shows that drags are not a huge part of the trout fisherman's world, nor do they need to be. The high-priced reels offer the best in construction materials—the lightest and strongest and most pleasing to the eye; but drags, generally, are made to be adequate, nothing more.

The amount of actual drag you can get from a ratchet-and-pawl device is quite limited. Certainly, no fish of real power would ever be worn down by pawl drag alone, and no experienced fisherman would expect it to. The clicker is for keeping the spool from overrunning itself and putting a modicum of pressure on fish.

For most reels, the true drag is not in the clicker but in the exposed spool rim, which you palm manually to slow a fish's run. Let's state categorically that you should avoid any reel that doesn't have this feature. Exposed spool rims are just about mandatory for the proper playing of a good fish.

The second type of drag, rarer and really not required for most trout fishing, is the disc style. There are different designs, but the best works much like a car brake, utilizing cork or Teflon pads to place pressure on the revolving reel spool. A spring and adjusting nut allow you to increase or decrease pressure as you require. The effect can be startlingly smooth and powerful. Again, while such braking ability is crucial in a steelhead or bonefish reel, and is a pleasure to use for any species, it's not required for most trouting. A click drag and a trained palm, in my opinion, will subdue any trout you're likely to encounter.

▶▶▶ *Right or Left?* In the grand manner of flyfishing tradition, right-handed anglers are supposed to reel with their left hands, and vice versa. The idea is that fish should be fought with your strong arm holding the rod. Also, if you cast with your right hand, you can reel in slack line with your left without shifting the rod from one hand to the other. This has always made sense to me, though there is no point in being dogmatic about it.

If you're starting out, there's wisdom in doing things the "right" way from the beginning. However, most reels come set up for right-hand cranking (which, again, is really more suitable for left-handed casters). Luckily, it's easy to change the crank direction on most ratchet-and-pawl reels. Usually you need only flip the pawl, or one of the pawls, over to reverse direction. See the instructions that come with the reel for the exact adjustments. Disc drags are usually more difficult to convert, and some can be changed only at the factory. Be sure a disc reel is set for the proper crank direction *before* you buy it.

➤➤➤ *What About Multipliers?* Most flyreels are single-action, which means the spool turns one complete circle for each turn of the handle (a 1:1 ratio). Multiplier reels are geared to provide faster line retrieve. In other words, with a 3:1 retrieve ratio, you can pull in three times as much line with a single turn of the handle.

Multipliers come into their own whenever you need to zip in slack line quickly, such as when a large rainbow is running back toward you, or when you're working a lake or big river with long casts and want to pull excess line in fast to make a new cast or approach a different lie or fish.

—Anthony Acerrano, December 1989

[**7**]

Knots, Lines, and Leaders

~

"A visit to a first-class fishing-tackle shop

is more interesting than an afternoon at the circus."

–Theodore Gordon, 1906

<<< *An angler shucks line for a long cast on the Yellowstone River.—**Photo**
by Andy Anderson*

Tips for Knot Tying

A generations-old knot-tying practice of fishermen: spitting on the knot before drawing it down. They say it makes the knot stronger: Does it? No, it actually weakens the tie by about 5 percent. But doesn't the spit lubricate a knot, enabling it to be drawn down tighter, thus minimizing slipping? No, this is also a misconception. Just remember the most important factors when knot tying are the skill and care you exercise. Take the time to practice tying the knots of your choice, the ones you trust to bring back that catch of a lifetime. Practice until you know the look of a knot that has the strands in order. Then, when a knot does break, you'll know it was an internal foldover impossible to detect—or a faulty piece of line.

–From Sports Afield's Freshwater Fishing, *1992*

Very Necessary Knots

A POOR OR BADLY chosen fishing knot can weaken the strength of your line by more than half. The basic overhand "granny" knot, for example, is not effective with fishing line. A good fisherman should master a half-dozen necessary patterns, and none of them are complicated. This is an important and all-too-often overlooked subject, yet for no need. The following knots are easy to tie and can be memorized in a few evenings of practice. Once you learn how to tie them, you can fish with added confidence, knowing that the link between you and your lure is solid.

>>> *Clinch Knot (and Improved Variation):* This is perhaps the most-often-used knot for attaching line to a hook or lure. The standard clinch knot uses five turns of line before the standing end is passed back through the opening loop and tightened, but with very heavy lines the knot will gather more easily if three or four turns are used. This knot is normally given 85 to 90 percent strength rating (meaning the finished knot is only 10 percent weaker than the line itself). The improved variation is said to be 5 percent stronger than the ordinary clinch knot. Tie both and test them on a spring-type weight scale to see which you prefer. Note that either variation can be further strengthened by doubling the line before tying (moisten the line and press it tightly together—don't spin it—to form an easily worked double strand). The double-clinch knot is especially useful with lines lighter than 6-pound-test.

Clinch Knot

The clinch knot—perhaps the most-often-used knot in fishing—is tied by wrapping the line around itself five times, then passing the standing end back through the opening loop.

Improved Clinch Knot

Said to be five percent stronger than the standard version, the improved clinch is tied by simply passing the tag end of a clinch knot back through the larger loop.

>>> *Trilene:* This is really yet another improved version of the basic clinch knot, and if tied properly, it forms a knot of nearly 100 percent strength. Because it uses two loops inside the hook or lure eye, you get substantially more resistance to wear and breakage at that point, which is particularly valuable for ultralight lines and light tippets.

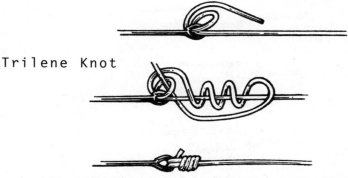

Trilene Knot

Pass the line twice through the eye; pinch the loop and make 3 or 4 turns around the standing line; then insert the tag end through the double loop, and slide tight against eye.

>>> *Palomar Knot:* Many anglers use this one because it's quick and easy to tie; it can be tied simply by feel, even in the dark. Flyfishermen like it because it produces a strong but small knot at the fly head.

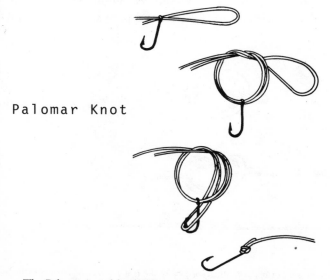

Palomar Knot

The Palomar is tied by doubling the leader, passing it through the hook eye, forming a simple overhand knot, then passing the hook through the tag end loop and tightening.

>>> *Duncan Loop:* When you want to emphasize the side-to-side or wobbling action of a lure or streamer fly, use a loop connection instead of a standard-fixed position knot. The duncan loop is a good choice because it's easy to tie, strong, and will jam down tightly once a fish is on, after which it can easily be pulled open again, to any size you desire.

Duncan Loop

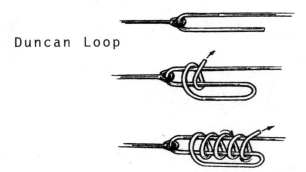

Pass 6 or 8 inches of the tag end through the eye of the hook; form a loop, then pass the tag end around the loop five times and tighten, so that a small loop remains at the hook eye.

>>> *Double (or Triple) Surgeon's Knot:* This is the fastest, easiest way to connect two lines, either of equal or disparate thickness. It's particularly useful (and headache-saving) for building flyfishing leaders—much easier than the traditional, time-consuming blood knot. Many fishermen rely on the double version; I prefer the triple because it provides added proof against slippage.

Surgeon's Knot

Place leader tips side-by-side in opposite directions; twist the two together to form a loop; then pass both ends through the loop two more times; wet the loop wraps and tighten.

—Anthony Acerrano, June 1994

More Knots to Know

FIRST, LET'S EXAMINE the world's worst, weakest knot. It's a simple overhand knot tied in a line—the first part of the bow knot you use to tie shoelaces. This knot will cause line to break at about 50 percent of its given test. Ten-pound test will break at 5 pounds of pull. So never tie a fishing knot with an overhand knot in the main line, especially if the line tests 25 pounds or under. The lighter the line, the more potentially damaging an overhand knot is.

Before looking at specific knots, let's examine some properties of lines from early fishing days until the present. Here are the "breaking loads," measured in pounds per square inch of line diameter:

The earliest material was braided horsehair, which yielded 20 to 40 psi; later came braided silk at 40 to 60 psi. Nylon emerged in the 1930s at psi levels slightly higher than those of silk, but modern nylons rate 60 to 100 psi. Incidentally, our most advanced lines today pale when compared with a spider's monofilament, which checks out at 200,000-plus psi.

Today's miraculous nylon monofilament lines are twice as strong as yesteryear's silk and linen lines. Even poorly tied knots will hold ordinary fish. But let's talk about knots that will hold that behemoth you hope to catch.

A PAIR OF PARAGONS

▶▶▶ *The Brinson Knot:* Not only does the Brinson knot prove stronger than the line at least three-quarters of the time, but it is the only knot that remains true to itself. Often it's difficult to tell if other knots have drawn down properly; not the Brinson. When it's tightened, it will break easily to let you know it's misbehaving. When it draws down properly, you can see and feel it pop through itself and lay a neat row of parallel strands. Just try tying it a few times.

Brinson Knot

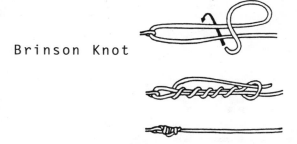

(1) Pull 6 inches of line through the eye, and lay a 3-inch length of tag end against the main line; (2) make five wraps with the tag end around the doubled line, holding the wraps with your thumb and forefinger while inserting the tag end through the loop; (3) pull lightly on the tag end to slightly tighten turns, then pull the main line and eye in opposite directions.

➤➤➤ *The* Sports Afield *Knot:* This knot is fairly involved, but easy once you get the motions worked out. In force-gauge tests, it checks out at 100 percent—meaning the line will break before the knot fails most of the time.

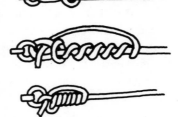

Sports Afield Knot

(1) Feed 6 inches of line through the eye, and tie a half hitch in the tag end around the main line and snug it down, leaving an opening between it and the eye; (2) wrap the end around the main line 6 times and thread it through the opening; (3) draw down the knot by pulling the tag end and main line in opposite directions; make sure the wraps are parallel.

KNOTS FOR JOINING TWO LINES

Often it's necessary to join line to line, or leader to line. The knot for this purpose needs to be minimal in size, tapered at both ends to flow through rod guides, and passably strong. Here are some good ones.

➤➤➤ *Joiner Knot:* The joiner knot, recommended for lines below 30 pounds, is extremely versatile. It was originally used by commercial fishermen for suspending dropper lines at right angles to the main line, to reduce tangling.

Joiner Knot

(1) Join the ends by tying an overhand knot; (2) form a loop that stands above the knotted ends; (3) make six foldovers with lapped lines, keeping the center loop open; 4) pull the knot through the center loop, pull on each section of main line, and draw it tight.

>>> *Dropper Loop:* The dropper loop is superior to the usual figure eight knot because it suspends dropper lines at right angles to the main line to minimize tangling. A dropper can also be tied by leaving 6 inches on the leader-to-tippet section of a surgeon's knot, or on a blood knot.

Dropper Loop

(1) Use the same procedure for making six foldovers as in the joiner knot, then pull the loop through to the desired length of the dropper; (2) snug the knot tight and the loop will stand at a right angle to the main line, reducing the dropper line's tendency to tangle.

>>> *The Blood Knot:* The blood knot is an old favorite of flyfishermen for tying tapered leaders and for joining lines of equal diameter, such as when your fishing line breaks for some reason after you have out 20 or 30 feet of it. It's a good idea to practice tying this knot on scrap monofilament before you ruin a good leader, but once you get the hang of it, it's a very simple and useful knot to know. The blood knot is also suitable for joining fresh line to spool backing.

Blood Knot

(1) Lap the ends of both lines about 6 inches (more if it's your first time); (2) make 5 turns with each end, holding open the middle loop with your thumb and forefinger; (3) insert the tag ends in opposite directions through the loop; (4) draw down the knot by pulling down alternately on the tag ends and main lines until the knot is snugged tightly.

Tying Backing to Flyreel
>>> *Slip Knot:* You probably won't tie this knot very often, since you don't need to change your backing often, but here's how.

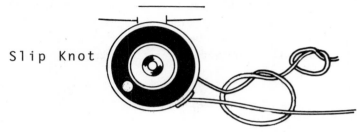

Slip Knot

(1) Loop the backing around the reel arbor; (2) tie an overhand knot around the lower strand and then tie another overhand knot at the end of the line; (3) pull on the line, and the knot will slide right up against the arbor; the knot at the end prevents slippage.

Tying Flyline to Backing

>>> *Nail Knot:* This knot was originally tied with a nail, but a simpler method is to use a small tube, such as a basketball air valve needle.

Nail Knot

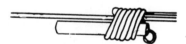

(1) Arrange the flyline, tube, and backing as shown—allow plenty of backing extended for wrapping; (2) hold all parts firmly, and wind the backing line around itself, the flyline, and the tube; (3) holding the turns in place, push the end of the backing line through the tube; (4) continue to hold the turns as you carefully slide the tube out; then draw the knot tight.

Tying Leader to Flyline

>>> *Perfection Loop:* Most commercial leaders come with a loop already attached to the butt. If not, or if you want to make your own, here's how.

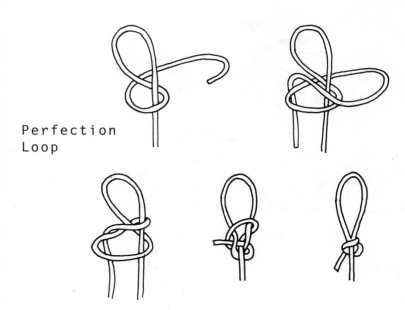

Perfection Loop

(1) Take one turn around the monofilament forming the upper loop, then hold it at the crossing point with your thumb and forefinger; (2) take a second turn around the crossing point and bring the end around once more between turns, forming the lower loop; (3) pass the lower loop through the upper loop; pull on the lower loop until the knot jams.

>>> *The Jam Knot:* This is a simple way to tie the leader to your line and can be used for all ordinary fishing conditions. However, if you expect to catch big fish, it is best to tie a heavy mono butt to the flyline with a nail knot. Tie the other end of the butt to the leader with a blood knot and coat with Pliobond.

Jam Knot

(1) Tie an overhand knot at the end of the flyline, and thread this under the leader loop, over one strand and across and under both strands, over the other strand, across the line and under the loop; (2) draw the knot tight until the overhand knot is tight to the loop.

Tying the Fly to the Leader

>>> *Double Turle Knot:* Although this knot has about 8 percent less breaking strength than the improved clinch knot, it is preferable for attaching a trout fly because it holds the fly straight, makes it ride naturally, and improves hooking.

Double Turle Knot

(1) Thread the leader tippet through the hook eye, and slide the fly up the leader; (2) turn back the end of the tippet and make a slip knot, but bring the end around twice instead of once before sticking the end through both turns; (3) draw the knot tight and push the fly through the resulting loop. Tighten again until the loop slips up over the head of the fly.

Easy Twist Knot

HERE'S A QUICK and easy way to make the twists of the knot that attaches a fly and leader. Pass the leader end through the eye of the fly. Place the end between the thumb and index finger, exposing approximately one inch at a right angle to main line. Hold the main portion of the leader between your other thumb and index finger, keeping the fly centered. Using the thumb and index finger that are securing the main portion of the leader, roll the line. Bring both hands together, and lines on both sides of the fly will automatically twist together. Pass the end through the loop at the eye of the fly. Pull at the main portion of the line to tighten.

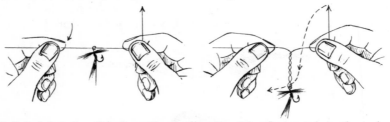

Roll the left portion of the line with your finger tips. Bring the two ends together and pass the tag end through the loop at the eye of the fly.

—Dennis L. Brisson, May 1983

How to Fish Two or More Flies

OLD-TIME WET-FLY ANGLERS often fished two or three flies at once, but then this practice fell out of favor. Now, however, multiple wet-fly fishing seems to be undergoing a slight revival; you might want to try it. The way to attach additional flies is by tying one or two lengths of monofilament (known as droppers) to the leader with a dropper loop knot.

To attach the droppers, tie a perfection loop at the end of a length of monofilament. Pass this loop through the dropper loop, thread the end of the monofilament through the perfection loop, and pull tight. Tie a fly to the end of the monofilament.

➤➤➤ *Blood Knot Extension:* This is an even better way to tie a dropper to a leader. It is tied the same way as a blood knot.

When making your own leader, you can form the dropper by allowing an overlap of about eight inches when you start to tie the knot. When the knot is tightened, you will have an extension to which you can tie an additional fly.

—*From* Sports Afield's Freshwater Fishing, *1992*

Understanding Flylines

➤➤➤ *Line Color:* Flylines come in virtually every hue in the rainbow. Opinions vary widely on whether bright, visible lines or dark, drab ones are preferable.

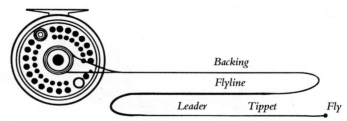

A standard flyline is comprised of five parts—backing, flyline, leader, tippet, fly—all of which play a significant role in your ability to hook and land a trout.

The issue is largely one of personal taste. In most cases, a bright line is not likely to hinder your chances for success. This is particularly true when you're surface fishing and using long leaders. Your line is rarely over the fish; just the leader and fly are.

There are also some advantages to using highly visible lines. During periods of low light or when fishing a nymph, brighter lines help you control your fly drift better and detect strikes more readily.

When working flies below the surface, with shorter leaders and the line closer to the fish, darker, drabber-colored lines are generally preferred. With sinking-tip lines, you can get the best of both worlds: a light-colored floating section, which helps in line control and detecting strikes, and a dark sinking portion, which is closest to the fish.

➤➤➤ *Matching Flylines:* In the past, matching a flyline to a rod was always a bit of a challenge. Today manufacturers mark flyrods with a number designating the exact line weight the rod was designed to cast. Buy a line with the number indicated on the rod, and you should have a well-balanced outfit.

That's the safest approach, and the one to start with. But individuals differ in their speed and style of casting, and sometimes a line one weight heavier or lighter than that indicated on the rod may work better for you. If you don't feel you're getting the potential from your rod, try experimenting with a brighter or heavier line. Generally speaking, for casting small, feather-weight flies, a line one weight lower in number might be more effective. For fishing heavy nymphs and streamers, you may do better with a line one step heavier.

>>> *Connecting Backing and Leaders:* The knot most commonly used to connect flyline to backing is the Albright knot, while the nail knot is generally preferred for securely fastening leaders to the flyline.

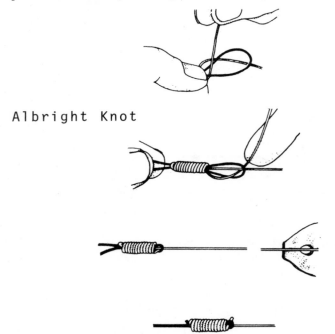

Albright Knot

(1) Make a U-loop in the flyline and lay the end of the backing alongside—allow enough backing to extend for wrapping; (2) hold the loop in place with your left hand, and wrap about a dozen turns of the backing around itself and the loop; hold the turns in place and push the leader through the loop; (3) tighten the knot slowly with pliers.

>>> *Tapers:* The angler must understand the basic difference between fly-lines and spinning or baitcasting lines. In flyfishing, the weight of the line

*The **double taper** is especially useful for rollcasts, and performs best on small streams when casts of no more than 30 or 40 feet are necessary.*

*The first flylines made were **level lines**, but because of their inefficient design, they were good only for short casts, and are seldom used today.*

*Because of its shape, the **weight-forward line** allows for longer, more accurate casts; it is particularly useful for casting large streamers, heavy nymphs, or bushy dry flies; it's probably the best bet for virtually all trout fishing.*

Shooting tapers are specially designed for very long casts, with thirty or forty feet of heavy line, for the falsecast, followed by second, thinner segment of shooting line.

itself is cast; the fly is simply pulled along by the line. This is the opposite of spinning or baitcasting, in which the weight of the lure pulls out the line, and the lighter the line, the farther the lure can go. That's why flylines are thick and heavy, while spincast and baitcast lines are thin and light in comparison.

The flyrod is flexed, or loaded, by the pull of the line's weight during false-casting. When that energy is released on the final forward power stroke of the cast, the rod sends the line out over the water, carrying the fly behind. Depending on the fly's size and the distance you're casting, different tapers are utilized. These are designated by letters on the flyline box: L stands for level, DT stands for double taper, WF for weight forward, ST for shooting taper.

The first flylines made were level lines—they had the same diameter from end to end. This is the least efficient design, good only for short casts—and even on those, the lines do not cast smoothly or delicately because they don't narrow at the end. A tapered line provides more efficient energy transmission; the narrowing diameter eases energy out of the line and into the leader at the end of the casting cycle. This allows much more delicate and efficient fly deliveries.

The double-taper line is even and fairly thick in the middle, but tapers down gradually to a finer point on each end. This is an improvement over the level line and can be useful for casting over wary fish such as trout on small streams, where casts no greater than 30 or 40 feet will be required.

The thinner line near the leader on a double taper allows even more delicate casts than a level line. With the same taper on both ends, the fisherman can also reverse the line on the reel when one end becomes worn—getting, in effect, two lines for the price of one. Double tapers are also effective for

Easy Slider Knot Worms

The junction of the fly-line and the leader usually requires a nail knot or some variation of it. Leader links are okay but are not as effective as a good, tight knot. A problem arises, however, when the leader-line connection is drawn through the guides of the rod. Without custom treatment, the knot will often hang up in the guides—unhandy and frustrating in most circumstances, disastrous in big-fish situations.

The knot can be coated with Pliobond, but it takes several coats of that messy stuff because of shrinkage.

I prefer Shoe Goo and Sportsman's Goop, both excellent knot coverings.

A bead of goo is squeezed out of the tube onto the knot and left to dry for a moment or two. When it's pliable but not too tacky, it can be formed into a nice little worm, tapered on both ends, completely surrounding the knot. Shrinkage is minimal, and the goo stays flexible, even in frigid weather.

–Deke Meyer, April 1987

roll-casting, since this cast gains its momentum not from a backcast, but from a downward and forward snap of the rod. The heavy line near the tip of the rod provides more weight to cut through the air and carry the gradually tapering tip forward.

Weight-forward lines are also known as rocket or torpedo tapers. In most modern lines, weight forwards are identical to double tapers for the 30 feet closest to the fly. But they quickly taper down to a thinner running line for the remainder of their length. Because of their shape, switching ends with weight-forward lines when they wear out is impossible. In most fishing situations, however, the advantages the WF taper offers are worth the extra cost.

The finer running line of the WF shoots more easily on long casts than a double taper or level line does. Its thinner diameter creates less friction with the rod guides and less air resistance on the cast, and also offers less weight to be carried forward. This makes the weight forward the line of choice over a double taper when you're casting more than 30 or 40 feet. Weight-forward lines are also particularly useful with large streamers, heavy nymphs, or bushy dry flies. Here the efficiency of the final power stroke is critical, since weight and wind resistance are added to the leader by the heavy flies.

Some people believe that double tapers allow gentler fly deliveries than weight forwards do. But as I mentioned, the final 30 feet of line in both taper designs is identical, so the same delicacy can be achieved with either line.

Shooting tapers (ST) are the final major flyline type available. These are specialty lines useful where extreme long-distance casting is required—such as

Type of Angling	Weight
Small-stream trout	1–5
Medium trout streams and rivers	3–6
Large trout waters and steelhead rivers	5–8
Salmon rivers	7–9

on a broad, deep steelhead river where the only way to reach a rainbow's holding lair is with an 80- or 90-foot cast. This flyline setup consists of two parts. Called a head, the section closest to the fly is 30 or 40 feet long. It's designed much like the end of a normal weight-forward line. This is connected, usually by interlocking loops, to a second thinner segment called the shooting line. The angler falsecasts the head; then, on the final downward stroke, shoots the thin remaining line. Because of the shooting line's extremely fine diameter (sometimes even monofilament or braided nylon is used), it goes out even more easily than a normal weight-forward line, enhancing the angler's ability to make very long casts.

➤➤➤ *Floating and Sinking Lines:* When you're shopping for a flyline, check the letter code on the box to determine if the line is designed to float or sink. The letter F stands for floating; S for sinking; F/S means that the forward or tip section of the line sinks and the remainder floats; and I stands for intermediate or neutral density line—one that stays near the surface or sinks very slowly.

A line designated WF-6-F, for example, means a weight-forward Size 6 line that floats. A WF-6-S is a weight-forward Size 6 line that sinks. A WF-6-F/S is a weight-forward 6 line that has a sinking forward section and a floating mid and rear section. A WF-6-I designates a weight-forward 6 line with neutral density; it hangs near the surface or sinks slowly.

Full-sinking lines are useful when fishing deep in lakes or large rivers, particularly when drifting, trolling, or fishing from an anchored boat where flies are left suspended in the current, as in some forms of shad or tarpon fishing. Here precise line control is not demanded and very little casting is done. A slow full-sinking or intermediate line is also good for working flies over weedbeds or along the edges of dropoffs. Intermediate flylines are also favored by many saltwater flats fishermen who don't want the line on top of the water but don't want the fly to sink quickly, either.

Use sinking tips when you want to get your fly down deep but have most of the line floating where you can detect strikes. These lines are less tiring and troublesome to use when you have lots of casting to do. The floating part lets you keep better track of the drift of the fly, control the line more effectively, and lift the line out of the water more easily for the next cast. These lines come in 10-, 20-, and 30-foot sinking-tip lengths, with the remainder of the line floating. For probing deep sections of lakes or deep rivers with heavy currents, choose the longer sink tips.

In addition to different lengths of sinking tips, these lines come in sink rates ranging from slow sinking (around 1.25 to two inches per second) to fast, extra fast, and superfast sinking. These latter lines descend at speeds of three to six inches per second and are particularly useful for nicking a streamer along a riverbottom for trout.

If these lines still aren't getting far enough down for the fish you're seeking, it's time to turn to specialty lines, which are made by Cortland, Scientific Anglers, and other companies. These will all probe the deepest lake waters and stay down close to bottom even in heavy river currents. They can be useful for some Pacific salmon and steelhead fishing, tarpon angling in deep rivers, probing offshore wrecks and going after low-hanging summer lake trout.

➤➤➤ *Care and Storage of Flylines:* Modern flylines don't need much care, but they do require occasional attention if you want them to deliver optimum performance. To prolong the life of your line, for example, avoid casting without a leader, stepping on the line, pinching it between the frame and spool of your reel, snapping it in the air behind you by starting your forward cast too quickly, and allowing it to make contact with insect repellent, gasoline, and suntan lotions.

The only care necessary to keep your line in top condition is occasional cleaning. You may see a dirty film developing; the flyline may stick in the rod guides and not shoot as well as it should; or, if it's a floating line, it may begin to sink. In all of these cases a cleaning is in order, since algae and microscopic particles of dirt have likely built up on the line. These attract and hold water and reduce the line's buoyancy and shootability.

Some flylines come with cleaners and conditioners. If yours didn't, you can buy several types for only a few dollars, use soap and water, or apply an auto vinyl upholstery cleaner such as Armor All.

Flylines do not require any special care during the off-season. You can remove the line from the reel if you like and store it in larger loops around a wooden peg, but the easiest storage method is to simply leave it on the spool. Be sure not to put the spool in an airtight container while it's still wet, or mildew may develop.

—Gerald Almy, January 1989

Leader Logic

THE LEADER CAN be a critical factor in catching fish, yet anglers concern themselves with the rod, reel, and breaking strength of the line—and then hang a leader that doesn't make sense.

Not every situation demands a leader, and you can often tie your hook or lure directly to the line. If you need more strength, try doubling the line by using the Bimini Twist or the Spider Hitch. For those who use braided line on casting reels, a monofilament leader should be incorporated at the terminal end.

A leader serves a specific purpose; it's vital that you analyze that purpose. It may be to protect against the teeth or gill plates of a fish. You may need an extra length to prevent abrasion. In some cases a heavier piece of material cushions the shock from casting, and there are times when you may want a leader that is lighter than the line. If you are using a sinker, it's a good idea to attach it with mono that has a finer diameter than your line. That way the sinker will break off and you won't lose the whole rig if it gets snagged.

Flyfishermen often let tradition saddle them with handicaps. Gossamer threads help to make the presentation look more natural than larger strands, of course. The primary purpose of a leader, however, is to create a separation between flyline and fly.

It's hard to convince trout purists that they can catch their quarry on extremely short leaders. I have taken rainbows on leaders less than six inches long. Remember that the leader should be adjusted to the conditions. A long leader is much more difficult to cast and handle than a shorter one.

Adjusting a leader holds the key to success. When you're fishing a sinking flyline and want your offering to be swept right over bottom, long leaders will defeat your purpose. The weighted line will hug the gravel, but the leader will float the fly well above it: A short leader of a few feet should keep the fly in the payoff zone.

Some flyfishermen seldom use tippet material that's lighter than 6X, and they often prefer 3X or 4X. The key lies in presentation and not in how fine a tippet is. When the water is extremely low and placid, conditions may demand a longer leader. Ask whether it is more important to be able to cast a shorter leader on the mark or stray with a longer one.

A fallacy in dry-fly fishing insists that the leader must turn over and the fly must land at the end of a taut tether. You want the fly to alight on the water with serpentine curves in the leader behind it. This prevents drag, and spells trout on a dry fly. Use a stiffer butt section and a softer tippet end. You actually want the tail end of the cast (meaning the leader) to collapse.

Once a flyfisherman tailors a leader, he might assume it can handle any pattern or size, but as the size and bulk of a fly increase, the leader has to be stouter. You'll also find that too long a leader frustrates casting efforts as fly sizes get larger.

–Mark Sosin, Sports Afield Fishing Secrets, 1986

A New Theory of Leaders

I T SEEMS TO ME that the development of terminal tackle has been based largely on the assumption that trout don't see particularly well. We use light leaders in hopes that they won't be seen and we tie on bright flies to make sure they will be.

Is the reasoning behind this sound? I doubt it. A trout may take your fly because he doesn't happen to notice the leader, or because he does see it and doesn't become suspicious, but the thought that we conceivably could use gut too fine for trout to see is preposterous.

Sometime when they are rising, but hard to catch, sacrifice a half-dozen flies in an experiment. Drop them into the stream well above rising trout and let them float down to them. Few flies unattached to a leader will escape being taken. Yet you can cast the same pattern to the same fish and never get a touch. It is the leader that makes the difference.

Learn to Tie the Orvis Knot

Shown here is a knot every fisherman should add to his basic repertoire. The Orvis knot retains 94 percent or so of the line's rated strength (compared to 82 percent for a standard clinch knot, and 90 percent for the improved clinch), and is particularly useful for tying on small flies.

–Anthony Acerrano, May 1996

(1) Form a loop by bringing the tag end down in front of the leader, and up through loop.

(2) Rotate the tag end to the left and wrap it twice through the second loop.

(3) Pull the fly with one hand and the tag end with the other until the knot tightens.

Thorns for Flytying

A tool that should be in every flytying kit is the often condemned thorn. Good-sized thorns have a number of uses. They are ideal for applying glue. The taper readily brings a droplet of glue to the point; after a few practice dips, you can get just the right amount. The hard point of the thorn can be used to clean out the eyes of all but the smallest hooks. They can fluff up wool or other tying materials. The point is also perfect for undoing knots in monofilament, clearing up backlashes, and linking leader to lines with a nail knot.

–Jim Casada, October 1989

All of us have seen trout rising to midges, tiny gray flies so small they become invisible to a man at a distance of a few feet. Yet the trout can see them, and on evenings when the rise continues through the dusk, the fish feed on them after we can no longer see anything at all.

Even more convincing is the knowledge that trout feed on plankton, usually on such tiny crustaceans as daphnia, which are smaller than the head of a pin and nearly transparent. Of course, all young fish utilize this food, but it is not so commonly known that good-sized trout in some waters feed extensively upon it.

One day while my brother Burtt and I were camped on the shore of a wonderful trout lake near the continental divide, I noticed big fish feeding in the shallow water before our tent. We tried a number of flies, but failed to interest them. Finally, in desperation, I set up a casting rod and took a three-pound cutthroat on a spoon. He was gorged with daphnia.

Experiences such as these—and many others—have led me to the firm conviction that it is impossible to use a leader so fine that trout can't see it. Fine gut is less conspicuous, less alarming, but not invisible.

It was Al Klotz, of Boise, Idaho, an expert and thoughtful angler, who gave me the solution. "You know," he said one evening after I had outlined my idea, "most of the good streams that we fish have a lot of moss. Even clear mountain brooks have some. "Trout aren't afraid of moss. They're used to it. I've seen them take damsel flies that were sitting on it. I don't believe they'd think it unnatural to see an insect—your fly, that is—drifting along clinging to the end of a piece of moss. If the leader were dyed exactly the right color . . ."

"I think it would work!"

He chuckled. "As a matter of fact, I know it will. I've tried it. I've been dyeing my leaders the color of moss for some time."

I bought some ordinary household dye in brown and green. The stringy moss I wanted to imitate was not a clear bright green, but rather a dull shade, strongly tinged with brown. I dissolved a piece of the green dye and a fourth as much brown dye in a quart of water, simmering hot.

The first scrap of nylon that I soaked in it came out too green. I added a little more brown. Finally, after coloring innumerable pieces of leader material and adding a pinch of blue dye, one took on the color I wanted. I dyed several leaders and extra tippets and bottled the solution for future use.

A few days later I went to Silver Creek. It is a crystal-clear spring-fed stream with an abundance of moss, countless small hatchery trout, and a few wise old lunkers. I spent most of the day fishing with wet flies and nymphs because only little trout seemed to be rising. Not once did I use a leader finer than 2X. When I walked back to the car after sunset, I was completely satisfied. The moss-dyed leader worked. I had released 21 trout. I had kept one, a three-and-a-half-pound rainbow.

That was three years ago. I have since used the brown-green leaders in a variety of streams and lakes. Some of them contained a great deal of moss. Others, especially the granite-bottomed, churning mountain rivers, were almost devoid of vegetation, except for algae on the rocks. In most waters I found that I could hook fish on tippets a full size larger, and occasionally two sizes larger, than before.

—Ted Trueblood, September 1951

Fishing Fundamentals

M OST OF THE expert anglers I know—and I'm fortunate to be acquainted with some of the best in the world—are surprisingly simple fishermen, tactically speaking. That they catch fish in numbers and sizes many anglers only dream about is seldom a result of esoteric technique or late-breaking "miracle" lures and equipment. Besides having an astute knowledge of the quarry and its environment, superior fishermen pay almost samurai-like attention to some unglamorous but vital tackle fundamentals.

1. Line: Since the line is the link to the lure and the fish, experts are scrupulous about choosing and inspecting it. It's also what typical fishermen tend to think about least.

Selecting the right line for the species and the situation is important. For example, stiff, abrasion-resistant line works in heavy cover or salt water; but limp, thin line is best for long casts, light lures, and clear, open-water presentations. Before buying line, read the packaging box carefully to decipher the specific qualities of the line and the kind of fishing or conditions that it's designed for. Also make sure your line is neither too heavy for the necessary presentation (clearwater fish will often spook from, say, 10-pound-test line, but strike eagerly at the same bait presented on 4-pound-test) nor too light (8-pound-test might not be able to hold a good bass in heavy cover, whereas 14-pound-test will).

Inspect all of your lines before each fishing trip. Nicks, frays, kink, yellowing, and hardening all mean the line should be replaced immediately. Too many fishermen try to cut costs by buying the least expensive line they can find, or by using good line past its prime. I've seen trophy fish lost, sometimes after hours or days of effort and expense, because an old or worn line popped. Buy quality line; carry a good array of strengths and types (soft, stiff, thin, thick, tinted) suitable for the conditions you expect to encounter; while fishing, check frequently for nicks and frays, particularly in the terminal six feet (trim it back as needed); replace the entire spool slightly before, rather than after, it needs changing; and load your reels to their correct capacity, usually about a quarter of an inch from the spool rim.

2. Knots: You don't need to know 50 knots to be a good fisherman, but you do need to master at least two or three, or as many as a half-dozen, depending on the type of tackle you use and your range of angling interests (see box below). A good guide to knots will provide instruction. I suggest Mark Sosin and Lefty Kreh's *Practical Fishing Knots* (Lyons & Burford).

3. Hooks: Keep your hooks sharp. This may be old advice, but it's rare to see a companion actually take 30 seconds to hone a hook point. Sharpening may be less important with softmouthed species (crappies, panfish, even small trout) but it's essential with pike, bass, salmon, steelhead, tarpon, and the like.

Whether the shape of the hook point is round or triangular (three sides honed flat toward the point) is up to you, as is the choice of using a small whetstone or a handheld battery-powered grinder. Sharp points are what matter. Be sure to check your hooks periodically, especially after catching fish, hauling in snags, or making contact with rocks or a gravel bottom.

4. Rods: Using the wrong rod can make it difficult to impossible to make the proper presentation or hook-set. I recall trying to fish for king salmon in Alaska's wide Nushagak River, using only a 5 1/2-foot bass/pike-style bait-caster. The short rod limited my casting distance and hampered my ability to

Tippet Size		Fly Size
X4	.015 inches	6/0-3/0
X3	.014 in.	5/0-2/0
X2	.013 in.	3/0-2
X1	.012 in.	2/0-2
0X	.011 in.	1/0-2
1X	.010 in.	2-8
2X	.009 in.	6-10
3X	.008 in.	6-14
4X	.007 in.	6-16
5X	.006 in.	8-18
6X	.005 in.	10-22
7X	.004 in.	14-26
8X	.003 in.	18-32

"long-line drift" a lure (much aided by a long rod's ability to lift a substantial portion of the intermediate line from the river's current) and my leverage for quick and effective striking. I got skunked while those fishermen around me, properly equipped with seven-foot, long-handled, ultra-fast-action drift rods, caught a pair of kings each.

Long rods not only improve casting distance and line control, they also absorb shock and stress better than short rods. But short rods highlight the advantages to quick leverage. Everything else being equal (such as angler competence and sufficient line strength), a short rod will subdue a fish faster than a long rod will. It will also provide better lure feel and allow quicker strikes on a short or submerged line; more casting maneuverability in tight places; and quick, powerful leverage to haul fish out of cover.

—Anthony Accerano, May 1996

You Must Use the Right Flyline

OUT OF 20 fly fishermen that I meet on the streams, I rarely find more than one who is doing good, graceful, effortless casting. The rest will be flipping around short pieces of line so awkwardly and ineffectively that it's more luck than skill when one of them catches a fish.

Furthermore, it would be totally impossible for most of these to learn real fly casting, since their lines come nowhere near fitting their rods. Nobody living can do good casting with mismatched rod and line.

When, oh, when will these poor fly casters learn this? Angling writers for years have been trying painstakingly to teach them, but they refuse to learn—simply can't get it into their heads that the matter is all-important if they want to stop flubbing around and really learn to cast a fly. And catch fish.

About 99 times in 100, the trouble is that the line is much too light to bring out the action of the rod. So all anybody can do with it is flip that short piece around, with a lot of tiring, unnecessary, and ungraceful arm waving.

Clerks in tackle stores are largely to blame for this, I believe. In spite of the omniscient air on all matters pertaining to fishing that most of them assume, few are good fishermen. They usually recommend line too light, almost never too heavy, and still more rarely, the right size. As a matter of fact, most rodmakers, in their catalogs, recommend line too light for best and easiest casting with their rods.

No set of tables can be of any real use except for rods of the company that compiles the tables. In fact, they're rarely useful even for that, since most rod companies put out rods of different models, with different actions, in similar lengths and weights.

Many quite experienced anglers use a line one size too small, because they learned with such, and are used to it. Put on one of the correct, larger size, and it will probably seem all wrong at first—it will confuse him. He'll have to learn to slow down his timing, let the rod do most of the work, not his arm. He may not use that line long enough to get accustomed to it; he'll take it off, say it is too heavy for his rod. If he'd stick with it a while, and get used to it, he wouldn't go back to the lighter line for anything. He'd find that with the heavier one he could cast more accurately, farther, and with much less effort.

—Jason Lucas, December 1954

A New Strong Knot

ANGLERS ARE ALWAYS experimenting with new knots. Occasionally, a truly strong and different one is discovered. Joe Miller of Buena Park, California, has done it. When tied to a hook at one end of a short length of monofilament line, the Miller Knot consistently outpulled the competition by breaking Improved Clinch, snell, and Palomar knots tied to a hook at the other end of the line. The Miller Knot takes a little longer to tie than most popular knots, but the result can be more fish in the boat. It's workable on lines testing under 60-pounds breaking strength, but becomes unwieldy on heavier lines.

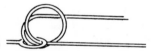

Hold the hook or lure in your left hand. Pass the end of the line through the hook eye twice.

Loop the tag end of the line under and over the line twice.

Pass the tag end through the coil next to the eye.

Pass the tag end through the single coil from underneath, taking it over the two lines twice.

—Chuck Garrison, January 1986

Add Forty Feet to Your Flycasting

M AYBE YOU HAVE always admired the angler who can throw a long fly line and hoped someday you could do the same.

With a simple trick, requiring little outlay of cash, you too can throw your fly line an impressive distance, catch those fish you now find just out of reach, and do it all easily—if you have any basic knowledge of fly casting.

Novice fly casters may not realize there is considerable difference in the construction of various fly lines. Basically, there are level, double-taper, and forward-taper lines. A level line is just what the name says: level throughout its length. A double-taper has a level section in the mid-portion and tapers to a rather thin point at each end. The forward taper-line has most of the weight and size concentrated in the forward end, near the lure, with a much thinner portion toward the reel.

It is important that the caster understand a little about forward-taper line. A forward-taper fly line has three distinct segments. Beginning at the end nearest the fly there is a short tapering section that gradually swells in diameter to a rather heavy, thick portion called the belly or head. This head is somewhere between 15 and 30 feet long, depending on the manufacturer and the purpose of the specific line. Beyond this head, toward the reel, is a thin section, the longest portion of the fly line, called the running line.

Here is briefly how a forward-taper works for distance casting: Coils of running line are pulled from the reel and allowed to lie at the caster's feet. To throw the line a long distance the angler must develop line speed with the head portion of the line, which is kept waving back and forth outside the tip-top guide of the rod. As the head is brought forward with a sweep of the rod, the left hand holds the running line. When the rod has been brought down and points nearly at the target, the left hand releases the running line. The rapidly moving head pulls the running line through the guides and out over the water. The speed and inertia of the movement of the head are enough to pull many coils of the running line at the angler's feet through the guides and make the long cast possible.

The running line, while thinner than the head, is still rather heavy. A lot of line speed has to be developed with the head to drag this relatively thick running line through the guides. Unfortunately, most anglers cannot get the head section of the fly line moving rapidly enough to pull the running line through the guides well, so they never make long casts.

The method suggested here will allow the angler using a relatively slow-moving head still to throw a fly line a considerable distance.

Spare Flylines

Carrying all the extra flylines, in various sink rates, needed to probe all the depths of a lake or large river can take up most of the room in your vest. It can also cost a bundle: You need to buy a spare spool for each line.

However, if you use a shooting-head system, you can keep your spare lines coiled and labeled in plastic bags. Whip a loop to the back end of each 30-foot line, another to the front end of your shooting line, and you can also change heads without reeling all the way in and restringing the rod every time. This approach saves space in the vest, fishing time, and money. It also gives you more options: When you need a specific line, you are more likely to have it with you.

—Dave Hughes, October 1989

Basically, you can attack the problem in two ways. Either develop more line speed to drag the running line easier to pull through the guides; or make the running line easier to pull through the guides by changing its basic construction. I have selected the second method.

Let's replace that relatively heavy conventional running line with something slick, smooth, light, and thin which can be pulled with little effort. Thirty-pound monofilament is the answer.

If you take a forward-taper line and cut it just back of the head, you will see that the heavy head is much larger than the remainder of the line. If you are still confused, measure back 30 feet from the forward end and snip the line and you'll be close enough to make the idea work well.

Using a nail knot [see page 220], splice in 40 feet of 30-pound monofilament fishing line where you made the cut. Then attach the other end of the monofilament to the running line. What you should have is a head section in front, 40 feet of monofilament spliced in with a nail knot at each end, and the running line completing the connection to the reel.

You can do the same thing with a level line, although it will not cast quite so well. Use the level line if you don't want to experiment with an expensive forward-taper.

A rule of thumb that works well on level line is to cut it about 25 feet back from the forward end, unless you are planning on trout fishing. Then 15 feet works well. Make the cut, splice in the monofilament as has been outlined, and you have, actually, a forward-taper line.

How will this arrangement help the average fly caster obtain more distance? Simple.

Assemble the line on the rod and reel and take it to the nearest water. Place outside the rod tip the entire forward section called the head, plus about 18 inches of the monofilament. Make the normal back cast, throwing the line high and straight behind you. Then make a normal forward cast. During all of this time you have the 40 feet of mono lying at your feet, with your left hand firmly holding the mono during the back and forward casts below the largest rod guide. As the rod comes forward and extends almost parallel with the ground, release the monofilament in your left hand. The heavy-fly-line head section finds little difficulty in pulling the 40 feet of slick, thin monofilament through the guides and toward the target.

Add together the 30-foot head and the 40 feet of monofilament and you realize that you have thrown 70 feet of fly line—that's way out there!

There are several things that will simplify the whole procedure. I always take Pliobond, or some other supple, rubber-base glue, and roll a little over the two nail-knot connections. This makes them slide smoothly through the guides.

You should always stretch the monofilament before you begin fishing. Manufacturers of nylon fishing line say it has a "memory," which is another way of saying that it tends to stay in the position in which the line was stored on the reel spool. In this case the line will lie at your feet in coils that will tangle if not stretched well. Pulling tightly on the line does eliminate nearly all of this problem.

I find that Stren Fluorescent monofilament has a fantastic ability not to tangle during the shoot. It is much superior to anything else I've used. I've noticed, however, that after a number of fishing trips, usually a dozen or more, any kind of nylon gets "stale." For ease of casting I replace it with fresh nylon, a simple trick I accomplish by tying two nail knots. Two dozen trips, of course, is at least a season for the average angler.

Make sure the nail knots are tied tightly. If not, they could slip and lose you a good fish. Then snip the knot closely, so that they feed easily through the guides.

Always leave about 18 inches of the forward portion of the monofilament outside the guides when you make ready for the back cast. It helps little, however, to have much more than that outside, since the monofilament weighs next to nothing and cannot develop any force to pull running line through the guides.

What's the difference between a shooting-head line and this idea? Not much—and plenty.

Shooting-heads, conventional types, are made by attachment of a section of fly line to 100 or so feet of nylon monofilament line. A shooting-head allows the angler to cast farther. But on windy days; or when he's wading a swift river; or when he's in a boat, where all sorts of "things" stick out and grab line, it takes a man of strong religious convictions to remain pure as he solves the tangles of yards of monofilament after each cast. Wind, too, can blow the light monofilament in every direction.

With the 40-foot piece inserted between the running line and the head you have an entirely different proposition. Here is the way it works.

The angler shoots the line to 70 feet, or closer if he wishes. Then he strips the 40 feet into the boat or onto the water at his feet and drops it. The 40-foot length is short enough not to tangle easily or blow around. When the head portion comes up near the rod tip, the angler simply lifts the rod, swings back, swings forward, and shoots. Then he repeats the whole operation again, and again, with a minimum of line trouble.

Shooting-heads are made for extremely long casting. The method suggested here is for the nonexpert fly angler fishing at practical fishing distances. It creates a minimum of casting problems—and affords a maximum of casting efficiency.

–Bernard "Lefty" Kreh, December 1966

Foul-Ups

FEW THINGS CAN muck up the bliss of fishing like the appearance of unwanted knots, tangles, and snags. Tangles particularly plague the beginner and come in many forms, but they are usually associated in one way or another with line twist. Twisted monofilament has its own "energy" and wants to curl up and wrap around itself or jump in loops from the reel spool. The best way to eliminate many tangles is to watch for, prevent against, and deal with line twist before it gets out of control.

First, it's important to load line correctly onto a reel. Another way to reduce twist and tangles is to favor limp lines over stiff ones. (Exceptions occur in salt water; in heavy-cover situations, where line is easily abraded; and for trolling, where stiffer lines offer less stretch and more lure-to-rod sensitivity.) Limp lines have less memory than stiff lines and thus lie down more tightly onto the spool.

Note also that line twist is cumulative. Repeated casting with lures that spin will eventually wind the line to a trouble point, as will the bad habit of reeling against a fish's pull or a snag's resistance. (Use the rod to pull against dead weight or an opposing force, reeling only after, or as, slack is created.) With lures that revolve, such as spoons and whirling jigs, use a swivel to reduce line twist. Whenever twist accumulates, unravel it by removing the lure and dragging the line behind a boat, or by letting it straighten in a current.

What else causes tangles? Poor line handling, for one thing. This includes reeling up large amounts of slack without guiding the line through your fingers while maintaining tension and feeling for loops and knots. Flyfishermen create tangles by letting flyline accumulate at their feet or on the water during retrieves, or by looping it sloppily in their line hands.

No matter how careful you are, sooner or later tangles are going to occur—hopefully not too often, but even once can be too much if you compound the problem with an inept response. On the bright side, remember that a lot of messes can be untangled neatly if you respond with patience. Tangles are not helped by anger and irritation. Take a few moments to calm down and study the mess. The wrong approach is to start yanking and jerking, which only makes everything worse. Figure out the logic of the tangle as best you can, then work slowly to pick it apart. Pick and pull lightly, because tightening usually locks down incipient knots. Never try to cut your way free unless the tangle is near the end, and never cut a tangle on the reel unless you intend to replace the entire spool.

Another category of common foul-ups occurs when your hooks stick in things other than fish, such as weeds, snags, and bankside brush. The remedies:

(1) Practice casting in the backyard until you have precise control and accuracy. (2) Use the proper lure for the conditions. For example, don't try to drag a treble-hooked crankbait through thick weeds; go to a weedless spoon, plastic worm, single-hooked plug, or jig. (3) Carry lure-retrieving devices. (4) If a multihooked plug lands in bankside brush, don't try to yank it free, as this only sets the hooks deeper. Instead, jiggle your rod tip lightly. If the lure rattles, you're in luck. Keep jiggling, keep the lure rattling, faster and faster. Eventually the hooks will loosen and the plug will jump free of the brush.

—Anthony Acerrano, June 1994

Inflation Needle Knot

T HE NAIL KNOT has always worked well for attaching the leader to the flyline, but carrying around a sharp and usually rusty nail can be a bit of a nuisance. Try instead a blunt, stainless-steel basketball inflation needle, which can be found at most sporting goods stores.

Cut or grind one-eighth to one-quarter inch off the tip to create a hollow

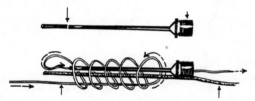

An inflation needle can simplify—if not improve—the process of tying a nail knot.

tube. After that, the procedure for tying the nail knot is pretty much the same as it would be if you were using a common nail: Hold the modified needle above the free end of the flyline and run the butt end of the leader back in a parallel fashion so you can wrap the tag end around the flyline, needle and leader. The hollow inflation needle allows you to shove the mono completely through the needle tube. After making five wraps and running the leader into the tube, simply remove the needle, pull the lines tight, and trim the loose ends.

A plastic ink magazine from a ballpoint pen will also work for this technique, but the large threaded end of the inflation needle makes removal much easier when you pull it free from the completed knot.

—Gene Trump, December 1990

One-Way Flyline

Let's suppose you've just arrived on the river, the evening hatch is on, and you're trying to fumble flyline through all those tiny rod guides. If you drop the line at the last guide, the whole mess will shoot backward to land in a snarl at your feet. All this can be avoided by doubling the flyline a foot or two before threading it. If you drop the line, the springiness of the loop stops its fall at the first guide.

—Lewis Watson, April 1988

[8]

Spin Tackle

~

"All fish are not caught with flies."

–John Lyly, 1579

Snelled Hooks

Trout fishermen should avoid snelled hooks and use leader lines at least six feet long, with monofilament testing not more than six pounds. In high or muddy streams, use one or more split-shot to sink the bait to bottom. Worm fishermen should use short-shanked Size 8, 10, or 12 hooks. You only need one worm on the hook for best results.

–William Fodiak, April 1988

Quick Hookups

When fishing with a float, the line between the rod and float sinks into the water, causing extra drag when you try to set the hook. Try coating your monofilament line with flyline dressing so the line will float on the surface. This procedure will reduce drag, enabling you to set the hook more quickly. The sinkers that you use with floats will pull the line down between the float and the hook.

–Donald Seeley, August 1994

Successful Spinning

USED PROPERLY, A spinning rod can catch an amazing number of trout. And the craft aspect of spinning entails much more than pitching out a lure and cranking it back. Indeed, the full dimensions of the game are wider and more complicated than many think.

▸▸▸ *Where the Trout Are:* Before you begin casting, you must know where the trout are—which is to say, you must know how to read water. The skill has many subtle dimensions, but the basics are fairly straightforward. Look for places where the push of the current is broken or altered by obstructions or other currents. An obvious example is a boulder sitting in the midst of a fast run. The boulder breaks the current and creates a downstream pocket of "cushion" water, in which trout will lie. Less obvious, perhaps, is a "seam," where two currents of different speeds meet, creating a band of flat surface water. Also look where slow water near shore or a midstream island meets the fast water of a main riffle. Trout will rest in the calm perimeter while watching for food carried down in the faster current.

Another easy-to-see example is where a tributary creek enters a stream or river. You can follow the seam of the different flows quite easily, and this is where trout will often be. Brown trout like the shade, cover, and cushioned water of undercut banks—which are easy to fish with lures. Rainbows will rest and feed in shallow riffles that are quite fast, using dips and gouges in the streambottom for cushion water; they also rest in the lee of submerged or partially submerged rocks. This again is a kind of "pocket" water. If you study a stream or river very carefully, you'll begin to see the many shapes and forms and subtle ways in which these two kinds of "good" water—seams and pocket cushions—are manifested.

▸▸▸ *Presentation:* It's common to read or hear advice like "an upstream cast is better than a downstream one" or "The best cast is across stream and up." But I think the true picture is more complicated. A good spinfisherman will use every approach possible, and in one stretch of water may cast upstream, downstream, across-and-up, across-and-down, or directly on target. It all depends on the specific demands of the water. The key is to cast a lure so that it approaches a fish or prime lie in the most tantalizing fashion. Let's look at some examples.

▸▸▸ *Up-and-Across Casting:* Imagine a comparatively open stretch of water—let's say a long seam that separates bankside slow water from a fast mainstream riffle (such seams commonly occur below sharp bends in the stream). The first thing to remember is that the trout might be cruising the quiet pool water itself. Approach stealthily, from the downstream side if possible, keeping a low profile, casting first near shore and then working upward and outward toward the seam, making essentially upstream and up-and-across casts. Cast long, to keep yourself as far from the fish as possible, and retrieve swiftly. (A good rule to remember: In slow water, you should favor a quick retrieve, which excites a trout's predatory instincts while allowing less time for close lure inspection.) Try to keep the lure near bottom. Once you've probed the calm water, move up closer and explore the stream itself. The best approach is to begin at the tail of the run and cast upstream-and-across at a 45-degree angle, dropping the lure in the swift current and retrieving slowly as the current swings it into and through the seam. The retrieve aspect here is minimal: You're mainly tight-lining while the current drifts and tumbles the lure, reeling just enough to keep tension on the line and maintain the lure's action.

▶▶▶ *The Turnaround:* A more offbeat but very productive method is to creep around to the upstream side of the run (walking far up on the bank if necessary to avoid spooking the fish) and approach the seam with successive down-and-across casts. Again, the lure is dropped into the fast water, where it's allowed to sink and drift for a few feet until the slack is gone and the line tightens. On a downstream approach the actual drift time will be very short. As the line tightens, the lure swings around in the current and lifts toward the surface, creating what is called the "turnaround" effect—something trout find irresistible, possibly because it so closely resembles the actions of a wounded baitfish trying to adjust itself in the current. The trick is to calculate your cast and drift angle so that the turnaround occurs right in the prime lie—that is, right in front of the fish's nose. This is a deadly technique, suitable for all kinds of situations on a trout stream. Once mastered, it will change your life as a spinfisherman—no exaggeration.

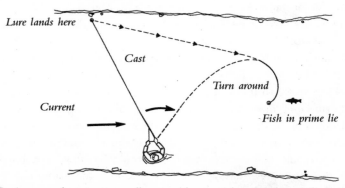

Casting up-and-across stream allows your lure to sink and drift until the line tightens. The lure then swings around and comes towrad the surface, creating the turnaround effect.

What happens on a turnaround is this: A trout sees the lure swing and instantly swings up right behind it—a wonderful sight. If you're lucky, the fish hits as soon as the lure swings through the lie or straightens out in the current. But sometimes the fish hesitates, and this is why you should begin a slow retrieve, pausing every few moments to lower the rod, allowing the lure to drift back a foot or two. Sometimes the current will swing the lure through the lie and back into fast water, where line tension pops it to the surface. In that case, all you can do is reel in and cast again.

The turnaround technique doesn't always require a downstream approach; in fact, whenever possible, it's better with an up-and-across initial cast, which provides a longer drift and gives the lure time to sink. It also gives you time to adjust your retrieve speed to position the lure for the desired swing.

Bank water—which is often excellent trout water—may be such that a drift of any kind is impossible. This is true for undercut banks or for lies made by fallen logs or branches. For undercuts, the secret is to drop the lure precisely on target, as close to the bank as possible. This means literally scratching the bank soil with the hooks. A soft cast is best here—you don't want to spook the fish—and the retrieve should begin instantly.

>>> *Fluttering:* When casting to fallen logs, submerged branches or root tangles, the best bet may be a "fluttering" approach. Here, you cast as close to cover as possible and simply let the lure sink, without creating tension or retrieving, so that it flutters to the bottom. (Obviously, this implies a spinner or spoon—a lure capable of fluttering.) Trout find the simple flutter appealing and will often dart out to grab the falling lure.

Some water may demand a combination of drift and flutter casts. A boulder cushion amid fast water, for example, can be fished several ways. You may first want to cast well above and past the boulder, bringing the spinner back across the upstream side of the rock—where there is also a cushion, albeit a smaller one, that sometimes holds trout. On the next cast, you might make the lure drift past the rock on the side opposite you—you may have to raise the rod high to let the line clear the boulder's peak—and turnaround inside the downstream cushion. Angle successive casts to cover as much of the cushion as possible. Then move to the inside edge and work it as best you can (the turnaround drift being more difficult here because of the rock's interference in the necessary line of drift). Next you might pinpoint some direct-drop casts into the center of the cushion, starting at the tail and working up toward the underside of the rock. Retrieves should be slow or minimal, essentially a fluttering presentation, to keep the lure in the prime holding water as long as possible.

—Anthony Acerrano, April 1989

Finessing the Spin Rod

TROUT FISHING IS more popular now than ever. Tackle companies love it, of course, and many are enthusing over soaring profits. However, having the right gear is only part of the equation; you also have to know how to use it. The following tips can help all spin rodders finesse their technique.

➤➤➤ *Stream Craft:* Take pains not to alert trout with loud wading or a high bankside casting profile. Examine the water for visible fish and prime lies before you approach, then plan a strategy. Move quietly and carefully, using cover to keep out of obvious view. Cast to close water first and slowly emerge cast by cast. Make the first cast while hunkering behind a bush, the next while kneeling at bankside, the next after wading softly a few steps in, and so on.

➤➤➤ *Fine Presentations:* Whenever possible, cast above a visible fish or prime lie. How far depends on the weight of your lure and the speed and depth of the current. The point is to cast so the lure drifts or swims past the fish's nose, not much above or below it, not very far to either side. This is true in lakes as well as streams.

Another approach that can improve any spinfisherman's success rate requires mastering the underhand, or pendulum, cast. This cast delivers small lures softly and precisely on target, at a low trajectory. With it you can shoot a lure under an overhanging branch and into a cup-sized pocket with only a blip of surface disturbance—perfect for situations that require accurate presentations, when the lure can't be retrieved or drifted to a fish or lie.

➤➤➤ *The Right Lures:* Top spinners include the Panther Martin, Mepps (bare and squirrel tail), Vortex, Blue Fox Vibra, and Rooster Tail. Sizes 00, 0 and 1 are best for ultralighting and small-stream situations. Also carry 2s and 3s.

Safety-Pin Rod Guide

Anglers carrying an extra safety pin in their pockets have saved many a fishing trip. Beyond its obvious uses (emergency hook or line swivel), the pin can also replace a damaged rod guide. Clip off the safety pin's head and align its spring, or eye, along the shaft of the rod. Once straightened, the pin's arms can be attached with tape or fishing line; the eye is large and smooth enough to let even heavy-test line pass through freely.

–Jeremy Pearce, November 1995

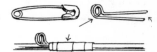

For a quick and easy rod-guide replacement, bend a safety pin so both arms are straight, clip off the head, and tape the arms to your fishing line.

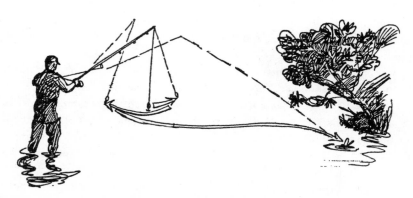

The pendulum cast: Let the lure dangle below the rod tip, then swing it back under the rod and, with the reel in freespool, cast by swinging the lure back and out toward the target.

Left Is Right, If You're Right- Handed

Right-handed reels with right-handed handles have been around a long time (spinning reels came from Europe with left-handed handles). The fact is, the right-handed caster with a right-handed reel wastes time by casting right-handed, switching the reel to the left hand for a right-handed retrieve, then changing hands to cast again. Although the choice is a personal one, expert anglers advise fishermen who are starting with casting reels to learn with left-handed-retrieve reels.

—Gerald Almy, November 1988

Favorite spoons? The Kamlooper, Wonderlure, Cyclone, Pixie, Krocodile, and Dardevle, all rarely more than two inches long. Spoons have the edge for fishing fast currents since they sink quickly and maintain their fish-appeal when tumbling along.

Also carry an assortment of minnow-shaped plugs—Rapalas, Rebels, and the like—from the smallest you can find to three-inchers. Another hot, infrequently used trout lure is a plastic-bodied jig, the kind designed and marketed for crappie and bass fishing.

—Anthony Acerrano, May 1995

Spinners and Spoons

SPINNERS AND SPOONS are lures no angler can afford to ignore. An assortment should be in every tackle box. Many are made of plain, smooth-surfaced metal, while others are decorated in various ways. Some are painted with one or more colors on the convex side, others are fluted or hammered. Hammered blades reflect the most light, fluted blades somewhat less light, and plain blades the least.

The June Bug's leaf-shaped metal blade revolves around the spinner's shaft when retrieved.

Since we consider the glitter and flash of a spoon to be its principal attraction, it might be thought that the hammered blades would be the most desirable, while the fluted and plain blades could be dispensed with. But this isn't necessarily the case. The strength of the light, the clarity of the water, and the type of food that the fish are seeking all have bearing on what will produce best.

On bright days, and in very clear water, the spoon that doesn't flash much is usually the best choice. The darker the day and the cloudier the water, the greater the need for a flashy spoon or spinner. Often when fishing in extra-clear water on a very bright day, it's helpful to scour the spoon blade with an abrasive so the finish is dulled and reflects light as would the scales of a natural minnow. More than once I've seen a fish frightened by a flashy spinner strike at one with dull blades.

Size can also make a difference. The general rule is to use smaller spoons for bright conditions and larger spoons for the opposite.

—Bill Palmroth, May 1984

Ultralight Trout

ULTRALIGHT SPINNING IS not only fun, but it offers tactical advantages as well. In the spring, when flyfishing is difficult on swift, high-water streams, working spinners, spoons, plugs, and jigs is a fine way to catch trout. When insects aren't hatching and rainbows and browns swim along the bottoms of river pools and lakes, probing the water with lightweight, quick-sinking lures often puts you into trout.

Also, ultralight spinning is a boon on low, crystal-clear waters. Casting fine line that is nearly invisible, you can present lures accurately and delicately without spooking skittish fish.

➤➤➤ *Ultralight Tackle:* For years, the standard ultralight outfit has consisted of a tiny rod/reel combo utilizing 4-pound-test line. Such a setup is middle of the ultralight road today. Manufacturers have developed versatile spin rigs that, in the hands of dexterous anglers, are capable of casting 1/64- to 1/4-ounce lures on 2- to 6-pound-test monofilament.

When refining an ultralight rig, begin by choosing a quality rod. Hand-test a variety of models; the one you want should be sensitive but not too wispy. Modern graphite and graphite-composite rods are strong and well-balanced and flex well from tip to butt.

These rods typically measure 4 1/2 to 6 feet. Choose a short rod when probing for trout in creeks and small streams. A long rod allows you to cast feathery lures 50 to 70 feet on large rivers and lakes.

Ultralight spinning reels weigh only six to eight ounces, but top-quality models offer big-time features.

Constructed mainly of graphite, these reels are durable and function smoothly. Many employ popular "quick-cast" and extended-range casting designs. Most important, these reels feature first-rate front or rear drag systems that, when set properly, release line at the slightest hint of pressure. This is imperative to success when playing trout on hair-thin monofilament.

Fill the main spool with 4-pound-test mono, which will prove adequate for most trout fishing. Scale up to 6-pound test on rivers and lakes where you have a realistic chance of tackling one- to five-pound rainbows and browns. Carry a spare spool with 2-pound-test line when angling for wild cutthroats and brookies and any time you go for pressured trout on clear waters.

Modern monofilament lines are small in diameter, yet high in tensile strength. Regardless of brand or test, choose a premium line: It will cast smoothly; provide superior strength and elasticity; and its abrasion-resistant coating is an excellent feature, since lightweight, quick-sinking lures tend to rub line on rough bottoms and underwater structures.

>>> *Ultralight Tactics:* Ultralight spinning is a delicate game. Sensitive tackle and feathery lures mean that success depends on the angler's dexterity.

After quietly approaching an obvious trout lie, open the tiny reel's bail, cradle the monofilament lightly in your forefinger, and flick your wrist to send a spinner or spoon sailing out across the water.

Direct the lure to your target by placing your forefinger on the reel's spool before turning over the bail. Your finger will touch the line spiraling off the spool, "freezing" the lure in midair. This has two major advantages.

First, it promotes precise, delicate presentation. With practice, you can stop a lure inches from structure or well ahead of where you anticipate trout to be. Once the lure clips the surface, you can maneuver it strategically through prime water, or let the current drift it naturally in front of a trout's nose.

Freezing the line also eliminates troublesome slack. A taut line is key to keeping a quick-sinking lure from snagging the bottom in shallow water.

And you will bump bottom. Spinners, spoons, and jigs sink relatively fast when using small-diameter line, and subtle trout strikes can be hard to detect on retrieve. Keep a tight line and hold the rod firmly to feel subtle takes. You'll have to pay close attention to the condition of your hooks as well, because the points will abrade quickly—or even break off—when striking bottom.

Raise the rod tip sharply when you feel a take. Modern graphite rods have the muscle to set a hook effectively.

When a brown runs deep or a rainbow writhes across the surface, the reel's drag, which should be set very low, will work freely. Let the line go, and touch the spool with your forefinger if you must turn the trout.

Hold the rod at an angle to the water and pump it gently to near vertical. The flexing of the rod, combined with the line's elasticity, will tire the fish.

Never attempt to land a trout before it's ready. Be cautious, however, not to overstress a fish if you intend to release. Coax it in after a reasonable battle. You'll feel grand as it fins away in healthy condition.

—Michael Hanback, May 1993

Nymphing with Spinning Tackle

THE USE OF nymphs is not restricted to fly tackle; they can be fished effectively with spinning gear. And for the angler who prefers spinning tackle, they are great on waters with flies-only restrictions.

A good nymph rig for spinning tackle consists of a monofilament tippet about 12 or 14 inches long tied to the spooled line with a blood knot, leaving a three-inch dropper at the knot. On the dropper, clamp a split-shot or two for weight (having the weight on the dropper rather than on the main

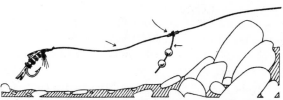

A nymph tied on the end of a 12- to 14-inch tippet weighted with split-shot is capable of landing many good-sized trout.

line enables you to pull the rig free should a split-shot get caught on a rock). Tie a good nymph, such as a Zug Bug or Hare's Ear, to the end of the tippet.

Fish the nymph as you would worms or salmon eggs. Cast upstream and across, bouncing the nymph along the bottom and maintaining a tight line, lifting the rod as the fly swings by. At the slightest hesitation of the nymph, set the hook. It may just be a rock—or a trout.

Using spinning tackle, I have landed bragging-size rainbows that I could not have gotten with traditional flyfishing gear.

–Robert Drew, June 1984

How to Spin a Fly

EVER TRY CASTING flies with spinning tackle? As mentioned above, you must weight the wispy trout fly and its hairlike leader so the spinning rod can cast it. Yet to be effective, the fly—wet or dry—must perform as perfectly as it does with a flyrod.

While fishing Connecticut's Farmington River, I discovered a simple system that works perfectly.

The trout wouldn't look at my spinning lures but were feeding eagerly on a hatch of gray-blue mayflies. I had dry flies of a similar pattern, but no way of fishing them. I dug in my tackle box and found a battered HCF torpedo-taper flyline. Snipping off about 15 feet of it, I tied the heavy end to my spinning line, and tied a leader and fly to the other end.

The first rainbow weighed one and a half pounds. The second took the rig; I hadn't tied the flyline securely enough to the monofilament, so I used the other end of the taper.

The heavy flyline provided the needed weight. The rest was easy. Here's the system:

Prepare an end of any heavy tapered flyline—about 15 feet or so—with terminal loops for quick tying and untying when converting from spinning to spin-fly casting and vice versa. The cast is a combination of flycasting and spinning techniques.

The Basic Spinning Outfit

Most trout water can be fished with a 5- to 5 1/2-foot ultralight graphite rod (fast-action, on the stiff side rather than whippy) with a matching mid-ultralight reel. Use 4-pound-test monofilament to start, but carry spare snap-on spools of 2- and 6-pound-test line in case you need to modify—in the first instance, for tiny-lure, small-fish, brook situations; in the second, for larger lures, obstructed waters and/or heavyweight trout.

–Anthony Acerrano, May 1995

One difficulty is flimsy spinning line that you must hold in your left hand. If it has any twist, it's tough to keep from tangling. Here's a way to beat it.

Hold the flyline only in your left hand, working it through the guides with the reel's pickup closed. When all of the flyline is out of your hand, strip the spinning line from the reel against the spool's drag and work it out until the attaching loop is beyond the rod tip. Then, while you make false casts, the forefinger of your right hand picks up the spinning line against the rod handle to hold it. Now release the pickup with your left hand, and make the cast.

On the retrieve or when you're playing a fish, the spinning line is wound in on the reel in the conventional way. But when the attaching loop reaches the reel, the flyline is taken in with our left hand as with a flyrod. The flyline should not be wound on the reel, even if there seems to be room for it.

A difficulty of this technique, which also is true of conventional flycasting, is preventing the line from reaching out farther than the fly and striking the water first. You can solve this problem by stopping the line short of the mark, thus allowing the leader and fly to swing out ahead. The simplest way to do this is to turn the reel handle so the pickup stops the line so you can quickly wind in any slack and be prepared.

Next time you take to the stream with your spinning gear, take along some flies and a dressed taper prepared this way. It can really pay off.

—Gilbert Paust, April 1955

Spin Control

A FIRST-RATE SPINFISHERMAN working a piece of water is a sight to behold. Well-versed in basic and advanced streamcraft (knowing how to read and approach the water), he or she uses specialty casts as needed; has pinpoint accuracy (is able to drop a small lure into tiny pockets, near or far); understands trout behavior through observation; knows which lures to use in which situations; uses tackle that's sporting and appropriate; and catches, handles, and releases trout with care and efficiency.

➤➤➤ *Equipment Choices:* My first choice for fishing in streams and natural lakes would be a 5 1/2-foot graphite spinning rod—ultralight, with a fast action; firm rather than willowy, not stiff, but bending mostly in the upper third when loaded. I would match this with a long-cast-style reel capable of holding spools of 2-, 4-, and 6-pound-test line. For a second outfit, I'd want a "light"-rated spinning rod, six feet long, same action as the graphite rod, matched to a light freshwater reel and using 4-, 6-, and 8-pound-test spools. I could fish brooks, small-to-midsize streams, shallow lakes, and moderate rivers with the first rod, whereas I'd use the larger rod for deep lakes, large rivers, or any situations where I'd need to cast large or weighted 1/4- to 1/2-ounce lures. Most fishermen use tackle that's too stout for the conditions, thereby muting casting efficiency and the pleasures of hooking and playing a fish.

➤➤➤ *Spinner Logic:* When putting together a lure selection, I start with all-purpose in-line spinners in an array of colors and styles—Panther Martin, Mepps, Blue Fox Vibrax, Rooster Tail, Luhr-Jensen Tiger Tail, to name a few—in Sizes 00 to 3/0. The smaller the water and/or trout, the smaller the spinner. Just as important as the length of the spinner or the size of the blade is what might be called "necessary weight"—the weight needed to get the lure to the desired depth. Not all 1/0 spinners are equal, in other words. If I need to get down in a current or to reach deep stillwater fish, I favor compact spinners with thick lead bodies that plummet quickly. But for situations where a heavy splashdown might spook nearby trout, I choose light-bodied spinners.

➤➤➤ *Automatic Spoons:* The same logic applies to spoons, which can be thumbnail small or two to three inches long. (Kamloopers, Blue Fox Pixees, Woblures, Tor-P-Do's, Acme Thunderbolts, and Dardevles are some favorites.) I like spoons for trout when I need to get deep fast, or when I want a lure that has automatic action—meaning it can attract fish when tumbling along in a fast current, or when fluttered and retrieved slowly in deep, still water.

With metal lures, choose high-gloss finishes such as silver or polished gold when fishing in dull-light or dark-colored water; and brass or black-chrome in clear water or on bright days, when flashy finishes can spook fish. Specific body colors, blade shapes, and tail adornments can be determined only by location, season, and, to some extent, daily experimentation. (Carry a variety of weights, colors, and styles to facilitate the process.)

➤➤➤ *Crappie Jigs:* Crappie-style jigs and spinner-jigs round out my tackle kit. Trout rarely see these lures, which in 1/16- to 1/4-ounce sizes catch fish when spoons and in-line spinners are ignored. Jigs and spinner-jigs cast well, sink quickly, are snag-resistant, and can be drifted, bounced, or retrieved over otherwise hard-to-fish rocky bottoms and deep runs in deep and shallow lakes. Black and brown marabou jigs with dark heads can represent stonefly and mayfly nymphs, leeches, or small baitfish. I'm unsure if jigs with soft-plastic tails represent any natural food, but I do know that trout love them. I wouldn't be without a selection of orange heads with white tails; red with white; orange with black; black with white; all white; and all black. But this is just a starting point. Experiment not only with color combos but different styles and shapes of tails (Twistertails, forked grubs, and so on) and dressings (marabou, marabou with Mylar, and Flashabou) to find the hottest combination for a given day.

➤➤➤ *Casts and Strategies:* Good spinfishermen approach the water carefully, keep a low profile, and study the area to be fished with an eye to visible trout and possible lies, as well as a strategy of cast sequences. The idea is to work the close water first, moving gradually outward. This often means starting right at your feet, with the bank water. The quieter the water (i.e., the less current and surface disturbance), the more cautious your approach should be.

>>> *Spot-Casting:* To my tastes, spot-casting is the most pleasurable and skillful way to stalk stream or shallow, stillwater trout. Move carefully up- or downstream, reading the water for current cushions such as undercut banks, shore cover, midstream boulders, partially submerged tree trunks, weirs, and gravel bars; seams, where currents of differing speed meet and create a slick or foam line on the surface; and pools large and small. Once you have located these targets, plan a route or sequence of positions that makes it possible to cover each lie without alarming the trout.

Spot-Casting: Use a sequence of casts that gradually move the lure closer and closer to the prime lie. Soft, accurate casts are vital when lies are small.

Accuracy is vital to spot-casting. In cases such as bank and pocket-water, it's necessary to drop the lure precisely atop the lie, which may be no larger than a dinner plate. To do this the cast must not be only accurate but soft; the lure should not splash down heavily. While an underhand or pendulum cast works best, you can soften a cast by feathering outgoing line through the half-closed palm of your free hand, then clamping down on the line and giving a sharp tug just as the lure descends on the target. The tug negates a lot of the forward momentum, stalling the lure so it plops gently into the water.

On mid-sized to large rivers and streams, spot-casting will cover only part of the water. The rest, and some of the best trout-holding sections—deeper riffles and runs—must be worked with controlled drifts.

>>> *Controlled Drifts:* Select a lure that will drift near bottom, or use a lighter one with weight attached. Trout in these heavier flows usually lie close to the streambed, where friction creates a slower, more comfortable current. Compact, solid-body spinners and spoons should be favored over elongated, lighter ones; or try bouncing a marabou or soft-plastic jig along the bottom.

Make most casts across- and slightly upstream, above the suspected fish zone. As the lure sinks in the current, reel to control slack and form a tight-line connection that lets you feel the lure working, bumping bottom, and ticking off rocks—evidence that you're reaching the fish zone. The retrieve at this point can be minimal, just enough to keep the line tight on a free drift. Or you can speed it up to guide the lure past a visible fish, or into a particular zone. A general rule: The faster the current, the slower the retrieve; the slower the current, the faster the retrieve.

Trout love to strike a lure as it swings around in the current at the end of the drift, a fact smart anglers use to their advantage by timing the turn-around so that the lure swings right by the fish's nose, or into prime-lie water. This old trick is very effective and could hook you up with the most cautious—and largest—trout in a stream.

—Anthony Acerrano, April 1996

Spinfishing with Streamers

THE STREAMER TACTICS used by flyfishermen are easily modified for use with lightweight spinning tackle. The most basic approach is to simply buy weighted streamer patterns. Flyfishermen often use streamers that are weighted with lead fuse wire that's wrapped around the hook shank before the body dubbing is applied. Weighted streamer patterns in all but the smallest hook sizes are heavy enough to be cast with lightweight spinning tackle and can be fished using a standard across-and-downstream presentation. Many spinfishermen attach the streamer to the line with an improved clinch knot, although a swivel is sometimes used.

Smaller streamers and unweighted streamers can be fished by attaching strip lead or split-shot 10 to 30 inches above the streamer. The amount of weight required will depend on stream conditions.

Some anglers feel the streamer acts more lively if the weight isn't in line with the fly. They attach a three-way swivel to the main line. A five-inch length of mono is attached to one ring, with a split-shot crimped to the tag end. A two- to three-foot leader is then attached to the other ring, with the streamer tied to that.

Streamer patterns such as the Muddler Minnow, which is tied to imitate bottom-dwelling sculpins, are particularly well-suited to spinfishing gear. Simply tie the Muddler to the end of the line with an improved clinch knot and crimp a split-shot directly above the eye of the hook. The Muddler is fished by quartering the cast upstream and allowing it to bounce along the bottom. The fly should occasionally be jigged off the stream bottom to attract strikes. Also try fishing the Muddler under cutbanks and jigging it as it moves downstream.

Light-Line Leaders

Light-tackle anglers often use a leader to take the abrasion from rocks and other structures. By using a leader that is stouter than the line, you can enjoy long casts with lighter lures and greater casting accuracy. But sometimes you want a leader that's lighter than the line, especially with sharp-eyed fish like brown trout and steelhead. In either case, attach the leader to the line with a barrel swivel. For 6-pound-test use a Size 12 or 14 swivel. For 8- to 15-pound-test, I like Size 7.

—Fred Everson, March 1996

For lake trolling, try weighted streamers or streamers weighted with lead on the leader. An alternative method is to attach a casting bubble filled with water two to five feet above the streamer. A swivel can be attached above the bubble to prevent twisting. Some anglers attach a spinning blade above the streamer, particularly when working deeper water.

Longer rods in the 5 1/2- to 7-foot range are preferable for spinfishing streamers. The added reach is useful in rivers and streams where Muddlers are being worked under cutbanks or a streamer is being guided through narrow channels.

—Ed Engle, February 1994

Spinning the Hatches

WHEN INSECTS HATCH on the water and trout are feeding actively, a spinfisherman can feel left out of the party. All those bugs, all those feeding trout, but only lures to throw at them. Here are two remedies:

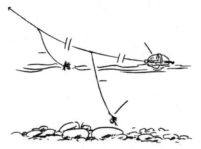

To fish flies with your spinning gear, use a standard spinning bubble with an emerger on a dropper and a dry fly up on the line.

1. If all you have is hardware, make good use of it by fishing below the hatch. While small and mid-size trout feed on surface insects, the largest trout in a given stretch will hunt closer to bottom, either gobbling up preemergent nymphs or preying on the small trout and baitfish that are also out to feed. If you mimic these smaller fish with a spinner, spoon, or jig, you can catch some of the best trout in the run. Cast upstream of the rising fish, rather than over them; and work your lure below the zone of surface activity.

2. The second response to a good hatch is to fish flies with your spin rod. Use a standard spinning bubble, and rig both a dry and an emerger-style wet pattern off a dropper. (You'll catch as many, and sometimes more, trout on the wet emerger pattern, even during the peak of the hatch.) Ask a local flyshop to help you put together a generalist kit of flies for the area.

—Anthony Acerrano, April 1996

Tackle Care Made Easy

ACCORDING TO TRADITION, winter is the off-season and the perfect time for getting fishing gear in shape. But for many modern anglers, there is no "off" season; we fish year-round and must tackle our tackle when we can.

>>> *Line:* The first thing I check is my line, because it's the most fragile part of the overall fishing outfit. Fresh line casts smoothly, resists memory (which is to say, it doesn't coil and tangle easily), and retains its full breaking strength; whereas old line does the opposite in every category. Furthermore, line doesn't take long to age. Ultraviolet sun rays and heat make quick work of even the highest-quality monofilament. So if line is more than a year old, or if it's been used frequently in bright light conditions, I pull it from the spool and reload with fresh stuff. I always err on the side of throwing a line out too soon rather than too late, a lesson learned the hard way—by losing trout of record-book proportions—that I prefer not to learn again.

>>> *Rods:* Modern graphite rods require little maintenance. One-piece rods can be wiped clean with a damp rag after each trip, then stood in upright racks. Breakdown models are returned to their sacks and cases. Before storing, I inspect each rod for surface damage to the blank. (Graphite shatters easily if nicked or fractured.) I also check the guides and guide wraps. In the old days it was common for guide rings to become rusted and/or pitted, but modern materials make this less of a worry. Still (and especially with lower-quality or older-model rods), I run a swab through each guide ring and look for signs of wear or damage to both the ring and the wrap, just in case. If the reel seat and clamping rings are metal, I wipe these too, periodically lubricating them with a light film of oil. On multipiece rods I check the ferrule joints for tightness. Loose joints are fixed by applying a rub or two of wax (parrafin, candle, or commercial ferrule wax) to the male portion of the joint. Then, for graphite rods only, twist the connection firmly together to join the ferrule properly.

>>> *Reels:* A reel is the workhorse and most mechanically sophisticated part of an outfit. Hence reels require the most care and attention. General maintenance is fairly simple, however. Once a year—or whenever the reel fails to operate smoothly—disassemble the outer housing to expose the main gearing. Be sure to use some kind of system to ensure that any parts you remove go back correctly. For simple take-downs, I lay the parts on a left-to-right line on my workbench; to reassemble, I simply work back from right to left.

When the gears are exposed, the first step is to clean away dirt and old lubricants. Alcohol-based gun-cleaning solvents, which are sprayed or wiped on, work best. I use an old toothbrush to scrub the solvent into the

To maintain spinning and baitcasting reels, disassemble the outer housing to reveal the gears, clean away any build up with an alcohol-based gun-cleaning solvent, and re-oil.

gears, wiping away the excess with a clean rag. Don't ignore the line-guide mechanism on baitcasting reels, including the worm gear—where lots of dirt and grit tends to build up.

Next comes re-oiling, an important step. Most anglers slop on too much lube, which only serves to attract and hold dirt and grit that mess up the smooth flow of the gears. Place one light drop of oil on each gear (using a toothpick for the hard-to-reach areas); no more. As you reassemble the reel, place a touch of oil on each housing screw; this helps lock them tightly.

For spinning reels, be sure to check that the bail-return mechanism trips properly when you turn the handle. If the bail hesitates or requires sharp force to turn over, you may need a new bail spring or bit of linkage, which can be ordered from the manufacturer. (Always save the reel's instructions, which can be helpful for re-assembly and ordering new parts.) Spin reels with frontal drags can accumulate grit that hampers smooth braking, so when cleaning such a reel, remove the drag knob and swab its underside and all exposed inner-spool surfaces thoroughly. Pull the spool free from the reel; then clean and lightly lubricate the under-spool gearing.

—Anthony Acerrano, December 1991

A Close Look at Spinning

MANY SPINFISHERMEN, WHEN they are ready to cast, do not hold the line properly. The average angler grips the line tightly against the rod handle with his forefinger. This makes for a slow and improper release when the lure is snapped free on the cast. Instead, the angler (if right-handed) should reach for the line with his forefinger and push it to the left of the center of the reel spool. The finger should then be held as stiff as possible. If the line is pushed to the left of center, it will never slip free. Then, when a cast is made, the finger has only to move a fraction to release the line.

After the line is released, the finger should stay pointed down along the side of the spool. When the lure is at the target, the finger can then reach down and catch the line. Only after the finger has caught the line is the handle turned to close the bail. If this procedure is followed, the spinfisherman can get extreme accuracy.

One trick that helps in accurate casting is to begin feathering the line with the finger as it nears the target. This slows the lure's flight and gives the angler more reaction time to make up his mind when to stop it. Baitcasters often argue that they can get more accuracy than a spinfisherman. This is not true if the spincaster uses his finger as described. Finger control is considered essential to good spinning by all who are expert at it.

Many anglers are fed up with bails that constantly fail at the wrong times. Little springs that are expected to function hundreds of times a day will break, slip from the catches, and so forth. This makes it impossible to use the reel until the trouble is corrected.

Once the trick of using your finger to catch the line at the end of the cast is mastered, you can solve your bail problems with no trouble. Simply remove the bail from the reel. Sometimes it is necessary to saw it off. But don't remove the roller guide or the part that grips the line and runs it around the spool during the retrieve.

The roller guide will flop around uselessly unless it is made stationary. This is an easy project accomplished by placing a washer or two under the bail screw to prevent it from swiveling.

Once the bail has been cut off and removed and the roller guide has been made stationary, the angler is ready for trouble-free casting.

Grasp the line with your forefinger as you always do. With your other hand move the spool a half turn. This will cause the line to slip from under the roller guide so it will be held by your finger only. Make a conventional cast, but catch the line just before the lure strikes the water. Then, pull back slightly with your finger and turn the reel handle. The roller guide will come around, remove the line from your finger, and begin spooling it before you realize what happened. There's nothing to break or wear out; and just as important, with a little practice, you will find that you can get into action much faster.

Sometimes it's necessary to stretch a cast so you can reach a distant target or feeding fish. You can get additional yardage on a cast if you place your left hand (if you are right-handed) on the lowest portion of the rod butt, bring the rod swiftly forward, and stop sharply. Use of your left hand in this manner nearly doubles the power you can generate for a cast. This same technique is useful for women casters and for youngsters who use outsize tackle. Of course, nearly all salt-water fishermen use the two-hand trick, but freshwater fans have all but ignored this gimmick for better casting.

Many spinfishermen don't understand how those loose loops appear many yards down in their reel spool. These loops can cause a real tangle if the bail is opened and the angler pulls line off by hand until the loop is encountered. Try to cast the loop free instead. These loops appear most frequently when a fisherman works a surface lure. Many anglers impart action to the lure by snapping backward or upward with the rod tip, retrieving the line by moving the rod forward and then winding in the slack. Then they repeat the operation. This is when the loop appears—when the rod is brought forward and the slack gathered. After the rod is flipped backward or upward, the angler should strive to reel in the line as he moves the tip forward, never allowing any slack to appear. When slack doesn't occur, neither do loops.

Loops are also created at the end of the cast. If a high, arching flight is made with the lure and it strikes the water before the bail is turned, the falling slack line will cause a loop when the bail is turned. Making sure that the lure keeps traveling in a straight line, plus catching the line with the finger before the flight's end, will eliminate these loops.

—Bernard "Lefty" Kreh, March 1967

A Steelheader's Sinker

WHILE SEASONED STEELHEADERS consider the loss of lead sinkers an occupational hazard, the search continues for ways to reduce time-consuming—and costly—hangups.

I make no claim that my method guarantees the recovery of every snagged sinker. However, I have found it to be far more effective than any previously used.

You need either three-sixteenths or a quarter-inch-diameter lead wire, rubber surgical tubing that fits tightly over the wire, and monofilament leader material testing two to four pounds less than the main line. Rigging steps are simple, but should be done ahead of time to save fussing when you should be fishing.

1. Cut lead wire to the desired length and squeeze one end slightly flat with pliers.

2. Punch or drill a small hole through the flattened end, then tie on a short length of monofilament as a dropper.

3. Cut an eighth-inch-wide O-ring from the rubber tubing.

4. Fold the dropper back against the sinker body, slip the O-ring over the flat end, then roll it to within an eighth of an inch of the opposite (round) end.

5. Tie the dropper either onto the front eye of a barrel swivel or onto a three-way swivel, with the end of the sinker hanging about one to two inches below.

If the sinker hangs up during use, a sharp jerk on the line stretches the O-ring, which causes the sinker to "pole-vault" over the obstruction.

Should the sinker jam tightly—between two rocks for example—a steady pull will either cut through the O-ring, or cause it to slide down the sinker and pop off the end. Changing the direction of pull is usually enough to free the weight.

As you lose far more O-rings than sinkers, it pays to carry spares.

—Robert H. Jones, July 1982

Drag Dos and Don'ts

DESPITE THE MOLDY cliché about "screaming reels" (as in "my reel screamed as the huge fish beelined for Tahiti. . . ."), there is, in fact, nothing finer than the sound of a good fish kicking in the afterburners; the sound, that is, of a reel's drag being put to the test. It's not as much a scream as it is a shrill whine embellished by the voice of the angler, who really is screaming more often than not.

The vocal effect intensifies when good fish break off, as many do because of improper adjustment and use of the reel's mechanical drag. This is a shame, because that very same drag can be your friend once you understand its function and limitations, and apply that understanding sanely.

When set properly, a drag allows you to set the hook as hard as possible or necessary without snapping the line. When a fish is on, the drag provides consistent, sturdy resistance to the pull of line. This tires the fish out faster, without endangering the breaking test of the line.

A good drag slows the rotation of the spool, evenly and smoothly, whether at the sudden jerk-start from inertia or during a high-speed run. The drag doesn't inhibit line flow, however; it merely slows it with smooth, firm resistance.

▶▶▶ *Drag Testing:* The emphasis on smoothness isn't arbitrary. A drag that jerks and hitches is going to cost you fish for obvious reasons. A slip in tension means loss of control; a hitch in drag rotation means the spool has suddenly, if only momentarily, been given a complete brake—at which time the line is exceedingly vulnerable to snapping.

Make a habit of testing your drag before you hit the water and, when possible, before you buy a new reel. One basic test is to remove the reel from the rod and set the drag to a point of resistance slightly lower than the weight of the reel itself. Pull off a foot-and-a-half of line, hold the end, and allow the reel to lower itself against the drag. The "fall" should be smooth and even, without jerks, hitches, or stops, any of which indicate an inadequate drag mechanism.

An even better test is one I call the "dry land run." Attach the reel to a rod and string it up. Have a friend grasp a hookless casting plug tied to the end of the line and turn him loose around the yard. Adjust the drag to about one-third of the line's rated strength (using a weight scale or De-Liar, for example, to measure). Whether your "fish" runs slowly, jerkily, or quickly, the reel should give up line smoothly. Slips or hitches should not occur at all on a new reel; on an old one they may indicate that the drag mechanism needs cleaning or that the tension spring needs replacement.

➤➤➤ *Setting and Using the Drag:* Most of us are guilty of checking our drags with a quick pull or two of the line just above the reel. "Feels right," we say. But this is less than an educated guess.

Conventional wisdom advises that a drag should be set at a tension level of one-fourth to one-third of the line's breaking strength; that is, set for three pounds or less of tension for 10-pound-test line. This is not a bad basic reference point, though specific conditions will require adjustments. In thick cover, for instance, you may need more drag to horse fish away from potential tangles. Or, when using very light lines in open water, you may prefer a looser setting that allows the fish to wear itself out without severely stressing the line.

Another easy adjustment procedure is to fasten the line to an immovable object 15 or 20 feet away. Then tighten the drag fully and exert full-bend pressure on the rod. Slowly loosen the drag until you find a point of tension that allows maximum rod leverage but releases line before it reaches the breaking point.

After the Strike . . . Points to Remember When You Hook a Trout:

1. Avoid making drag adjustments while fighting fish. Fishermen who fiddle with their drags usually regret it. Begin with a safe drag setting and fight the fish from there.

2. If you need additional tension while fighting a fish, use your hands. That is, rather than tightening the drag, put more thumb pressure on the baitcasting spool or cup your fingers lightly around the turning spool of a spinning reel.

3. Remember that, in addition to the drag, the rod angle also exerts pressure on the fish—and the line. A heavy fish that runs suddenly, or surges, can pop a line that's already stressed near the breaking point, especially if the angler reacts reflexively and lifts the rod to stop the fish. The better reaction is to do the opposite: Lower the rod and point the tip at the fish. That is, let the fish fight the drag only.

4. If, during a fight, you do adjust the drag for some reason—say, for an unexpectedly large fish—be sure to readjust the drag tension before you begin casting again. In short, know exactly where your drag is set, and how much pressure you can apply, before—not after—a good fish strikes.

—Anthony Acerrano, February 1991

A Fall River rainbow taken on a Zug Bug nymph comes into the net.—Photo by R. Valentine Atkinson

[9]

Trout Miscellany

~

"The old drunk told me about trout fishing.

When he could talk, he had a way of describing trout

as if they were a precious and intelligent metal."

–Richard Brautigan, Trout Fishing in America, 1967

The Best Rainbow Trout Fishing

RAINBOW TROUT FISHING is as different from brook fishing as prize fighting is from boxing. The rainbow is called *Salmo iridescens* by those mysterious people who name the fish we catch and has recently been introduced into Canadian waters. At present the best rainbow trout fishing in the world is in the rapids of the Canadian Soo.

There the rainbow have been taken as large as fourteen pounds from canoes that are guided through the rapids and halted at the pools by Ojibway and Chippewa boatmen. It is a wild and nerve-frazzling sport and the odds are in favor of the big trout who tear off thirty or forty yards of line at a rush and then will sulk at the base of a big rock and refuse to be stirred into action by the pumping of a stout flyrod aided by a fluent monologue of Ojibwayan profanity. Sometimes it takes two hours to land a really big rainbow under those circumstances.

The Soo affords great fishing. But it is a wild nightmare kind of fishing that is second only in strenuousness to angling for tuna off Catalina Island. Most of the trout too take a spinner and refuse a fly and to the 99 percent pure flyfisherman, there are no one hundred percenters, that is a big drawback.

Of course the rainbow trout of the Soo will take a fly but it is rough handling them in that tremendous volume of water on the light tackle a flyfisherman loves. It is dangerous wading in the spots that can be waded, too, for a misstep will take the angler over his head in the rapids. A canoe is a necessity to fish the very best water.

Altogether it is a rough, tough, mauling game, lacking in the meditative qualities of the Izaak Walton school of angling. What would make a fitting Valhalla for the good fisherman when he dies would be a regular trout river with plenty of rainbow trout in it jumping crazy for the fly.

There is such a one not forty miles from the Soo called the—well, called the river. It is about as wide as a river should be and a little deeper than a river ought to be and to get the proper picture you want to imagine in rapid succession the following fade-ins:

A high pine-covered bluff that rises steep up out of the shadows. A short sand slope down to the river and a quick elbow turn with a little flood wood jammed in the bend and then a pool.

A pool where the moselle-colored water sweeps into a dark swirl and expanse that is blue-brown with depth and fifty feet across.

There is the setting.

The action is supplied by two figures that slog into the picture up the trail along the river bank with loads on their backs that would tire a pack horse.

These loads are pitched over the heads onto the patch of ferns by the edge of the deep pool. That is incorrect. Really the figures lurch a little forward and the tumpline loosens and the pack slumps onto the ground. Men don't pitch loads at the end of an eight-mile hike.

One of the figures looks up and notes the bluff is flattened on top and that there is a good place to put a tent. The other is lying on his back and looking straight up in the air. The first reaches over and picks up a grasshopper that is stiff with the fall of the evening dew and tosses him into the pool.

The hopper floats spraddle legged on the water of the pool an instant, an eddy catches him, and then there is a yard-long flash of flame, and a trout as long as your forearm has shot into the air and the hopper has disappeared.

"Did you see that?" gasped the man who had tossed the grasshopper.

It was a useless question, for the other, who a moment before would have served as a model for a study entitled "Utter Fatigue," was jerking his flyrod out of his case and holding a leader in his mouth.

We decided on a McGinty and a Royal Coachman for the flies and at the second cast there was a swirl like the explosion of a depth bomb, the line went taut, and the rainbow shot two feet out of the water. He tore down the pool and the line went out until the core of the reel showed. He jumped and each time he shot into the air we lowered the tip and prayed. Finally he jumped and the line went slack and Jacques reeled in. We thought he was gone and then he jumped right under our faces. He had shot upstream toward us so fast that it looked as though he were off.

When I finally netted him and rushed him up the bank and could feel his huge strength in the tremendous muscular jerks he made when I held him flat against the bank, it was almost dark. He measured 26 inches and weighed 9 pounds and 7 ounces.

That is rainbow trout fishing.

The rainbow takes the fly more wittingly than he does bait. The McGinty, a fly that looks like a yellow jacket, is the best. It should be tied on a No. 8 or 10 hook.

The smaller flies get more strikes but are too small to hold the really big fish. The rainbow trout will live in the same streams with brook trout but they are found in different kinds of places. Brook trout will be forced into the shady holes under the bank and where alders hang over the banks, and the rainbow will dominate the clear pools and the fast shallows.

Magazine writers and magazine covers to the contrary, the brook or speckled trout does not leap out of the water after he has been hooked. Given plenty of line he will fight a deep rushing fight. Of course if you hold the fish too tight he will be forced by the rush of the current to flop on top of the water.

But the rainbow always leaps on a slack or tight line. His leaps are not mere flops, either, but actual jumps out of and parallel with the water from a foot to five feet. A five-foot jump by any fish sounds improbable, but it is true.

If you don't believe it tie onto one in fast water and try to force him. Maybe if he is a five-pounder he will throw me down and only jump four feet eleven inches.

—Ernest Hemingway, September 1970 (Reprinted from the Toronto Star Weekly, August 28, 1920)

Releasing Trout

MANY TROPHY WATERS exist only because of catch-and-release, limited bag, slot limits, or other special regulations that require you to release at least some of the fish you catch. In addition, many trout fishers release most or all of the fish they catch even on waters where that's not required; and many lodges and guide services severely limit the number of fish they kill, in some cases allowing clients something like one trophy fish per week, period.

When releasing a trout, always handle the fish carefully, and never squeeze it or grab it by the gills for a better grip. If you want to take photos, do it quickly.

Here are a few tips for releasing fish unharmed:

1. *Use reasonably stout tackle.* Ultralight spin rods and tiny 2-weight flyrods are fun, but if you catch a big trout on one you may end up playing it so long that it'll be too worn out to survive after release.

2. *Use single, barbless hooks.* Most fisheries managers say fishermen struggling to unstick barbed hooks do more damage to the fish than the barbs themselves. (By the way, there's a school of thought that says a barbless hook sinks deeper with less pressure, so you'll have fewer missed strikes.)

3. *Use a soft-mesh landing net.* It doesn't damage a trout's scales and is quicker and less clumsy than hand-landing.

4. *Handle trout carefully and gently.* Don't remove a fish from the water and don't squeeze it or grab it by the gills for a better grip.

5. *If you're going to take photos, do it quickly.* Don't leave the fish out of water while the photographer changes lenses and fools with the settings on his camera.

6. *Release the fish by holding it gently in the water*—face into the current—until it swims off under its own steam.

—John Gierach, April 1997

Flyrod Lightning

SUDDENLY I WAS flying through the air, smelling a horrible burning odor, hearing a high-pitched whine in my right ear. I thought, "My God! I've been struck by lightning! I'm going to die!" That's how my yearly Vermont fishing vacation ended.

The last evening of my trip I was fishing the Connecticut River northeast of Beecher Falls. I noticed a huge, black cloud boiling over a hill and since I couldn't possibly make it back to the car before the storm hit and there was no bush that offered any protection, I sought shelter under a small tree.

The bolt of lightning struck me with incredible suddenness. The next thing I remember was the realization that I was five feet from the tree and that I was paralyzed.

Gradually, my right leg and both of my arms began to tremble and then feeling returned to part of my body. I was nearly deaf in the right ear and most of the hair on my body had been singed.

The little tree had been split down to the point where my fishing rod had been leaning against it. And that brand new 6-foot Fenwick Blackhawk graphite spincast rod was mangled into a nearly unrecognizable shape. The lightning had melted the first four eyes as well as the material that held the graphite strands together. Just below that the rod was broken, and above

Hollywood Flies

When Dorothy Lamour, a movie actress once famed for her long black hair, cut her tresses, the strands were cut into small sections and sent as a publicity stunt to various fly tiers and trout fishermen to be made into streamers.

–Bill Wolf, March 1956

The Royal Hackle

In the early days of English flyfishing for trout, one pattern called for "8 or 10 hairs of Isabella-colored mohair." This color, described as "whitish-yellow or buff color, somewhat soiled," had a most peculiar origin due to a vow taken by Infanta Isabella of Spain in 1602. Her husband, Archduke Albert, lay siege to Ostend, and Isabella, who accompanied him on the expedition, vowed that she would never change her garments until Ostend was captured. However, three years passed before the city was reduced and her linen became, let us say, discolored. Her court copied the shade—with dyes, not fortitude—and the fashionable Isabella "buff color, somewhat soiled," was born.

—Bill Wolf, March 1956

the rubber pistol grip the high-impact plastic handle was totaled. My Johnson 710 reel was lying next to me completely undamaged. The ten live minnows that were in a jar of water had been fried and were sticking to its sides. I thought to myself, "I have to get this pole out, or no one will believe what happened." So I picked up the three largest pieces and, dragging my left leg, began my trek. I spent over 30 minutes stumbling, tripping, falling, and climbing up slippery banks before I finally made it to the car. By then feeling had returned to my left leg.

My fishing companion, Bob Bailey of Mansfield, Pennsylvania (he'd been fishing upstream), drove me to the motel where I showered some of the muck off and discovered pieces of graphite burned fast to the right side of my face and neck. Those minor burns and the hearing loss seemed to be the only damage.

We drove ten miles to the hospital in Colebrook, New Hampshire. A doctor checked me over thoroughly, prescribed an antibiotic to fight off possible infection in my ear, and told me there was no way for him to tell if the hearing loss was temporary or permanent.

Back in the motel I noticed the trail the lightning had etched on my skin—an inch-wide red welt. It entered the right arm, traveled down the right side, and crossed my body just below the rib cage. The welt continued diagonally across my abdomen and down my left leg. It exited just above where my hip boot had been.

Why was I so lucky? First of all, those hip boots offered no ground for the lightning. Second, the rod, which was leaning against the tree with its tip just to the right and above my head, took the brunt of the lightning's force. And third, that Man Upstairs had to be watching very carefully over me.

—Roddy A. Fisher, March 1983

2000 Words of Heartfelt Advice for Absolute Flyfishing Beginners

ONE SPRING MORNING fifteen years ago, I woke up urgently needing to fish with a flyrod. I was 29. I'd never been flyfishing, and I hadn't fished at all since I was 12, a boy with a bait rod in a boat. All I remembered about fishing was that sunfish have spines and bullheads have barbels and that it's better to eat lunch as soon as you pull away from the dock, before the sandwiches start to smell like bait. That wasn't much to go on. I called my dad, a longtime flyfisherman. He gave me some good advice. "Start fishing," he said. But I lived in Manhattan. I had little money and no car. All I had was an appetite for an unfamiliar sport, an appetite aroused by the sudden dreamlike memory of sitting on shore when I was very young, watching my dad cast a wet fly in the White River near Meeker, Colorado.

An angler and his son fish Silver Creek in Idaho. Matching the hatch on this stream is quite a challenge; a dozen different bugs may come off the water at the same time.

As it happened, I learned to flyfish much as my dad had: I figured it out for myself. But there was a difference. He learned on the high mountain lakes and streams of Colorado. I built a flyrod—it was cheap and I wanted to build one, anyway—and took it up to the roof of the building I lived in, which was narrow but nearly a hundred feet long. There in the swirling wind four stories above Third Avenue, I taught myself to cast, using a kiddie pool as my target. I practiced almost every evening for an entire summer. It would have been a ridiculous thing to do, if it hadn't been so effective.

The hardest part about being a beginner in any sport is knowing nothing. The problem isn't just what to learn, it's how to learn, a problem that's even worse in a sport like flyfishing, where a lot of emphasis is laid on tradition and on the supposedly scientific rigor of its best-known modern practitioners. In fact, flyfishing is often presented as a form of connoisseurship, which can be—and is often meant to be—very intimidating. But to some people, the apparent elitism of the sport is part of its attraction. So here's a rule of thumb. If you come across anglers, or angling writers, who make it sound as though the art of the dry fly gets passed down from firstborn to firstborn, ignore them. No one ever inherited a prose style or a casting stroke.

Flyfishing is basically a simple sport, no matter what you hear to the contrary. Casting is easy, not half as hard as learning to swing a golf club or rope a calf. Compared to spinfishing and baitcasting gear, the equipment is mechanically simple. Flyfishing becomes elitist only if you want to own or lease private water, and in this country that's strictly a matter of cash, not breeding. The thing to remember is this: People spend enormous amounts of money for access to easy fishing. Really hard fishing is usually free. And no matter how far you progress in the sport or how exalted your ambitions become, there's no pleasure in angling as pure as the emotion you feel when you catch your first fish with a flyrod. That moment will echo down your sporting life, whether you find yourself casting for bluegills in a farm pond or for permit on Ascension Bay.

It's natural to want to sign up for flyfishing school right away, and there are good reasons for doing so. The level of instruction and camaraderie at fishing schools can be very high, even though the enormous network of fly-fishing courses these days resembles a giant intake valve sucking beginners and their cash into the sport. I say, teach yourself instead. You'll be giving the tackle companies enough of your money anyway. Professional instruction can save you some time, but you learn nothing from the mistakes you don't make. Flyfishing isn't a product you consume while worrying about the shortness of time. It's a pursuit that gets interwoven with time itself. Teaching yourself, you learn about the techniques of flyfishing, of course, but, more importantly, you also get a chance to rediscover how you learn. That will be important on the stream. To paraphrase Heraclitus, you can never fish in the same river twice. Conditions are always different, minute by minute, cast by cast, and the ability to adjust to changing conditions—to instruct yourself quickly—is a good measure of an angler's success. If that sounds like mere philosophizing, wait till you find yourself at the onset of a Baetis hatch on the Bighorn River in early May.

Learning isn't just a matter of absorbing information. It's the act of win-nowing information. I think the best, though not the fastest way to learn to flyfish is to read widely in the literature of the sport, which is a long-lasting pleasure in itself. Subscribe to the magazines; buy or borrow the books. (Watch the videos too.) Read everything and believe nothing until you've tried it out. Then keep what you can use and throw out the rest. Experience teaches you to read skeptically, and reading makes you a better judge of experience. Practicing on my rooftop long ago, I tried to copy the dissimilar casting styles of Joan Wulff, Lefty Kreh, and Charles Ritz. I also tried to ape every diagram in every flycasting article I saw. Ultimately the dynamics of the cast itself—how a double haul felt when I did it right—taught me what I needed to know; but by trying out so many different casting styles I discovered that there is no single right way to cast. There is, instead, the broad range of what works.

Over the years, I've spent almost as much time watching anglers as I have fishing. It's a habit I picked up as a beginner, partly because I was lucky enough to be fishing with friends who were, and still are, vastly more skillful than I am. They never gave me advice, and I never asked for it, and yet their example meant everything to me. But in a way I've learned almost as much from watching men and women who were struggling with the sport. In their clumsiness, I could see my own, and I began to correct it little by little. I saw anglers for whom the loss of a fly or a tippet provoked a crisis, because it meant they had to tie an improved clinch knot or, worse, a blood knot. I saw anglers standing in water they should have been casting to, anglers casting to utterly barren stretches of river, anglers lashing the pool behind them with every backcast, anglers hopelessly entangled in the slack they had stripped from their reel, anglers whose rudeness had earned them the contempt of everyone around them.

And what I learned was that there's no substitute for practice or awareness or economy of motion or courtesy. Those are the fundamentals of flyfishing. These days, for instance, it's a fairly common habit to buy prefabricated leaders, knotted or knotless. When I began flyfishing I decided I wanted to tie my own leaders, following the same logic that led me to build my first flyrod and tie my own flies. I bought Art Lee's *Fishing the Dry Fly on Rivers and Streams* and made up a couple of dozen leaders according to his formulas. (Tying leaders in the evening allowed me to pretend that I was fishing.) When I began, a blood knot was merely an aspiration, something I hoped one day to achieve. When I was done tying leaders several nights later, it was an instinct. Now I buy knotless leaders, but I still have a bombproof blood knot. The peculiar thing about learning to flyfish is this: every shortcut you take when you're a beginner ultimately diminishes your feel for the complexity, the subtlety of flyfishing. That's why, if at all possible, you should also learn to tie your own flies. The joy of catching a trout on a flyrod is compounded many times when you do it with a fly of your own making.

When I think back over my flyfishing education—thus far, that is—the single most instructive moment was an evening in June more than a decade ago. I

Travel Rods

If you're going on a long-distance fishing trip by air, wrap several rod tubes together with duct tape. This makes a larger package that's sturdier and less likely to get misplaced or overlooked by baggage handlers.
–Gerald Almy, March 1996

Reshaped Rod Grip
Fishermen whose hands tire easily while flycasting may find the cause is an ill-fitting rod grip. Try a different shape. Often there is no need to remove the old grip. It can be reshaped by sanding. A full-wells grip, for example, can be changed into a cigar shape, a style referred to as the "perfect" grip by some rodmakers. Sanding with medium-course sandpaper does the trick. The reshaped grip will have a distinctly different feel, more like that of a new rod, and it should fit your hand better and cause much less fatigue and cramping.
–Don Shiner, July 1985

had driven to the Catskills to interview a famous angler, and he invited me to go fishing with him. We drove along the Beaverkill, pausing here and there to look at the stream, and then we parked, geared up, and walked down to the river. I was tense with impatience, with nervousness. I wanted to wade right in and begin to pretend fishing, because, of course, what I really wanted to do was to watch this man fish. Instead, we sat down on a big rock near the high water mark. He didn't say much. He smoked a cigarette all the way down, and then he lit another one. He watched the water, and he tried to help me look where he was looking, although he couldn't actually make me see what he was seeing.

The current ran heavy along the far bank, and the river thinned out over a flat that ended on the near shore, so that most of that broad, beautiful river was in fact very shallow. Well upstream, at a picturesque distance, a couple of anglers were drifting dry flies along the edge of the deep current, a place that looked naturally inviting—to humans, at least. But that wasn't where this man was looking. His gaze ended at a line of rocks in water only a few inches deep, just a dozen yards upstream from us. I can't explain to you how long it seemed before I saw what he was looking at, but when I finally saw it I felt very stupid. It was the tail of a large brown trout, the tail an almost iridescent brown, glowing as it wriggled, half out of water. The fish was nymphing, nosing around in the sediment beneath the rocks. After offering me the chance, the man stood up, paid out line, made a single cast, and caught the fish, which he released.

It wasn't the cast, the catch, or the release that mattered to me, though they were elegant and unhurriedly efficient. It was the lesson about observation. Like most beginners, I had spent so much time thinking about gear and technique that I neglected the most important thing of all: the fact that my real subject was the river. I had watched the water every time I went fishing, watched it as I waded out to what I thought would be a good starting point, watched it as I made my backcast, as my fly drifted downstream. But I had never taken the time to sit down and absorb the river, to realize that what I should really be watching was the way the river differed from itself instant by instant. I had never realized that those differences—in light, in current, in sound—would show me trout, if only I could be patient enough to look for them. It was time to begin fishing in something besides my preconceptions.

That's a hard shift for most of us to make. It's easy enough to emphasize the rituals of flyfishing, its daily and seasonal rhythms, the languorous, almost supplicating beat of a long casting stroke. These are some of the things that make flyfishing a lifelong sport, a sport of ever-deepening complexity. But those rituals and rhythms inevitably belong to the everyday world we inhabit, and they overlay, on the stream, a world we perceive only in flashes, when, for a moment, we're able to concentrate on the swiftness, the abruptness, the almost unimaginable profusion of what nature has laid before us. It is to lengthen those moments of concentration that one goes flyfishing, and a lifetime is barely long enough to learn what they contain.

—Verlyn Klinkenborg, August 1996

A Flyfishing Library (12 Must-read Books)

>>> *Gwen Cooper and Evelyn Haas,* **Wade a Little Deeper, Dear** Lyons & Burford, 1989. Originally intended for female anglers, this book is a superb introduction to flyfishing tackle and techniques, no matter what your gender might be.

>>> *Joe Humphreys,* **On the Trout Stream with Joe Humphreys** Stackpole Books, 1989. Humphreys taught flyfishing at Penn State, and his book is full of practical, on-stream insight.

>>> *Mel Krieger,* **The Essence of Flycasting** Club Pacific, 1987. This is the clearest, most concise instruction on the art of flycasting available.

>>> *Art Lee,* **Fishing the Dry Fly on Streamers and Rivers** Atheneum, 1982. Lee is a longtime resident of the Catskills, and his book is a distillation of his experience.

>>> *Eric Leiser,* **A Book of Fly Patterns** Alfred A. Knopf, 1987. For beginner and expert alike, this is the most comprehensive—and beautifully produced—book about flytying on the market.

>>> *A. J. McClane,* **McClane's New Standard Fishing Encyclopedia and International Angling Guide** Holt, Reinhart & Winston Inc., 1965. The Oxford English Dictionary of angling, a little outdated, but endlessly informative.

>>> *Vince Marinaro,* **In the Ring of the Rise** Lyons & Burford, 1987. Marinaro was one of the masters of spring creek angling, and this book represents a level of intelligence and observation to which angling literature rarely rises. For advanced beginners, as well as those just beginning the sport.

>>> *Dick Pobst,* **Trout Stream Insects** Lyons & Burford, 1991. This is the new standard in concise, on-stream insect identification, as useful at the flytying desk as it is in a fishing-vest pocket.

>>> *Tom Rosenbauer,* **The Orvis Fly-Fishing Guide** Lyons & Burford, 1988. Perhaps the best all-around introductory guide to the world of flyfishing.

>>> *Tom Rosenbauer,* **Reading Trout Streams** Lyons & Burford, 1988.

This is an introduction to what is perhaps the greatest art in flyfishing: learning to read the face of a river or stream.

>>> *Mark Sosin and Lefty Kreh,* **Practical Fishing Knots II** Lyons & Burford, 1991. Everything you need to know about fishing knots. The only thing this book will not do is practice tying knots for you.

>>> *Dick Talleur,* **Mastering the Art of Fly Tying** Stackpole Books, 1979. This sounds like, and is, an advanced book about flytying, but it is also full of useful ideas and hints for the flytier who is just learning his way around a vise.

—Verlyn Klinkenborg, August 1996

The Return of the Creel

THE TRADITIONAL WICKER fishing creel has, for the most part, been replaced by the canvas bag. With its wide shoulder strap and large pockets (usually equipped with a steel spring closure), the creel is an excellent choice for outdoorsmen. Occupying a niche similar to the  traditional possibles bag of the mountain man, the creel can replace or augment the popular daypack seen so commonly today. The creel is especially handy when you need to access small items repeatedly and since a creel is made to naturally drain out water, it is an extremely handy bag to carry in the wetlands. Keeping this in mind, I have found a creel especially handy while waterfowl hunting to carry shells, calls, gloves, and detachable decoy weights; and while trapping to carry lures, baits, gloves, wire, tools, etc. Use your imagination and you may find the creel is not just for fishing.

—Donald A. Smith, December 1994

Fishing for Emergency Food

SURVIVAL FISHING—LIKE all other emergency procedures—is simpler if you're prepared, infinitely harder if you're not.

Make a kit consisting of assorted hooks (two each) in sizes ranging from 12 to 1/0. (The small hooks are for minnows and fingerlings, which are easy to catch. The large hooks are for big fish, in case the opportunity arises.) Include a bare leadhead jig in the 1/16-ounce range and another adorned with a white or black soft-bodied (grub-style) tail. Add 6 pinch-on split-shot of various sizes, and two small spools (leader spools work fine) of monofilament line: one of 12-pound test, the other 20 pound. To keep the kit as small and weightless as possible, coil 20 feet of each line into a small bunch and secure it with a twist-tie. This way the entire kit can be stored in an empty film canister and easily carried in your pocket.

➤➤➤ *Tactics:* Since you will likely be using either a handline or a green branch pole, your "casting" range will be limited. This makes stealth a crucial factor to success. Keep your profile low, off the skyline. If necessary, crawl to a bank on all fours or on your belly.

Most times you'll have more casting range, longer drift potential, and a better chance of landing your quarry if you use a pole. Look for a seven-foot or longer green branch with natural butt-to-tip taper, then clean it of all projecting offshoots and twigs. Don't tie the line to the extreme tip of the pole. Instead, knot it to the center, reinforce it with a few wraps, then move up toward the tip a couple of feet and repeat the process. The last knot and wrap will be at the extreme tip of the branch. This way, should the tip break, the line will hold firm to the lower rod and the fish can still be landed.

In streams or creeks, lob the jig lure or baited hook (weighted with split-shot if necessary) upstream of prime fish lies and let it drift through. Look for undercut banks, current cushions below midstream rocks, and seams where two currents of different speed meet. Be patient.

In still waters—lakes, ponds, sloughs—probe carefully around weeds, logjams, stickups, and rockpiles. Vertical jigging in heavy cover with the lure or bait rig is a good way to entice reluctant baitfish, panfish, or trout.

➤➤➤ *Best baits:* Bait is everywhere if you know precisely where to look. In streams, try kicking over rocks in mid-riffle to dislodge various nymphs and larvae. Spread a sieve of some sort (an undershirt, handkerchief, or piece of netting will work just fine) downstream to catch bugs, which make an excellent source of live bait. Earthworms live near banks and can be dug out with a stick or by hand. Grasshoppers are commonly found during the warm months (into mid-fall) in open, grassy areas. Grubs, caterpillars, and assorted larvae can be found in rotted tree bark and stump wood and under terrestrial rocks.

When no fish can be had and you're facing desperation, you can always eat your bait. Unpleasant as it may sound, research has proved that many insects actually have higher protein levels than beef or soybeans. Grass-hoppers, grubs, worms and aquatic nymphs can all be eaten as a last resort. To prevent the possibility of accidentally ingesting harmful internal parasites, be sure to cook the bait you have gathered by boiling, frying, or roasting it in wet leaves in a fire.

—Anthony Acerrano, February 1990

Survival Fishing Kit

Anyone spending time in the outdoors should carry a survival kit that includes gear to catch fish for food. A simple kit should contain a few hooks of various sizes and styles, maybe a couple of trout flies (Woolly Worm patterns in Size 6 to 8 are excellent choices), 10 feet of monofilament line of at least 10-pound test, and a couple of rubber bands. These items will fit nicely inside a 35-mm-film container, which can double as a float. Just wrap the rubber band around it to secure it to the fishing line.

—Thomas C. Tabor, February 1989

Measure Before Release

Once in a great while we take a trophy fish on a fly and release it without getting a picture of it, or even an accurate idea of its size. The next time you hook such a fish, lay it gently in the shallows and measure it with your leader, the fly still attached. Then cut the leader at exactly the fish's length. Over the years you will build a collection of chewed flies with various lengths of leader attached, each with a story behind it, something to be preserved forever in a display case instead of in your memory.

–Greg Roberts, August 1979

Measure the fish you catch, then save the proof forever.

Traveling with Tackle

I'VE LONG HAD WHAT can loosely be called a "system" for getting fishing tackle to and from distant places, and my track record—knock on a wooden reel seat—has been pretty good: virtually nothing lost, nothing broken, and only a couple of misdirected items of baggage.

However, I've seen a lot of other people's stuff get side-railed, stolen, or broken, so my luck is not really luck—knock on a walnut fly box—but may actually be the result of doing something right. With that in mind, consider the following suggestions:

First, pack it wisely. This brings us to the heart of travel-tackle success: Whenever possible, get all your equipment, even the rods, into self-contained duffel bags. Avoid long rod cases and tubes that must be packed or airline-checked separately from your main luggage. Rod cases have a way of falling off baggage carts, of being run over by those long baggage-cart trains you see whisking all over the tarmac. Also, rods inside long cases eerily tend to get broken—it's not always clear how. And long, separate rod cases have a way of calling attention to themselves, making them more prone to theft. They're also clumsier to pack, whether in a car or a floatplane or a packsaddle. Outfitters groan at the sight of long rod cases, and I don't blame them.

If you're a traveling angler, even if only by car, duffel bags are your friends. I mean high-quality duffels, not the cheap $20 kind that burst under a tough load. I keep a stable of good bags and choose them according to the needs of the moment. All are made from high-denier, water-resistant Cordura and have reinforced zippers and seams. If possible, I stow everything in two bags: one large, one medium.

How do you get fishing rods into duffel bags? By using travel rods whenever possible. New designs and materials have brought us multipiece rods that sacrifice no performance quality. Travel flyrods are easy to find (though hard, sometimes, to pay for), and there's an increasing number of telescoping and breakdown spin and plug rods, too.

Now for actual packing. Use the large duffel for your rod tubes. I usually pad the base area with clothing—pants and shirts, for instance. The rod tubes are laid in lengthwise along the outer edges, in a sense forming a protective frame for the bag's other contents. I use comparatively small tackleboxes—the see-through snap-lid types—for lures, pliers, and such. The largest of these boxes goes into the big bag, near the bottom, and the rest of the bag's space is used mainly for other clothing and software. The smaller duffel becomes essentially a tackle bag—it holds all the various small lure kits, pouches, and sacks. I use lots of stuff sacks when traveling: one for spools of

line, one for encased reels, and so on, because loose gear is gear you'll lose.
—*Anthony Acerrano, April 1991*

Cold Weather Trouting Problems

>>> *Problem 1:* **Ice in the guides.**

Solution: Dip the tip of the rod in the water and swish it around. This should thaw the tip enough to get you through one more cast, after which you'll probably have to do it again. If the tip ices up immediately, it's probably too cold to be fishing anyway.

>>> *Problem 2:* **Cold or wet hands.**

Solution: There are myriad fingerless gloves on the market, all of which work fine in moderately chilly weather and somewhat less fine when it's really cold. The traditional glove material is wool, which does a good job of keeping your hands warm. Unfortunately, most wool fishing gloves are missing the tips of all the fingers when, for dexterity, all you really need open are the tips of the thumb and first finger. An alternative is to wear regular wool gloves and remove them as needed.

Synthetic fishing gloves work well and don't sag like wool when they're wet, but do not keep you warm when soaked, as the manufacturers invariably claim. For that matter, neither will anything else, including wool. Synthetics will keep soaked fingers from freezing, however, and most of those that are available are reasonably priced.

Neoprene gloves are not reasonably priced but are quite warm, and some sport fingertips that can be left on or off, as you choose—a good feature. Most neoprene gloves will also keep your hands dry when immersed in water, the only type of fishing glove to do so. Their main drawback is their tight fit, which restricts the circulation of the blood in some people, resulting in cold hands.

>>> *Problem 3:* **Sunburned face.**

Solution: This can be a serious problem in the winter, when the combined glare from snow and water is often intense. Always apply a heavy-duty sunscreen before leaving home. If you can find it, zinc oxide will further protect the sensitive skin on your nose. Wide-brimmed hats will shade your face and cut down on glare, improving your vision.

>>> *Problem 4:* **Leaky waders.**

Solution: You're in trouble. Nothing I know of will make an instant patch, and by the time you discover the leak, you're probably already soaked anyway. Hard-core types will continue to fish, but those who don't enjoy flirting with hypothermia should go home and warm up before they freeze to death.

—*Dave Carty, February 1991*

Backtrolling for Steelhead

FEW METHODS OFFER more potential for taking fall and winter's aggressive steelhead than backtrolling—working lures downstream behind a boat moving slower than the current.

The classic West Coast version of this approach is done in a driftboat with one person at the oars controlling the action and presentation of the lures, another one or two people in the middle of the boat handling and battling fish.

To backtroll efficiently, you should know the locations of the runs, channels, and pools in which steelhead like to hang out, so the bulk of your lure-pulling efforts can be expended on areas with high strike potential. Basically these will be reaches with a steady but not overly swift current (about the speed of a person walking) in runs and in pools from the point where the riffles end to where they tail out and start to become shallow.

Rods of eight to nine feet with sensitive tips and heavy butt sections are preferred, with large-capacity baitcasting reels and line testing 8 to 17 pounds. The lighter the line, the deeper the plug will run. Add a swivel 36 to 48 inches up the line to reduce twist, increase lure action, and catch leaves and debris that could otherwise foul the plug, then tie in your offering.

Some fishermen like to hold their rods while they backtroll, but I've found you'll catch more steelhead with the rod left in a holder until the fish strikes.

The trick to successful backtrolling is moving the boat at the speed at which the lures dive and wobble enticingly at the proper depth to tempt strikes from steelhead. To determine this speed, let out a small amount of line and watch the lures beside the boat. Find the upstream rowing speed that gives them maximum action and then watch how the rod tips quiver and vibrate. Then, when the lures are downstream wobbling out of sight, you can tell by the action of the tips and bend of the rods if they are working properly. It's important to position all of the lures (usually two to five of them) so they run at the same distance behind the boat, usually 50 to 75 feet. This approach presents a line of plugs moving down toward the fish.

You'll be moving downstream slower than the current, so the lures dig in with their large lips and produce the shimmying action that elicits strikes. When you reach a particularly good spot, move the boat sideways back and forth across the flow, then ease down a short ways and repeat the side-to-side sweep.

If you fish with spawn sacs or flies, you're presenting the fish with something it will want to eat. Backtrolling works on the opposite principle. The fish usually doesn't want to eat these plugs; instead, it looks at them as intruders.

Therefore the best lures for backtrolling are diving plugs that have an aggressive, wide wobble and run at prime steelhead depths of three to fifteen feet. The most famous lure used for this fishing is the Luhr-Jensen Hot Shot. In fact, this lure is so well known for its backtrolling prowess that the technique is often referred to as Hot-Shotting.

Hot Shots come in a variety of sizes, but the most popular is the Size 30. The slightly smaller Size 40 is also good, particularly in low-water situations or for heavily pounded fish. The Size 20 can be good for high, roily water. A top choice for big rivers is the deep-diving Size 35.

Hot Shots aren't the only lures effective for backtrolling, however. Other top plugs include Strom's Hot'N Tot, Wee Steelie Wart, and Wiggle Wart; Heddon's Tadpolly, the Lucky Lady, Hawg Boss Super Toad, Flatfish, and Fire Plug; and Rebel and Bagley crayfish lures.

When choosing a lure for backtrolling, consider the depth it runs in relation to the water you're probing. Lures that run 3 to 6 feet deep are great for shallow rivers or when the fish are hanging in thin water at the heads and tails of pools. If fish are deep, go with a plug having a bigger or steeper-angled lip that makes it dive deeper, in the 8- to 15-foot range.

—Gerald Almy, November 1990

Keepers

A COUPLE OF years ago, we were camped on a famous river in Alaska, fishing for rainbows and silver salmon on one of the remotest stretches of trout water in North America. We'd pitched tents and had been catching—and releasing—native rainbow trout up to 7 pounds, beautifully marked wild fish with raspberry-hued center stripes and copper-green backs. The legal limit was five rainbows per day, but we weren't keeping any.

On the third day, a floatplane from a well-known outfitting operation flew in with three sports and a guide inside. They parked the plane near a stashed aluminum boat, got in, fired up the outboard, and jetted off heading upstream from us. We happened to be nearby when they returned a few hours later. We watched them load 15 dead rainbow trout, not one of them less than four pounds, into the plane just before they roared off, heading toward cocktails and a chef-prepared dinner at their lodge.

▸▸▸ *Was It Legal?* At that time, on that river, yes. At least from what we could see, and referring only to the legal daily limit. We had no way of knowing how they caught them, but it's pretty safe to assume that they took the fish legally. In the far northern rivers, the open-water season lasts for just a few months, and the fish in those waters have such a short time to feed that they'll eat anything that presents itself.

Low Backing Indicator

Powerful fish such as large Atlantic salmon and steelhead trout can make runs downstream that can rip line off your reel and, when taken on a fly, can have you quickly into the backing. Once the spool is emptied, the tippet will surely break, and your trophy fish is lost.

When backing is critically low, you can give chase or follow the fish downstream in an attempt to regain some backing for the fight to resume.

A useful time to help in deciding when to stop fighting and to start chasing is a low backing indicator. Simply mark a 6-foot section of the white dacron backing with the pen, 20 yards from its end. Though your eyes are likely to be focused on the fish water, the bright red color of the indicator zipping by is easily seen with your peripheral vision.

—Robert Drew, October 1988

Okay, let's say they caught the fish legally, the rules allowed five fish per man, and they had a boat limit of 15 fish. So, at least as far as the regulations go, they were in the clear.

Let's step away from that Alaskan river for a minute. You and I and another guy are drifting for walleyes over some reefs on East Deeplake. Our friend lifts the hatch on the fishbox and peers inside. "Thirteen," he counts. "Two more and we got a limit." You don't have to be a mathematician to figure that, with 13 fish in the boat, at least one of us has already caught his five-fish limit. So why are all three of us still fishing?

The regulations are universal on this one: There is no "boat limit." There are three individual limits to be observed in our boat. Each of us gets five, and when he does, he's finished. That, at least, is the law.

But wait a minute, you say. Just because I'm good enough to catch my five while you're still looking for number one doesn't mean I have to quit fishing. It just means I can't keep any more. I'll just release them.

Every now and then you'll want to keep a big one; use your best judgment.

Fine. Put them back. Except that, in some states, you'll be breaking the law by continuing to fish while in possession of that day's limit. So while you're flipping pages in the regs, trying to figure out if you can legally keep fishing, our under-the-limit friend snaps another walleye into the boat. He takes out the hook, opens the livewell, and compares his latest catch to what's in there. "This is a better fish than half these minnows," he announces. "Now we don't have to keep that runt I got on the last pass." He puts the new fish in, takes out the smaller fish, and puts it back in the lake.

Maybe. If he still has his license. Colorado's fishing regulations read like this: Any fish caught and placed on a stringer, in a container, in a live-well, or not returned to the water immediately will be counted as part of the daily bag and possession limits. Indiana's law is even clearer: It is illegal to sort and release any fish in the daily bag to replace it with another.

Depending on where you live, this rule may be astonishing to you. That's okay; it's far from universal. In fact, the law is just the opposite in Ohio: Anglers may also choose to release fish that they do not intend to eat or save for a mounted trophy. Selective harvest can help maintain good fishing.

So now we're drifting aimlessly across East Deeplake, noses buried in the fishing laws and ignoring the bottom-fouled walleye rigs below us as we try to figure out how soon we'll be eligible for parole. Probably a fine time to get back to Alaska, to our three counterparts having cocktails in the fly-out lodge as they relive their day, bragging about the 50 pounds of rainbow trout they brought back.

>>> *Was It Right?* Of course not. It probably, as we've just learned, wasn't legal either. The odds of three individuals each catching exactly five rainbows, all over four pounds, without "selecting" out some smaller fish, defy credulity. In that hasty northern summer the little fish are just as hungry as the big ones.

But the point here is not whether these "sports" were able to tiptoe legally through the Alaskan regulatory tripwires in order to fill their floatplane with keepers. Possibly they did. But those regulations, like every fishing regulation ever written, have one intent: to prevent excess. It's clear, too, that those three guys had one intent: to achieve excess.

>>> *The Decision:* In America we don't have paid riverkeepers, the private wardens traditional in Europe who "keep" their specific waters safe from excesses and unauthorized users. Here, we're all authorized by the purchase of a fishing license. Here, when we say "keeper," we mean a good fish that's going on to the stringer.

But the license which authorizes us to snap that stringer closed carries with it ancient and continuing sportsman's obligations. To exercise restraint; to use judgment; to be a keeper.

—Ed Gray, December 1992

How to Catch the Big One

EVERY FISHERMAN WANTS to catch some big trout if only to achieve a kind of balance. I mean, there are big ones and little ones and most of us have caught more than our share of the latter.

Of course, "big trout" is a relative term. When most fishermen say "big trout" they're probably thinking of something in the 20-inch or 2- to 3-pound class, and a few headhunters reserve the term for kype-jawed wallhangers. In most of the small mountain creeks I fish near home, a foot-long trout is big and a 16-incher is enormous, but on the Minipi River drainage in Labrador, where I've fished a few times, a 4-pound brook trout is just a "nice fish."

All I can say about that is, the more forgiving you are about size, the happier you'll be.

Try the tough spots, and you might come up with a 19-inch rainbow like this one.

It seems to me there are two ways to get big trout. One is to spend the thousands of dollars it costs to fly into some remote wilderness camp and, once there, do what the guide tells you to do. The other is to fish for big trout close to home. It's an article of faith among anglers that there's always a trout in the water you're fishing that's bigger than the biggest one you've caught so far. As articles of faith go, that's probably truer than most.

➤➤➤ *Read the Water:* I guess the best way to catch big trout is to fish for big trout, and that takes a degree of dedication. My old friend, Koke Winter, is famous among flyfishers for dredging two-inch-long, heavily weighted stonefly nymph patterns while everyone else is casting pretty little dry flies. He hardly ever catches as many fish as the rest of us, but some of the ones he does catch are real pigs.

Koke also knows where to find the bigger trout because he reads water well—a valuable and hard-won skill. All things being equal, a big trout wants cover, shade, or low light, good food availability, and he doesn't want to work too hard, so he'll want a fast current carrying food next to a slower current that he can rest in.

The classic spot is a deep plunge pool in the shade of a cliff or a stand of trees, but many good spots aren't nearly that obvious. Remember that it all works in three dimensions: Bankside currents are usually slower than those out in the middle of a stream, and the current is slower along the bottom than at the surface.

Remember also that cover can be almost anything: a fallen tree, a logjam, deep water, deep shade, cloudy skies, or broken water. One of the biggest rainbows I ever caught was lying behind a surprisingly small rock in 18 inches of fast water under a bright afternoon sun. As a friend of mine once said, "A big trout can be in any spot where you could hide a football."

>>> *Try the Hard Spots:* One way to find larger trout on heavily fished waters is to look for the most difficult places to fish, something like a deep, shady slot overhung with alders way over on the far side of a ripping fast current. Lots of fishermen pass up spots that are too hard to get to or where the cast is too difficult; consequently, that water is lightly fished and is more likely to hold a nice trout.

There's an interesting paradox here: Because the trout in a hard spot aren't fished for very often, they can be less spooky and selective than the fish in easier water. They can be tougher than usual in one way, but easier in another.

This is where the good caster outfishes the poor one, and I've learned that one way to become a good caster is to suck it up and try the hard spots. I figure, if I screw it up I'm no worse off than if I didn't even try, and in the long run I think I've actually learned a few things. Along the way, I've caught some nice trout, too.

Sometimes getting a good cast to a hard spot involves some adventurous wading, and "adventurous" is as relative a term as "big trout." My friend, Ed Engle, is a big, strong guy and a fishing guide with lots of experience. I'm not as big as Ed, I'm a bit older, and I have a bum knee. The point is, what Ed might think of as adventurous would be suicide for me. I'm smart enough to know that and secure enough not to feel as if I have anything to prove.

I don't care how big a trout is, it's not worth drowning for. As my friend A. K. Best once said, "Death can really cut into your fishing time."
—John Gierach, April 1997

An Early Call for Catch and Release

SINCE THE INCREASED population of this country has rendered meat fishing for wild trout clearly impossible, and since, as I have said in the past, meat fishing for little hatchery trout is—*Sniff*—well, we must train fishermen to fish for sport and gradually to accept laws making trout fishing almost purely sport fishing. That is, to fish in a sportsmanlike manner and to release, uninjured, practically all that they catch—at first, in some places, every last one, until wild trout have multiplied and become quite large.

All this will sound strange to the meat fisherman, who seems to think that this is the year 1864, when the bison, the passenger pigeon, and the trout were still legitimate provisions for the frontiersman's larder. But he must be gradually taught to refrain from eating most trout that he catches—which means, if they're strongly hatchery-flavored, doing so with a wry face anyway and only because he feels that he *should* eat them.

But after all, a bowler can enjoy his sport without trying to eat any pins that he knocks down. Why, even a pool player doesn't want to swallow all the balls that he knocks into pockets—so he's really more a sportsman than are many who fish.

Fishing principally for sport, with lures (mainly flies) that would not injure the fish, and liberating all under a quite large minimum size, was common before the turn of the century among members of some angling clubs. These owned private stretches of streams and so could bar meat fishermen from rushing in in hordes to ruin the fishing there practically overnight.

However, the idea of applying the same rules to public waters, to restore *real* sport there too, was first widely publicized in an article by that noted fish biologist and angler, Dr. Albert S. Hazzard, which was given the lead place, and highly featured, in the August 1952 issue of *Sports Afield.* . . .

So let me here (as I've done before) formally present the Park Service with a large bouquet of sweet-scented posies for the exceedingly tactful way in which it is gradually training anglers in national parks who have grand sport catching wild, hard-fighting trout from unstocked rivers and to release most of them, leaving real sport for the next fellow—and for themselves when they next return there. It is largely because of this good example set by the Park Service that many states—those in which conservation officials aren't too fossilized for new ideas to penetrate their heads—are taking it up more and more.

—*Jason Lucas, October 1964*

The Magic of Trout Fishing

TROUT FISHING GIVES a man time for meditation; a chance to absorb the meaning of a blue sky and pines sighing to the breeze. Tiny mosses on a streamside boulder, just placed right for resting, hold tiny scarlet flags above their soft green; in a cluster of forget-me-nots a shimmering green tiger beetle waves his antennae to a nether world of charm a man needs to know.

Trout fishing is the whirr of a hummingbird probing the columbine; a chipmunk staring curiously from a rock crevass; a phoebe darting from a limb to snatch an insect in mid-air; a small snapping turtle crawling along the bottom.

Trout will often congregate near waterfalls because the tubulent water stirs up food.

Trout fishing is trout at their stations, slowly finning, watching the surface where the stream smoothes out into a pool. Trout fishing is a mayfly dappling the water. Watch there as the trout turn; one moves to break the surface. Slowly widening ripples mark the spot where the mayfly tried to leave its eggs.

Resist the urge to cast as two other mayflies touch the water and slowly drift. Perhaps the trout you see shows no interest. You wonder why until a large dark shape materializes where nothing was before. You sit, tree-still, heart throbbing, planning your next move. This is trout fishing.

There are trout fishermen who never seem to reach the released tempo of effective trouting. One sees them hurrying from pool to pool in a rush to cover as much stream mileage as time will allow. Others may stay at one pool and flail the water for hours without interruption, impatient over the lack of rises. True, there is a magnetic attraction to the stream ahead, the next riffle. There is a hungry desire to round the bend where a bigger trout must be waiting. This is a part, an important part, of trout fishing, the spirit to explore, to seek the new. Just as it is an important part to return to old, treasured spots. But how much of the in-between flavor we miss if we overlook the little things? In fact, a man is trout fishing only if each day's success is not measured by the creel alone.

This does not mean that trout should be caught, or that a day in which no trout are caught is more enjoyable than one with abundant rises. Rather, it means that the sting of disappointment when trout do not readily take can be tempered by the observations of the wonders nature parades for those who will but look and see.

There are streams to which I have returned so many times the trout in each pool have become familiar companions. And I have found that a cast placed so and a fly drifted such will renew a pleasant acquaintance. If it doesn't, I wonder if someone else, more creel-conscious than I, has tempted them. I have tagged trout with a device available from the Fish Tagger's Association, and in one season took the same 15-inch rainbow six times. Each time the thrill of catching him was stronger than the last.

There is a stream in the Blue Ridges where I once caught an 18-inch brookie and released it. For several seasons afterward, I tried for that same fish. Once he rolled short of the fly, but never struck. I'm glad he didn't. He made me a better fisherman.

A stream I often fished in Colorado contained a particularly beautiful pool that had never produced a trout for me. The water was so deep and turmoiled by a waterfall that I could not see into the pool, even with Polaroid glasses.

It became a spot where I liked to rest and study the view of the canyon. I'd fish the pool more out of respect for good-looking water than from any faith in results. Only once did I raise a fish. My fly had finished its drift, and I paused to watch a deer drinking from the stream below. When I looked back, a trout was turning with my fly in its mouth. As if in slow motion, the trout continued to turn, exposing a rainbow-lined side not less than a foot wide. Finally its tail, as broad as this page, made one twisted flip and disappeared from view. The rod and my arm were in position to set the hook but I was completely unable to move. The trout did not hook itself. I fished that pool many times but never raised the gigantic rainbow again. That fish also made me a better fisherman.

Yet I'm not sure that if the same thing were to happen this season, I might again fail for the same reason. For such is trout fishing that you can fully prepare only for what has happened. Future days hold only the unexpected.

While I often wonder what would have happened if I'd hooked that trout, my life is no less full for failing to do so. In fact the outcome of that surely prodigious battle gives me a special daydream I use when things get dull at Congressional hearings. It also helps me fight harder to save similar places others cherish.

Although I have caught many trout, it seems the ones I remember best are those I did not catch. There is a delight in recalling the streams and pools. Each one is a world of its own with a particular charm surrounding it. Fishing is real fun . . . all kinds of fishing. But the places where trout live have a special appeal that gives fishing for them the extra plus.

There is a bond between trout fishermen. Like every well-knit family, relations seem strained only to an outsider. It's not only true, but entirely as it should be that an artificial lure trouter speaks curtly to the live-bait fisherman—if at all. A dry-fly purist may cross the street to avoid being seen with a known wet-fly man. I have known friends to fall out over spoken preferences between brook and brown trout. I know two members of a trout club who don't like to sit at the same table because one uses a nine-foot instead of a seven-foot rod on a certain brook-trout stream. They, of course, are considered a little extreme. One even has been seen bass fishing.

But let someone make a slur about trout as compared to other fish species, and let him beware. Trout fishermen close ranks like a herd of maddened bison. Only when the infidel is in full rout do they realign in their individual compartments and sneer at all the other compartments.

With the growth of this country and its population, the unspoiled environment for trout is becoming scarcer. Those who appreciate trout fishing and the quiet beauty of the places of trout must unite to help protect those values. It means too that we must appreciate the trout themselves.

There are many kinds of natural beauty, from the expansiveness of a sky showing through a covering of multigreen forest, to the myriad forms of wondrous natural life. But there is a special something, a washing of the spirit, a re-creation of the individual, for those who take to the streamside where trout waters sing.

—Mike Hudoba, March 1956

Appendix

Trout Fishing Schools

~

A.A. Pro Shops Fly Fishing Schools
R.D. 1, Box 78
White Haven, PA 18661
717/443-8111

Adirondack Sport Shop
Rte. 86
Wilmington, NY 12997
518/946-2605

George Anderson's Yellowstone Angler
P.O. Box 660, Hwy. 89
South Livingston, MT 59047
406/222-7130

Anglers Engineering
Rte. 6, Box 27
Eureka Springs, AR 72632
501/253-7850

Dan Bailey's Fly Fishing School
P.O. Box 1019
Livingston, MT 59047
1-800/356-4052

The Battenkill Anglers
P.O. Box 2303
Manchester, VT 05255
802/362-3184

L.L. Bean Fly Fishing School
Outdoor Discovery Program
Casco St.
Freeport, ME 04033
1-800/341-4341

Beaver Kill Angler
Steward Ave.
P.O. Box 198
Roscoe, NY 12776
607/498-5194

California School of Flyfishing
P.O. Box 8212
Truckee, CA 96162
1-800/58-TROUT

Catskill Fly Fishing Center and Museum
P.O. Box 1295
5447 Old Rte. 17
Livingston Manor, NY 12758
914/439-4810

Al Caucci Fly Fishing School
R.D. 1, Box 102
Tannersville, PA 18372
717/629-2962

Clearwater House on Hat Creek
P.O. Box 90
Cassell, CA 96016
916/335-3530

*Colorado School of
Flyfishing*
P.O. Box 1848
Estes Park, CO 80517
303/586-8812

*Columbine School of
Flyfishing*
4305 Hwy. 50
Salida, CO 81201
303/539-3136

*Cutter's California
School of Flyfishing*
P.O. Box 8212
Truckee, CA 96162
916/587-7005

Jack Dennis Fly Fishing
P.O. Box 3369
Jackson, WY 83001
307/733-3270

*Diamondback School of
Flyfishing*
Rte. 100 South, P.O. Box 308
Stowe, VT 05672
802/253-4358

Dirt Road and Damsels
Teeny Nymph Co., P.O. Box 989
Gresham, OR 97030
503/667-6602

Ephemera
P.O. Box 629
Roscoe, NY 12776
607/498-4508

Fish Tech Institute
P.O. Box 807
Walker, MN 56484
218/547-1882

Fishing Creek Outfitters
R.D. #1, Box 310-1
Benton, PA 17814
1-800/548-0093

Fly Angling Services
5897 Loon Lake Loop
Rose City, MI 48654
517/685-3841

Fly Box Fishing School
1293 N.E. 3rd St.
Bend, OR 97701
541/388-3330

Fly Fish Vermont
804 S. Main St. #4
Stowe, VT 05672
802/253-3964

Fly Fishing Outfitters
463 Bush St.
San Francisco, CA 94108
510/284-3474

*Fly Fishing with Bert
and Karen*
1070 Creek Locks Rd.
Rosendale, NY 12472
914/658-9784

The Fly Hatch
90 Broad St.
Red Bank, NJ 07701
908/530-6784

The Fly Shop
4140 Churn Creek Rd.
Redding, CA 96002
1-800/669-3474

The Flyfisher Ltd.
252 Clayton St.
Denver, CO 80206
303/322-5014

Greg Lilly Fly Fishing
270 Tuke Lane
Twin Bridges, MT 59754
406/684-5960

High Country Flys
P.O. Box 3432
164 North Center St.
Jackson, WY 83001
307/733-5382

Hunters North Country Angler
P.O. Box 516, Rte. 16
North Main St.
North Conway, NH 03860
603/356-6000

Indian Springs Flyfishing Camp
Upper Delaware River
RR1, Box 200AA, Warren Rd.
Hancock, NY 13783
215/679-5022

Bob Jacklyn's Fly Shop
105 Yellowstone Ave., P.O. Box 310
West Yellowstone, MT 59758
406/646-7336

Joe Humphreys Fly Fishing Schools
P.O. Box 7
Boiling Springs, PA 17007
717/258-1464

Kaufmann's Fly Fishing Expeditions, Inc.
P.O. Box 23032
Portland, OR 97281-3032
1-800/442-4359

The Mel Krieger School of Flyfishing
790 27th Ave.
San Francisco, CA 94121
415/752-0192

Madison River Fishing Co. Fly Fishing Schools
109 Main St., P.O. Box 627
Ennis, MT 59729
406/682-4293

Maggie Merriman Fly Fishing Schools
P.O. Box 755
West Yellowstone, MT 59758
406/646-7824

McLeod's Highland Fly Fishing, Inc.
191 B Wesser Heights Dr.
Bryson City, NC 28713
704/488-8975

Michigan Academy of Fly Fishing
P.O. Box 70, Wellston, MI 49689
616/848-4163

Montana State
University Fly Fishing
Institute
204 Culbertson
Bozeman, MT 59717
406/994-4820

Montana Troutfitters
1716 West Main St.
Bozeman, MT 59715
1-800/646-7847

Murray's Fly Shop
P.O. Box 156, 121 Main St.
Edinburg, VA 22824
540/984-4212

Orvis Fly-Fishing
Schools
Historic Rte. 7A
Manchester, VT 05254
1-800/235-9763 Ext. 844

Parade Rest Ranch Fly
Fishing School
7979 Grayling Creek Rd.
West Yellowstone, MT 59758
406/646-7217

Pintail Point
511 Pintail Point Farm Lane
Queenstown, MD 21658
410/827-7029

Points North Fly
Fishing School
P.O. Box 146
169 1/2 Grove St., Rte. 8
Adams, MA 01220
413/743-4030

Reed's Orvis Shop
5655 Main St.
Williamsville, NY 14221
716/631-5131

Reno Fly Shop
294 E. Moana La., #14
Reno, NV 89502
702/825-3474

Rocky Mountain
Institute of Fly
Fishing
8403 145 Ave.
Edmonton, AB
Canada T5E 2J1
403/475-8139

The Rod Rack Fly
Fishing School
181 Thomas Dr.
Frederick, MD 21702
301/694-6143

The Royal Coachman, Ltd.
P.O. Box 642, 1410 East Genesse St.
Skaneateles, NY 13152
1-800/359-9992

Sage Fly Fishing Schools
and Fly Casting Clinics
8500 NE Day Rd.
Bainbridge Island, WA 98110
206/842-6608

The Santa Fe Flyfishing
School/Guide Service
P.O. Box 22957
Santa Fe, NM 87502-2957
1-800/555-7707

Scott Fly Rod Co. Fly Fishing School
200 San Miguel Drive
P.O. Box 889
Telluride, CO 81435
1-800/728-7208

Mark Sedotti Fly Casting
59 South Regent St.
Port Chester, NY 10573
914/939-5960

Silver Creek Outfitters
P.O. Box 418, 500 N. Main
Ketchum, ID 83340
208/726-5282

Sportsmen's Den of Greenwich, CT
33 River Rd.
Cos Cob, CT 06807
203/869-3234

Thomas and Thomas Fly Fishing School with Jason Borger
1211 Horn Ave., Suite 204
West Hollywood, CA 90069
310/647-7765

The Thornapple Angling School
c/o Thornapple Orvis Shop
1200 East Paris
Grand Rapids, MI 49546
616/975-3800

Trout and Grouse
300 S. Happ Rd.
Northfield, IL 60093
847/501-3111

Vermont Bound Outfitters and Guide Service
HCR 34, Box 28
Killington, VT 05751
1-800/639-3167

Westbank Anglers Fly Fishing Schools
P.O. Box 523
Teton Village, WY 83025
1-800/922-3474

Western Angler
532 College Ave.
Santa Rosa, CA 95404
707/542-4432

Western Sport Shop
902 Third St.
San Rafael, CA 94901
415/456-545

White River Artisans School
202 South Ave.
P.O. Box 308
Cotter, AR 72626
501/435-2600

The Wright Schools of Fly Fishing and Rod Building
P.O. Box 27, 45 Churchill Rd.
Websterville, VT 05678
802/476-6125

The Wulff School of
Flyfishing
P.O. Box 948
Livingston Manor, NY 12758
914/439-4060

Yellow Breeches
Outfitters Fly Fishing
Schools
2 First St.
Boiling Springs, PA 17007
717/258-6752

Trout
Fishing
Contacts

~

American Casting
Association
1773 Lance End Lane
Fenton, MO 63026
314/225-9443

American Fisheries
Society
5410 Grosvenor, Suite 110
Bethesda, MD 20814-2199
301/897-8616

American Rivers
1025 Vermont Ave., NW
Suite 720
Washington, DC 20005
202/547-6900

American Sportfishing
Assn.
1033 N. Fairfax St., #200
Alexandria, VA 22314
703/519-9691

Anglers for Clean Waters
c/o B.A.S.S.
P.O. Box 17900
Montgomery, AL 36141
334/272-9530

Atlantic Salmon
Federation
P.O. Box 807
Calais, ME 04619
506/529-4438

Catch & Release
Foundation
P.O. Box 556
Pound Ridge, NY 10576
1-800/63-CATCH

Federation of Fly Fishers
502 S. 19th
Suite 1, Box 1595
Bozeman, MT 59771
406/585-7592

FishAmerica Foundation
1033 N. Fairfax St. #200
Alexandria, VA 22314
703/548-6338

Fish Unlimited
Box 1073
1 Brander Pkwy.
Shelter Island, NY 11965
516/749-FISH

Flyfisher Apprentice
Program
407 West Seneca St.
Ithaca, NY 14850
607/272-0002

Future Fisherman
Foundation
1033 N. Fairfax St., Suite 200
Alexandria, VA 22314
703/519-9691

Hooked on Fishing
P.O. Box 691200
Tulsa, OK 74169-1200
918/366-8318

International Game Fish
Association
1301 E. Atlantic Blvd.
Pompano Beach, FL 33060
954/941-3474

International Women's
Fishing Association
P.O. Drawer 3125
Palm Beach, FL 33480

Izaak Walton Fly
Fisherman's Club
2400 Dundas St. West, Unit 6
Mississauga, Ontario
Canada L5K 2R8

Izaak Walton League
707 Conservation Lane
Gaithersburg, MD 20878-2983
301/548-0150

National Fish and
Wildlife Foundation
1120 Connecticut Ave., NW
Suite 900
Washington, DC 20036
202/857-0166

North American Fishing
Club
P.O. Box 3405
Minnetonka, MN 55343
1-800/843-6232

Theodore Gordon
Flyfishers
P.O. Box 978
Murray Hill Station
New York, NY 10156-0603

Trout Unlimited
1500 Wilson Blvd., #310
Arlington, VA 22209
703/522-0200

United Fly Tyers
P.O. Box 2478
Woburn, MA 01888

U.S. Fish and Wildlife
Service
P.O. Box 25486
Denver, CO 80225
303/236-7904

Washington Trout
P.O. Box 402
Duvall, WA 98019
206/788-9634

Index